HOW HIGH IS UP?

The Rise, Fall, and Redemption of a Sam M. Walton SIFE Fellow

―――

Curtis L. DeBerg

D1279604

Memoir
BOOKS
Chico, CA

Dedicated in loving memory to my father,

James L. DeBerg

=====

Contents

THE REDEMPTION

Foreword

by Dr. Manuel A. Esteban

I met Professor Curt DeBerg shortly after I assumed the presidency at California State University, Chico, in 1993. From my earliest conversations with him, I was impressed by his boundless and creative energy, charisma, and determination. He also struck me as a rather atypical faculty member in that he was constantly trying to modify and improve his teaching to have a greater positive influence on his students. The more I dealt with him, the more I realized that he was a nonconformist, irrepressible, blunt, and undeterred by bureaucratic hurdles. Above all, he convinced me that whatever he did, he did it out of devotion to his students. It was also obvious that he not only was able to think outside the box, as the saying goes, but that he had a vision that would ultimately push him well beyond the confines of CSU, Chico.

When he approached me about becoming involved in Students in Free Enterprise (SIFE), I was immediately supportive of the idea. I believed and professed that students learn more and better by actually applying textbook theory with hands-on experience. SIFE allowed students, faculty, and the community to become directly involved in the free enterprise system by providing students with the opportunity to teach what they learned to others. Through such cooperation, students improved their communication and management skills, creativity, and team building. I was so impressed with the work done by Professor DeBerg that I nominated him for the Leavey Award from the Freedoms Foundation at Valley Forge, an award he deservedly received.

As I became more involved and better informed about SIFE and its guiding principles, I wondered how Professor DeBerg would fit into a system that appeared to rely heavily on right-wing dogma, religiosity, a corporate and club-like culture, and a system that manifested itself as rather dictatorial and inflexible.

While the Chico State SIFE teams were racking up honors and successes and Professor DeBerg was quickly becoming one of SIFE's greatest ambassadors, the seeds of conflict between Dr. DeBerg and SIFE's CEO, Alvin Rohrs, began to bloom. Sam M. Walton Fellows, like Dr. DeBerg, were the heart and soul of SIFE. However, the powers that be, headed primarily by Rohrs and Wal-Mart's former executive Jack Shewmaker, were not really interested in taking into account the concerns and advice provided by these Fellows. The more Professor DeBerg attempted to mobilize Fellows to push for changes, the more he was perceived by Rohrs and others at the helm of SIFE as a unionizing-type person, anathema in their corporate world, and frankly, as a troublemaker. When Dr. DeBerg created Students for the Advancement of Global Entrepreneurship or SAGE, and SAGE began quickly to expand nationally and internationally, his fate within SIFE was sealed. SAGE was slowly but surely becoming such a force that Rohrs perceived it as in direct competition with SIFE. This was not to be permitted

How High Is Up? is a book that details CSU, Chico's, SIFE's incredible successes and Curt DeBerg's rise and fall within this organization. It is also a story of David and Goliath, a lowly Walton Fellow against the powerful machinery of SIFE and, partly, of Wal-Mart. It is also an exposé of what Professor DeBerg perceived to be a culture of corruption. It is a fascinating account that should be of interest to educators, entrepreneurs, advocates of service learning, and to humanitarian capitalists.

This book should also be of interest to anyone who pulls for the underdog. It is clear that Professor DeBerg was the underdog in his clash with SIFE leaders.

In the final analysis, *How High Is Up?* is also a book about dedication to student learning and devotion to students.

I have always been impressed with Professor DeBerg. After reading this book, I am more impressed and filled with admiration. Read this book.

Author's Note

─────────

Reviews in the next few pages suggest *How High Is Up?* has become controversial. As a terminated Sam M. Walton Free Enterprise Fellow for SIFE who helped found SIFE's rival, SAGE, I narrate the conversations, emails, meetings, and national competitions that lead to the controversy.

This memoir will have you asking yourself, how high is up? *How High Is Up?* provides the impetus for nonprofits to practice greater transparency and accountability. It is a story of merging corporate needs with students for entrepreneurship using tactics taken by two competing nonprofit organizations—one heavily funded and one smaller.

How High Is Up?

Book Reviews

Curtis DeBerg has written three books in one. First, [*How High is Up?*] is an unusually intriguing story of an academic life, which actually makes the accounting profession seem exciting! Second, it provides a spirited, inside account of a scandal plagued organization, Students in Free Enterprise. ... And finally, Professor DeBerg's narrative offers readers important insights into the conservative, evangelical business culture propagated by companies like Wal-Mart. ...

—Nelson Lichtenstein
University of California, Santa Barbara.
Author of *The Retail Revolution: How Wal-Mart Created a Brave New World of Business.*

This book is a compelling read about [DeBerg's] struggle to nurture SAGE [Students for the Advancement of Global Entrepreneurship] and grow it to more than twenty countries and counting—one part educational, two parts suspenseful, and three parts uplifting. It certainly wasn't easy: His personal, unsavory experience with SIFE could easily have left him bitter. Instead, it just made him more tenacious.

—Jerr Boschee
Cofounder, Social Enterprise Alliance
Founder and Executive Director, The Institute for Social Entrepreneurs

There is a valuable message in *How High Is Up?* For me, the message was about overcoming adversity and pressing on to reach your goals. It was about the trail you take to reach your destination and about how to stay true to yourself. ... Dr. DeBerg's memoir is definitely worth reading.

—Adrian Lazaro Sherrod
Student, CSU, Chico, Two-Time All-American, Cross-Country (2012, 2013)

How High Is Up? is an excellent piece of work. ... Professor DeBerg educates readers about how a great vision has become reality ... he provides a unique, insider's perspective about the real world of corporate politics and the practice of self-proclaimed servant leaders. ...

—*Kofi A. Obeng*
Assistant Financial Analyst
University of Westminster, London, U.K.
Member of the SAGE Ghana Board of Directors
President, 2004 University of Cape Coast SIFE president (Ghana national champions)

This is a good read, a revealing reflection on organizational dynamics from a passionate believer in the global vision of civic engagement and entrepreneurship education.

—*Alfred Konuwa*
Vice President, Academic and Student Services,
Woodland Community College
Former Sam M. Walton Free Enterprise Fellow of the Year, Butte College

Part memoir, part expose, part manifesto, it takes the reader on an intellectual journey into the uses and abuses of community service programs. DeBerg is a fine storyteller, and his personal energy and vision radiate from every page. The story he tells is especially timely given the choice our country—and our planet—faces as to how and for whose benefit we marshal the creative energies of a market economy.

—*Edward A. Zlotkowski*
Professor, English and Media Studies, Bentley University
2010, Lifetime Achievement Award for Service Learning and Civic Engagement, International
Conference on Service-Learning and Engaged Research

This book gives a glimpse into the potential of service learning to do good, for both students on a campus and residents in a community. Just as importantly, this book tells me that academics and scholars can have a laudable, palpable impact upon society if they make applied research the highest priority, for which, after years of service learning, there is still much room for growth.

—*Van Ajemian, JD*
SAGE Board Member

All entrepreneurs will relate to Professor DeBerg's story in *How High Is Up?* It is one of fighting the odds, challenging authority, and being tagged the "wild one" because he dared to think outside the proverbial box. Like most entrepreneurs DeBerg did not give in or give up. He followed the path he knew to be right—first, to show high school students the power business ownership has to transform lives and offer hope, and second, to help stimulate youth entrepreneurship on a global scale.

—*Rieva Lesonsky*
CEO, GrowBiz Media.
Former Editorial Director, *Entrepreneur Magazine*
Former Board Member, Students in Free Enterprise (SIFE)

With Curt's inspiration, dedication and energy, he has created the SAGE program. SAGE taps into the creative energy of all its participants. Most importantly, he gives young people the chance to reach their full potential and to truly believe that they can change the world for the better.

—*Irina Dannikova*
Tula Teachers' Retraining Institute, Tula, Russia
SAGE Asia Continental Co-Coordinator

This book should be required reading for emerging leaders in academia, as well as the public and private sectors, particularly in Africa. In Africa, there is an urgent need to create and mobilize social entrepreneurs, who are beginning to tackle the numerous challenges of poverty and conflicts that visionless leadership has, for decades, spread throughout the continent. … *How High Is Up?* is a valuable source of inspiration and motivation for change makers.

—*Agwu Amogu*
SAGE Nigeria CEO
SAGE Africa Continental Coordinator, Abuja, Nigeria

Prologue

Hold Onto Your Socks

────────

The team of five California students marched boldly to the front of the packed conference room at the Hilton Orlando to make a twenty-four-minute business presentation. The young women were all wearing matching skirts and neatly pressed black blazers, each sporting a lapel pin bearing the crimson flame logo of their alma mater, California State University, Chico. The room of over 150 people consisted almost entirely of white, male, middle-aged executives who had come to this meeting at the personal invitation of one of the world's most respected men in the retail business: Jack Shewmaker.

It was May 1999 at the International Mass Retailers Association annual meeting at the Orange County Convention Center in Orlando, Florida. The IMRA has since changed its name to the Retail Industry Leaders Association, but its mission today is the same as it was in 1999—to serve as one of the retail industry's most powerful lobbyists in Washington, D.C.[1] And no one carried more clout with IMRA than Wal-Mart.

During his Wal-Mart career, Shewmaker had served as a member of IMRA's board of directors. After retiring from Wal-Mart in 1988, he continued to speak at IMRA conferences and meetings that it sponsored.

Shewmaker, though long since retired as president and vice chairman of Wal-Mart and now in his early sixties, was still going strong as a member of Wal-Mart's board of directors. In Orlando, Jack Shewmaker was to mass retailing as Michael Jordan was to basketball—a superstar among superstars. His role at Wal-Mart was sine qua non: Sam Walton's right-hand man; Discount Retailer of the Year, 1981; Retailer of the Year, 1985; and, later, Retail Hall of Fame, 2007.

Anyone who met him couldn't help but be charmed. With his deep, soft Missouri Ozarks drawl and piercing blue eyes, he commanded people's attention and could spin a good story. People hung on his every word, like how he still won his age division in downhill ski races in Colorado. Or how he and "Mr. Sam" would go quail hunting and how it was good for his personal "bidness" not to outshoot Wal-Mart's legendary boss. Or when Sam Walton drove seventy miles to meet him halfway between their respective hometowns of Buffalo, Missouri, and Bentonville, Arkansas, to convince Shewmaker to join Wal-Mart in 1970. Such was an example of Walton's leadership that Shewmaker often used it in his countless public speaking engagements as an anecdote to support his own "servant leader management philosophy."

Shewmaker never tired of cajoling fellow business leaders to join the board of one of Wal-Mart's favorite nonprofit organizations, Students in Free Enterprise—SIFE. SIFE's mission in 1999 was "to provide college students the best opportunity to make a difference and to develop leadership, teamwork, and communication skills through learning, practicing, and teaching the principles of free enterprise."[2] Since its founding in 1975, SIFE invited "college and university SIFE teams" to make multimedia presentations to a panel of business leaders at the end of each academic year. The presentations described activities undertaken in their local communities by students, under guiding themes provided by SIFE in support of its ostensible mission to support free enterprise.

Such leaders included other big names in the retail industry: Len Roberts, CEO of RadioShack, David Bernauer, CEO of Walgreens, and Tom Coughlin, future Wal-Mart vice chairman and president of Wal-Mart Stores, Inc. SIFE judges ranked the teams according to several judging criteria. The top SIFE teams won praise, prize money, and opportunities to repeat their presentations to audiences like the one in Orlando.

Even though Shewmaker had long since retired from Wal-Mart's executive management team, he still played a crucial role as chairman of Wal-Mart's strategic planning committee of its thirteen-member board of directors in 1999. The board was chaired by Sam Walton's oldest son, Rob. Shewmaker's role, arguably, was one of the most important jobs in the Wal-Mart organization, given the company's new strategy to expand globally—which meant, of course, to build more stores and supercenters outside the U.S., while at the same time, buy from international vendors who could out-compete American manufacturers because of substantially lower labor costs.

In addition to serving on Wal-Mart's board, Shewmaker also served on SIFE's board since 1985, always as a member of its Executive Committee and, for two years, as its chairman. By 1999, he had been SIFE's leading cheerleader for almost fifteen years, and its strongest advocate among fellow executives in the retail industry.

The energy in Orlando was palpable—seats were arranged theater-style, with a narrow aisle down the middle. The young women about to make their presentation weren't fazed, though. Only ten days earlier, they had made a similar presentation to an audience of over twelve hundred CEOs, senior business leaders, academics (known as Sam M. Walton Free Enterprise Fellows), and fellow students at the Bartle Hall Convention Center in Kansas City, Missouri. Their presentation was deemed to be the best presentation out of over two hundred university SIFE teams, earning them the title of SIFE International World Cup Champion. With the title came a round-trip ticket to represent SIFE, and Chico State, at the prestigious retail conference in Orlando.

Wal-Mart had just reported revenues of over $137.6 billion, up 17 percent from the prior year. In January 1999, it boasted 1,869 domestic stores, 564 Wal-Mart Supercenters, and 910,000 employees. The retail giant—with Shewmaker serving on its Executive Committee—was poised to go full steam ahead in pursuing international markets.[3] Brazil, China, Germany, England, Mexico, and Canada appeared foremost on Wal-Mart's radar. One strategic way to penetrate these markets was attracting young, ideological business students who wanted, as SIFE proclaimed, to change the world by practicing the principles of free enterprise.

Shewmaker started off the Orlando meeting by giving a brief and lofty speech about how businesses could support the future of America, and the world, by supporting SIFE. "SIFE students," he said, "teach free market economics to others. If we share the knowledge we have that helps people support and provide for their families, we could eliminate the need for war." He then introduced Alvin Rohrs, SIFE's president and CEO. Rohrs, son of a Southern Baptist preacher, was a rotund man with soft hands, a fishy handshake, and cascading chins. Confidently taking the stage, Rohrs had participated in his share of revivals. Like a pastor delivering a sermon, he said, "What you are about to see is a group of college students from California who are changing the world. They have done some incredible work, from helping elementary kids start their own lemonade stands and learning about free enterprise, to helping the elderly learn how to use computers to keep in touch with their grandkids."

Seated in the back of room, Bruce Nasby had to smile. Nasby had seen Rohrs work this magic before, and it made Nasby's role as SIFE's senior vice president of development a whole lot easier. The formula worked like this: Alvin introduces the students; the students put on a great performance; the executives are impressed, so much that they want their companies to be part of this world-changing idea. That's when Bruce steps in: for only $25,000 your company gets an honorary seat on SIFE's board of directors, right next to Jack Shewmaker and, by extension, Wal-Mart's powerbrokers. Make the check payable to SIFE. By writing the check, you can help university students become missionaries, spreading the gospel of free enterprise.

Rohrs, then in his early forties, had been at the SIFE helm for almost twenty years. He took on the job in 1982, when SIFE was struggling to stay alive. At the time, Rohrs had just become the director of Southwest Baptist University's (SBU) new National Free Enterprise Center, as well as SBU's SIFE faculty adviser. The economic downturn in the previous few years had reduced SIFE teams from over one hundred to just eighteen and a handful of sponsors. SIFE's founder, Robert T. "Sonny" Davis, and main funder, William "Bill" Seay, were looking for someone to breathe new life into the floundering organization. They were also looking to move SIFE's home office out of Dallas, Texas, and into a permanent location.[4]

After a meeting with Rohrs in St. Louis, Davis approached the president of Southwest Baptist, James Sells, about a possible move. Sells was keen on expanding SBU's curriculum to include free-enterprise education, and he was thinking about how SBU might work with local business leaders to further this agenda. SIFE looked like a natural fit for this, and the SIFE board promptly hired Rohrs as its national director. Not long thereafter, Rohrs met Shewmaker, who was soon to become SIFE's patron saint.

Before the Chico State team began its presentation, the team captain,

Dawn Houston, stepped to the microphone. Houston had been a busy woman. She caught a red-eye flight to Orlando directly from a vacation in Hawaii. An economics major who would later go on to get a law degree, she had graduated from Chico State two weeks earlier. The male-dominated audience waited for her to speak.

At twenty-six years of age, Houston did not lack confidence. "Ladies and gentlemen," she announced, "before I begin, I'd like each of you to please do me a big favor." She asked them to lean forward and reach down to their ankles. "In the next half hour, we're gonna blow your socks off!"

With that, the presentation began. Houston and her SIFE teammates—Suzanne Cozad, Danielle Emis, Rachel Muzzall and Kelby Thornton—described, in great detail, the projects completed by the Chico State team during the previous academic year. At the end, Shewmaker rose to his feet from the front row and began a slow, loud clap. The remainder of the audience followed suit, and the slow claps grew to become a rousing, standing ovation.

Rohrs seized the moment. He lumbered to the stage to close the loop on this day's work. Scanning the audience, he stepped to the microphone. He tried to speak, but no words came. He tried again, and still nothing. Something was happening. His shoulders began to shake, and then he adjusted his glasses. As one, the audience understood—he was overcome with emotion!

Finally, he sputtered, "Aren't these young people marvelous?" he said, tears flowing, no longer able to choke them back. Then, regaining himself, he said, "The projects that these students are doing are changing people's lives. The children in the entrepreneurship camp; the people in the old-folks home, and ..." He stopped, took off his glasses, rubbed his eyes, and then sputtered again, "And the teens in the juvenile hall facility, learning how to write resumes and how to become responsible members of society."

Nasby smiled. He knew, once again, that he would be getting a big bonus at the end of the year.

But something was nagging at Rohrs. He had done this dog and pony show dozens of times. Crisscrossing the country, he, Shewmaker, and now Nasby, had logged hundreds of thousands of frequent-flier miles speaking

to groups of executives exactly like this one. Together, they made a powerful team. SIFE was now collecting about $7 million a year in donations,
and Rohrs was raking in $238,000 (not including employee benefits of
$48,000), and Nasby $188,000 (not including benefits of $32,000).[5] Most
of the donations were coming either from Wal-Mart, its army of vendors,
or other retailers like Walgreens and RadioShack.

But the Chico State team was different. It didn't feel ... Christian-enough,
like private Sun Belt universities such as Harding, La Sierra, Southwest
Baptist, College of the Southwest, Houston Baptist, John Brown University,
College of the Ozarks, or Union University. Chico State was secular; as a
public, comprehensive university from northern California, the students
seemed ... too liberal. And their faculty adviser, their Sam M. Walton
Free Enterprise Fellow, was a real California-lefty. Rohrs made a mental
note—this guy had to be shown his place in the organization, or be shown
the door—preferably the back door.[6]

That guy was me.

Part I

THE RISE

COLLEAGUES AT CSU, CHICO, SPRING 1992
The U.S. Department of Education awarded our accounting department a three-year, $380,0000 grant to reengineer our introductory accounting courses. Left to right: Professors Richard Lea, Lee Pryor, Curt DeBerg, Paul Krause, and Brock Murdoch. Photo by Sally Adams, courtesy of author.

SAM M. WALTON FELLOW
Each faculty adviser is recognized for his or her service to their SIFE team and called a "Sam M. Walton Free Enterprise Fellow." Photo courtesy of author.

Chapter 1

To Be a Saint, a Sinner or a Teacher?

As a teenager, I loved three things: attending Sunday school at the Tabernacle Baptist Church, dealing poker and pitching quarters with my irrepressible buddy Scott Slade, and playing basketball every chance I got. As I dreamed about my future, I considered being a preacher, a professional poker player, or a coach.

But deep down, I knew I wasn't an organized religion kind of guy, especially during my freshman year at university. One weekend, when I returned to my little farming community in northwest Iowa, our self-righteous youth pastor informed us that all other religions of the world were works of the devil. That didn't make much sense given one of my new friends was an atheist from Sweden, another was a Jew from Chicago, and a third was a Lutheran from Lake Wobegon. I also knew there wasn't a future in professional gambling, especially after learning that the only game you can ever win money is blackjack, and this is true only if you have the patience and sobriety to count cards.

That left basketball. Because I was only five feet eleven inches and couldn't jump or make a layup or dribble with my right hand, playing for the Chicago Bulls wasn't an option. But that didn't rule out a teaching career, with coaching on the side. In 1974, near the end of my high school senior year in Rock Rapids, Iowa, two of my favorite teachers—Bruce Lubbock, an English teacher and baseball coach, and John Massa, a math teacher and basketball coach—pulled me aside. Each knew that I planned to go to college to become a teacher and coach. They both gave me the same message: if you want to support a family and see the world, high school teaching is not recommended. And to prove their point, both fine gentlemen left the teaching profession a year or two after I went away to college.

So off I went to the University of Northern Iowa (UNI) in Cedar Falls, a sleepy campus of about thirteen thousand students in northeast Iowa, thinking about the advice proffered by Mr. Lubbock and Mr. Massa. If I chose to ignore it, I would probably major in English or journalism. But if I followed their counsel, what then? My brother Craig, only one year ahead of me in school, suggested I take an accounting course. He said, "It's not hard, and there are plenty of good jobs for accountants."

If I couldn't win money playing poker or blackjack, it didn't sound like such a bad idea to keep track of other people's money.

Craig was right. Accounting came easily for me and I sailed through the CPA exam on my first try. But my mentor at UNI, Dr. Darrell Davis, suggested I consider becoming an accounting professor. To do that, he said, I had to go on to get a master's degree and, if I wanted to shoot for the stars, a doctorate.

Roll the clock forward from 1974, the year I enrolled at UNI, to 1981. I ended up majoring in accounting, became a CPA, and went to work at one of the Big 8 professional accounting firms, Ernst & Whinney (now Ernst & Young). Not long before I graduated and accepted the position at Ernst & Whinney, I called my favorite accounting professor.

"Dr. Davis, shall I take the GMAT exams now and apply for graduate school, or should I go to work for a CPA firm?"

"To be an outstanding accounting professor, you have to experience the real world of accounting," he replied. "Go be a CPA for a couple years, then give me a call. But don't get too comfortable with the lifestyle," he warned. "You better save some money because graduate school isn't cheap."

So off I went to Des Moines in the summer of 1979, with a whopping starting salary of $16,200. It was a heady time, earning a steady paycheck, driving my '67 Chevy Bel Air named Bertha, and living with three other recent graduates from UNI. Two of my housemates were Rich Johnson and Steve Marlow. Like me, they had also majored in accounting and now were colleagues at Ernst & Whinney. The fourth person in the house was Tim Hermsen, who taught at nearby Urbandale High School and was the head baseball coach.

We were all single, working hard, making money, playing city league basketball during the week and partying on the weekends. Dr. Davis was right—I could easily get used to this.

But public accounting wasn't for me. I yearned to be a teacher, like

Dr. Davis. I also saw how much Tim enjoyed coaching baseball. So in the spring of 1981, I gave my mentor a call. "Dr. Davis, I need your advice. I just took the GMAT test and I scored pretty well. What should I do now?"

He suggested that I send my graduate school application and test results to several universities. "Ask questions like what they can offer you in the way of research or teaching assistantships. Ask them if they require a foreign language component. And check out the cost of living in the area," he added.

"Where did you get your PhD?" I asked.

"Oklahoma State University," he said. "They have an outstanding department chair named Wilton T. Anderson. And they have some great faculty there."

"Alright," I said. "I will do as you say, Dr. Davis."

"It will be a pleasure to welcome you to the teaching profession, Curt," he said. "And one more thing," he added. "Knock off the Dr. Davis bullshit. My name is Darrell."

What a show of confidence! I was thrilled that *Darrell* now considered me a peer. Such was the power of mentorship. I respected and admired this man so such. I thought to myself, "He's more than a professor. He is a coach. He is a mentor. And now he is a peer and friend. Maybe someday I can affect young people the way he has impacted me."

After submitting several doctoral applications and being accepted into PhD programs at Kansas, Kansas State, Nebraska, and Oklahoma State, I decided to enroll at Oklahoma State. In August of 1982, my dad, a farm equipment dealer, helped pack all my belongings and we loaded them onto his trailer. Off we went to Stillwater, which seemed like a different planet to me.

The drawn-out Oklahoma accent had a way of making one syllable into two (e.g, "Ya'all want to go a movie?"), and adding superfluous words to a sentence (e.g., "I'm fixin' to go to bed."). It seemed that, for men, chewing tobacco and wearing cowboy boots was the norm, and for women, one of life's highest aspirations was to win a beauty pageant. Country and western music dominated the radio waves and the (dry) bar scene. The two-step dance was the only way to boogie. Late-night radio featured hellfire and brimstone evangelists—reminiscent of the occasional guest evangelists proselytizing to the flock at Tabernacle Baptist Church—my home church in George, Iowa. It didn't take long for me to find out I was, as they say in Oklahoma, sum-mack dab in the middle of the Bible Belt.

Notwithstanding the culture shock, Oklahoma State was a lot like UNI in that it was the anchor institution of a relatively small city. Within a week after moving to Stillwater I was enrolled in engineering calculus, statistics, and industrial organization—fast on my way to earning a master's degree in economics. These courses also served as fine preparation classes for future doctoral courses such as multivariate regression analysis, advanced economics, and the math-dominated research design courses in business administration. At the same time, I was assigned to teach two courses in introductory financial accounting each semester as part of my assistantship, which paid a paltry $600 a month. Good thing I was single.

After the first day of teaching, I knew I had made the right decision. I absolutely delighted that when I spoke, students actually wrote down what I had to say. No longer only a student, I soon became accustomed to my new role as subject-matter expert and teacher.

Three and a half years flew by and before I knew it, the city population sign for Stillwater faded from Bertha's rearview mirror as I headed west to Tempe, Arizona. I had accepted my first position as a tenure-track professor at Arizona State University. Now twenty-nine years old, I was about to jump from a $6,000 a year teaching assistant to a whopping $37,000 job as an assistant professor. With that salary, I knew Bertha and I were nearing the end of our line together.

Tempe was nothing like Cedar Falls or Stillwater. Arriving in early January 1985, I found Tempe to be at the hub of economic development. Centrally located, Tempe was just east of the booming metropolis of Phoenix, west of the winter snowbird destination of Mesa, and south of upscale Scottsdale. Nestled in the heart of Tempe was our relatively small campus bursting at the seams with over 40,000 students.

Within a few months I bought a new Mazda pickup and purchased a townhouse five miles from campus. As a tenure-track professor, I was required to do just one thing to keep my job forever: publish the results of my dissertation in one of the top two accounting academic journals.

Unfortunately, when I started my dissertation in 1983, inflation was still a hot topic and editors of accounting journals still welcomed research in this area. But by the time I defended my dissertation in April 1985, inflation had dropped to a rather insubstantial level. That summer, I submitted a manuscript to *The Accounting Review.* After surviving two requests to revise the manuscript and one change in editorship, I received a note from the new editor in 1988: "Our journal is no longer interested in manuscripts about the stock market effects of inflation accounting reporting requirements. I suggest you find a new line of research."

My magnum opus had languished at *The Accounting Review* for two years and eight months! Thanks to the letter from the new editor I knew my chances of tenure at Arizona State were nil—it was time to look around for a new teaching position.

I had been dating a wonderful woman for nearly two years. Marriage was a distinct possibility. I didn't know how she'd take my news of possibly leaving Arizona. "I've been in the desert for fifteen years," she said. "It's too hot for me. Let's get out of here!"

My contract with ASU was set to expire after the 1990 spring semester. Kristine and I decided to get married in Sedona in October 1988. We waited until the following August to start job interviewing. The market for accounting professors was robust, and wherever I ended up I would likely get a pay bump of about five or ten thousand dollars. To test the waters, we interviewed at Western Washington University, Seattle University, Northern Arizona, and the University of Nevada, Reno.

As an afterthought, I decided to interview at one more university. We learned there was a financial accounting teaching position at a little campus about ninety miles north of Sacramento. It was California State University, Chico—or Chico State for short. Chico State was known to be a teaching campus, first and foremost, and while I still enjoyed research, the thought of prioritizing my time for undergraduate students rather than erudite journal editors had great appeal. Expectations for research and publication, compared to ASU, were minimal, and there was very little doubt that tenure would be an issue. So in the fall of 1989, we accepted the offer from the dean at Chico State. Kristine, my stepdaughter Julie, and I planned to make our move to Chico in June 1990.

Around this time, the environment was ripe for education reform, including accounting. In 1989, the Big 8 accounting firms pungled up $1.5 million to fund a handful of grants to be awarded to universities brave enough to dramatically alter their curricula. The firms were clamoring for accounting graduates who were more than the stereotypical rule-following, bean-counting nerds in green eyeshades. Sure, they wanted new accountants to know generally accepted accounting principles—GAAP—but they also wanted graduates to be stronger communicators, better problem solvers, adept decision-makers, and lifelong learners.

This was perfect for me. Now, as a teaching professor first and research professor second, I was more than happy to see how we could spice up the accounting curriculum to be more than debits and credits. Not yet thirty-five years old, I had arrived on the Chico State campus with a new zest for teaching. Instead of relegating my teaching duties to the back of the bus, I could now give most of my attention to teaching rather than research. I always considered myself an innovator in the classroom.

It was refreshing to find student-centered kindred spirits on my new campus. Several like-minded colleagues saw accounting as the language of business, and perhaps like other foreign languages, we believed we could enhance the traditional stand-and-deliver lecture approach by employing active-learning strategies and cooperative learning techniques. At one of our department meetings I asked my colleagues if we should chase one of the $200,000 grants from the Accounting Education Change Commission. "Let's go for it!" they agreed.

As it turned out, we came very close to winning the grant in 1991 but we were too broad in scope. Undeterred, we repackaged the proposal in early 1992 and submitted it to the U.S. Department of Education's prestigious Fund for the Improvement of Postsecondary Education "FIPSE" [fip-see] program. We were one of about 150 finalists out of over two thousand proposals. In the end, the reviewers said, "Nice job. Don't give up. Narrow your focus and resubmit next year."

Still unwilling to throw in the towel, we tried one more time in the spring of 1992. A few months later in June, we received the good news—of over seventeen hundred proposals we were one of the seventy-nine FIPSE grants funded. Result: we had won a three-year grant for $380,000 to reengineer our first two courses in accounting, and I was one of the two project codirectors.

As codirectors, Richard Lea and I had to lead countless department meetings, delegate roles, coordinate authorship of new lesson plans, oversee their implementation, and encourage alternative teaching strategies (educators call teaching techniques *pedagogy*). In the spring of 1993 Rich and I were invited to Washington, D.C., to attend a conference exclusively for FIPSE project directors. This was a watershed event for two reasons. It was eye-opening to learn that some of the same problems my accounting colleagues were dealing with were also being confronted by faculty in other fields including medicine, engineering, architecture, chemistry, and the liberal arts. But the most interesting thing I learned at the conference was many educators were starting to employ a new pedagogy called community *service learning.*

Then, as now, I have always been a firm believer that students learn best by actually applying textbook theory with hands-on experience. The service-learning pedagogy fit neatly into this philosophy. The National and Community Service Trust Act of 1993 defined service learning as follows:

> A method under which students or participants learn and develop through active participation in thoughtfully organized service that is conducted in and meets the needs of a community, and is coordinated with the community and with an elementary school, secondary school, institution of higher education, or community service program; helps foster civic responsibility; is integrated into and enhances the academic curriculum of the students or the educational components of the community service program in which the participants are enrolled, and includes structured time for the students and participants to reflect on the service experience.[1]

After we returned from Washington, I wondered how I might integrate service learning into my accounting courses. Clearly, sending students into the community to perform "service" while they "learned" accounting could be a disaster, especially introductory students. But these students could perform other services, couldn't they? The stew was simmering.

Shortly after my return, Chico State's business dean, Dr. Arno Rethans, circulated a brief memorandum with a letter attached. The letter was from a nonprofit organization in Springfield, Missouri, called Students in Free Enterprise—SIFE. Dr. Rethans asked if any faculty members in the college might want to become a Sam M. Walton Free Enterprise Fellow.

In exchange for the title bearing the name of Wal-Mart's iconic founder and a $1,000 stipend, the Walton Fellow was expected to organize a small team of students, conduct training sessions, show videotapes, and set up a structure so these students could complete community service activities that met SIFE's mission: for college students to teach Americans of all ages a better understanding of how the free enterprise system works.

The letter, authored by SIFE CEO Alvin Rohrs, added: "SIFE's purpose is accomplished through the SIFE teams' outreach projects that involve students, faculty, and the community, in the free enterprise system, providing the students with an opportunity to teach what they have learned to others. This unique experience provides the SIFE students with better communication skills, creativity, team-building, and management skills to become the leaders of the future."

This clinched the deal—I had become a staunch service-learning advocate, and had now found a unique organization to help implement it into my courses. I marched down to the dean's office and told Dr. Rethans, "I want to do this." The dean replied, "No problem, as long as it doesn't cost me any money."

I faxed my Walton Fellow application and soon received a big box of materials from SIFE Headquarters with a return address from The Jack Shewmaker SIFE World Headquarters in Springfield, Missouri. This sounded impressive. "And who is this Jack Shewmaker guy?" I wondered. The box contained a dozen information handbooks, a few videos, a hundred or so brochures, and a cover letter from SIFE's manager of university relations, Sidney Lilly.

Soon thereafter, on May 6, 1993, I received a warm welcome letter personally signed by S. Robson Walton congratulating me on becoming a Fellow named after his father. Rob Walton, Sam Walton's oldest son, was now Wal-Mart's chairman of the board. His father had died only a year earlier on April 5, 1992. Carbon copied on the email was Mr. Joey Jones, Wal-Mart's director of college relations.

What's up with this? Why are these fellowships named after Sam Walton? Why am I getting a personal letter from one of the most powerful and wealthiest business leaders just by signing up to be a SIFE faculty adviser? Why is Wal-Mart involved? Why does my becoming a faculty adviser merit the attention of Sam Walton's son? I was anxious to find out. I got my answer less than a year later, in May of 1994.

As a college professor, I was happy to have chosen education as a career. But now I could also fulfill one of my dreams—I was not only a Sam M. Walton Fellow, I was now Coach DeBerg. Not a basketball coach, mind you, but a free enterprise coach—a coach named after one of the twentieth century's most influential capitalists.

Chapter 2

Free Enterprise "Coach"

———

As our accounting department began implementing the FIPSE innovations in fall of 1993, we decided to enlist the help of upper-division undergraduate accounting majors to serve as teachers' aides. We called these students accounting *mentors*; one mentor was assigned to each section of introductory accounting. The mentors provided tutoring to the younger students, which included training sessions on how to use Excel spreadsheets. Microsoft had recently released its famous Version 5, and the progressive members of the accounting faculty jumped at the opportunity to use Excel to teach accounting knowledge and skills.

At the same time, I was one of the Chico State representatives on the Chamber of Commerce's Education Committee. Also serving on the committee was Dr. Rob Barbot, superintendent of the Chico Unified School District. At one of our monthly meetings, I said, "Rob, do you think any of your middle school math teachers would be interested in having a few business students help them with their lesson plans?"

"As a matter of fact," he replied. "Chico Junior High has a dynamic young principal who'd be glad to talk to you. His name is Jeff Sloan."

The next stop for me was Chico Junior High. I explained my idea to assign Chico State business students to teachers, much like we were doing at the university.

"This sounds really interesting," Sloan said. "I'd like you to meet with our four, pre-algebra teachers. We call this Math 3." Math 3, I learned, was for the kids who couldn't hack regular algebra.

"It's not that most of these kids can't do it, but, you know, at age thirteen and fourteen it's really hard to get them to pay attention," Sloan admitted. "Maybe your college students can get them back on track."

A few days later I met with the teachers and we set up the plan. During the fall semester 1993, 93 percent of the eighth grade algebra students were

Caucasian, while 64 percent of the Math 3 students—our target student audience—were Caucasian. Many of the Math 3 students had failed seventh grade math. One teacher said, "If you can teach just a handful of these kids that math is relevant to their lives, your project will be a success."

My next step was to find and train at least ten Chico State students to team-teach the junior high kids. I promised the teachers that Chico State students would come to Chico Junior High once or twice a week and deliver a set of lessons called *Using Math to Make Business Decisions.* This was a great deal for the teachers; it not only gave them a break from the often unruly junior high students, but it might also give the kids a new reason to pay attention. However, there was a small dilemma. Where were these lessons?

Only in my head.

Two of the accounting mentors were Heather Tatton, an outgoing junior from Stockton, and Julie Millett, a smart young woman from San Juan Capistrano in Orange County. Heather and Julie were close friends. They often hung out together with Julie's boyfriend, Chris Coutant. Chris was from Cypress, also in Southern California. He was a political science major with aspirations to get a law degree down the road. A lover of debate, he wore shoulder-length hair that looked more like he was from the mid-'60s than the mid-'90s.

One day I spotted the three of them in the hall. "Hey, you guys want to grab a cup of coffee? I have something I want to run by you." When we met the next day, I talked about the SIFE team I wanted to organize.

"How would you like to do some community service work by teaching some basic concepts that you're learning here?" I asked. "Junior high students all take algebra, but a lot of them are in a pre-algebra class. The teachers are looking for a new source of energy to ignite a spark in them."

I promised if they could pull this off, I would bring them to San Francisco the following April to compete against other universities participating in SIFE. "The most creative and innovative teams receive an invitation to Kansas City, Missouri, to compete against regional winners from eleven other cities around the country. But we need at least seven or eight more Chico State students if we want to do this right."

Like many university students, Heather, Julie, and Chris were idealistic, and they believed that they could truly make an impact in their communities. By participating in SIFE, they could fulfill an innate desire to give back. And there was the bonus of competition and travel.

"We're in!" they unanimously agreed. Within the next two weeks they recruited three more accounting mentors: Sara Reynolds, Dave Caraway, and Lara Dean, and three computer science students: Joe Pena, Maricella Torres, and Sathya Maturi.

While they recruited students, I had a chat with Chico State marketing professor Dr. Richard Davis. When we first met a year earlier, Dick and I struck it off immediately and became friends.

In his late forties, Dick was handsome, fit, and sported a salt and pepper beard. He easily dusted off men in their thirties and forties on his weekend road bike races. Dick had just returned from a two-year unpaid leave of absence from Chico State to serve as an overseas consultant for small and medium enterprise development. Less than a year earlier he had been in Somalia serving as a consultant for the United Nations Development Program, but civil unrest there resulted in mandatory evacuation from Mogadishu in late 1992. Before returning to his teaching duties at Chico State, the UN assigned him to Bali for a few months.

Over a beer at Sierra Nevada Brewing Company, I asked, "Hey, do you know any good marketing students who might want to do this SIFE thing with my accounting students?" After I explained the SIFE concept and my junior high idea, he said, "Count me in! I'll get you a few more students. And do you want a co-adviser?"

Before I knew it, Dick recruited two of his best students, Stefan Hackett and Megan James. Chris Coutant recruited one more liberal arts major, Steve Harrington, and in less than two weeks the first Chico State SIFE team was born.

By December, the nascent SIFE team developed an overall master plan for the next five months and submitted it to the Chico Junior High math teachers. In January 1994, I authored the first ten lessons, and on January 28 we hosted an in-service workshop for the SIFE mentors and junior high teachers.

Until February 22, one pair of SIFE students entered each math class to deliver the first ten lessons in ten consecutive school days. After February 22, the project called for the SIFE students to return each Friday throughout the semester. I had a great time authoring lessons such as "Good Business Is Good Business," "Data vs. Information: The Two-Dice Game," "Einstein's Second Greatest Theory: The Time Value of Money," and "The Penny Experiment."

March 11 was a key day—the seven junior high students in each class who authored the best business plans were awarded $25 startup loans. The kids came up with some creative ideas for businesses. Among the more memorable were "*Chico Kids Magazine*," "Animal Exercise," "Two Musketeers Babysitting Service," "Candy Shack," "JAAM Car Wash," "Erin's Bobbles and Beads," "The Lawn Mower Dude," and "The Flintstone Factory." Contracts were signed by the winning students promising to fulfill the spirit of their plan by the end of the semester, at which time the $25 debt would be forgiven.

By the middle of April most of the lessons had been taught and the rookie Chico State SIFE team finished its preparations to go to San Francisco. With help from Dick and me, the SIFE students authored a mandatory four-page annual report and prepared PowerPoint slides to back up their twenty-four-minute presentation.

The regional tournament took place at the beautiful Hyatt Regency on the Embarcadero. For some students it was the first time they had been in a luxury hotel. The cascading mirror pond in the middle of the lobby left many mouths agape, including mine.

I thought, "First I receive a letter from Sam Walton's son, and now my students and I are staying at a luxury hotel. This SIFE organization seems to be well-connected, and it doesn't hold back when selecting event venues." At the same time, though, I wondered why a nonprofit organization espousing economics and fiscal austerity didn't avail itself of more economical venues, such as university campuses or lower-cost hotels.

Of course, SIFE Headquarters wasn't footing very much of the bill. SIFE's home office in Springfield, Missouri, had promised to reimburse each SIFE team for only three hotel rooms (we needed six). All transportation costs were the responsibility of each team.

SIFE tournaments today are not much different than they were back in 1994. At a regional competition, teams are put into "leagues" named after one of SIFE's board member companies. Individual colleges and universities are assigned to a league of between four to eight teams, with two winners advancing from each league. Winners are determined by a panel of judges recruited in advance by SIFE Headquarters. The more money a company gives, the more prominence they receive in recognition. Companies represented in San Francisco included Wal-Mart, of course, but also corporations that sold products to Wal-Mart such as Goodyear, General Electric, Unilever, American Greetings, Hallmark Cards, Co-ca-Cola, Kraft Foods, and more. Each regional champion team wins a prize of $1,500, contingent on the team using these funds toward air and hotel travel expenses to the national competition, to take place in Kansas City the following month.

I did the math. If we were fortunate to win our regional competition, eight students, Dick Davis, and I would be traveling to Kansas City. That's ten airfares and five hotel rooms for three nights, I worried. Conservatively, travel costs would be about $6,000. How would we come up with the other $4,500? One answer: prize money from special competitions.

At SIFE regional competitions, SIFE provided "special competitions" as additional incentives to complete projects meeting specific criteria. In 1994 there were two special competitions. One was called "Halt the Deficit/ Reduce the Debt" and the other was "Success 2000." These competitions were usually sponsored by SIFE board member companies or by individual philanthropists who leverage SIFE teams as a delivery vehicle to support a particular cause sanctioned by SIFE. Some of these causes, I saw with some degree of consternation, supported conservative political ideology. No special competitions supported progressive or liberal causes.

If a team completed a project or activity that met the specific criteria for these special competitions, it was encouraged to submit a one-page summary to the judges in addition to the four-page annual report required for the overall competition.

Besides judging the overall competition, the business managers and executives judging the teams in each league would also evaluate the special competition entries. If a team won its league in one special competition category, it picked up an extra $1,000. If it won both special competitions, it brought in $2,000.

Our team arrived the night before competition. The next day there was a palpable energy in the conference area buzzing with enthusiastic students visiting with recruiters at exhibit booths set up by sponsoring companies. Staffing the largest booth was Wal-Mart's Joey Jones, a long-time Wal-Mart associate. He was charismatic and friendly.

"Interesting way to recruit, don't you think?" he smiled at me. "What better way to find highly motivated, articulate university students at one spot? We can interview students from several campuses in one day, rather than us sending recruiters to each individual campus. Supporting SIFE is one of our innovative strategies to get first shot at star students."

Chico State was placed into a league of five other SIFE teams. When it was our team's turn, the five presenters confidently took their places in the front of the room. As a new team, Chico State only had one substantive project to talk about and our goal was to convince the judges we had done the best job of meeting the main criteria. The first and most important criterion was: how creative, innovative, and effective were the students in implementing in-depth free market economics and business educational programs on the campus and in the community? Did they ensure the continuation of these programs in the future?

This criterion mapped perfectly onto my interest in community service learning. How better to involve undergraduate business students than having them implement economics and business programs to at-risk math students at an ethnically diverse junior high? My enthusiasm was reinforced when I discovered an article on the Internet—which was just then beginning to make its way into mainstream society as a research and communications tool. Richard Riley, secretary of the U.S. Department of Education, made a speech to the *Fortune* Magazine Education Summit Conference in September 1993. He described several objectives he would like to accomplish at the federal level in order to increase workplace lit-eracy. One question posed by Riley was, "How do we involve the entire community by creating partnerships at every level, from child development and school-to-work programs and to afterschool and summer programs, working with community groups, business, and others?"[1]

Another source that reinforced my new interest in service learning was the Wingspread Group on Higher Education. Unlike Secretary Riley, who focused on K-12 education, the blue-ribbon panel of the country's leading academics and business leaders focused on higher education's vantage point: "What does society *need* from higher education? It needs stronger, more vital forms of community." The group offered a recommendation in order to achieve these goals: "There is no substitute for experience. Academic work should be complemented by the kinds of knowledge derived from firsthand experience, such as contributing to the wellbeing of others, participating in political campaigns, and working with the enterprises that create wealth in our society."[2]

At the SIFE regional competition in San Francisco, it didn't take long for our team to learn that the elite SIFE teams such as La Sierra University in Riverside, California, had completed dozens of SIFE activities. These teams hurried through their well-rehearsed presentations, shot-gunning judges with an almost overwhelming array of facts and figures, finishing their multimedia presentations just seconds before their allotted twenty-four minutes. Presenters on these teams brought in their own sound systems and microphones, wore matching business suits and ties, and worked from well-rehearsed scripts, only occasionally looking at their note cards.

Comparatively, the Chico State team was a motley crew. Chris Coutant, the long-haired liberal arts major, was the team leader, and he didn't exactly look like the kind of conservative recruit Wal-Mart would want for its fast-track management program. The Chico presenters were hodge-podge, wearing their own non-matching business attire—some with clip-on ties. Each student worked from overhead slide transparencies rather than note cards. And rather than a catalog of projects, the Chico State SIFE team's junior high math project was a one-horse pony. After about sixteen minutes, the team ended its oral presentation—compared to other teams, this was abbreviated. I worried that the judges—numbering about twenty, mostly men—might deduct points because we ended early. But this was, indeed, our first year in SIFE, and in actuality, we had only been operating our project for less than three months.

Nonetheless, I was like a proud father. The Chico State team described how our project met all three of the main judging criteria.

Criterion two focused on evaluation, asking how well students measured the results of their educational programs. This criterion fit neatly into what I was learning as project codirector of the FIPSE grant, and also into the total quality management (TQM) philosophy taught in management courses. The father of TQM is J. Edwards Deming. In the early 1990s, business schools were just beginning to teach Deming's approach, which emphasized the importance of outcomes assessment and statistical quality control. I soon came to be a staunch believer in Deming's credos: "In God we trust. All others must provide data," and "What gets measured gets managed." SIFE's second judging criterion was consistent with Deming's philosophy.

The third criterion required SIFE teams to get out in the community and hustle. Not only must the team implement outreach projects, but it also had to enlist the support of community leaders to serve on business advisory boards (BABs). Teams were encouraged to get as much publicity for their projects as possible. SIFE Headquarters was more than helpful in this regard, as the SIFE information handbook included sample templates to use in press releases. The SIFE name and mission, of course, was prominently included throughout the template.

Because our junior high project was not yet finished for the semester, we didn't have any outcomes assessment results to report. Everything was anecdotal. Compared to other, more experienced teams, we were weak there.

As for use of a BAB and the media, we were much stronger. We had recruited sixteen members of the business community to serve as our advisors. We also had some favorable attention from three local newspapers.

After all presentations were made and the exhibit booths closed, the teams gathered in a big conference room. Joey Jones took the stage. "Let me tell you, SIFE students are the future leaders of this country," he said. "I have seen some presentations today that give me great hope for America. And I know many of our sponsors have hired some SIFE students today. Thank you for your continued support of the SIFE mission."

After that, Jones called out the winners of each league. When he got to the Chico State league, we all held our breath. "And the league winner is … Chico State! And the winner of the Kraft General Foods Success 2000

Special Competition is … Chico State! And the winner of the Jules and Gwen Knapp Halt the Deficit/Reduce the Debt Special Competition is … Chico State!"

The judging criterion for the Success 2000 special competition sponsored by Kraft General Foods was based on how well a SIFE team taught the economically disadvantaged an understanding of the free enterprise system. Our junior high math project nailed that criterion. When our name was called I was relieved and added $1,000 to our Kansas City travel fund.

The second special competition was sponsored by the Jules and Gwen Knapp Charitable Foundation. It was called the Halt the Deficit/Reduce the Debt Special Competition. As the title implied, SIFE teams entering this competition were asked to educate their community about the federal budget deficit and national debt, along with their impact on the U.S. economy. Our entry for this competition was entitled *Profits, Taxes, and Government Spending: The Penny Experiment.* This entry was based on two lessons at Chico Junior High. By winning this competition, I added another $1,000 to our travel fund.

The penny lesson was among my favorites. Each junior high student was provided fifty pennies, representing $50 of income tax on an assumed $250 of pretax earnings. Students voted on how they wanted their tax money to be spent, such as a class party, new uniforms for athletic teams, a big screen TV for the student lounge, or tax refunds to those who paid the taxes. A Mason jar provided a visual prop for the most popular programs; the more popular the program, the more pennies went into the jar.

In a follow-up to the first lesson, I created a situation where the class inherited a large class debt from prior years. One of the Mason jars was labeled, "Interest on government debt," and before the students could allocate their funds to government programs, the interest on the debt had to be paid first. The first seven pennies, out of fifty, represented 14 percent of the federal budget, the same percentage being paid by the federal government in interest. My SIFE students liked teaching the lessons, and the students loved it.

The Penny Experiment was intentionally designed to be nonpartisan. I wanted students to see for themselves that, when they became adults, they had a role to play in a democracy through their democratically-elected officials. These officials establish tax policy, including setting tax rates and determining how tax revenues are to be spent.

While absorbing the goings-on at my first regional competition, I observed companies like Kraft Foods and Sherwin-Williams were among the long and growing list of SIFE corporate sponsors. I noticed most sponsors were conservative business leaders like Jules Knapp. He and his wife, lifelong Chicago residents, were now philanthropists. Earlier in his life, Jules Knapp had gained his initial fortune by starting a private-label paint firm, United Coatings Inc., with his brother. Knapp was one of the first paint producers to market to mass merchandisers like Wal-Mart.[3] In the mid-'90s, United Coatings merged with a Buffalo company, Pratt and Lambert, which was subsequently sold to Sherwin-Williams in 1996. Knapp was typical of the members of SIFE's executive board of directors: white, older, rich, politically conservative, and strongly connected to Wal-Mart.

In comparison to the board of directors I was also white, but much younger, not nearly so well off, and politically independent. Later, as I got to know other Sam M. Walton Free Enterprise Fellows, I realized I was in the distinct minority. Like SIFE's management and board, most Walton Fellows were free market devotees, and not proponents of big government. Many, in fact, were proponents of little or no government.

Philosophically, I was neither a left-leaning Keynesian, a right-learning acolyte of Milton Friedman, nor a libertarian from the Austrian school of economics championed by Friedrich von Hayek. My parents taught me to work hard, to work smart, to create a budget, and to live within it. Government should strive to do the same, I reasoned, but they should also avail their power to implement available monetary policies to maximize employment, minimize inflation, protect its citizens, and increase standards of living for its people—even if it meant incurring budget deficits and debt. This view, I would soon learn, was considered radically left of most people associated with SIFE.

Though it was clear to me in April 1994 that SIFE leaned to the right politically, I wasn't to learn just how conservative SIFE really was until the Chico State team went to Kansas City a month later. And, much later, I discovered that SIFE was founded in 1975 as a young Republican club encouraging university students to propagandize for conservative political ideologies.[4] I would also learn—the hard way—that when one gets too close to the seat of money and power, those threatened by your presence may look for ways, directly or surreptitiously, to mitigate your influence.

In spite of my political misgivings, though, I enjoyed our first SIFE exposition and career fair. The San Francisco event felt similar to a sports tournament, with nervous tension building until the team's performance. And there was something heady about learning Sam Walton supported SIFE before his death in 1992, and knowing that his son Rob was now actively recruiting new SIFE fellows named in his father's honor.

After Joey Jones announced our league results, the Chico State SIFE team took the stage, collecting three large trophies, a check for $3,500, and an invitation to Kansas City on May 10–12.

It was to be the first of twelve annual trips to Kansas City, exactly equal to the number of years I would serve as a Sam M. Walton Free Enterprise Fellow. Now, almost thirty-eight years old, I was more than an accounting professor. With the FIPSE grant and SIFE, I had discovered a way to fulfill my lifelong coaching passion. Service learning was the name, and SIFE was the game.[5]

Chapter 3

Kansas City, Here We Come

——————

Ten of us—eight Chico State SIFE students, Dick Davis, and I—departed from the Sacramento airport early May 7, 1994, to catch a flight to Kansas City, Missouri, with a stop in Denver. I felt like Bobby Knight taking his Indiana Hoosiers to the NCAA basketball tournament. In our carry-on luggage we included forty copies of our team's annual report, a laptop computer, and a clunky video overhead projection system. We arrived at the Hyatt Regency late in the afternoon, freshened up, and walked over to the Crown Center to check out the welcome reception for students and Sam M. Walton Fellows.

In the heart of downtown Kansas City, the Crown Center was connected to our hotel by street walkways. The Crown Center includes another luxury hotel, three levels of high-end stores and restaurants, and the world headquarters of Hallmark Cards, Inc.

Hallmark was one of SIFE's board member companies; a seat on the board cost each board member company $25,000 a year. The title for the event put the company in the spotlight, ahead of other donor companies and on the same playing field as one of its most significant customers, Wal-Mart. The official name of the event was the Hallmark Cards/Students in Free Enterprise (SIFE) International Exposition and Career Opportunity Fair.

The SIFE expo had been in Kansas City since 1988. It was a convenient place to host a national event; centrally located in the heart of the nation's breadbasket, a two-hour drive north of SIFE's home office in Springfield, Missouri. It was also a favorite place for Wal-Mart, where its annual meetings took place.[1]

As we sauntered from the Hyatt to the Crown Center we didn't quite know what to expect. But we soon found out. The Westin ballroom was abuzz; it seemed like every SIFE team except ours was wearing customized T-shirts with their school colors. The SIFE staff members from Springfield were all wearing new polo shirts and SIFE donor-company reps—mainly from human relations or campus recruiting—proudly wore their company casuals. Joey Jones from Wal-Mart's People Division was there, too.

Before long, a rotund man of about 230 pounds with rosy red cheeks and dark-rimmed glasses lumbered to the stage. After welcoming the group, he invited a friend to come to the stage to offer a prayer asking Jesus Christ to guide and help us over the course of the next two days.[2] Following the prayer, he stepped back to the microphone and drawled, "Do y'all wanna do the SIFE cheer?" Clearly, most of the veteran SIFE teams knew what he was talking about, but rookies like us had no clue.

"Well, it goes like this," he boomed. "Give me an S!"

The group replied, enthusiastically and in unison, "S!"

"Give me an "I"!"

After the F and the E, he shouted, "What's that spell?"

"SIFE!" everyone cried.

"Who are we?" he thundered.

"Students in Free Enterprise!" the herd responded.

"And what's that mean?" he implored.

"Success is where we specialize!" which the crowd immediately followed with a Tiger Woods fist pump and a corresponding "Yesss!"

Dick Davis and I looked at each other, eyebrows raised. "What the hell, is this a sideshow or a professional business conference?" I asked.

Chris Coutant, non-conformist and agnostic to the core, saddled over. "Do you believe this? Are we at a revival?"

Approaching forty years of age, the marshmallow of a man leading the cheer had natural curly hair and a double chin begging for a third. If he were younger, he could be a spitting image of cherubic movie actor Jonah Hill, before Hill went on a diet.

This man was not a professional cheerleader, nor was he an evangelist. His name was Alvin Rohrs, SIFE CEO. The big dog.

Shortly after the prayer, two men in their mid-fifties joined Rohrs on the stage. Both seemed to be cut from the same cloth—each wore a business suit, was well-tanned, tall, handsome, and athletic. Rohrs introduced them as SIFE's two strongest advocates: Jack and Jack.

In the next twelve years, I would learn a lot more about Alvin Rohrs,

Jack Shewmaker, and Jack Kahl. In their own way each has had an indelible impact on my professional career. In many ways they have had a hand in shaping the direction of my personal life.

Each man was an ardent believer in a leadership philosophy, called *servant leadership*. Each was an advocate for free enterprise and conservative political ideology. In SIFE, they found a perfect outlet to leverage their advocacy by tapping into the idealism of college and university youth who, in turn, would continue to advocate for the same causes. As Wal-Mart was expanding beyond the Ozarks, the Bible Belt, and the Sun Belt in the mid-1980s, the retailer needed a fresh army of enthusiastic young managers.[3] In short, Wal-Mart made SIFE a vital part of its human resources strategy. What better source than a highly-motivated, passionate group of recent graduates who already bought into the SIFE cheer? Give me a W, give me an A, give me an L, give me a squiggly.

Born and raised on a farm in the Ozarks, and son of a Baptist minister, Alvin Rohrs was the SIFE CEO—*le grand fromage,* the big cheese. He had been with the organization since August 1982 when he was asked to take over the floundering organization that, a few years earlier, had boasted over a hundred university SIFE teams. In late 1981, the number had dropped to just eighteen, and SIFE was in big trouble. It needed a new home and new energy.

SIFE found its new home at Southwest Baptist University (SBU) in the Ozarks, and gained its energy from Rohrs, who graduated in 1979 from SBU (then known as Southern Baptist College) with a business/political science double major. As an undergraduate at SBU, he was a member of the SIFE team and participated in debate.

A few years later, by June of 1982, he had earned his law degree specializing in tax law and business regulation and graduated cum laude from the University of Missouri Columbia School of Law. Degree in hand, a career as a lawyer no longer seemed appealing. When he received a call from his undergraduate alma mater to head up the new free enterprise center on SBU's campus in Bolivar, he happily accepted. In October, the SIFE operation moved its headquarters from Dallas to Bolivar, and Rohrs also accepted the additional responsibility as SIFE's new director.[4]

SBU's entrepreneurial president, James Sells, welcomed Rohrs back to SBU with open arms. With the new Gene Taylor National Free Enterprise Center, dedicated to the service of Christ by Vice President George H.W. Bush, Sells saw a new opportunity to link private businesses with his campus by making free enterprise education a cornerstone of SBU's curriculum.[5] In an interview with Sells on March 17, 2005, Sells told author Bethany Moreton, "In my opinion, these students are often terribly naive about finance—all aspects of finance, personal and institutional. They would have a general pull toward Christian work but little sense of how it is organized and funded."[6] The new curriculum included a heavy dose of servant leadership as a management technique, which fit nicely into SBU's mission: a Christ-centered, caring academic community preparing students to be servant-leaders in a global society.

The emphasis on Christian-centered free enterprise education had great appeal to local business leaders. At the time Rohrs was hired, SIFE's annual budget was only about $200,000 per year. But that was going to change. Rohrs used his social networking skills to create the Leaders of the Ozarks program where local business leaders each donated $1,000 annually for the "mutual fellowship and social interaction" provided by the SIFE organization. Among its members were Wendy's fast-food chain founder Dave Thomas and the governor of Missouri, John Ashcroft.[7]

SIFE's first main financial backer, Bill Seay, joined the Wal-Mart board of directors in 1984. During a meeting in Sam Walton's office in Bentonville, Seay convinced Walton and his most trusted lieutenant, Wal-Mart vice chairman and CFO Jack Shewmaker, to come to SIFE's aid. Walton liked the idea of helping SIFE, but Walton knew he didn't have the personal time to commit. According to Shewmaker, Walton told Seay the SIFE concept sounded like something Jack would like to take on. "If Jack wants to take this on," Walton told Seay, "I can promise you and him that I'll support him in that endeavor."[8]

Shewmaker grabbed the reins with gusto, immediately bringing cash, connections, and leadership to SIFE. According to historian Bethany Moreton's 2009 book, *To Serve God and Wal-Mart: The Making of Christian Free Enterprise*, "Shewmaker was the man on horseback. In 1985 he accepted the organization's chairmanship and brought with him a

$50,000 donation from the Wal-Mart Foundation. He augmented the $1,000-per-member Leaders of the Ozarks by launching the Chairman's Club for donors of $20,000 or more. The goal was to bring in up to fifteen private contributors who wanted to support a major marketing drive with backing for new videos, word processing, toll-free phone lines, recruiting staff, and PR materials."[9]

With Wal-Mart providing the wind, the SIFE ship started sailing. Rohrs began depositing large checks and, with Shewmaker at his side, he gained direct access to dozens of Wal-Mart vendor companies, all wanting to curry favor with the retail giant. SIFE soon outgrew its offices on SBU's campus in Bolivar and moved thirty miles down the road to Springfield in 1987. Under Rohrs' direction, SIFE was now flush with cash. In SIFE's fall training workshops, its founder Sonny Davis applied servant-leadership theories to recruit more SIFE teams and corporate sponsors. Davis had been honing this human-centered management philosophy since 1963 in Texas where, as assistant attorney general, he had worked with juvenile delinquents to help them be more cooperative and accepting of society norms.

Servant leaders (as we will see in the next chapter) have three main things in common: they are willing to share power and listen to subordinates; they constantly express their appreciation and recognition of subordinates; and they project an "I am no holier than thou," self-deprecating humility to earn respect and trust. If successful, the servant leader creates a culture of unabiding loyalty to the organization. Such loyalty and obeisance result in a trade-off, wherein the intangible rewards from the higher purpose over-ride more tangible material rewards. Many rank and file workers believe so ardently in the higher purpose that they are willing to forego higher pay, better working conditions, or improved health insurance benefits.

By the time the Chico State SIFE team arrived in Kansas City in May 1994, the SIFE organization claimed to field 250 active SIFE teams, reaching over twenty thousand individuals. Earlier in the year, each Sam M. Walton Fellow had come to know Sidney Lilly as the amiable voice at the end of SIFE's toll-free line. Lilly, in her late fifties, was Rohrs' academic office administrator. She handled a multitude of faculty queries through-out the year. With some faculty, especially enthusiastic new ones like me, she developed a bond. Lilly also was in charge of mailing big boxes of promotional handbooks, brochures, and videotapes to all SIFE campuses.

While Lilly handled the operational side of the house, Rohrs was the money man—he much preferred it that way. He didn't really enjoy interacting with SIFE advisers, most of whom were instructors and adjunct faculty members. And, for the most part, he wasn't a natural around students, it seemed, especially those from nondenominational public colleges and universities. When he did take an interest in SIFE teams he had a parochial view, appearing much more at home with students and faculty from nonsecular universities such as nearby Drury University, John Brown University, College of the Ozarks, and Harding University.

Rohrs was not shy about interacting with potential donors, though. He appeared thrilled to be in the presence of high-powered CEOs, and he loved canvassing the country and racking up frequent-flier miles. What he undoubtedly enjoyed most, however, was cashing the ever-increasing number of checks made out to SIFE.[10]

Not long after Bill Seay introduced SIFE to Walton and Shewmaker in early 1985, Rohrs invited Shewmaker to make a speech at one of the local SIFE team's campus. Shewmaker showed up in his pickup and cowboy boots. Rohrs, looking down at his own cowboy boots, thought, "This is someone I can relate to." The two had another thing in common—both were Ozarks boys—Shewmaker growing up in Buffalo, Missouri, just twenty miles east of Rohrs' hometown of Bolivar.[11]

As a teenager, Jack Shewmaker learned the value of hard work by working at his father's grocery store after school each day. On Saturdays he worked from 7 a.m. to 7 p.m. Smart and athletic, he accepted scholarships to study engineering at Georgia Tech but early in his freshman year his high school sweetheart suffered a life-threatening car injury. He dropped out of Georgia Tech to be at her side, and before long he decided to forego college altogether and get married.[12]

Shewmaker's career started with Wal-Mart in 1970, the same year the company went public with only thirty-two stores. Prior to that he worked for a Springfield manufacturing company for a couple years, then tried his hand at retail. After a brief stint with Montgomery Wards he accepted a job as field manager with Coast to Coast. Impressing the brass with his tenacity, curiosity, and ambition, he was promoted to company training director. Then, switching gears and taking a job with a large food chain—a job that proved a bad fit for Shewmaker—he was anxious to get back into retail. Sam Walton had heard about the young wunderkind's work at Coast to Coast and invited him to Wal-Mart's home office for an interview.

Shewmaker and Walton had an unforgettable first encounter, as related by Shewmaker in a SIFE newsletter in 2008:

> I got in the car and interviewed with Wal-Mart and was of-fered a job as a store manager, but I wanted to be a district manager, so I declined. That night I received a call from Sam Walton. He said, "I understand they were pretty impressed with your ideas." I agreed and told him I was impressed with Wal-Mart. He suggested we meet, and I said, "Well, Mr. Walton, I don't see a lot of merit driving all the way back to Bentonville." Instead of just closing the door, he said something that I'll never forget. He said, "Will you meet me halfway?" We both drove seventy miles and spent six hours in a Howard Johnson's restaurant talking about how we wanted to build Wal-Mart, shook hands, and I started my career with the company. An important part of leadership is to be genuinely interested in the attitudes of people you are with. Sam's idea of meeting halfway was very different than most—he considered what the other person's impression of halfway was, not his own. That's the kind of diplomacy that works with businesses trying to merge or even during negotiations between countries. He saw that if you took one more step or drove ten more miles, it could make all the difference in the world. It became part of the management principles that still govern Wal-Mart today.[13]

At Wal-Mart, Shewmaker quickly rose through the ranks including district manager, vice president of security, vice president of store operations, and executive vice president of store operations, personnel and merchandise. Early on, he played a key role in shaping the "Wal-Mart Culture" by authoring the company's first policies and procedures manual. He continued to earn his stripes, adding a long list of innovations to his resume: Wal-Mart's "Everyday Low Prices" pricing strategy; coining the term "Rollback"; convincing Walton to invest heavily in the company's first satellite communications system; and implementing bar code standards for products. In 1978, he became president and chief operating officer; six years later he became vice chairman and CFO. By the time of his retirement he had won numerous awards during his career, including *Discount Store News* Discount Retailer of the Year in 1981. When he retired in 1988, over five hundred retail executives gathered at the Howard Johnson motel in Springfield to honor him. Wal-Mart was then the nation's second largest discounter. The event was cohosted by Wal-Mart … and SIFE.[14]

With Wal-Mart's contributions starting in 1985, and Shewmaker's prodding of local business leaders to join the Chairman's Club, SIFE's annual budget quickly exceeded $600,000. With the largesse, twenty-five SIFE faculty advisers were provided a $1,000 stipend from Wal-Mart and honored with the title of "Sam M. Walton Free Enterprise Fellow." At the national SIFE competition in 1985 with eight hundred people in attendance, one participant said, "I feel like I'm ready now to go out and evangelize the country for free enterprise."[15]

The year 1985 was also significant because it marked the first time SIFE created special incentives for teams to undertake projects with a specific theme. Over fifty teams competed for a prize money pool of $10,000 for projects designed "to educate Americans on the need to reduce the federal deficit caused by government waste."[16] The sponsor of the special competition, the Business Roundtable, consisted of over two hundred CEOs and business leaders advocating for conservative government policies and legislation. Business Roundtable support to SIFE included $10,000 in cash along with such materials as SIFE team handbooks, posters, bumper stickers, and postcards to Congress. These materials were mailed to all 170 participating SIFE teams. At the national SIFE exposition in 1986, SIFE graciously thanked the Business Roundtable's executive director, James Keogh—formerly President Nixon's chief speechwriter.[17]

Though he would remain one of the most significant board members of SIFE's Executive Committee until his untimely death at age seventy-two on November 17, 2010, Shewmaker stepped down as SIFE's chairman in 1988—the same year he retired from Wal-Mart at age fifty.[18]

Taking Shewmaker's place as SIFE board chairman was Stanley Gaines, the recently retired CEO of GNB, Inc. GNB was an automotive and industrial battery company. Like Bill Seay, SIFE's cofounder, as well as many of the CEOs serving on SIFE's board of directors, Gaines was conservative and politically well-connected. His strongest connection was his wife, Gay Hart Haines.

Mrs. Haines had an impressive resume in Republican politics. Among her credentials: chair of the board for William F. Buckley's National Review Institute; positions at think tanks like the American Enterprise Institute, the Heritage Foundation, and the Hudson Initiative. She was chair of GOPAC, Newt Gingrich's political action committee, a role she relished in helping to raise funds to sweep Republicans (many of them belonging to the New Christian Right) into Congress as part of Gingrich's Contract with America in 1994.[19]

Stanley Gaines held the SIFE board chair until 1992 when he passed the torch to SIFE's second Jack—Jack Kahl. Kahl was to hold the position for five years. With Kahl at SIFE's helm, the number of regional competitions grew, the number of participating teams hit an all-time high, and SIFE's board of directors grew to more than a hundred members in 1997.[20]

Shewmaker had turned the reins over to Gaines, and Gaines to Kahl, at a propitious time. By 1989, SIFE was growing rapidly and its treasury was bulging. New marquee supporters were signing up, including the international accounting firm KPMG, which began its sponsorship in 1990.[21] Clearly, SIFE had outgrown its first home in Springfield—it was time to move. So SIFE—in keeping in practice with the servant leadership principles of lavish recognition and praise—built a new building in Springfield and promptly named it the Jack Shewmaker Center/SIFE National Headquarters.

Jack Kahl and the company he founded, Manco, weren't household names but its flagship product certainly was. Kahl was known to veteran SIFE faculty and companies involved with SIFE as the "Duck Tape Man," and the largest customer for his famous duct tape was Wal-Mart. When he first met Walton and Jack Shewmaker in 1976, Kahl was not yet forty years old.[22]

Walton and Shewmaker immediately took a liking to Kahl, and about the time Wal-Mart started buying duct tape by the truckloads from Manco in 1985, Kahl was quick to jump on the SIFE bandwagon. Manco, too, wanted fresh-faced graduates right out of college to enter its management training program. SIFE's philosophy of servant leadership mapped directly onto Kahl's, and the friendship he forged with Wal-Mart executives had two main benefits: it was certainly good for his own bottom line and, impressed with the Wal-Mart culture, he picked up some effective motivational techniques and adapted them at Manco.

Like Shewmaker, Kahl did not grow up with a silver spoon. His father was often hospitalized with tuberculosis, so his mom declared young Jack the man of the house. He got his first job at age seven as a newspaper carrier, and before long, his mom helped him open his first bank account.[23] Born and raised in the Cleveland area, Kahl went to the all-male, college preparatory St. Edward High School. Like many Catholic schools, St. Edward "emphasized the importance of a Christ-like commitment to servant leadership." In 1962 Kahl graduated from John Carroll University to which, shortly after selling Manco in 1998, he contributed $1 million to endow an entrepreneurship fellowship in honor of his father.

Soon after his wedding, Kahl used $10,000 originally intended to furnish his new house to help finance his investment in Manco. Together with the cash savings and a loan for $182,000, Kahl founded Manco in 1971 by buying out a company with revenues of about $800,000. Manco was selling pressure-sensitive tape products to retail outlets when he met Walton and Shewmaker in 1976. At the time, Manco was generating between $4 and $6 million a year in revenues. Soon thereafter Kahl's company began selling to Wal-Mart and within a few years sales skyrocketed to $21.5 million.

Like his new friend and mentor, Jack Shewmaker, Kahl was an innovator. He insisted on using an eye-catching, green packaging-set, and in 1985 he introduced the Manco Duck as the company mascot. Against the advice of market researchers he labeled his "duck tape" with the cuddly green duck mascot. In 1993 he was named one of "America's Most Admired CEOs" by *Industry Week* magazine. *Cleveland Magazine* named him the "Best Boss in Town" in 1996. In 1998, with Manco now generating annual sales of $180 million, Kahl sold his company to German-based Henkel Group.

A gregarious, fun-loving guy, Kahl had a quirky sense of humor and a gravelly voice. Eccentric in a way similar to his mentor, Sam Walton, Kahl had been known to swim across a duck pond in icy weather or shave his head when Manco achieved its company goals. Manco did not call its employees "associates"; rather, they were "partners." And like Wal-Mart, it had a company cheer, spelling out M-A-N-C-O followed by, "Who's number one?" Answer: "Partners and customers first, always, (fist-pump) yessss!"

Kahl, employing servant leader principles, said, "We ring bells to praise people, and we pat them on the back. We recognize all the unsung heroes."[24] In his book about leadership, Kahl said, "But as important as Manco Duck has been to our company as a symbol of servant leadership, he only came onstage after that crucial element had become embedded in our corporate psyche."[25]

He ended his book: "Leading is about making a choice in your heart to help, coach, and serve others. Leading from the heart is the only path to serving the team. And when the well-served team wins success, they will find that their servant is their master."[26] In 1999, I was on hand in Springfield when SIFE dedicated a wing of its new world headquarters and called it the Jack Kahl Entrepreneurship Center.

Such were the three men—Rohrs, Shewmaker, and Kahl—on the stage at the Westin Hotel in Kansas City in May 1994. When my Chico State SIFE team and I first saw these three men on stage we didn't know their background or their current positions. But after two full days of activity, we knew. In extolling the virtues of SIFE at the welcome reception, two lunches, and two banquets, Rohrs was undoubtedly an articulate and emotional fundraiser. Frequently, he would get so choked up that tears would flow.

We also learned that Shewmaker and Kahl were the powerbrokers on the board. Both took the microphone at lunch and dinner in three capacities: making speeches, handing out honors and awards, and being presented with them. In short order my Chico State companions and I all knew that these three men made up the SIFE troika—a power triumvirate.

More than just a bit unsettling, though, was that on at least two occasions in Kansas City, participants were asked to bow their heads as one of SIFE's volunteers or faculty advisers led a prayer. Three of my students were not Christian—Heather was from a Jewish background, Sathya was a Sikh from India, and Chris was an atheist. All three of them wondered why SIFE was *so Christian?* At the time, I couldn't answer them.

La Sierra University, a Seventh-Day Adventist campus in Riverside, California, ended up winning the SIFE USA championship in 1994, starting what would be a string of national championships in 1995, 1996, and 1997. Its oral presentation in 1994 set a new benchmark for SIFE, using state-of-the-art multimedia technology to support its dazzling twenty-four minutes in front of CEOs and senior executives. The La Sierra team, in black business suits accented with red, white, and blue ties and U.S. flag lapel pins, described a long list of activities and projects that it had completed during the year; many of these activities were designed to teach the community about the importance of halting the federal deficit and reducing the debt.

Democratic president Bill Clinton had been in office less than two years, but there was an undercurrent of contempt for Clinton in Kansas City. Speeches included unveiled criticism of his policies and leadership abilities. After holding the Oval Office for twelve years under President Reagan and the first President Bush, Republicans were gearing up to recapture the House of Representatives and, should Clinton stumble before 1996, the presidency.

While it was true that SIFE teams in Kansas City were honored and recognized, the SIFE exposition put just as much emphasis on lavish rewards and praise on its business leaders. These leaders all seemed to share similar business and political views. Honors for the CEOs and companies included SIFE Eagles Club, Legend Award, Guardian of SIFE, Double Eagle Award, and Champion of SIFE. The vast majority of the business leaders were men.

Overall, the Chico State team did very well in 1994. We came in second place in our league on the first day (I think the league was sponsored by Fruit of the Loom underwear!), finishing behind SIFE powerhouse Pittsburg State University from Kansas. Pittsburgh's faculty adviser, Tom Payne, was an accounting lecturer and a salesman extraordinaire. Just one year later, Alvin Rohrs would snag Payne from academia and make him

SIFE's vice president of university relations. In this capacity Tom and I would soon get to know each other very well.

Though the 1994 Chico State SIFE team was one of the few teams not wearing matching business attire, we did win first place in one special competition, and second place in two others. A total of eight competitions were sponsored by the GE Foundation, with each competition targeting one of eight national education goals designed to improve America's education system by the year 2000. Each competition had two criteria; the first criterion asked students to create a project explicitly targeting the education goal. The second criterion asked students how well they integrated an understanding of how the free enterprise system works into their efforts to achieve the goal.[27]

My justification for helping the first Chico State SIFE team deliver the Math 3 project was based, in part, on a 1989 national report called *Everybody Counts: A Report on the Future of Mathematics Education*, which stated: "In spite of the intimate intellectual link between mathematics and computing, school mathematics has responded hardly at all to curricular changes implied by the computer revolution." Furthermore, "The ideas of mathematics influence the way we live and the way we work on many different levels: Practical knowledge that can be put to immediate use in improving basic living standards. The ability to compare loans, to calculate risks, to figure unit prices, ... brings immediate real benefit."[28]

To become an elite SIFE team, I quickly understood that a team would have to emulate and exceed the exuberant evangelizers for free enterprise from one year to the other. I had to ask myself, did Chico State want to be one of these teams—the kind of team described by Nelson Lichtenstein in his 2009 book, *The Retail Revolution: How Wal-Mart Created a Brave New World of Business*. In his book, Lichtenstein observed that SIFE teams complete "activities during the school year [that] are essentially ideolog-ical and propagandistic: the students develop skits, games, and exercises, often for use in elementary and middle schools, which explain and justify markets, entrepreneurship, deregulation, low taxes, and business ethics."[29] It was clear that the business executives in Kansas City loved SIFE. But could they come to love a team led by someone who didn't share their economic, political, or religious views? Or did I even want to continue my affiliation with SIFE?

Yes, I decided, Chico State would continue in the SIFE program. The benefits outweighed the costs. I saw SIFE as a vehicle for university students to be recognized and rewarded for their service-learning activities; my challenge was to identify appropriate activities. Though I didn't know what servant leadership was at the time, I certainly had seen it in action in Kansas City—the sharing of business success stories; the prayers offered up by its servant leaders, among them business leaders and Sam M. Walton Fellows; the endless praise and recognition for participants; the self-deprecating humor of its leaders, including the humility demonstrated by Alvin Rohrs actually crying for joy in front of some of the U.S.'s most powerful captains of the retail industry—not once, but many times. In spite of my uneasy feelings for SIFE back in 1994, I believed I could put up with the hokey cheers, the long-winded speeches by aging CEOs, and even the underlying religiosity.

With service learning gaining new prominence in higher education, I was willing to swallow some of the more distasteful tenets of servant leadership in order to advance my own educational philosophy of student involvement. SIFE's philosophy may have been something along the lines of: "People support what they help create, and when they do, recognize the shit out of them." But my philosophy was: "Students learn best when applying theory to actual problems, and if solving these problems helps the community, all the better." These two philosophies could coexist, I surmised.

I eagerly read Bethany Moreton's book in 2009, five years after I left SIFE. She provided a fascinating account of Wal-Mart's history, especially as it related to "a complex network that united Sun Belt entrepreneurs, evangelical employees, Christian business students, overseas missionaries, and free-market activists."[30] She acknowledged that the Walton family "did not embrace a Christian identity in the evangelical sense, but the people in their stores were in the midst of realignment, and it was their values that Wal-Mart came to represent."[31] Especially interesting to me was how evangelical employees began to adopt the servant leadership philosophy as part of their Christianity:

For different reasons, many who met inside Wal-Mart stores and offices could see a significant victory in the company's gradual identification with its Christian constituency. In the stores, Christian women on both sides of the Wal-Mart checkout line successfully incorporated many of their priorities into the new workplace. More generally, many found appealing the growing religious identity of the discount store, which produced distinct experiences of mass consumption, low-wage work, and managerial ideology. This new identity did not cater to the citizen-consumer, that Northern shopper who defined her rights and responsibilities to the nation by way of the marketplace. Nor did it radicalize the descendants of the Populists to pocketbook politics in the formal policy arena. Rather, people within Wal-Mart learned to revalue shopping as selfless service to family, and service in turn as a sacred calling. In this context, the salient identity became not citizen-consumer nor worker of the world, but Christian servant. [32]

Especially interesting were two entire chapters linking Wal-Mart, SIFE, Christian free-enterprise, and the Christian servant leader.

Shortly after reading Moreton's book in 2009, I received another book in the mail, the one by Nelson Lichtenstein. Lichtenstein and I had crossed paths in early 2005 when he accepted my invitation to attend the SIFE USA exposition in Kansas City. I knew this was going to be my last trip to Kansas City as part of the SIFE organization, and Lichtenstein wanted to see SIFE teams in action. When SIFE learned he would be accompanying me, it sent him a short note: "This is a private event, by invitation only." SIFE was a closed event, and he was definitely not welcome.

Lichtenstein is a well-respected professor of labor and politics at the University of California, Santa Barbara. We had talked in the spring of 2005, when he was finishing up his editorship of a much-cited collection of essays on Wal-Mart.[33] In 2009 he was finishing up his *Retail Revolution* book.

The Moreton and Lichtenstein books were the result of detailed research and painstaking references, and I found a treasure trove of information. I learned more about servant leadership, SIFE, and how Alvin Rohrs came to be a key player in Wal-Mart's recruiting strategy as it expanded globally. Comparing the information they uncovered with my own personal experience, I knew that someday I would write my own book.

Chapter 4

Servant Leadership, SIFE, and the Big Three

As I began writing the first draft of this chapter from the sixth floor of a seven-story apartment building overlooking the city center in Manama, Bahrain, I received a CNN breaking news email bulletin. The October 5, 2011, bulletin stated, "Sarah Palin said she is not seeking the 2012 Republican nomination for president, according to a statement read on the Mark Levin radio program. 'This has been prayerfully considered,' the statement said. 'I can be on the right path without being a candidate.'"

While governor, Palin and her family were members of the conservative evangelical Wasilla Bible Church, in Wasilla, Alaska. Like thousands of similar churches across the United States, its members believe "in the Bible as the only inspired, inerrant Word of God." According to its website, its members "will serve Christ together. We will pray for one another, we will encourage one another, we will serve one another, even, if need be, we will admonish one another, and above all we will love one another."[1]

It is not unusual for politicos in the United States, especially the more conservative Republicans and tea party advocates, to openly believe in creationism—or two of its offshoots: creation science and intelligent design—instead of evolution.[2] Thus, it was not out of the ordinary to learn that Palin had sought divine guidance in making her decision; however, what caught my eye was when I read her full statement.

"When we serve, we devote ourselves to God, family and country. My decision is based upon a review of what common-sense conservatives and independents have accomplished, especially over the last year," Palin wrote. "I believe that at this time I can be more effective in a decisive role to help elect other true public servants to office. I will continue driving the discussion for freedom and free markets ... we must reduce tax burdens and onerous regulations that kill American industry and our candidates must always push to minimize government to strengthen the economy and allow the private sector to create jobs."[3]

Public servants? Given what I had personally experienced with SIFE and its Big Three leaders—Alvin Rohrs, Jack Shewmaker, and Jack Kahl—all claiming to be servant leaders—I wondered if Sarah Palin had been trained in the management philosophy of servant leadership. Googling Sarah Palin and servant leader, I found this passage from her September 3, 2008, acceptance speech as John McCain's running mate, "No one expects us to agree on everything. But we are expected to govern with integrity, goodwill, clear convictions, and ... a servant's heart."[4] Peggy Noonan of the *Wall Street Journal* gushed at Palin's speech and picked up on how conservatives somehow are better public servants with bigger hearts. Noonan wrote:

> It was the old-time conservatism. Government is too big, Obama will "grow it," Congress spends too much and he'll spend "more." It was for low taxes, for small business, for the private sector, for less regulation, for governing with "a servant's heart"; it was pro-small town values, and implicitly but strongly pro-life.
>
> This was so old it seemed new, and startling. The speech was, in its way, a call so tender it made grown-ups weep on the floor. The things she spoke of were the beating heart of the old America. But as I watched I thought, I know where the people in that room are, I know their heart, for it is my heart. But this election is a wild card, because America is a wild card. It is not as it was in '80. I know where the Republican base is, but we do not know where this country that never stops changing is.[5]

Palin's statement, along with Noonan's endorsement, helped me organize my thoughts for this chapter of my memoir, because one of my goals is to explain how Christianity is linked to the management philosophy of servant leadership. In October 2011 I had already spent nearly five weeks in the Middle East and was intrigued by a culture as unwaveringly devoted to Islam as the United States is to Christianity.

No doubt, I was enjoying my sabbatical leave from Chico State—I no longer stumbled on cable TV evangelicals preaching the gospel; no longer did I see automobiles with chromed loaves and fishes affixed to the trunk; and no longer did I pass by churches with slogans inviting me to Sunday services.

But that didn't spare me from ubiquitous religious reminders. Instead of Christian solicitations, I was now bombarded five times a day with Muslim prayers blasted from the minarets of nearby mosques. Bahrain, like other nearby Muslim countries, was a strange land for an Iowa boy. Like Saudi Arabia, the United Arab Emirates, Qatar, Oman, and Kuwait, Bahrain was dripping in oil wealth—Mercedes, BMWs, Bentleys, Lamborghinis, Porsches—the norm.

Part of my sabbatical duties was to introduce youth from the Middle East to American business and entrepreneurship, but from what I could tell most of the youth in the Gulf Coast countries didn't have to worry very much about making money. The government provided natural citizens with free health care, education, utilities, housing, and monthly living expenses. As long as you didn't question the king and his sheiks, you pretty much had it made.

Unfortunately for many of the Shiite youth in Bahrain, they had recently questioned the Sunni-controlled kingdom as part of the Arab spring uprising, and the huge Pearl Roundabout and monument adjacent to Manama's city center were dismantled. The monument consisted of six "sails" reaching high into the sky, representing the six member nations of the Gulf Cooperation Council. In its place now sits a forty-acre plot of packed sand, encircled by barbed wire fences, empty except for a handful of police cruisers, a few tanks, and desert tents housing the young army men patrolling the hot spots around the city. The Bahraini armed forces were ordered to tear down the monument and cordon off the main meeting place for Bahrain's disenfranchised youth, especially when, on March 1, 2011, Saudi Arabia came to Bahrain's aid by sending thirty tanks across the fifteen-mile King Fahd causeway linking Bahrain to Saudi Arabia.

As I read Palin's announcement, I thought about my own religious upbringing and how the Tabernacle Baptist Church helped shape my early worldview. I also thought about how most U.S. presidential candidates—Republican or Democrat—would have no chance of winning the coveted prize if they claimed to be anything but Christian. Ruminating in my Bahrain apartment, I wondered, "Would a Gulf Coast country ever claim a Christian king?" Not likely.

Even with religious differences, though, I wondered if Christian and Muslims could coexist peacefully and prosperously in a post-modern world with a new form of value-creating capitalism—capitalism that Whole Foods founder John Mackey calls *conscious capitalism*. Or what Bill Gates refers to as *creative capitalism*. I call this *humanitarian capitalism*. One reason I was in the Middle East was to plant this seed of capitalism into the hearts and minds of Middle East youth.[6]

When the Chico State SIFE team and I were in Kansas City in May 1994, I was able to glean that its executives subscribed to the fuzzy notion of servant leadership. Further, most of them seemed to be, to one degree or another, Christian and politically conservative. When I signed up to be a SIFE adviser in 1993, I was under the impression that SIFE was a nonprofit organization with one main mission: to serve as an outlet for university students to achieve their dreams through free enterprise education. What I didn't know was the extent to which SIFE seemingly served three other purposes, and how they were prioritized. One purpose: to act as a public relations and advertising group advocating neoconservative political views, with university students strategically on the front lines, trying now to break through to public universities like Chico State. Second, to promote servant leadership as practiced by Christian CEOs. And third, to serve as a primary way for Wal-Mart and its army of vendors to recruit young and enthusiastic talent who shared these same values.

Today, if you go to SIFE's website at enactus.org, you won't find much about SIFE's history, and you certainly don't find much about servant leadership. But if you dig deep enough, you will learn that the SIFE originated in the mid-'60s under the leadership of Robert T. "Sonny" Davis, who was then heading up an organization that worked with delinquent youth. Davis believed that these difficult youth would be better managed if the adults who supervised them ceded some of their traditional control.

Though SIFE wasn't officially created until 1975, its progenitor entered the picture in August 1963, when Sonny Davis was assistant attorney general in Texas. In this role Davis helped launch what was to be a successful youth program to curb juvenile delinquency by channeling teenage energy to respect social norms. As Bethany Moreton said in chronicling SIFE's history, "Sonny Davis tackled juvenile delinquency with the same fresh ideas that proved so compatible with servant leadership: the human relations school of management, which encouraged intimate teamwork and nonauthoritarian control." One key element of this school was "to shift the responsibility for learning from the teacher to the student." This worked so well with the troubled youth because "the point was to dispense with both the individual striver and the authority figure of the teacher, and thus demonstrate the superior outcome of cooperation."[7]

A cooperative, rather than authoritative, theory of management ran parallel to the intuitive way that I managed my classrooms at Chico State, and this was the direction my accounting colleagues and I were taking in our introductory accounting courses. We believed in a Socratic classroom environment, where students are encouraged to ask probing questions and to question authority. In this environment, the teacher's role is to help students master concepts through "discovery learning," with the teacher guiding students to the best answer. Furthermore, this learning environment is, in a way, consistent with game theory, which I had been exposed to in my doctoral program at Oklahoma State. The gist of game theory—made famous when one of its championing mathematicians, Nobel Prize winner John Nash, was featured in the Hollywood movie *A Beautiful Mind*—stipulates that cooperation between players in a game will lead to an overall better outcome for the group than if each individual acts alone.

Instead of requiring individual students to line up in rows and take copious notes from the *sage on the stage*, we developed a more interactive Socratic learning environment where the teacher became more of a *guide on the side*. Lessons were designed such that students often worked in groups, where stronger students could assist weaker students in mastering learning objectives. We believed that, when teachers give up complete control of the classroom, we could concentrate more on getting students to consider how the information they learned could be used to help make personal decisions. Some of the class time still consisted of lecture, but the majority of each class consisted of student groups working together, with teachers listening in on group interactions and intervening when necessary. Natural leaders emerged within each group, who were then in a position to help their teammates. Once students saw how accounting could be useful in their own personal lives, we were then in a position to take this to the next level. If individuals could use accounting information to make personal decisions, then business leaders could use similar information to make organizational decisions. So far, so good.

In Sonny Davis's training manual he wrote, "So how does one become an effective leader? Simply by helping the uninvolved grow and experience a sense of belonging and contribution to the organization … [P]eople support what they help create."[8] The term "servant leader," however, wasn't coined until 1970, when Robert K. Greenleaf wrote an essay, *The Servant as Leader*.

A longtime manager at AT&T, Greenleaf had spent most of his career in the area of management development training. Taking an early retirement from AT&T, he became a well-traveled consultant, serving as a visiting lecturer and management consultant. In 1964 he founded the international nonprofit foundation, the Center of Applied Ethics, which was renamed The Robert K. Greenleaf Center for Servant Leadership in 1985. The Business Roundtable, an influential group of business leaders, was one of Greenleaf's clients; the Roundtable was also one of SIFE's sponsors in the mid-1980s.[9]

By humanizing management theory, Greenleaf explicitly included human emotions as part of the factors of production, as compared to the management theories espoused by Frederick Taylor. Taylor viewed humans more as machines from whom efficiency of motion was paramount; human feelings and morale were irrelevant.

In his essay, Greenleaf relates the story of a servant named Leo, based on a fictional story written by Herman Hesse in 1958. According to the story, Leo is a servant who accompanies a party of men on a mythical journey. Not only does Leo do the chores, but he provides energy and sustenance to the group with his spirit and songs. But then he disappears. Shaken, the group falls into disarray and the journey is abandoned. Later, after some years of wandering, the narrator of the story—a member of the group—finds Leo, only to discover that he has now become the great and noble leader of the organization that originally sponsored the journey.

The moral, Greenleaf surmised, is that a group cannot exist without its servant; the role of a good leader is to be a good servant. In his book, Greenleaf explains how his theory differs from autocratic forms of management.

> The servant-leader *is* servant first. ... It begins with the natural feeling that one wants to serve, to serve *first*. Then conscious choice brings one to aspire to lead. That person is sharply different from one who is *leader* first, perhaps because of the need to assuage an unusual power drive or to acquire material possessions. ... The leader-first and the servant-first are two extreme types. Between them there are shadings and blends that are part of the infinite variety of human nature.
>
> The difference manifests itself in the care taken by the servant-first to make sure that other people's highest priority needs are being served. The best test, and difficult to administer, is: Do those served grow as persons? Do they, *while being served*, become healthier, wiser, freer, more autonomous, more likely themselves to become servants? *And*, what is the effect on the least privileged in society? Will they benefit or at least not be further deprived?[10]

The concept of the servant as leader has great appeal in Christianity with Jesus the ultimate example. The Bible is replete with references to Christ as servant. For example, Matthew 20, verses 27 and 28 state, "and whoever wants to be first must be your slave. Just as the Son of Man did not come to be served, but to serve, and to give his life as a ransom for many." Also, John 13, verses 12 to 15, read, "When he had finished washing their feet, he put on his clothes and returned to his place. 'Do you understand what I have done for you?' he asked them. 'You call me "Teacher" and "Lord," and rightly so, for that is what I am. Now that I, your Lord and Teacher, have washed your feet, you also should wash one another's feet. I have set you an example that you should do as I have done for you.'"

In 1970, the same year Jack Shewmaker joined Wal-Mart, Bill Seay was the chairman and CEO of Southwestern Life Insurance Company based in Dallas, Texas. Seay was typical of Sun Belt Christian business leaders, many from the oil, banking, and insurance industries. He eventually became director of the Dallas Theological Seminary and Billy Graham Evangelistic Association. He was also politically well-connected—in 1980 he would become the chair of George H.W. Bush's presidential bid in Texas.[11]

Seay had learned about Davis' training workshops. In 1970 Seay invited Davis to conduct a training weekend for company executives, their wives, and about twenty-five student leaders from nearby universities. As Moreton reported, Seay "had been disturbed by the gathering clouds of anti-business attitudes in college and university classrooms. The intensive weekend institute was to impress emerging campus players while they were still reachable and provide them with human relations skills for influencing peers." At the concluding banquet, participants applied Davis' management techniques by giving the food service providers a standing ovation.[12]

Though SIFE wouldn't officially be born for another five years, "Davis and Southwestern had united the elements for a fantastically successful endeavor: a nonprofit organization backed by corporate PR departments that raised the status of business among potentially rebellious students through the efforts of their own peers; that saluted the contributions of the humblest service workers; and that employed an antiauthoritarian, cooperative human relations model taken from law enforcement and management theory."[13]

I enrolled at the University of Northern Iowa in fall of 1974. In the aftermath of Watergate and the illegal corporate donations to the Committee to Re-elect the President, big business was not highly regarded. A 1973 poll showed business ranked last in prestige among the professions, even below lawyers. In January 1975—about the same time Alvin Rohrs was entering the second semester of his freshman year at Southwest Baptist College in Bolivar, Missouri—Davis formed SIFE as a nonprofit organization. With Bill Seay and Southwestern providing the initial funding, one hundred students from ten Sun Belt campuses gathered in Arlington, Texas, to discuss "what they might do to counteract the stultifying criticism of American business which was flowing from the campus, the press, and elsewhere, seeking to tear down the very system which gave the critics their jobs and their warm, comfortable homes. ... The kids loved it."[14]

In the spring term of 1975, students were to return to their home campuses, develop projects for promoting capitalism, and return to Dallas at the end of the school year to showcase their free enterprise projects to Dallas businessmen recruited by Seay. The winning team would receive a grant of $2,500.

Other events shaping SIFE's future were soon in the works. For example, Milton Friedman won the Nobel Peace Prize for his support of laissez faire economics in 1976. A few years later, Friedman aired his ten-part PBS television documentary series, *Free to Choose*, which became the basis for many SIFE projects. The Business Roundtable, then consisting of over two hundred CEOs of major American corporations, became one SIFE's most significant beneficiaries. Among the Roundtable's primary objectives was to resist organized labor's drive to strengthen the National Labor Relations Board, and to do so, it used new PR techniques like direct mail. Before long, SIFE teams would use direct mail and other techniques to bombard local students, citizens, and Congress with simple free market messages echoing the same messages proffered by conservative business and political action groups like the Business Roundtable.

SIFE gained steam in the late 1970s, and soon became a public relations arm for President Reagan's campaign. Moreton said, "An explicitly ideological organization that trained young activists, SIFE offered an outstanding laboratory for the elaboration and dissemination of Christian free enterprise. Just as young Americans for Freedom was the poster-child organization of the electoral Reagan revolution, SIFE was its economic counterpart."[15]

However, with the recession of 1980 and 1981, SIFE lost many of its sponsors and dropped from about a hundred participating colleges and universities to only eighteen. That's when Davis connected with Alvin Rohrs at a meeting in St. Louis and together with the president of Southwest Baptist University, made a deal to move SIFE's home from Dallas to the sleepy little Baptist university in Bolivar, Missouri.

Servant leadership has been, and still is, central to Southwest Baptist University's mission, and Alvin Rohrs was among its strongest advocates.[16] As an undergraduate at SBU, Rohrs, by his own admission, had been a small player on SBU's SIFE team. But now, in his new role in 1982 as SIFE's director, he had internalized servant leadership. When Rohrs was a student, SBU espoused the philosophy in its curriculum and cocurricular activities, and now, as SIFE's director, he had an outlet to practice these principles.

On the surface, there is much to like about a leadership philosophy where the boss starts out in life with a servant's heart, but only later becomes a leader because of his earnest quest to serve others. Such a boss isn't too big for his britches; he is willing to be a humble servant to his associates; he is the first to roll up his sleeves and get into the trenches with frontline employees. He has strong enough self-esteem to lead a hokey cheer to start the day; he would gladly accept his employees' dare to swim in freezing water. He would dress up in a Hawaiian skirt and do the hula, or he might even shave his head, if the company's goals are met.

There is a great deal to like about a boss recognizing and appreciating the hard work and dedication of the employees. Such bosses are usually charismatic and self-deprecating. By their words and deeds, they instill a sense of loyalty, both to the boss himself, but more importantly, to the organization for which the boss has pledged his devotion.

But there is also much to dislike about servant leadership, especially when its servant leaders attempt to demonstrate to subordinates their commitment to a *higher purpose* in order to extract higher returns for their companies. Also, self-avowed servant leaders tend to have inflated egos.

James Hind wrote a guest column in the *Wall Street Journal* in 1989 entitled "The Perfect Executive." According to Hind, Christ was a perfect executive because "[H]e did not use his miraculous powers to obtain power, honor, or glory. Yet he won the crown of glory and honor because of his strongest leadership trait: the servant attitude. This means cultivating a supportive role *that puts self-serving interests and ego gratification aside* (emphasis added)."[17]

SIFE's "Big Three"—Alvin Rohrs, Jack Shewmaker, and Jack Kahl—all claimed to be servant leaders, but anyone who has been to a SIFE exposition could readily see that none of them was keen to put ego gratification aside. For twelve straight years, from 1994–2005, my SIFE teams and I traveled to Kansas City. After the first few years, SIFE noticeably relaxed its religious and right-learning political tones, mainly to accommodate a growing list of stakeholders who did not necessarily share the same religious and political beliefs. Such stakeholders included prestigious U.S. universities—many of them public—and international participants entering the SIFE picture in 1999.

But Shewmaker and Kahl weren't looking only for Christian students to work for Wal-Mart or Manco. These companies were happy to hire as many SIFE students as they could, because these students had the requisite can-do, problem-solving attitude and work ethic demanded by these companies. In a *Time* magazine article May 1987, Shewmaker was asked what made Wal-Mart different from other discount stores. "It's attitude, give me workers with the right attitude," he said.[18]

At SIFE expos, especially in the mid- and late-1990s, the Big Three dominated the show. At the time, the Jacks each had an award named after them. Kahl's award went to the Sam M. Walton Fellow of the Year, and Shewmaker's name was attached the Spirit of SIFE Award. It wasn't until about 2003 that an award was named after Rohrs. With ego and all due modesty *not* pushed aside, the award was dubbed the Alvin Rohrs Servant Leader Scholarship.

Unable to hold ego in check, SIFE's board of directors—led by Shewmaker, Kahl, and Rohrs—named SIFE's world headquarters in Springfield after Shewmaker, and it also named one of its two large wings after Kahl. In August 2008, executives from around the world gathered in Springfield to dedicate the expansion of one of its buildings to longtime sponsor Robert Plaster. Among those making remarks were John Ashcroft, former U.S. attorney general under George W. Bush, and powerful Republican Congressman Roy Blunt from Missouri. The press release issued by SIFE concluded, "The program concluded with the Board Room being named in honor of Alvin Rohrs, who has served as SIFE's CEO for twenty-five years."[19]

Ego gratification aside?

To be fair, Shewmaker and Kahl did their share of recognizing SIFE teams at the SIFE expos, but they were on the stage more often to give rousing speeches to peer business leaders. Rohrs' comments, however, were usually reserved at the final luncheon when he would tearfully and unashamedly try to drum up more money from corporate sponsors.

Looking back, I can't really blame the Jacks. Had I been in their shoes, I may have done a little chest-thumping and fist bumping, too. They earned it, having come from modest backgrounds and demonstrating business savvy throughout their careers. They had become multimillionaires, and to the thousands of SIFE students, they had become examples of how free enterprise, practiced morally and ethically, could help them, too, some-day become servant leaders. By doing good work and subscribing to the principles of servant leadership, Shewmaker and Kahl had achieved great prosperity for themselves, their shareholders, and some of their employees.

Shewmaker and Kahl, I am quite sure, practiced servant leadership in a way that they truly believed could make the world a better place. Both men enjoyed being around students and faculty, although Kahl was much more natural around them.

Shewmaker seemed a little stiff and out of place in informal discussions, but he could give rousing speeches. Kahl, on the other hand, was easygoing and gregarious. One time—I think it was at the welcome reception at the 1998 expo—Kahl led the championship team from the prior year onto the stage at the Kansas City Convention Center. Kahl charged in front of the pack while lugging the huge traveling trophy with him. Approaching sixty years old at the time, Kahl clearly reveled in the moment, but after huffing and puffing up to the stage, he bent over to catch his breath. He reminded me of a racehorse beyond his prime, which is ironic. One of his favorite stories was how Triple Crown winner Secretariat had made a major impact on how he ran his business. After witnessing the great horse pull away by thirty lengths at the Belmont Stakes in 1973, Kahl had an epiphany. "Chills washed through my body and the hair on my arms stood on end as I saw this wondrous animal push himself to be the best," he said. "What was astonishing, though, is that this intensity did not come from any external threat, but rather from some hidden, internal desire to simply be the best. I made a choice right then to always pursue my personal best. I made a choice to let my passion for success lead my decisions."[20]

Of the Big Three, though, it was Alvin Rohrs who had no experience in the real world of for-profit business. But as a lawyer he was razor-sharp when it came to social networking, and the two giants in his sphere of influence, clearly, were Jack Shewmaker and Jack Kahl. SIFE's revenues were not generated by the free market, but instead through donations from retail corporate leaders who, in many cases, identified with the Christian servant leader philosophy.

It didn't take me long to believe Rohrs didn't consider faculty and students worthy of his servant leadership skills. We were not employees, associates, or partners, but pawns to further another agenda, it seemed. From my perspective, he certainly was not a servant leader for many students or faculty.

But he needed us. Prior to 1995, Rohrs had delegated almost all responsibility for university relations to the amiable Sidney Lilly. With Lilly's impending departure, Rohrs hired two well-decorated Sam M. Walton Fellows to come on board to take over university relations. One fellow—Tom Payne of powerhouse Pittsburg State University—would later become a close personal friend of mine. The other—Dick Laird of four-time champion Lubbock Christian University—was deeply religious and prone to wearing expensive gold rings. Both men had led their respective SIFE teams to national championships in the late 1980s and early1990s.

In 1994, Laird jumped at the chance to be on SIFE's payroll full-time, and Tom followed suit in June of 1995. As former SIFE advisers, they could better relate to prospective new faculty as SIFE began its incredible growth.

A few years later, in February 1998, Rohrs hired a professional fundraiser, Bruce Nasby, as his sidekick to help raise more funds for the burgeoning SIFE organization. Rohrs was an effective fundraiser, but in Nasby he had found someone with vast experience in the area, having made a career of shaking the money tree as top dog for Junior Achievement of Southern California, the Greater Los Angeles Zoo Association, and Non-Profit Management Resources. On the LinkedIn website, he lists his specialties as "Major Gift and Capital Campaign Fund Raising." In short, he was just the right guy to help Rohrs in what appeared to be Rohrs' most important role with SIFE—raising money.[21]

When Chico State joined the SIFE program in 1993, SIFE claimed to have about 250 teams.[22] For the 1994–1995 year, it claimed 343 teams and an annual budget of $1.9 million; and in 1995–1996, 460 teams and a $2.8 million budget. Rohrs had lofty goals for SIFE, planning for 1,000 teams by the year 2000, and dreaming to have "SIFE activity at each of the nation's 2,080 two-year and four-year colleges that offer a business course."[23]

The key word here is activity. Many of the teams SIFE counted as part of the organization were not active, but had shown some type of "activity." This could mean that a campus may at one time have fielded a team, but was now dormant. Or maybe one student made up a "team," and a faculty adviser accompanied the student to the SIFE regional expo in order to collect a $1,000 stipend.

In other words, SIFE publicized big numbers and big growth in its quest to show impressive results to its board. Further, SIFE executives were more than happy to count schools with little or no real SIFE activity. Though the number of participating teams reported by SIFE was possibly overstated, the amount of donations pouring in from corporate sponsors clearly was not.

Rohrs had an impressive model that worked like this: Walton Fellows and their students do all the heavy lifting during the academic year, for which SIFE paid a paltry $1,000 stipend to the adviser. SIFE teams put on snazzy multimedia presentations in April and May. The May expos have been described as "two parts pep rally, one part patriotic revelry, one part affirmation of corporate support, and one part recruiting frenzy."[24] And with the two Jacks by his side and a powerhouse board of directors that included such companies as KPMG, Walgreens, American Greetings, and RadioShack, Rohrs recruited like-minded, patriotic CEOs to observe the passionate students in action—many of whom were hired on the spot. At the same time, Rohrs and, later, Nasby, were busy doing their own networking, collecting more big checks from new corporate sponsors.

Under this system, SIFE's corporate sponsors not only hired tremendous talent, but the CEOs had the chance to hobnob with one another during the expositions—good old-fashioned, face-to-face social networking before there was texting, tweeting, LinkedIn, and Facebook. Most importantly for SIFE and its sponsors, though, was SIFE's ability to harness the energy of idealistic young SIFE students to become part of a huge, inexpensive public relations juggernaut for conservative corporate America.

In the next few years, I would get a firsthand look at how Rohrs treated subordinates and Sam M. Walton Fellows who challenged his authority. He needed faculty, much the same way, I believe, as Wal-Mart's management needed store managers. The faculty members were essential to help SIFE achieve its annual projections to report at the Board's annual meeting, much as Tom Sawyer relied on his friends to whitewash Aunt Polly's fence.

But Rohrs had a small problem. SIFE advisers like me were not employees, but volunteers, and as Sam M. Walton Fellows, we were the heartbeat of SIFE teams. Walton Fellows organized students, helped them identify community projects, garnered resources to travel to competitions and, in many cases, became as close to students as coaches get to their athletes.

Before long, I began to feel like an underpaid, overworked Wal-Mart associate. Nevertheless, I chose to continue my participation despite SIFE's conservative ideology and Alvin Rohrs' brand of servant leadership. The benefits outweighed the costs. I saw the powerful, positive effect on my students as they completed hands-on, real-world projects. The Chico community showed its appreciation by recognizing the team at the Rotary Club and Chamber of Commerce. And not least of all, SIFE provided a structured environment where I could pursue my pedagogical interest in community service learning.

Even though it was apparent to most SIFE advisers that we had very little voice in the organization, most were okay with that. But for some of us who wanted more input and feedback, there was frustration. We had no seats on the board of directors, nor were we invited to serve in an advisory capacity. In 1994, there was no outlet for us to provide constructive feedback to SIFE headquarters, except for phone conversations with Sidney Lilly. In a few years, I would ask other faculty to join me in lobbying for more input into SIFE's policies, especially as they affected our students. When I confided to Lilly that I might do so, she was prescient when she warned, "Curt, be careful, be very careful. You don't know what you're getting into here."

As the Chico State SIFE team got stronger over the next five years, scoring higher at the national event and gaining attention for our performance in special competitions, we started gaining a larger audience of influential executives at SIFE expos. Other faculty started asking me for advice, and I happily obliged. One of servant leadership's rallying cries, and adopted as SIFE's credo, is "people support what they help create." My desire to be more involved in SIFE's policies and procedures was consistent with the credo, but my efforts to be more involved with SIFE didn't look like servant leadership to Alvin Rohrs.

It must have looked more like something else. From Rohrs' vantage point, maybe I was trying to form some type of *union*—which is anathema to servant leaders like him, and to the Jacks.

Chapter 5

Go Ye Forth and Preach the Gospel

$$\equiv$$

Upon our SIFE team's return from Kansas City in May 1994, we were excited to start another year. But before we did, the SIFE mentors had some final business to attend to. They still had to go to Chico Junior High and teach three more math lessons.

After the last lesson was delivered at the end of May, the team assessed the program and found that the thirteen- and fourteen-year-old students did well with their micro-businesses. The young entrepreneurs had grossed $2,340 in revenues, with net income of $1,264. A total of eighty-one students started businesses and completed financial statements. After the program ended the junior high teachers received favorable letters from parents, and they were ecstatic.

"We want you back," Julia Smith said. Smith was the Math 03 coordinator. "Some of these kids had failed math in seventh grade, and now they are excited to come to class."

This was all the more satisfying to us because Chico Junior High had a large percentage of economically disadvantaged students. And on top of that, the Math 03 classes contained a disproportionate number of underrepresented students.

The positive reinforcement was rewarding, and before diving into planning the fall's lessons, Heather Tatton, a returning Chico State SIFE veteran and now team captain, insisted that the team come up with a mission statement. It read: "Our mission is to work together with our partners in business, education, and government to help the citizens in our community become business literate, so that everyone has the opportunity to live happy and productive lives."

I was proud of the returning team leaders, as they were now doing something that most university students wouldn't get to do until well into their business careers. They were beginning to think like leaders.

At the same time, we received some press coverage in the *Chico Enterprise-Record*, a conservative daily newspaper, and we decided to parlay that into a creative fundraising scheme. The marketing strategy resulted in the implementation of the "Adopt-an-8th-Grade-Entrepreneur" program, where local business owners were teamed up with eighth grade entrepreneurs. Each student was asked to write a thank you letter to the sponsor, and Chico State SIFE supplied the sponsor with a copy of that student's business plan.

Dick and I didn't want our SIFE team to become the next SIFE USA champion if it meant completing, or claiming to complete, over a hundred projects and spending hundreds of hours preparing for competition—hours that could best be devoted to impactful community projects. Instead, we insisted that the team focus most of its energy on the math project.

"We may not have the numbers to win the overall SIFE competition, but we're going to have more depth than anyone else," Dick and I told the team. "Quality over quantity."

By the time the fall 1995 semester rolled around, the second-year Chico State SIFE team was raring to go, with five new members. One was a junior finance major from Southern California—he was a bright, though sometimes incorrigible, young man named Greg Mills. Returning to Chico Junior High with twenty improved lessons, pared from twenty-eight the semester before, the SIFE team delivered the lessons to 350 eighth graders much to the delight, once again, of Julia Smith and her cadre of teachers.

Early in the fall semester, we continued to generate community support by hosting the first annual Business Advisory Board banquet. The theme for the banquet—cohosted by nearby Butte Community College SIFE and its energetic, hard-charging adviser, Al Konuwa—was "Forging Partnerships for Progress." We recruited Dan Daniel, an executive with Konica Quality Photo West, to be our keynote speaker. Daniel was a member of SIFE's board of directors. We had met him earlier that year in April at the SIFE regional competition in San Francisco. He had been one of the judges and took a liking to Chico State. Other featured speakers included presidents of Chico State, Manuel Esteban, and Butte College, Betty Dean, along with conservative California Assemblyman Bernie Richter. The banquet was one of the lead stories on the eleven o'clock news on ABC affiliate KCPM-TV.

Near the end of the semester, November 17–20, four of Chico State's SIFE leaders traveled with me to a national conference in Washington, D.C. This was to be the first of many trips I would take with students on behalf of the math program and service learning. The conference, sponsored by the American Association of Higher Education, solicited papers and poster session topics about school/college collaboration. It was designed to help individuals and teams from colleges and school districts launch K-16 change efforts. Our abstract was a perfect fit:

> The project entails a unique partnership between several constituencies interested in improving the quality of middle school education in Chico. The partnership includes: university students and faculty; area business representatives; and junior high school teachers and administrators. College students are directly involved in community service activities aimed at improving the *business literacy* of Chico's eighth graders. We have focused our efforts on junior high students because these students have little or no exposure to business concepts. In order to live happy and productive lives, it is essential that all students learn how to properly manage their money. These students will someday be employers or employees, and it is essential that they learn the *language of business* at an early age.[1]

Nationally, service learning was gaining momentum as an acceptable teaching strategy, and SIFE provided the structure to get university students excited about giving back to the community. At the same time, SIFE provided an avenue to reinforce the concepts and skills that university students were just now mastering. The best way to truly master something is to be able to explain it to others.

At the conference in Washington, we conducted an abbreviated form of the Penny Experiment, one of the more fun junior high lessons. Each member of our audience—mostly high school teachers—was asked to allocate fifty pennies according to various categories of hypothetical government spending. If a teacher wanted most of her money to go toward K-12 education, she could put most of her pennies in the K-12 Mason jar. If she wanted some of her pennies to go toward other categories, like higher education, the prison system, welfare, or better roads, she could divvy up her pennies accordingly. This exercise, like most of our lessons, was hands-on and interactive.

In the case of the Penny Experiment, audience members themselves identified categories of state government spending of their tax dollars, and then voted with their pennies to inform elected officials where they would like to allocate their tax monies. It was a lesson about percentages and decimals, to be sure, but it also integrated the concept of civic engagement and the importance of voting.

In spring semester 1995, we were invited to deliver the *Using Math to Make Business Decisions* lessons at another school in Chico, Bidwell Junior High. To conform to their specific schedules, we pared the lessons down to fourteen and taught them to 110 eighth grade math students. Three of the math teachers at Bidwell joined our business advisory board, and all three of them shared Julia Smith's enthusiasm about the program. One of teachers, Debra Cowan, said, "The Chico State students provide our school with a great liaison with the university, and the kids are excited and enjoying the program. They are actively learning about math outside of the school, which is one of the primary goals of our state framework in teaching mathematics."[2]

In mid-April, the Chico State students took a break from the math lessons and headed back to San Francisco for the SIFE regional competition. A week or so before the trip, Heather, Dick, and I discussed whether the presenters should invest in *team* business attire.

"No, I don't think so," Heather said. "It seems too conformist. And besides, do business people go into their offices each day wearing matching suits?"

Dick and I agreed. No matching suits or ties for our team, and we certainly weren't planning to do the SIFE cheer. The Chico State team, once again, worked hard on its presentation in the couple days leading up to the trip. Dick and I helped Heather write the four-page annual report.

The team's hard work paid off. Unlike 1994, the 1995 team was much better prepared. And the tech crew, unlike many of the teams still using overhead transparencies, helped the presenters with their PowerPoint slides. In 1995, PowerPoint was a relatively new presentation tool. Led by Heather and Greg Mills, the team cakewalked through its league and was again crowned regional champion. Also, like the previous year, we won first place honors in the two special competitions. Same song, second verse—we were headed back to Kansas City.

One thing Dick and I tried to instill in our team was the importance of focusing on one major project, but doing it very well. We especially helped Heather and Greg with the last page of the annual report, where we stated:

> This year, our team has continued to pursue and test exciting new "service learning" ideas in a collaborative fashion. By identifying, planning for, and capitalizing upon the often underutilized resources within our campus community—the end result is a set of learning experiences which will make us better leaders tomorrow.
>
> In closing, consider a quote by current Secretary of Labor Robert Reich (*The Work of Nations*, Knopf Publishers, 1991): "Sharing risks and returns ... is a powerful creative stimulus. Few incentives are more powerful than membership in a small group engaged in a common task, sharing the risks of defeat and the potential rewards of victory. Rewards are not only pecuniary. The group often shares a vision as well; they want to make their mark on the world."[3]
>
> Our SIFE team wants to make our mark on the world, and we know we are off to a promising start. By continuing to use our junior high business literacy project as our "wheel," other projects have naturally emerged as "spokes" in the wheel. We will continue to move forward as we strive to forge new partnerships for progress in teaching America's citizens the value of free enterprise.[4]

Returning to Kansas City a month later in May 1995, we arrived at another highly-charged welcome reception at the Hallmark Crown Center. Once again, Rohrs and the Two Jacks seemed to be omnipresent and, once again, Rohrs couldn't hold back the sobs.

On the first day, Chico State drew a team from Union University, a small evangelical Christian college from Jackson, Tennessee. Union University was one of five campuses that formed a consortion of campuses with similar missions—among them, Southwest Baptist University in Bolivar, Missouri. Union's adviser, Robert Wyatt, was an accounting instructor. He knew SIFE and Wal-Mart country well. He received a master's degree in accounting from the University of Arkansas at Fayetteville in 1989, and a bachelor's degree in business administration from the University of Central Arkansas in 1983.

In 2001, Wyatt became dean of Drury's business school, putting him in a unique position to throw his full support behind the SIFE program, and it paid off. In 2001, 2003, and 2005, Drury won the SIFE USA title and, in 2001 and 2003, it went on to win the international SIFE World Cup. Its success was in no small measure due to major contributions from one of Drury's trustees. That trustee, whose wife graduated from Drury, was Jack Shewmaker.[5]

Back in 1995, Union University's SIFE team was led by a caped mascot—SIFEMAN. Their free enterprise superhero made a greater impression on the judges than our abbreviated rendition of the Penny Experiment. To our chagrin, we were eliminated in the first round. We licked our wounds by going to the same watering hole and restaurant as last year—Kansas City's famous Gates Barbeque.

It was Heather Tatton's last year, having just graduated from Chico State and taking a job with Price Waterhouse, one of the Big 6 accounting firms. She planned to hand the reins over to Greg Mills next year.

Heather hadn't been impressed with the top teams, which reported dozens of SIFE projects with more flash than substance. She took the results with a stiff upper lip. "You guys might have to do more cute projects to be competitive," she advised the underclassmen as the team ate barbequed chicken and beef and downed a few pitchers of Budweiser. "But whatever you do next year, keep the math project going. It's our bread and butter."

"Don't worry," said Greg, "We'll keep it up. The Penny Experiment rocks!"

Greg's part of the Chico State presentation had been an animated one. Shortly after introducing the Penny Experiment, Greg unveiled a mystery jar from behind his back. The jar had a substantial number of pennies in it.

"What's in this jar?" he asked the judges, rhetorically.

With just the right dramatic pause, he answered, "It's the interest on the federal debt!"

Greg continued, "Fourteen percent of the pennies from each of the other jars get dropped into this one."

He explained how he and his fellow SIFE students had shown the junior high kids that interest on the debt reduces money that could otherwise be spent on government services.

"Because of inherited debt," Greg said, "we showed the kids that they must pay interest on this debt before they can spend money on new athletic uniforms, a student lounge with a big-screen TV, or even a class party."

No matter your economic hero—John Maynard Keynes, Friedrich Hayek, Ludwig von Mises, Milton Friedman—the lesson was a hit with the kids. By relating economics to them at a personal level, the kids could easily get a visual picture of how government debt affected discretionary spending. The lesson wasn't designed to make a political statement; rather, it was designed to demonstrate that interest is an expense that federal government must pay. Simple but effective.

The team had entered the Penny Experiment in the regional Halt the Deficit/Reduce the Debt special competition, and it was Greg's favorite lesson. He had fun with it, so much that between practice sessions in the hotel room, he peppered his fellow SIFE teammates by zinging pennies pressed tightly between his thumb and middle finger. He ended up leaving the maid with a pretty good tip in pennies, though I'm not sure she was too happy about it.

Though we didn't advance to the next round in the overall competition, our strategy of going deep with one quality project paid off—we won $4,250 in prize money, ranking us in the top ten universities in total prize winnings. We placed first in two national education goal competitions, second place in another, and third place in a competition sponsored by the National Federation of Independent Business, called "Teaching through Media." The NFIB is a lobbying organization representing small and medium-sized businesses, and today claims about 350,000 members, with offices in Washington, D.C., and all fifty state capitals. Though claiming to be nonpartisan, it is widely understood that it is a lobbyist for traditional austerity political issues, such as balanced budgets, lower taxes, fewer social welfare programs, and fewer regulations; in short, smaller government.[6]

Other SIFE teams noticed Chico State took the stage on five separate occasions. Also taking notice was Alvin Rohrs, who kept calling us the *University of California, Chico* when announcing the winners. In California, there are two distinct university systems: the University of California system, and the California State University system. No doubt, we were also on Shewmaker and Kahl's radar because California was not only an untapped market for SIFE, but a key demographic in Wal-Mart's growth strategy.

Early that summer, I was happy to learn that Chico State president Manuel Esteban had nominated me to receive a Leavey Award from the Freedoms Foundation at Valley Forge. With the success and attention Chico State SIFE was receiving for our junior high outreach project, the panel of Leavey judges was kind enough to honor me. The purpose of the award was "to recognize excellence in private enterprise education." It included a $7,500 stipend and a trip to Philadelphia, where my wife and I met the five other national award winners. We also enjoyed meeting Donald Trump and his wife Marla, who arrived at the heliport on the hotel roof to be the featured guests at Freedoms Foundation annual banquet.

Shortly thereafter, I received a letter indicating Jesse Williams, one of our eighth grade entrepreneurs, had won first place in his age bracket for a national award presented by the NFIB Foundation. Jesse's father was a computer technician, and he had turned obsolete computer hard drives into alarm clocks. Jesse sold a bunch of his refurbished clocks at the mall, making a tidy profit for himself and saving the Chico landfill from non-biodegradable hardware. The name of his company, cleverly, was Hard Times. Three awards were given nationally in his age category.

Career wise, it was a heady and exciting time as we entered the 1995–96 academic year. Chico State SIFE was rolling. My returning students were anxious to start their third year. Also, my accounting colleagues were being recognized for their achievements with the FIPSE grant. Results of our efforts to reengineer introductory accounting were presented at regional and national meetings, and the U.S. Department of Education invited us to submit a proposal to a new grants program called *Disseminating*

Proven Reforms, resulting in a new grant of $180,000. Six other colleges and universities adopted our lesson plans, and the accounting faculty at Chico State had a new role. With our guidance, these campuses decided to drastically change their first two courses using our discovery learning approach, with a heavy emphasis on collaborative learning and technology.

Our SIFE team's primary project continued to be our middle school math project, with two new twists that would affect my career dramatically from this point forward. First, starting in the spring of 1996, the Chico State SIFE students were been joined by twenty-three *associate* SIFE students from Chico High School as part of a high school initiative to encourage teachers to experiment with community service learning as a teaching strategy. The high school students worked as apprentices to their older peers to deliver the lessons to the junior high kids. The result was a cadre of university students working with high school students to become role models for middle school students. In a way, our program was providing an element of seamlessness between age categories.

Second, we adopted six new SIFE teams, sharing our best projects with them. This was not common practice, because SIFE's intense competitions didn't encourage sharing. But Dick Davis and I were pushing our team to buck the trend. We wanted to instill in them a mentality of "the more you give, the more you receive," admittedly a bit like servant leadership—*sans* the Christianity or the inflated egos.

Our team's annual report, once again, concluded with a passage about how university students could make a difference in the schools' system through community service:

> If we are serious about meeting the National Education Goals, it is imperative that today's teachers are business and computer literate. Many of our SIFE students are extremely knowledgeable in both areas. Equipped with the necessary knowledge, skills, training, hardware and software, these mentors can provide high school students, junior high students, and teachers with access to an integrated curriculum using new technology. In essence, the teachers can receive in-service training while simultaneously receiving assistance to help their students; at the same time, SIFE

mentors planning to become K-12 teachers can obtain valuable preservice training. Furthermore, SIFE students planning on careers in business can improve leadership, teamwork, and communication skills.[7]

Starting a trend that was to last for a total of twelve consecutive years, we again won the regional competition in 1996 and returned to the USA nationals. We weren't the only ones drawing a line; continuing a trend of its own was La Sierra University, the Seventh-Day Adventist team from Riverside, California. La Sierra took home first place honors in Kansas City for the third straight year.

Matching suits, smart ties, and their own sound system, La Sierra once again blew away the judges with the sheer number of projects reinforced by Hollywood-style technology. I almost wanted to break out the popcorn as La Sierra described its *Rent-A-Brain Consulting Company*, or its South American llama project (a barnyard pay-it-forward, where the munificent American students purchase a pregnant llama and donate it to a selected village; after the baby llama is born, it is donated to another village as its interest payment), or its on-campus cleaners, claiming revenues of over $100,000 per year.

La Sierra's faculty adviser Johnny Thomas was a hyperkinetic, entrepreneurial professor who saw how SIFE's performance in Kansas City could yield pecuniary rewards to his university. With each win, Thomas would receive dozens of letters from the CEOs and senior executives who judged the finals. In the final round, the CEO/judges now numbered over one hundred. They ran companies like Valvoline, American Greetings, Hallmark, Pepsi, Walgreens, and RadioShack. Almost all of the companies were retailers, with a few exceptions like *USA Today*, Kinko's, and, notably, public accounting firm KPMG. In a few years, when SIFE decided to expand globally in 1999, KPMG's annual support to SIFE increased. KPMG offices around the world were encouraged to support SIFE with funds and facilities. With each national title, Thomas and his La Sierra team collected more accolades, prize money, and business cards.

Although the Chico State SIFE didn't make it to the final round, we did well—again—by winning $4,750 from special competitions, placing us sixth in overall prize money. We won first place and two third places in the GE Foundation's National Education Goals three, four, and seven, and we won second place in the SHOPA Foundation Best In-Depth Education Project. Chico State continued to take the stage each time we placed in a special competition, but I was beginning to wonder if we needed a change in strategy.

To advance to the final round, and to present to a panel of coveted judges who were now on a first-name basis with Johnny Thomas, we might need to change things up. We would still focus most of our energy on a few main projects. But if we wanted to make the big show, we might have to rethink our approach.

Even though 1995–1996 had been a good year, my personal life suffered. My dad, Jim DeBerg, had a severe heart attack on December 23, 1995. Six days later he succumbed on an operating table in Sioux City, Iowa, while undergoing an emergency angioplasty procedure. The memorial service took place in the Tabernacle Baptist Church. The church was packed, overflowing well into the hallways. My three brothers and I laid Dad to rest on New Year's Day, 1996, in near-blizzard conditions in his hometown of Little Rock. Dad was only fifty-nine years old. As I write this book now—at age fifty-six—I think of his gentleness, kindness, sense of humor, work ethic, and our far-too-few fishing trips to Canada.

Some people say bad news happens in a series of three. The spring of 1996 gave credence to this superstition. After Dad left us, I had two more rough patches. My wife Kristine was growing unhappy with my long hours, and we were growing apart. Before long, we would separate.

If losing my dad and separating from my wife weren't enough, there was another emotional issue I had to deal with. I was starting my fifth year at Chico State, and I was required to submit my dossier and curriculum vitae to the dean's office to be used in the college's decision to grant me tenure and a promotion to full professor. During the FIPSE grant period, the head of Chico State's accounting department was a guy named Lee Pryor. Lee and I had some professional differences of opinion during the past couple years, and I was wary that he might put a few obstacles in my career trajectory.

One of the problems was related to the federal grant. About six of the senior accounting faculty were part of the development team, and each was assigned to write new lesson plans based on grant objectives. Lee wanted to be paid his share of the grant money up front, like a stipend. On the other hand, the FIPSE codirector, Rich Lea, and I had set up a system where we paid faculty at an hourly rate, and payment was based on periodic deliverables. We didn't make an exception for Lee, even though he was the department chairman.

Another issue involved the California Society of CPAs. A couple years earlier the society had picked me to become their academic fellow. The fellowship was a coveted position requiring the professor to serve as a liaison between California's practicing CPAs and accounting educators. It included an annual $15,000 stipend and a healthy travel allowance. Though he never said it directly, I had the feeling Lee was expecting to receive the fellowship, and when it came my way instead, he seemed resentful.

Tenure is the holy grail of being a professor. Receiving it is almost like being handed a lifetime contract. As one might expect, tenure has some negative aspects about it. No doubt, there are occasions where bad teachers are tenured because they are politically well-connected. But the good thing about tenure is that, once getting it, a progressive, controversial, yet very competent professor is no longer at risk of serving under a boss who might become vindictive, jealous, or hostile.

The end result is that Lee recommended against both tenure and promotion, which meant that I would be sent packing if the dean agreed. Fortunately, Dean Arno Rethans overturned the chair's recommendation against tenure. In academia, a dean's position is highly political. Going against a department chair's recommendation in tenure decisions is risky. Dean Rethans called me into his office and said, "I know you've been working really hard. Keep it up one more year and we'll promote you to full professor. Be happy with tenure for now. That's the big thing."

I had worked my ass off for five years, publishing research articles and receiving good teacher ratings. The fact that I was a leader of the FIPSE project and was now serving as a SIFE faculty adviser counted almost nothing to the department chair. His recommendation against the tenure and promotion left a nasty taste in my mouth, seeing for the first time how someone in a position of power, like Lee Pryor, can wield their power unfairly.

Entering the 1996–1997 year, Dick Davis and I, like all other Sam M. Walton Fellows, were beginning to think of ways to unseat La Sierra from the catbird's seat.

"Duke, what do you think? Shall we get theatrical, pile on the projects, give them creative names, and go toe-to-toe with La Sierra next year?" I asked him.

By now, SIFE students and I had started calling Richard "Dick" Davis by his nickname, which he picked up in our first year in Kansas City. Some of the new SIFE students who didn't know Dick very well were concerned about what to call him. All of them had been calling me Curt, but Dick was more than fifteen years older than me, and he looked much more like an erudite professor.

"What shall we call you, sir? Professor Davis? Dr. Davis? Dick?" Chris Coutant asked.

Dick scratched his beard and looked up at the ceiling as though in deep thought. Then he turned back to Chris, leaned forward, and with several SIFE teammates looking on, said in his best John Wayne impersonation, "My friends call me Duke."

And so Duke it was. Early in fall 1996, Duke and I decided to stay the course. We believed that, compared to teams like La Sierra, the Chico SIFE students should complete fewer projects, and our comparative advantage lied in K-12 education. However, we also knew that if we ever had a chance to make it to the final round in Kansas City, we would have to encourage our team to do more *one-pop* projects.

At the beginning of the school year, the team outlined ten goals. One goal was to cement our relationship with Chico High School by formally creating a high school program called *Cal-High SIFE*. Under this program, we would encourage high school students to complete their own projects based on the collegiate SIFE criteria. A second goal was to revise our junior high math lessons and teach them to at-risk teens at a local alternative high school. A third goal was to disseminate our lessons as widely as possible by adopting new SIFE colleges and universities.

Chico State president Manuel Esteban had been urging faculty at Chico State to design programs that contributed to what he called a *seamless education*. Leading a campaign to recruit and retain more Chico State students, Esteban encouraged faculty from across disciplines to be more proactive in working with K-12 educators so that incoming Chico State freshmen would be better prepared for higher education. With our SIFE team's presence at middle schools, and now a local high school, I jumped at this as an opportunity to implement my service-learning teaching strategy.

To help us accomplish the team goals, I offered three units of course credit to SIFE team leaders. In the syllabus I explained that I was not to be viewed as the professor. Instead, I explained that my role was that of an adviser, and linked it to baseball:

> The adviser oversees all aspects of the organization, with student leaders directing specific project areas. And while most of the students specialize in one or two areas, they all depend on one another to maximize team performance at the competitions. One of the most aspects of this project lies in its potential to contribute to a seamless education. Using a baseball analogy, university and community college students can be viewed as the major league players, high school students as AAA players, middle school students in the instructional league, and so on. In fact, the SIFE team's motto is "Students Helping Students." All players have a common goal: to serve and to succeed. How each team performs together, in a competitive setting, provides an independent measure of success.[8]

Only experienced SIFE students—those who participated in SIFE in a previous semester—were eligible for credit. To receive three units, students were required to complete at least fifty hours of service over the next two semesters. During the semester, students had to keep a log describing their activities. At the end of the semester, they were required to write a reflective essay and to offer recommendations to improve the course. About a dozen students ended up receiving course credit.

As the dot-com era was beginning its ascent, two technology firms became aware of our efforts. Intel provided a $5,400 grant, and Sun Microsystems showed its enthusiasm by providing a $10,000 grant. Chevron also contributed $2,500. Under the leadership of Todd Giammona, senior management information systems major from Grass Valley, California, the Chico State SIFE team accomplished its goals. Throughout the year, the Chico State students once again taught at the middle school and helped the Cal-High SIFE students from Chico High with their projects. The Chico State SIFE team was doing well. The university students and I were excited to share our best projects with other SIFE teams.

At the time, Alvin Rohrs was more than happy to help. A few years earlier, he implemented a program to leverage the enthusiasm of experienced Sam M. Walton Fellow's by providing them with an incentive to identify prospective new SIFE teams. If an existing adviser like me helped a new SIFE team participate in a regional competition, SIFE provided the team with a $1,000 *Adopt-a-Rookie* grant.

Most faculty members in professional disciplines like business, engineering, and computer science travel to regional and national academic conferences as part of their professional activities. I was no exception. In addition to participating in these conferences, I visited the six colleges and universities that were part of the second FIPSE grant. By now, I had become an ardent subscriber to service learning. I viewed accounting conferences as fertile ground to introduce service learning, the SIFE program, and Chico State's best SIFE projects. To this end, I became a road warrior.

In the 1996–1997 school year, Chico State adopted nine rookie SIFE teams. I traveled to six of these schools, usually with one or two students joining me. Our team also made several presentations locally. On a regional level, the team traveled to Long Beach in October to make a presentation to ninety California State University education faculty and K-12 administrators. Four students and I ventured to San Diego to present at the National Education Association-Higher Education Conference on March 6–8, with four hundred people in attendance. As a result of the San Diego conference, the Chico State SIFE team was invited to present at the National School Board Association Annual Meeting in Denver the following November.

By May 19–21, 1997, the annual SIFE USA event had outgrown the Kansas City Crown Center and had moved two miles north to Kansas City's huge Bartle Convention Hall. According to SIFE's Web page at the time, it boasted that the number of active SIFE teams had grown to encompass students on over five hundred college campuses across the country and beyond U.S. borders. Students reached more than 102 million people through their free enterprise outreach programs.

Much to the dismay of our students, La Sierra won for a fourth consecutive year. Chico State came in first runner up in our league on the first day. Once again, we would not make the final round. Again, we had outstanding individual projects, but the teams making it to the final round were much slicker.

Even though we didn't make it to the final round, we had vastly improved from 1995–1996. We had won $7,750 in prize money, placing first, second, or third in seven special competitions. Chico State may not have been making it to the final round, but everyone was wondering what we were up to.

Duke and I, like all other Walton Fellows, were disheartened. At a minimum, La Sierra's win confirmed what we had learned the prior three years—we would need to make some big changes if we wanted the big stage. Next year would be different, I promised myself.

Several signals pointed in a favorable direction. First, in May 1997 Chico State's College of Business was one of 230 finalists, out of 2,250 proposals, submitted to the FIPSE program. We had requested $165,000 for a project titled, *A Cross-Age Mentoring Program to Improve Math and Computer Skills.* Though we ultimately did not receive funding, we knew we had a competitive proposal and could very well parlay it into other support down the road.

Second, at an accounting conference in Southern California in April 1997, I met an interesting fellow by the name of Edward Zlotkowski. Zlotkowski, a nationally-recognized scholar from Bentley College, was heading up a major service-learning initiative. He had been commissioned by the American Association for Higher Education to edit a series of eighteen volumes, with each volume dedicated to a different academic discipline. Accounting was one of the volumes, and Zlotkowski was making presentations to drum up some interest from accounting faculty. We struck it off immediately.

I explained what I was doing in the area, and he was intrigued by the SIFE organization. I agreed to submit a manuscript to the accounting series, which was published the following year—summer of 1998. Before saying goodbye, I asked him if he'd like to attend the SIFE USA expo as my guest the following month.

"Sounds interesting," he said. "I'll see if I can make it."

He did, in fact, attend. As I was writing this book I asked Zlotkowski what he remembered about his experience. "What sticks in my mind is the incredible professionalism of the presentations," he wrote in an email to me in October 2011. "Indeed, the presentation polish often seemed to overshadow the service content. That is not to say there was no content. There was—though its interest and value to me differed considerably from team to team."

Zlotkowski also expressed some other reservations. "What I probably liked least were those presentations where the students' underlying assumptions seem never to have been seriously questioned," he said. "I remember one presentation where the students wanted to go to Mexico to teach the Mexican villagers how to work hard. Have you ever read Ivan Illich's *To Hell with Good Intentions*? Some—but not all—of the presentations modeled precisely what Illich warns against."[9]

Zlotkowski's reference to Illich gave me a different view of fresh-faced university students serving abroad, like those in the Peace Corps and SIFE. Under this perspective, USA students traveling to a developing country to teach about work ethic and free enterprise was patronizing and sanctimonious. Indeed, in many cases their service violated the notion of *reciprocity*, one of the cornerstones of service learning.

Ivan Illich was an Austrian philosopher, educator, and social critic of contemporary Western culture. He was deeply disturbed by the paternalism in voluntary service. To be effective, service learning must be reciprocal. The server learns from the served, and vice versa. Some SIFE teams, like the one that traveled to Mexico, took a one-way approach to service. Rather than learning from those being served, paternalistic SIFE teams were on hand to bestow clients with their superior knowledge and skills. According to the Council for the Advancement of Standards in Higher Education:

> Service learning avoids placing students into community set-
> tings based solely on desired student-learning outcomes and pro-
> viding services that do not meet actual needs or perpetuate a state
> of need rather than seeking and addressing the causes of need.
> Through reciprocity, students develop a greater sense of belonging
> and responsibility as members of a larger community. Reciprocity
> also eschews the concept of service that is based on the idea that
> a more competent person comes to the aid of a less competent
> person. Service learning encourages students to do things *with*
> others rather than *for* them. Everyone should expect to learn and
> change in the process.[10]

Our Chico SIFE team, I knew, was not one-way. Our university
students learned equally as much from the K-12 students and teachers.
Chico Junior High was a tough diversified school, and the students we
served were not the most gifted math students. Some of the Chico State
students had, in fact, come from privileged backgrounds. By entering a
challenging public school environment, they had a firsthand look at a
public education system unlike the one they had known, many of which
were in the solidly middle- or upper-middle class areas in San Francisco,
San Jose, or Sacramento.

I was especially excited about changes in California in 1997. One
change had direct bearing on our high school initiative. In the lead article in the February 1997 issue of *California Educator*, published by the
California Teachers Association, new emphasis was placed on real-world
knowledge and skills.

> In the '90s, school-to-work/career combines vocational educa-
> tion with academics and is no longer intended for just one group
> of students. It's for everybody—whether college-bound or not.
> The premise is that everyone will, after all, earn a living. And do-
> ing so will be easier if students know what career possibilities exist,

have the freedom to explore those opportunities, and are able to see, firsthand, how their school curriculum is related to "real life" and "real work."

It seemed that Cal-High SIFE—our high school project—fit right in here, especially if we involved university students as mentors to their younger protégés.

Another development in California was recognition of community service learning as a viable teaching strategy. Just before leaving for Kansas City on May 18, I sent Fresno State finance professor Jim Highsmith a memorandum outlining how California State University campuses could benefit from service learning by starting SIFE chapters. As chair of the California State University Academic Senate, Highsmith was intrigued by the idea. He had a direct line to Chancellor Barry Munitz, who headed up all twenty-two CSU campuses, ranging from Humboldt State in the north to San Diego State in the south.

With SIFE's board consisting of some of the country's leading retail CEOs, which now included Bernie Milano, executive director of the KPMG Foundation, I thought we might get Munitz' attention. And with SIFE handing out $1,000 grants to entrepreneurial SIFE teams like ours, I thought we might be able to launch SIFE teams on all twenty-two campuses, rather than just the four that were currently involved.

In the May 14, 1997, memo to Highsmith, I pointed out that very few CSU colleges of business pursued service learning, other than through internships and cooperative education programs. I proposed that we create a new program called *Service Learning in Free Enterprise*, and that all twenty-two business colleges create service-learning centers. Not only could such centers permit closer student-faculty interactions on projects with real-world benefits, I argued, but they could also forge stronger ties between the business, university, and K-12 communities. Further, these centers would provide students the opportunity to showcase their best projects which, when delivered in front of other students, could lead to benchmarking and replication of best projects at other campuses.

In 1997, when SIFE was just beginning to expand its operations beyond the United States, a few SIFE teams from other countries like Monterey

Tec from Guadalajara, Mexico, or a Polish team from Poznan, were invited to present at the USA event. As the Internet, email and listservs were beginning to revolutionize global communications, several SIFE teams were starting global projects. Instead of just thinking globally and acting locally, many SIFE teams could now act globally, too.

One of the Kansas City judges in May 1997 was Rieva Lesonsky, editor-in-chief of *Entrepreneur Magazine*. She had judged the Chico State team in the first round, and was impressed with our education projects. In her July 1997 "Editor's Note," she gushed:

> I have just returned from one of the most overwhelming yet exhilarating experiences of my life—the annual SIFE International Exposition—and I will truly never be the same. In their spare time, the students of SIFE create projects to promote free enterprise. At the heart of their projects is community outreach, tutoring and mentoring, and enriching and strengthening those that live around them, especially the young.

Rieva pulled me aside in Kansas City and said, "Your team was a razor's edge from making it to the final round. Keep up what you're doing and you'll make it next year."

As a teenager growing up in northwest Iowa, and attending the Tabernacle Baptist Church on Sunday mornings, I would gaze up at the world map attached to the wall at the front of the church. Below the map it said, "Go ye forth and preach the gospel," and guest missionaries would tell incredible stories of faraway places. The map had great appeal, and during the sermons I would daydream of traveling to places like Africa, Southeast Asia, Russia, and the Middle East. The thought of world travel had great appeal to me as a youngster, and the allure of international travel had not waned. By summer 1997, though, I hadn't really seen much of the world.

With my FIPSE project experience and now SIFE in the last five years, I was beginning to believe in a higher purpose for my professional career. I would, indeed, go forth and preach the gospel, but it would not be the gospel of Christian free enterprise. Rather, it would be the gospel of community service learning, practiced with reflection and reciprocity.

Though I had serious reservations about Alvin Rohrs and his brand of servant leadership, as well as many of the paternalistic do-good SIFE teams, SIFE was a handy card to be carrying in my quest to introduce service learning to other educators—starting in the United States.

Chapter 6

Nearing the Summit

====

A few Sam M. Walton Fellows, like Al Konuwa of Butte College and Lisa Borstadt of Northern Arizona University, were beginning to use email to correspond with each other, and I even created a listserv dedicated to SIFE advisers. If we banded together, I thought, we could ask questions, seek clarifications, and provide constructive feedback to SIFE's home office in Springfield. We heard that SIFE's board of directors was planning to change the judging criteria for the next year, and we wanted a chance to provide our input. Some of the faculty advisers were unhappy with La Sierra winning the show every year, and they wanted their concerns to be heard by Rohrs and his staff.

So, I was happy to receive a phone call in late July of 1997, one month before the start of the 1997–1998 school year. SIFE's new director of university relations, Tom Payne, was on the line. "Curt, we would like you to serve on the National Academic Council," Payne said. "Your team has done such good work the past few years, and we want you to join a select group of other Walton Fellows. Can you come to Springfield on August 30 and 31? We'll drive you down to Branson, Missouri, and show you a good time. Of course we'll pay for air and hotel. Whaddya say?"

Though it would mean missing the second day of class in the first week of the fall semester, I immediately accepted. This would give me a chance, I thought, to offer some direct input into SIFE's new policies and procedures. Maybe Al Konuwa and I could explain service learning to SIFE brass. Al was spearheading a new Service-Learning Center at Butte College, and he had recently won a big state grant to launch it.

The meeting in Branson would also give me the opportunity to finally meet Alvin Rohrs in a personal setting. Though we had shaken hands a few times, I got the distinct impression that he didn't like talking to me. And based on the many times I had seen him cry on stage, especially when monied people were in the audience, I can't say that I went out of my way to befriend him, either. I think he knew I sensed the ingenuousness of his tears.

Our team had done very well the past three years; in no small measure we were helping SIFE meet its growth numbers. Executive bonuses, including Tom's and Alvin's, were based on the number of new teams going to regional competition. In short, hard-charging advisers like me, who worked diligently to enlist new SIFE teams, were helping SIFE executives receive their bonuses. In this light, even if Rohrs had to hold his nose when he was around me, he was certainly pleased with the smell of the money he and the SIFE organization were raising by showing robust growth.

The West Coast was a growth market for Rohrs, especially golden California. Wal-Mart was growing, too. In 1997, it had become the largest private employer in the United States. With 680,000 employees domestically and 115,000 internationally, sales revenue topped $100 billion, and it replaced Woolworth as a member of the Dow Jones Industrial Average.[1] My invitation to serve on the academic council was, no doubt, part of Rohrs' strategy to have the Chico State SIFE team recruit more new teams. As a practicing servant leader, Rohrs had once again heaped lots of praise and recognition on a long list of people at last year's event in Kansas City. I was one such recipient of Rohrs' munificence in 1996 when SIFE presented me with a Champion of SIFE Award. Before calling each of us to the stage, the announcer said, "The recipients of the award go above and beyond the call of duty by volunteering their time to recruit other interested entrepreneurs, educators, and corporate executives to become part of the SIFE family." Included among the other recipients of this award were Frank Newman, president and CEO, Eckerd Corporation; Robert Plaster, chairman of the board, Empire Energy Corporation; Len Roberts, president, Tandy/RadioShack Corporation; and Robin Walker, assistant vice president, Merrill Lynch. I was honored to be included in this group.

In the summer of 1997, I was beginning to make noise. Some of my emails to other faculty were undoubtedly being forwarded to SIFE Headquarters in Springfield. Many of these missives suggested possible changes. I was adamant about Walton Fellows having a greater voice in matters affecting our students. Also, I wanted SIFE executives to learn more about service learning, and how projects could be improved with greater reflection and reciprocity.

After receiving Tom Payne's invitation to serve on the academic council, I sent Rohrs the following note on August 26, 1997.

> Alvin, I submitted the attached memo below to Jim Highsmith, chair of the CSU Academic Senate last May. Jim is also a finance professor at Fresno State, and likes the SIFE idea. He has a direct line to Chancellor Munitz. The memo describes how service learning and SIFE fit together, and how CSU students can benefit from participating in service-learning programs. As I mentioned to you in Kansas City, I am eligible for a sabbatical next year (1998/99). For your information, I am eligible for one semester leave with full pay, or two semesters leave with half-time pay. No travel money is included. The sabbatical proposal, which would need to be approved by my dean, would describe how I would promote service learning in California. Moreover, I would encourage schools to join SIFE.
>
> I believe I could recruit many more SIFE teams as part of this sabbatical, at very low cost to SIFE. If I apply for, and receive, a one-semester leave, all I would need is travel money. Air travel between Northern and Southern California is very inexpensive, using state rates. If I apply for, and receive, a two-semester sabbatical, I would need travel money and half-time pay. Please note that the CSU, Chico, SIFE team would continue to be active during my absence. Professor Richard Davis would take over the helm as faculty adviser. I look forward to talking to you about this in more detail in Branson.[2]

If Jim Highsmith were to accept the ideas put forth in my memo, I could be the vanguard of the service-learning movement in California, and maybe beyond the West Coast. If done right, SIFE could be an important part of the movement. My memo to Highsmith suggested that all twenty-two campuses create formal service-learning chapters withing colleges of business. I asked him to consider the benefits, including strengthening the links among higher education, K-12 education, and the private sector. Further, such chapters could provide CSU student with the opportunity to showcase their best projects which, when delivered in front of other students and private sector leaders, could lead to replication of best projects at other locations.

Tom Payne was a personable man of boundless energy. He knew SIFE inside and out, having taken his 1993 SIFE team from Pittsburgh State to the SIFE USA championship. He clearly enjoyed the human relations part of SIFE. But he would readily admit that he isn't a big fan of *Robert's Rules of Order.*

In Branson, Tom set the agenda and topics were trite. Sample topics: What size should SIFE make the team trophies? What gifts should be presented to Walton Fellows as a token of SIFE's appreciation? Should SIFE create a Hall of Fame? Even on these topics, the conversation would often meander off, willy-nilly.

I had my own questions, and the list was long. How are the new SIFE judging criteria determined? Why isn't there faculty input? Why aren't Walton Fellows represented on the board of directors, even if only in an advisory role? How can SIFE recruit more name-brand universities into the SIFE network? How can faculty publish their work in academic journals? Why don't we use service learning as a way to attract new schools? Could there be an informal venue where board members could meet Sam M. Walton Fellows?

Unfortunately, none of these questions was addressed. Rohrs made his brief appearance and he seemed preoccupied. We learned he had been out late the night before, at a special SIFE donor barbeque. "It would have been nice if we could have been there," I whispered to Al Konuwa. Immediately after his presentation, Rohrs exited the room. I was hoping to see him later to ask him about my idea for a sabbatical with SIFE, but he was nowhere to be found.

It was a sad day, not only because I felt that SIFE advisers were still left without a voice, but it was also the same day that Princess Diana died at age thirty-six in the car accident in Paris. It was August 31, 1997.

Upon returning to Chico, I found an enthused group of twenty returning veteran SIFE students ready to dive into the upcoming year. Over the summer the team leaders indicated they wanted to shift their emphasis from middle schools to high schools. There were three reasons for this. First, the university SIFE students reported that they could relate better to high school students. Second, high school teachers in our area's high schools began to seek out our team's services. The third reason was because California's new welfare-to-work legislation (called CALWORKS) put more pressure on our county to provide workplace literacy skills for middle school and high school students who, in all likelihood, were not going to college.[3]

Duke Davis had decided to take a break from SIFE starting fall 1997, so I was steering the SIFE program on my own. I created a new series of lessons, adapted from the middle school math project, and the SIFE team began teaching at Ridgeview High School. Ridgeview was a continuation school in nearby Magalia. Three of our SIFE student leaders were hired by the Butte County Private Industry Council to team-teach a class of twenty-two students—twelve of these students were teen mothers. Each Monday, Wednesday, and Friday from September through March, the SIFE students taught the lessons in one-hour sessions. The lessons were aptly called *Ridgeview SIFE: Turning Risk into Success*. As a class, the Ridgeview students formed a hypothetical corporation. They wrote a business plan, conducted market research, acquired supplies, and then opened the first school-wide snack bar. This snack bar earned a tidy profit.

In the spring of 1998, the principal of another continuation school—North County Community School in Chico—asked us to deliver the lessons at his school. North County's continuation school represented the last chance the enrolled teens had to shape up or be shipped off to juvenile hall in nearby Oroville, the county seat. The immediate goal of continuation schools is to get the students back into the regular school attendance with acceptable behavior and improved study habits.

Ridgeview and North County both entered the first Cal-High SIFE tournament, modeled after the university SIFE tournaments. The teens were joined by peers from Chico Senior High School and South County Continuation School in Oroville. Fifteen people from the local business community were recruited to serve as judges. One of the judges was Kathy

Lowdermilk of the Butte County Office of Employment and Training.

Chico High was crowned as champions of the inaugural Cal-High SIFE tournament. Cal-High SIFE was a resounding success. In April, the Coleman Foundation in Chicago announced it would provide funding to continue the program with a $25,000 grant. Lowdermilk promptly hired six SIFE students from Chico State to teach the lessons to eighty at-risk youth, all between the ages of sixteen and twenty-one. The lessons, set to start in early June, were to be taught in Chico and the nearby towns of Oroville, Gridley, and Paradise. We dubbed the project "Summer SIFE."

Based on the quality of our main projects, the 1997–1998 Chico State SIFE team once again cakewalked through regionals. Two dozen students and I headed to Kansas City with great confidence. Not only had we completed some high octane projects, but by this time in Chico State SIFE's existence, we had recruited a total of twenty-three new SIFE teams across the country.

Two of our four presenters, Todd Wells and Julie Rose, had been on the presentation team the previous year. Two rookie students on the team were Ed Person and Danielle Emis. Wells and Rose insisted that the team wear matching business suits, and I didn't argue. It had finally become clear to me that SIFE judges preferred team conformity over individual expression, at least with respect to attire. This was a price I was willing to pay to get a better shot at making the final round.

Lo and behold, our team won the opening round on the first day, and for the first time in five years, Chico State SIFE took the final-round stage on the second day. At the awards banquet the night before, on Sunday, we also claimed $11,000 in special competition prize money. We placed first, second, or third place in seven of the twelve special competition categories, which were now sponsored by AT&T, *Business Week,* and Del Laboratories. Everyone now knew who we were and I felt a heightened level of respect, unknown in prior years, from peer Walton Fellows and CEO-judges.

The announcement of 1998 SIFE USA champion at the Monday night awards banquet was bittersweet. On the one hand, I was thrilled that Chico State President Manuel Esteban was present to accept the award as SIFE President of the Year. On the other hand, Chico State was not among the top five teams. The 1998 champion team was the pre-La Sierra University powerhouse: Pittsburg State University.

La Sierra had taken a break from SIFE in 1997–1998. Its Walton Fellow, Johnny Thomas, stepped away as adviser to take on the more demanding role as La Sierra's business dean. That gave other schools a better chance. Five of the top ten teams were longtime SIFE schools—Pittsburg State from Pittsburg, Kansas; College of the Southwest from Hobbs, New Mexico; North Central College from Naperville, Illinois; John Brown University from Siloam Springs, Arkansas; and Lubbock Christian University from Lubbock, Texas. In addition to Chico State, relative newcomers to the top ten teams were Northern Arizona University from Flagstaff, led by their Walton Fellow, Lisa Borstadt; Centenary College from Hackettstown, New Jersey; Southwest Texas State University from San Marcos; and the University of Texas-Pan American from Edinburg.

This had been our year to take the big prize, I thought. But our presentation just wasn't as polished as the other teams' and a couple of them—especially Northern Arizona—had some exceptional projects. If La Sierra returned next year, they'd more than likely be the tournament favorites, but at least Chico State, Northern Arizona, and a few other public universities would now be considered serious contenders.

Following the SIFE USA Championship, the summer of 1998 was about to start, and I had a lot of work to do. On May 28, I sent an email to a few colleagues in the CSU system. One of them was to Cheryl Wyrick from California State Polytechnic University, Pomona. In the email I asked if she, or if anyone else on her campus, was interested in starting a SIFE team. I informed her that four campuses already had SIFE teams and Chico State would be helping CSU, Bakersfield, and Cal Poly, San Luis Obispo, start teams in the fall.

Her reply came later in the day, and it was none too supportive:

> Quite frankly, we have been unable to create enough interest here to get a SIFE chapter going. I have given other faculty members the SIFE handbook and other promotional information, as well as providing the opportunity to view the video. The response has been lukewarm at best. There is the feeling that the projects

shown on the video are not "rigorous" or "academic" enough, and that the conference/competition is basically a pep rally, with no significant merit. There is some confusion about the benefits of being associated with SIFE. "What's in it for us? (students and faculty)" and "Why do we even need this organization?" are two frequently asked questions. This, coupled with a person who is an advisor for a successful SIFE chapter stating that it is a lot of work, and not much payoff, did not do much to increase enthusiasm.

Although I am supportive of the idea, I cannot be the advisor. I am already faculty advisor for two student organizations. While I encourage service learning for my Not-for-Profit Organizations class, that class is only offered once a year. My initial idea was to house the SIFE chapter in our Center for Entrepreneurship and Innovation (CEI), but I'm not sure that that is going to work.[4]

In reply, I thanked her for her openness, but reminded her that service learning was becoming a priority item at the Chancellor's Office. SIFE offered a venue to use this teaching approach.

The Chancellor's Office had recently hired a full-time service-learning director, Erika Freihage, and she had invited me to serve on the system-wide Community Service-Learning Committee. The key to service learning, I told Wyrick, is to make sure that the activities are, in fact, desired by the community, and that the students complete and reflect on how their activities met the course's learning objectives. A well designed service activity, I told her, with a reflection component built in, can increase leadership, teamwork, and communication skills. It could also help make students more conscious of their civic responsibilities in a democratic society.

I wasn't willing to refer to SIFE as a pep rally, either. My students were getting too much benefit from it. I wrote, "As for the conference/competition being a 'pep rally,' I think this is an unfair characterization. It's more like a basketball tournament. Competition drives the quality and efficiency of the community outreach projects, and the tension and energy is similar to a tournament. The irony is that students are competing based on how well they present their community outreach projects."

As I was contemplating our email conversation, the dean of Chico

State's College of Business, Arno Rethans, and I were invited by Wal-Mart
to attend its carnival-like annual meeting in Bentonville, Arkansas. The
invitation was sent to only ten universities around the country, including
Duke, the University of Florida, and the University of Arizona. Florida
and Arizona had just started SIFE programs, and they were high on Wal-
Mart's list of recruiting universities. I learned that the other campuses on
the invitation list also had strong retail business programs.

Five years earlier, the University of Arizona had created a retailing center
on campus "to bring together the resources and expertise of academia and
the retail industry with a shared goal of developing strong future retail
professionals."[5] It was only natural that Wal-Mart would court these universities but why Chico State? We didn't have a reputation as a particularly
strong university in the retail area. I didn't believe Arno and I were invited
to the Wal-Mart jamboree because our SIFE team had fared well at competition. A better explanation was that Wal-Mart's top executives must
have seen Chico State as a possible strategic partner in its growth plans in
northern California. Domestic sales growth was beginning to slow, and
California was still ripe for the picking, especially for its Supercenters.[6]
Though California's unions were losing clout, they were still influential in
blocking Wal-Mart's growth.[7]

Whether Jack Shewmaker had anything to do with the invitation to
Arno and me, I can't say for sure. But he and Jack Kahl had now taken
an interest in our team, mingling amiably with my students after their
performance in Kansas City. At that time, Shewmaker was one of thirteen
members of Wal-Mart's board of directors, serving on its Strategic Planning
and Finance Committee.

Arno and I arrived at our Bentonville-area hotel late on June 4, 1998.
Rising before dawn the next morning, we were shuttled to the twenty-thou-
sand-seat Bud Walton Arena on the campus of Fayetteville, Arkansas. The
Wal-Mart annual meetings moved to the Bud Walton Arena in 1995 to
accommodate arena-sized crowds. Except for the rolling hills on the University of Arkansas campus, the campus reminded me of Oklahoma State
University in Stillwater, where I had received my doctorate degree in 1985.

Wal-Mart's CEO, David Glass, along with Tom Coughlin, president of
the Wal-Mart Stores division, were the masters of ceremony presiding over

an almost-full arena of raucous shareholders and associates from across the country. Later in the meeting, Lee Scott, another senior executive, would also provide a brief report. I learned later that Coughlin and Scott were vying to become the heir apparent to Glass's job, and the annual meeting was a chance for Wal-Mart's board to see how the throng reacted to the candidates. Joining the vocal crowd was a large contingent of associates from Mexico, which was now the number one country in Wal-Mart's international growth strategy, along with a handful of associates from Argentina, Brazil, Canada, China, and Germany—all countries that were soon to be at the center of SIFE's global growth strategy.[8]

About the same time Wal-Mart was conducting its annual meeting, Jack Shewmaker made a presentation at the International Mass Retailers Association's annual meeting. "Now is the time for IMRA members to develop and nurture a global perspective," Shewmaker said. He also said that retailers needed to recognize and fast-track promising employees from around the world, and urged retail executives to broaden their worldview by making at least one trip abroad each year.[9]

Neither Arno nor I could have predicted what we were about to encounter. The first thing we knew, Richard Simmons, the effeminate fitness guru, came running out to the stage in his trademark tight shorts and tank-top shirt. Simmons led the crowd in warm-up calisthenics, including the Wal-Mart cheer. Then, Glass and Coughlin took turns at the mike, praising the company for earning revenues of $118 billion for the year ended January 31, 1998, an increase of $13 billion from the prior year. In between reports the two executives would take time to introduce sports dignitaries in the crowd like NBA star Dikembe Mutombo and former NFL quarterback Jim Kelly. In between reports and introductions were one or two musical numbers performed by such country artists as Reba McIntyre and Faith Hill.

"How much does Wal-Mart have to pay these celebrities make an appearance?" I asked Joey Jones. Jones smiled.

"They'd pay us if we asked them," he grinned. "Who do you think is the number one seller of sports equipment and CDs?"

Of course.

After the meeting ended mid-afternoon, we were driven back to our hotel to rest a little while before going to dinner at the country club home of Coleman Peterson. Peterson was executive vice president of human resources for Wal-Mart Stores.[10] He had joined Wal-Mart in 1994. We had met briefly in Kansas City when he was chatting it up with prospective new associates at Wal-Mart's recruiting booth at the SIFE career fair. During dinner that night, I was seated at his table next to Peterson's wife.

"How do you like living in Rogers, Arkansas?" I asked Shirley Peterson. The Petersons had lived in St. Louis for sixteen years prior to moving to the bucolic hills of northwest Arkansas.

"It's been quite an adjustment for us," she said. "There aren't too many African American families here. But Cole really likes his job."

The next day, we attended one of Wal-Mart's famous Saturday morning meetings in the auditorium of Wal-Mart's general offices, followed by a tour of the computer facilities and the Wal-Mart Visitor Center in downtown Bentonville.

Our trip to the annual meeting left me with two vivid memories. One memory is the extreme pressure put upon regional managers to show positive results. Each manager gave a brief presentation on weekly sales in their area at the Saturday morning meeting. The presentation included a comparison of the current week's figures with last week's, and a comparison of these numbers with the prior quarter and year. When there were unfavorable variances, executives at the front of the room peppered the managers with questions. Such scrutiny each week, I thought, made my twice-a-semester, mid-term examinations seem tame. My accounting students were pretty lucky.

The second memory is how the Wal-Mart annual meeting itself reminded me of SIFE's events in Kansas City, including its evangelical "higher purpose" overtones. I wondered how much Wal-Mart's culture affected SIFE. Mary Jo Schneider, an anthropology professor from the University of Arkansas, wrote an article in 1998 about Wal-Mart's annual meetings and how these meetings were an important part of the company ethos. Schneider and her husband had attended twenty annual meetings, starting in the late 1970s. In her article, she said:

The annual meeting is an extravaganza held mostly for the benefit of associates. They, and some analysts, question the wisdom of using the shareholders meeting as a primary vehicle for perpetuating Wal-Mart's corporate culture. Wal-Mart, known for its penny-pinching, doesn't like to say what the meeting costs, but it does acknowledge that many expenses are born by vendors who use the occasion to display goods and who cover the costs of celebrities. Videotaped segments of the meeting are played in Wal-Mart stores to motivate associates and transmit the company message.[11]

Having attended the Wal-Mart annual meeting, my SIFE comparison troubled me. Were SIFE's annual expositions held mostly for the benefit of students—or for the benefit of corporate donors seeking a public relations outlet for their ideological and political causes? Sam M. Walton Fellows like myself, and historians like Nelson Lichtenstein and Bethany Moreton, would later question the wisdom of using students as a primary vehicle for perpetuating Wal-Mart's culture—a servant leadership culture that Lichtenstein and Moreton both saw primarily as benefiting corporations rather than students.

SIFE is also known for its penny-pinching—providing token $1,000 grants to faculty advisers and not paying for travel expenses for students and faculty to participate in their showcase events. At SIFE events, companies display their products and recruit students at the same time and, in exchange, take a vaunted seat on the honorary SIFE board of directors. The cost of a seat next to Jack Shewmaker and Jack Kahl on the SIFE board? A minimum contribution of $25,000.

Like Wal-Mart, SIFE drew celebrities, too. In my twelve-year ride with SIFE, I remember such folks as NFL quarterback Len Dawson and Olympic stars Eric Heiden and Sarah Hughes as featured guests at SIFE expositions.

I continued to question SIFE's overall motives and operations. Thanks to Bethany Moreton and Nelson Lichtenstein, my questions were eventually answered. Still, in 1998 I couldn't help but wonder where all of SIFE's money was going. Were the contributions made by SIFE's donor companies really being used to advance the goals of a noble nonprofit organization, or were they really just a tax-deductible contribution to attract future servant leaders sharing similar religious and political views? And now that SIFE was actively recruiting public universities into its network, did it truly qualify as a nonprofit organization? Lichtenstein had called SIFE a "front group" for Wal-Mart.[12]

Nonetheless, at this time in my career, SIFE offered a unique platform to pursue my evolving educational philosophy. I wanted to improve education by moving from the lecture mode (sage on the stage) to a mode where students are actively engaged in the learning process—where the instructor is a coach and facilitator (guide on the side). By providing students with out-of-class learning opportunities—in teams, and on real projects that they had an innate desire to participate—the students could make a positive impact in the community. I firmly believed that, while it might result in more work for the teacher, effective service-learning strategies could motivate students to do their best. Ultimately, I could see a world where "seat-time" would be replaced by a system that rewards students for demonstrating mastery of well-specified core competencies, no matter how long it takes them.

Before the 1998–1999 academic year had started, I let my SIFE students know that we would not be a group of performers or a cheerleading squad. If we didn't make the top ten, I cautioned them not to be jealous of others' successes. I also told them, "We are not going to be completely successful in everything we do; we will be successful, however, in teaching how risk can be reduced to increase the chances of success."

But I am competitive. So were my students, especially four student leaders returning to next year's team—all women: Dawn Houston, Suzanne Cozad, Danielle Emis, and Kelby Thornton.

Butte College's SIFE team, just down the road from the Chico State campus, was beginning to feed its SIFE students directly to us. One of its students—Rachel Muzzall, a single mother of two young children—would soon join the four Chico State coeds to make up the 1998–1999 Chico State presentation team. The five students would prove to be headstrong, brilliant, dedicated, and formidable.

Chapter 7

World Champions

As the Chico State SIFE team was gearing up for its first and most ambitious project for the fall 1998–1999 year, SIFE's board of directors handed the chairmanship to a young, smart executive from Cleveland. Like Jack Kahl, his predecessor, Michael J. Merriman ran a company that supplied Wal-Mart with one of its most popular household items. If Kahl was known as Mr. Duck Tape on the SIFE board, then Merriman could go by the name Mr. Dirt Devil.

Merriman had been CEO of Royal Appliance/Dirt Devil since August 1995, and Royal's famous Dirt Devil was among its full line of vacuum cleaners. Merriman also shared other qualities with Kahl. Both were personable and warm, both were graduates of John Carroll University in Cleveland, and both were highly regarded in the Cleveland community actively participating on various civic boards and serving on John Carroll's alumni board of trustees.[1]

But Merriman wasn't only a people person. He was a numbers person, too—he had been a partner with Arthur Anderson & Co. When he and I were to meet for the first time in Kansas City the following May in 1999, we immediately took a liking to each other. We were the same age, and each of us had graduated with an accounting degree in the late 1970s. And, like me, he passed the CPA exam and went to work for a Big 8 accounting firm.

When I left public accounting in 1981 to enter the doctoral program at Oklahoma State, Merriman was on the fast-track at Arthur Andersen. In his fifteen-year career in public accounting, he managed merger, acquisition, and audit engagements in Andersen's closely-held business division. In 1990, he became a partner in the Special Services Division, where he specialized in high-growth companies. With stellar credentials, he became Royal Appliance's vice president of finance in 1992, and was named president and CEO in 1995. He promptly recruited Kahl to sit on Royal's board of directors.

As SIFE's new board chairman, Merriman had big shoes to fill. Kahl had been chair of the board since 1992, and as the number of participating teams grew dramatically, so too did the SIFE donor base and its board, which grew to more than a hundred members.[2] While Merriman and I would only shake hands in May 1999, we would get to know each other much better in the summer of 2000.

At the end of the previous semester, in spring 1998, I insisted that our returning students create a code of ethics for the next year. While our team had finally cracked the top ten in Kansas City, and with it the coveted audience of business leaders who judged the final round of presentations, I was still concerned that some of the elite teams were more sizzle than steak. Some teams had stunning multimedia presentations and had completed dozens of projects with only a handful of team members. Either the teams were superheroes or guilty of hyperbole. I didn't want Chico State to be one of those teams.

As Edward Zlotkowski had astutely noted the year before, some teams appeared to complete projects for their own purposes rather than their community clients. Thus, I told my team that I would refuse to let them overstate their projects. I was pleased when the team submitted its ethics code. Led by senior accounting major Suzanne Cozad, the team submitted the code early in the fall. Three items were especially noteworthy. The team pledged that it would:

- Create and deliver projects in our community, and on campus that reflect our commitment to quality and continuous improvement.
- Never lose sight of the fact that the ultimate winners are the citizens we serve. While competition against other teams is a "carrot," we will not let winning overtake serving.
- Never complete projects for the sake of "show" and "flash"; rather, all projects will be undertaken because they can make a substantial difference.

Before the fall term began in 1998, the team had to wrap up its first big project, Summer SIFE. Kathy Lowdermilk, director of the Summer Youth Employment Program for Butte County's Private Industry Council (PIC), had recruited six SIFE students to teach a nine-week summer to youth between the ages of sixteen and twenty-one.

PIC was funded by the Job Training Partnership Act, a law passed during the first term of the Reagan administration to help prepare youth for meaningful jobs. It was administered by the U.S. Department of Labor. As mentioned earlier, Lowdermilk had observed our SIFE team in action the previous spring at Ridgeview High School. She asked us to create a similar series of lesson for her "at-risk youth/employment program" using a revised version of the Ridgeview lesson plans. Her request resulted in the 1998–1999 SIFE team's flagship project called Summer SIFE: Turning Risk into Success.

Starting mid-June, three pairs of Chico State SIFE students taught the lessons in Chico, Paradise, and Gridley, all in Butte County. PIC funds were used to pay SIFE students $8.65 per hour, and the thirty participating PIC students were paid the minimum wage of $5.75 an hour. At the end of the program, each class came to Chico to make an oral presentation of their hypothetical business plan to a panel of judges. The best business plans/presentations were awarded prize money.

The Summer SIFE program emphasized computer skills, including word processing, spreadsheets, presentation software, email, digital imaging, and using the Internet as a research tool. At the end of the summer, each of the university SIFE students authored a reflective essay. One student summed up the program from her perspective: "I have taken courses in college related to the subject matter that I taught in Summer SIFE, but having the opportunity to teach the material gave me a greater understanding of business in general. I have also learned to be patient with others and it has made me realize how difficult teaching can be. It has helped me with my public speaking skills and given me more drive to exceed in life." This was federal money well spent.

Such was the case that by the end of summer, the Chico State SIFE team had wrapped up its major project. I doubted that any other SIFE teams had even started their projects for the year, and ours was in the can.

I was feeling good.

G iven the rate of technology changes during this period, it is safe to say that most high school teachers, even those who taught economics and business, were less competent in computer skills than my Chico State students. With over thirty thousand SIFE students nationwide, could they be marshaled into providing high school students with access to new skills? SIFE had a veritable untapped army of college students who could contribute to K-12 reform through well-designed service-learning activities.

In the first weekend of September, Tom Payne once again invited me and about a dozen other Walton Fellows back to the Ozarks for a second Academic Council meeting. Northern Arizona University had come in first runner-up to Pittsburg State in 1998, and its advisor, Lisa Borstadt, had become a good friend of mine. Lisa was among the SIFE advisers invited to Branson. Shortly after the meeting, I emailed Lisa for her feedback. Now that our team had cracked the top ten and placed in so many special competitions, other Walton Fellows came to Lisa and me for advice—and I was feeling my Wheaties.

Once again, Rohrs barely made an appearance in Branson. So, after returning to Chico, I came up with a list of items that I thought should be addressed by SIFE's executives. I floated my suggestions to other SIFE fellows, like Lisa and Al Konuwa. If the Academic Council banded together, I thought we could pressure Rohrs and his board to seriously consider our suggestions.

One suggestion, which I emailed to Lisa and a few others, was, "Many faculty advisers don't feel connected to the SIFE Board of Directors. What can we do to narrow this gap (chasm?). Next year, the Academic Council could be part of a Board of Directors/Faculty Adviser barbeque? How about a Sunday night adviser/director get-together in Kansas City? Please do more to help us interact."[3]

Another suggestion was a plea to Rohrs to develop better relations with Walton Fellows. A closer relationship to Rohrs, I reasoned, could lead to better connections to the corporations that supported SIFE. In my letter I wrote, "Just like Sam Walton visited his Wal-Mart stores, we need Alvin to visit some of our campuses (e.g., at SIFE banquets). That way, when

Alvin shaves his head at competitions, at least some of the students will know who he is and what role he plays." At the May 1998 SIFE USA competition, Alvin had done what Jack Kahl had done at Manco to demonstrate his servant leadership qualities—he got a buzz cut on stage. His tears afterwards may have been as much about losing his hair as about adding to SIFE's lucre.

One way to help with my service-learning agenda, I believed, was to highlight a few best practices and use SIFE's publicity machine to spread the word. "To make SIFE better known," I wrote to other Walton Fellows, "some recognition must be accorded the best continuing projects (e.g., those that have national dissemination possibilities). Why not create a new competition, with evidence of success measured by adoption by other SIFE teams, or adoption by outside parties? We need to tell the world about our best projects. The best way to do this is by disseminating great programs that have potential for long-lasting value, to other SIFE schools. This takes coordination from Headquarters."

In 1997, Jack Shewmaker had been pushing hard to advance Wal-Mart's global initiatives, and he was doing the same with SIFE.[4] One former Walton Fellow, Robin Anderson, was hired as director of SIFE Global the same year.[5] In 1998, SIFE was launched in three of Wal-Mart's strategic growth countries, including Brazil, Mexico, and Canada. Jack Shewmaker, serving on Wal-Mart's Strategic Planning and Finance Committee of its board, also had his eyes set on other countries, most notably Australia.[6]

Also launched in 1998 were four countries in the former Soviet republic: Kazakhstan, Kyrgyzstan, Russia, and Tajikistan. At the end of 1998–1999, SIFE claimed 667 participating USA SIFE teams and 79 global teams.[7] Many domestic Walton Fellows were excited to see SIFE's international growth and wanted to be a part of it. However, very little information was forthcoming from SIFE's home office in Springfield. In my letter to the Academic Council, I said, "There is little knowledge of the international dimension. All inquiries are handled by saying, 'That's Robin Anderson's department.' We need better communication here. Some of us can help … use us … don't keep us in the dark. Robin needs to communicate with us, especially when we need answers quickly."

Until 1997, Robin Anderson had been a Walton Fellow at the University of Nebraska, and he had a gold-plated resume in the international grant arena. Between 1992 and 1998, he had won several federal and private grants totaling almost $1 million. A $200,000 grant helped him establish a center for entrepreneurship at Khujand State University in Tajikistan. Another federal grant for $226,000 helped strengthen his relationship with Tajikistan and expand it to a nearby university in Kyrgyzstan. A third grant, from 1996–1998, was for $111,000 from the United States Information Agency (USIA) to promote international trade of small and medium sized enterprises in APEC region.[8] APEC is the Asia-Pacific Economic Forum.

As SIFE had done when it hired former Walton Fellows Tom Payne and Dick Laird a few years earlier, it cherry-picked Robin Anderson to now become its new global director. By September of 1998, I was beginning to learn Anderson was none too excited about helping other faculty members introduce SIFE to other countries. In obeisance to Shewmaker and the board, Rohrs hired Anderson, but Rohrs was atavistic. He liked things the way they had been, when SIFE catered mainly to Christian-based colleges in the Sun Belt.

But now, Shewmaker was pushing the board to expand globally, and he insisted that SIFE become an international organization. Rohrs acquiesced, but that didn't mean he would direct Anderson to go full-steam ahead. Rohrs was very protective of "his" board, and the global initiative might give Walton Fellows freer access to SIFE's powerbrokers.[9]

My laundry list of suggestions was sent to the Academic Council. Many said, "Keep it up!" Lisa replied to my email, "If we address all these items next year, we'll need to add another day to the schedule!" I copied Tom Payne on my letter to the council, asking him to share it with Rohrs, which he did, from which Rohrs did—nothing.

The $25,000 grant we had received from the Coleman Foundation, under its Entrepreneurship Awareness and Education Grant Program,[10] helped make the Summer SIFE program a true winner. The purpose of the Coleman grant, recall, was to improve and extend our summer entrepreneurship program to at-risk high school students. Starting in the fall of 1998, the lessons were again adapted for four alternative high schools. Shorter versions of the lessons were also delivered to students detained in the Butte County Juvenile Detention Hall.

Early in that fall semester, Suzanne Cozad and Dawn Houston asked me if we could hold tryouts for SIFE presenter slots in October.

"Isn't that a little early?" I asked. Traditionally, we didn't hold tryouts until March in the spring semester, when we'd invite our business advisory board to help us select the presenters and an alternate.

"We want to win this year," they said. "And to do that, we need our presenters lined up, and we want to have a first draft script ready by the start of the spring semester."

I liked their enthusiasm. A few months earlier, I had read a quote by Peter Drucker, and repeated by John Sculley of Apple Computer. The quote said, "The best way to predict the future is to create it." With that in mind, I decided to help the SIFE students write the first draft of their script as though they had completed all of their projects. Hypothetical assessment data were inserted into the script draft, later to be replaced by the real numbers.

"And two more things, Curt," Houston said. "We are going to insist that all presenters memorize every single word. No more note cards."

Whoa, I thought, if they pull this off, they will be the first team in SIFE history to do this.

"Another thing," Suzanne added, "We want our own sound system with wireless mikes. Can you make that happen?" Indeed. Another SIFE first.

Eleven speaker candidates gathered in Glenn Hall room 209 on a Tuesday night in late October. On hand were ten business advisers, thirty more SIFE students, and me. Three of the advisers included Judy Sitton, who cofounded Bi-Tech Software with her husband Gary in the 1980s. Another was Kenneth Derucher, dean of engineering and computer science at Chico State. Ken was a short, stoop-shouldered man who reminded us of the Penguin, the supervillain of the old *Batman* TV show. Ken was student-centered and entrepreneurial. As dean, he aggressively sought out private sector partners for his college initiatives.

Derucher's son, Ken, Jr., was a senior at Chico Senior High School and a member of Chico High's Cal-High SIFE team. Kenneth Derucher had seen his son's self-confidence grow in the high school program, and he gladly served as an adviser for our SIFE team. For the Deruchers, SIFE became a family affair. Also serving on the advisory board was his wife,

Barbara, who became known to the SIFE students as "SIFE Mom."

By the end of the evening, five presenters were selected: Suzanne Cozad, Dawn Houston, Danielle Emis, Kelby Thornton, and Rachel Muzzall. Team alternate was Heather Rosdail. Later, when asked by a judge in Kansas City why Chico State had all women presenters, Dawn would reply, "Four guys tried out, too, but the women were superior. Next question."

About the same time we were selecting our presentation team, a visiting professor at the University of California-Berkeley was writing something of his own. His name was J. Gregory Dees. On October 31, 1998, he released a manuscript called "The Meaning of Social Entrepreneurship." I hadn't heard of this term before. Social enterprise? I read Dees' article with great interest. A social entrepreneur, he said, combines the passion of a social mission with an image of business-like discipline, innovation, and determination. According to Dees' view, a social entrepreneur does not necessarily have to make money to stay in business. Dees said:

> Any form of social entrepreneurship that is worth promoting broadly must be about establishing new and better ways to improve the world. Social entrepreneurs implement innovative programs, organizational structures, or resource strategies that increase their chances of achieving deep, broad, lasting, and cost-effective social impact.[11]

This view focuses on innovation and impact, whether or not the enterprise relies on earned income strategies. In other words, both profit-seeking businesses and nonprofit-seeking businesses can be considered entrepreneurial if they are innovative and seek social impact.

I was a bit puzzled about his definition. How can a social entrepreneur stay in business if he doesn't earn money? Isn't he beholden to patron saints or government grants if he doesn't sell goods or services? As for myself, I believed I was an innovative educator seeking social impact, but that didn't make me an entrepreneur—social or otherwise.

What about Alvin Rohrs? Was he a social entrepreneur? He certainly was innovative and worked for an organization that was making a social impact. But SIFE's revenues, which topped $5 million in 1999, weren't earned; rather, they were donations. If Jack Shewmaker and Wal-Mart bailed on SIFE, would the remaining board members fall like dominoes? If so, kiss SIFE goodbye. This was a question that I would wrestle with in the next decade but, for now, I could settle for Dees' general definition.

Then, nirvana! Service learning, as an active-learning pedagogy putting students into the community—combined with social enterprise, as subject matter unleashing student innovation to address community problems—made a perfect combination for my teaching philosophy. That potent combination would be the cornerstone of my professional career from this point forward.

The Chico State SIFE team wrapped up its fall projects. Near the end of January six women—the five presenters and Heather—met at Rachel's house in Chapmantown, a working class residential neighborhood in southeast Chico. Putting her two kids to bed as we arrived, Rachel returned and said, "Let's get to work."

The team labored for three hours over a rough first draft of the script. I left that night thinking, "I've never had a team as dedicated as this."

In a week or two, the script started taking shape, so I brought the team to the basement of Meriam Library, home to the Instructional Media Center (IMC). There, I introduced them to IMC director Rick Vertolli. A graduate of Kent State with a degree in painting and sculpture in the mid-1970s, Vertolli moved to Sacramento and began taking classes at Sacramento State. The new field of computer graphics was taking form in the early 1980s, and to get access to the university's computers, Vertolli enrolled in engineering and programming classes. He wanted to create art on computers. In 1982 Vertolli was hired as an animator for Chico State's new IMC to teach computer-assisted art in the Department of Computer Science. He first started teaching a computer animation class in 1992, and in 1997 he offered an advanced animation production class. [12]

After meeting with my team, Rick said, "Give me the script. I will have two or three of my best students storyboard this out for you."

As the presenters began to work in tandem with Rick's student animators, the Chico State SIFE students embarked on their spring projects with gusto. The students needed to achieve the outcomes already spelled out in the script. In other words, the future had been created, and it was now up to the entire team to make sure that the predictions matched reality. The campus community and the Chico community backed us completely.

In the February 1999 issue of *Chico Statements*, a magazine reaching over 100,000 alumni, President Esteban gushed:

> In my convocation speech to our faculty and staff in August 1998, I mentioned "service learning." This is an exciting new way of teaching by professors who identify community outreach projects that can be directly linked to their course objectives. The projects are structured so that academic theory is reinforced by real-world experience. We are fortunate on our campus to have an award-winning group called SIFE. ... With such program successes as SIFE and the commitment, hard work, and selflessness of the students involved, I have great faith in our future as these graduates take their place in the world.[13]

In the spring, Chico State SIFE focused on four main projects. First, we once again taught our high school lessons at Ridgeview High, with adapted versions taught to at-risk students in County Center Day School and Butte County Juvenile Hall.

Second, we partnered with Butte College to offer a youth entrepreneurship camp for thirty kids between the ages of ten and twelve. The camp, which took place for five consecutive Saturdays, emphasized business ethics and included a segment where students were asked to write a one-page essay on the topic, "The meaning of honesty in business."

Third, we continued adopting new SIFE teams; in the current year we adopted six more schools, making our cumulative a total of thirty rookie SIFE teams since 1994.

Fourth, we continued our Cal-High SIFE program, started a couple years earlier. It had now grown to include six Cal-High SIFE teams. The younger students came to our campus on April 7, 1999, during SIFE Week in Chico, using similar judging criteria as at the college SIFE level. Several members of our BAB served as judges. The overall winner was Pleasant Valley High School, and seven PV team members traveled with Chico State SIFE to Long Beach to observe their college "mentors" compete at the SIFE regional competition.

With arrows firmly ensconced in quivers, Chico State headed for the SIFE regionals in Long Beach on April 17. Knowing we had made the national top ten the previous year, the audience for our presentation was overflowing at the Hyatt Long Beach. Among the Chico SIFE guests that we invited to our teams's presentation was Erica Freihage, who had a very long title. She was Coordinator of Community Service Learning for the California State University, Office of the Chancellor. Erica had accepted this position only a year or two earlier, and she was in charge facilitating the implementation of the CSU's system-wide strategic plan for community service learning. She had been following our progress for the past year and saw SIFE as a potential avenue to introduce service learning to all twenty-three CSU campuses.

The team rehearsed late into the night on April 16. Mind you, I was chaperoning a large group. If one has ever traveled with a group of thirty university students and seven high school protégés, you might guess that things might be a little hard to control. Later, I discovered that one of the hotel guests had made some complaints about some of our more "unruly" students making too much noise. The guest was race car legend Mario Andretti. Whoops. Sorry, Mr. Andretti!

The presentation the next morning was flawless. The forty-second computer-animated introduction grabbed the audience from the outset, and the five women—identically clad in their matching business suits— proudly explained how Chico State SIFE met the judging criteria. After the presentation, Freihage came up to me and said, "We really need our service-learning people across the CSU system to see this presentation."

On May 15, 1999, three dozen Chico students, Rick Vertolli, five business advisers, and I headed to Kansas City for the SIFE USA expo. In addition to Judy Sitton and Barbara Derucher, the business advisers included in our delegation were Tim Colbie, a travel agent in Chico; Eric Ostrom of Butte County's Center for International Trade; and David Bunganich, a successful chiropractor in Chico. Not only were they along for the support but they also were needed to drive the vans. In previous years, the entire team stayed at the Hyatt near the Crown Center, or at the downtown Marriott. But I had learned something the past five years—staying in the same hotel as the hundreds of spirited undergraduates was not conducive to team preparation, or for myself getting much sleep.

This year was going to be different. Much to the disgruntlement of the presenters and the technology support crew, I assigned them to stay over at the Historic Suites of Kansas City, with Rick assigned to a room next door to chaperone. Barbara and Judy would stay with the rest of the team at the official conference hotel, the Marriott. Meanwhile, Tim, Eric, Dave, and I roomed at the Hyatt at the Crown Center. The Hyatt was less than two miles south of the Marriott, and it would make for a good reprieve from the rest of the action.

The presenters were perturbed upon arrival at their suite. They wanted to be part of the action at the Marriott. "After your presentation tomorrow, you can trade places with anyone at the Marriott," I said firmly. "Right now, I want you to stay together as a team, away from the distractions."

Early that night, at the jamboree welcome reception, Rohrs and the Two Jacks performed their usual ritual. After the reception, the team and I all agreed to meet at a favorite watering hole called Tanner's, on the corner of Tenth and Broadway. Tanner's was about five blocks northwest of the Marriott and eight blocks southwest of the presenters' suites—both within walking distance but not an easy walk for the women on our team wearing stilettos.

All five Chico State presenters are unforgettable, but Dawn Houston had a knack for the limelight. A year earlier, on Dawn's first trip to Kansas City, she made an impression on a competing team. As she later recalled, "My first trip to KC as a rookie I scouted out who would be our toughest competition in the first round, and that was San Diego State. I made an effort to knock on their door, introduce myself, and invite them out for drinks with us. When they declined because they had to 'practice' I proceeded to taunt them, indicating that Chico State was indeed a bigger party school than San Diego State. This made them determined to go out with us to prove me wrong. When we got to the first bar I offered to buy the first round. I went up to the bar and ordered six shots of vodka (for the SDSU team) and six shots of water (for us). After a few rounds like that the Chico team went home and the SDSU team proceeded to party. The next day the SDSU team was on first at 8 a.m. and they looked tired!

Chico State advanced, SDSU didn't. Sorry SDSU!"

All was going well that night, until about one in the morning. That's when I received a call from Danielle Emis, another presenter. "Curt, I've got a big problem, and I need you to help fix it."

"Dannie, this had better be something big," I said. "The main reason I checked into the Hyatt is so I didn't have to deal with minor issues. What's up?"

"I need you to run me out to Wal-Mart," she begged. *"I've got a run in my pantyhose!"*

Now you know why I had chosen to stay at the Hyatt.

Fortunately, Tim and Dave said they'd handle it, and I crawled back into bed. "Sheesh, pantyhose, really?" as I finally drifted back to sleep.

The next day, we were assigned to a league of six other SIFE teams. One of our main competitors, I knew, would be longtime stalwart, the University of the Ozarks. At my side the entire morning were four people—two of them were Johnny Thomas, now dean of La Sierra, and his handpicked successor as Sam M. Walton Fellow, Heather Miller. La Sierra had decided to sit out for a second straight year—Johnny and Heather wanted to see Chico State in action.

John Thornton also remained close; he was soon to take up the reins for SIFE Australia. The fourth person was Sergei Ravitchev of Moscow. Sergei had put together a SIFE Russia competition with six high school teams, and the Russian champion was competing in Kansas City—in our league.

Again, the Chico State presentation was flawless, in no small measure due to Danielle's new pantyhose. In their matching attire, stiletto shoes, and Chico State lapel pins, they ran through the presentation in exactly twenty-four minutes without note cards. Everyone in the room could hear each word clearly with the team using perfectly calibrated wireless microphones. Finally, the crucial seven-minute question and answer period went without a hitch. The Q and A often broke a SIFE team because if the presenters weren't thoroughly familiar with all of the projects, they could get caught cold, off-script. Not so with Chico State SIFE.

After the presentation, Johnny Thomas leaned over and said, "Your team has just set the new benchmark."

John Thornton and Sergei Ravitchev had questions about Cal-High

SIFE. "Taking the SIFE model down to high schools is a brilliant idea," John said. And Sergei couldn't argue—his Russian teams were from high schools in Moscow.

Late that afternoon, the winners of each of the sixteen leagues were announced in the second-floor ballroom of the Bartle Convention Center. It had been a successful year for the Chico State SIFE team, and if Chico State were to advance, it must be ready to present the next morning against three other outstanding semi-final teams. When the announcer came to our league, he called, "First runner-up, the University of the Ozarks. And the winner is … California State University, Chico!"

Our team was euphoric, but only for a few moments. We had come to Kansas City this year not only to make it to the final round of four, but to win it all. Other powerhouse teams advancing to the semi-final round included hometown favorite Drury College of Springfield, along with Northern Arizona, Pittsburgh State, Lubbock Christian, the University of Arizona, John Brown University, University of Texas-Pan American, and College of the Southwest.[14] The only non-USA team to make it to the semifinal round was the highly-regarded Mexico team from Monterrey Institute of Technology.

After all semifinalists had been called, the announcer asked for one student from each team to come to the stage, along with their Sam Walton Fellow. Each student randomly drew for final round league brackets and presentation times.

First up in our league was the Mexico team. Next, Chico State. Third, College of the Southwest, a small New Mexico team that had won the national championship a decade earlier in 1989. Rounding out our league would be Wichita State, another hometown favorite only three hours from Kansas City. Instead of fifteen judges in the first round, the semifinal round totaled about sixty judges, many of them senior executives and CEOs. With students from other teams checking each other out, the semifinal room was packed the next morning.

Monterrey was strong, very strong. Then we were up next, wobbling only when Rachel Muzzall forgot a line, got a bit off track, and then re-gained her composure. Next, College of the Southwest gave a presentation much along the lines of La Sierra in previous years—loud, flashy, and lots of projects delivered in staccato fashion. Would the judges favor an international team? Would they go for a La Sierra clone?

The judges took a fifteen-minute break, and I was nervous. Johnny said, "Don't worry—your team is the best so far."

But I had seen enough presentations to know judges' scoring is highly subjective, and the Wichita State team still had to present. As the break was coming to an end, Tim Colbie came back into the presentation room along with the judges. The judges were taking their seats at the front of the room. Tim came up behind me, leaned over my shoulder, and whispered, "I overheard two judges talking in the bathroom. They both said that the Chico State team was the best presentation they had ever seen."

Deep sigh. Wichita State presented and I breathed a little easier. The projects weren't nearly as substantive as ours, and the presenters stumbled on a few occasions. Maybe we would advance. We would know in about an hour. During lunch, I glanced at my presenters. Like me, they weren't eating much.

Near the end of lunch, the announcer called out the winning semifinal teams. With dramatic fanfare reminding me of the Wal-Mart annual meeting, the announcer called out the Final Four winners advancing to the championship round. The four teams invited to present in front of twelve hundred guests, including over a hundred CEO judges, were … Drury College … Northern Arizona University … Northeastern State University from Tahlequah, Oklahoma, and … California State University, Chico!

If "regular" euphoria had reigned yesterday afternoon, euphoria was now on steroids. My team went wild. We had made the Final Four. Just like NCAA basketball.

Again, one student from each of the four teams, along with their faculty adviser, was called to the stage. Up went Robert Wyatt, Lisa Borstadt, James Clark, and me, along with our student leaders. Suzanne Cozad stood proudly next to me. We drew slot number three. Northeastern was up first, Northern Arizona second, and Drury last. We all shook hands and wished each other well.

Onward. The final round of presentations was in a huge conference room across the street, and we hurriedly made our way over. If we weren't going to win it all, I was hoping that Lisa's team would. She and I were of similar minds—we both loved the service-learning aspect of SIFE, but we were both getting tired of Rohrs' disingenuous tears, and we made jokes about Shewmaker and Kahl loving the microphone like a teenager singing karaoke. Lisa and I sat together during Northeastern's presentation. On our left was a gentleman in a neatly pressed suit with a name tag that read, "David Bernauer, Walgreens." I asked him what his role was at Walgreens.

"CEO," he smiled. "I'd be judging the final round but I have a plane to catch right after the first presentation."

"Too bad," Lisa joked, "the best two teams are going next."

Northeastern did a great job, but they seemed to be a relatively new team. They didn't have the same track record or depth of projects as we did. After the question and answer period, Lisa and I looked at each other. We both knew our teams were better. Next up was her team. Having come in first runner-up last year, Northern Arizona had to be considered the favorite. They were confident and poised.

"Wow, this team is good," I thought. It looked like they had gotten some training from a drama teacher. Their gestures and delivery were perfectly choreographed. But would their projects carry the day?

Then Chico State took the stage. As the tech team was setting up our technology system in the first five minutes, audience members noticed two things that were different about our team. First, the tech guys, young Ken Derucher and Ed Person, removed all five standing mikes and turned off the existing sound system. What was up with that? Also, unlike the other teams that took the stage after their introduction and stood hovering over the judges for five long minutes before they could begin the oral presentation, our five women huddled on the side like a basketball team, sharing a bottle of water.

At the one-minute warning, the women took their assigned places. Sixty seconds later they began their crystal clear presentation. Again, perfect. Next came the Q & A period.

Seven more minutes. Come on, women, bring it home.

Question 1: "I really liked your Summer SIFE project. Tell us more about how these at-risk teens were selected."

Kelby Thornton, who led the project, stepped forward and parked it.

Question 2: "The Juvenile Hall project. Did you maintain contact with these youth after they were let out of jail?" Danielle Emis jumped all over that one.

Question 3: "The Cal-High SIFE project. Isn't this just like SIFE except that you encourage high school students to learn and teach about business?" Suzanne said yes, just like a minor league baseball league prepares its players for the Big Show.

And then the Big Question: "You mentioned that you taught the grade school kids about business ethics in your youth entrepreneurship camp. How do you know they learned anything?"

Dawn stepped forward. "Let me take this one. At one of our Saturday sessions, we taught the children a lesson about honesty in business. The next week, we randomly planted three envelopes with $10 in each one. On the outside of the envelopes, we simply had marked the word SIFE. The three kids who found the money could easily have kept it—we wouldn't have known who they were. I'm proud to say that we received all $30 back."

Spontaneous applause. Not just the judges, but the entire room. Big applause!

Dawn gave a slight nod in appreciation and stepped back.

One more team. Drury. Its new adviser, Robert Wyatt, had just come to Drury from Union University the year before, and he had built Union into a recent SIFE finalist the past few years. He knew how to play, and his team would be strong.

The next thirty minutes went as follows: Drury was introduced. The student presenters hovered over their standing microphone for five minutes. During the presentation the microphones often produced screeching, high-pitched sounds. Shaken, the question and answer period was marginal.

"Damn, we just might win this thing," I thought. But, then again, Lisa's team was really good.

We had about two hours between the last presentation and the final awards banquet, so the business advisers and I slipped across the street to the Marriott lounge. I was drained. Before long, Robert Wyatt and his co-adviser Robert Taylor entered the lounge. Wyatt came over to me and shook my hand. "Congratulations, Curt, your team is going to win it all," he said.

Not so fast. About 6:30, all members of the Chico delegation met the Chico State presenters at the ground floor elevator of the Kansas City Convention Center. Together, we rode up to the main floor and entered the banquet room. After a keynote speech by Schwan's chairman, Alfred Schwan, there were more speeches and awards.

In the next ten minutes I would experience a new career highlight. The announcer called out the results, with all four teams on stage huddled closely together, arm in arm, heads down, eyes closed.

"Third runner up goes to … Drury University."

"Second runner-up … Northeastern State University."

"First runner up … drumroll."

Don't start with a C; please don't start with a C.

"First runner up goes to … N … Northern Arizona University!"

Again, our team went wild. Confetti and balloons fell from the ceiling. Music blared. Bedlam. Hugs, tears, high fives and handshakes all around. The moment was surreal.

Kahl and Shewmaker came on the stage to congratulate us. But no Rohrs.

Daniel Shewmaker, Jack's son, sought me out and said our team was marvelous today. Sergei Ravitchev wanted to learn more about our Cal-High SIFE program in Russia. John Thornton asked if I could help him with SIFE Australia. Other Walton Fellows wanted to learn more about our best programs. Many of the CEOs complimented my students and handed them business cards.

The next thing I knew, one of SIFE's staff was on the stage next to me. "We'd like your team to make its presentation again soon. There's a big retailer's conference in Orlando. Want to go to Disney World?"

Chapter 8

How High Is Up?

========

With its presentation on May 18, 1999, Chico State SIFE had, indeed, set a new benchmark for future SIFE teams. To win it all, a SIFE team now needed projects with substance, to be sure. But a splashy, high-tech introduction and a flawless presentation were now the norm. From now on, the presenters had to throw away their note cards. These facts were not lost upon the twelve hundred guests in Kansas City, including SIFE delegations from ten other countries. Among the international guests: John Thornton of Australia, Sergei Ravitchev of Russia, and Yusuf Majidov of Tajikistan.

With a parochial worldview, Alvin Rohrs was nonplussed about his board's new global strategy. The Executive Committee of the SIFE board—including its erstwhile chairs, Jack Shewmaker, Stanley Gaines, and Jack Kahl—was calling the shots, and globalization was now in the hearts and minds of free-market capitalists everywhere. Nonetheless, Rohrs had to be excited about the pecuniary rewards likely to follow. With revenues of over $5.3 million in 1998–1999, Rohrs could foresee more money flowing into the coffers of his educational nonprofit organization.[1]

In September, SIFE published its annual yearbook with the Chico State team's jubilant photo on the four-color cover. The welcome letter, co-authored by Rohrs and new board chair Mike Merriman, was effusive: "Making dramatic strides on the global front, SIFE is flourishing in eleven countries, and we are clearly on our way to establishing a global organization. It's hard to believe that SIFE Teams in former communist countries eagerly practice and teach free enterprise because they firmly believe that their SIFE efforts will help them pave the way for strong futures for their countries."[2] Page five of the handbook added, "SIFE was given the green light by the Board of Directors to cultivate SIFE Global. SIFE Global has made dramatic strides in its second full-year effort. This year, fifty-three

Global Teams competed in their countries, and ten competed at the SIFE Int'l Expo."

The yearbook claimed 139 board members. Several pages were devoted to full-page advertisements for SIFE's most generous donors, including Manco, Kinko's, *Business Week*, RadioShack, Sprint, American Greetings, Unilever, and of course, Wal-Mart. Also notable among the big donors was the international accounting firm of KPMG, now listed as a *Friend Extraordinaire.* In 1999, Bernie Milano was directing the KPMG Foundation, and Tom Moser was the firm's vice chairman.[3]

KPMG involvement was a good thing for me, as I could point to its affiliation with SIFE as a way to recruit more accounting majors to Chico State's SIFE team. Of course, from KPMG's point of view, it probably thought it wouldn't likely find many superstar future CPAs in SIFE—most SIFE students were management and marketing majors. More likely, KPMG saw lucrative new audit and consulting business by hitching its star to the SIFE wagon commandeered by Wal-Mart.

At the end of the yearbook, six pages were devoted to the 1998–1999 contributions or pledges by giving level: Friend Extraordinaire ($100,000 and above), Hutch Club $50,000–$75,000), Enterpriser's Club ($25,000–$49,000), on down the line to Chairman's Club, Director's Club, Builder's Club, Advocate's Club, and Patriot's ($999 and below). I also noted accounting firm Arthur Andersen, which would soon go out of business with the ensuing Enron scandal, was listed as a Hutch Club member.

As our team was wrapping up its celebration at the Kansas City Convention Center on May 18, Geralyn Mason, SIFE's vice president of expositions and meetings, provided me with details about the trip to Orlando. In addition to the five presenters, she said, I could invite seven more students to go to Orlando. Just like a basketball team, I mused, a starting five and a deep bench.

Each year, the International Mass Retailers Association (IMRA) had their annual meeting in June. This year, Jack Shewmaker made sure that the winning SIFE team would be on the agenda. Not only did he want to help Alvin Rohrs and Bruce Nasby recruit new corporate supporters, but Shewmaker was also bringing a special guest with him to Orlando.

Upon returning to Chico on May 19, we were treated like winners of the NCAA basketball tournament. We received national cable TV coverage on CNNfn on its *Entrepreneurs Only* program. A press conference took place in the center of our campus with both local TV stations and the *Chico Enterprise-Record* on hand. President Esteban and Chico Mayor Steve Bertagna made glowing comments about the team.

Letters of congratulations came pouring in from SIFE donor companies, inviting our students to apply for jobs and internships. A total of 157 judges had scored us in the final round in Kansas City, and sixty judges in the semifinals. Now, over two hundred CEOs and senior executives knew where Chico was located, and they also knew Chico State would no longer be known solely for its party-school image. A senior executive from Manco, Jack Kahl's firm, wanted to come to Chico State and meet Rick Vertolli. The animated computer graphics in the Chico State SIFE presentation had impressed him enough to want to see our Instructional Media Center.

We shared the spotlight with the newly crowned Chico State baseball team, which on the preceding Saturday had claimed the NCAA Division II championship. For a relatively small city like Chico, such excitement was unusual. More than ten years later, Chico would have a brighter spotlight by claiming Pleasant Valley High's Aaron Rogers as its hometown hero. Rogers was the 2011 Super Bowl MVP quarterback for the Green Bay Packers. Chico Funeral Home director Shawntel Newton, who graduated from the same high school as Rogers, became a celebratory finalist on *The Bachelor* the same year.

There was a whir of activity. In between making plane reservations for a dozen students and myself to go to Orlando just two days away, Danielle Emis and I were finalizing a trip to Bergen, Norway. Danielle was the incoming SIFE president for 1999–2000, and she and I had submitted a paper to the Sixth Annual EDINEB Conference. EDINEB stands for *Educational Innovations in Economics and Business.* This trip was going to be a first for Danielle and me; neither of us had ever been to Europe. The title of the paper reflected my lobbying efforts in the service-learning area: "Service Learning: A Vehicle to Combine Action-Based Learning, Entrepreneurship, and Business Partnerships."

Only three days after returning to Chico from Kansas City, ten students and I headed for Orlando. Two more students—Dawn Houston and Frances Dove-Edwin—would meet us there. Dawn was coming to Florida directly from Hawaii. Frances would drive down from Atlanta where he was visiting relatives. The Chico State SIFE team was scheduled to repeat its presentation on May 23, immediately following a discussion panel entitled, "The Challenges of Employee Recruitment and Retention." The panel included a star-studded panel of retail executives, including Tom Coughlin, president and CEO of Wal-Mart and Tom Kroeger, executive vice president of human resources of Office Depot. Both men knew SIFE well; in two years, Coughlin would replace Mike Merriman as chairman of the SIFE board, and Kroeger was currently a board member.

The Chico State students and I waited in the lobby, along with Bruce Nasby, until the end of the panel discussion. Upon entering the room, we saw it was packed with about 150 retail executives in tailored business suits and power ties—mostly blue or red. Not surprisingly, almost all of them were white men over fifty.

The audience fit the profile of the SIFE Executive Committee—all fourteen members of SIFE's central governing body were Caucasian, male, and in their fifties and sixties, with the exception of a couple young whip-persnappers in their forties like Merriman and Lee Scott. In a few years, Scott would replace David Glass as CEO of Wal-Mart's entire operations.

Shewmaker took the stage and introduced Alvin Rohrs. Oddly, this was the first time we had seen Rohrs—no greeting at the airport, no welcome message at the front desk, no invitation to dinner or breakfast. And really, by this point in our relationship, I wasn't surprised.

Rohrs was just doing what I thought he did best, and that was shaking the money tree. Interacting with SIFE students and faculty—especially those from public, comprehensive, and liberal universities like Chico State—was not his bailiwick. Undoubtedly, he would have been much more comfortable with the likes of Lubbock Christian, Drury University, Harding, or Southwest Baptist.

Chico State wasn't from the Bible Belt or Wal-Mart country. In fact, the majority of Chico's citizens, in just a few years, would be lobbying hard to prevent Wal-Mart from expanding its regular big box retail store, built in

1994, to a supercenter.[4] And to top it off, I was getting the distinct feeling that Rohrs viewed me as a loudmouth rabble-rouser trying to meddle in his business. And now, with the Two Jacks—Shewmaker and Kahl—taking a shine to me, this had to be unsettling for SIFE's CEO.

Rohrs took the microphone. True to form when addressing new and potential donors, he quickly became overcome with emotion. It was showtime.

Rohrs introduced the team, and the five Chico State women presenters marched proudly to the stage. The tech crew—Ed Person, Ken Derucher, and Charles Brooks—had already set up the laptop and checked the sound system.

Dawn Houston approached the podium. Smiling and confident, she implored the audience to please do her a favor. "Reach down and grab your ankles," she said. "Everybody set? Hold on tight because in the next half hour, we're gonna blow your socks off!"

The team didn't miss a beat. At the end of the presentation, Shewmaker stood up and began a slow, loud clap. The short man seated next to him followed suit, and in a moment, the whole audience rose to their feet to join what quickly became a rousing ovation. The Chico State coeds beamed, and even bowed. The audience was ecstatic.

Seated next to Shewmaker was Roger Corbett. Earlier in the year— January 1999—Corbett had just been named CEO of Australia's second largest retailer, Woolworths. Shewmaker had met Corbett several years earlier and they became close personal friends. Since his retirement from Wal-Mart in 1988, Shewmaker and his wife Melba began traveling the world. One of their favorite destinations was Australia. They usually traveled there twice a year. When Corbett asked Shewmaker to be a consultant for Woolworths, he gladly accepted.[5]

It was obvious to the retail leaders in Orlando: one way to help their companies meet the challenges of employee recruitment was to become a member of the SIFE board. If their company was a Wal-Mart vendor, they could achieve two objectives. They could attract good talent and have a perfect reason to rub elbows with Wal-Mart's top dogs like Shewmaker, Tom Coughlin, and Lee Scott. If their company was not a Wal-Mart vendor, like Office Depot, RadioShack, or Walgreens, SIFE was also a good investment. They had as good a chance of recruiting superstar seniors like Dawn Houston, Suzanne Cozad, or Kelby Thornton as Wal-Mart.

The Orlando convention seemed almost like a fraternity party for retail executives, and Shewmaker was its leader. SIFE was Shewmaker's baby, and he was proud to show it off. That night, before dinner, he clearly enjoyed interacting with my students and me. He also introduced us to the man who sat next to him at the presentation.

"Roger has something he'd like to ask you," Shewmaker said to the presenters.

Roger Corbett was a gregarious man. With his charming Aussie accent he said hello and shook hands all around. Barely containing his enthusiasm, he said, "How would you like to be my guests in Australia? Jack and I would like to start a SIFE program down under."

Though Corbett and Shewmaker were far different in physique and stature, they were two peas in a pod when it came to retail. They had met soon before Shewmaker retired from Wal-Mart in 1988 and before long, Shewmaker was consulting for Big W, Woolworths largest discount chain.[6] The two men immediately took a liking to each other, as did their wives Rosemary and Melba. Four years younger than Shewmaker, Corbett was short and balding compared to Shewmaker's lanky six feet, two-inch frame. Shewmaker also had a full head of black hair, though he sometimes wore it in a crew cut. Corbett, now age fifty-seven, had become Woolworths' CEO earlier in the year.

Corbett considered himself to be a Christian servant leader. In the July 23, 2006, interview with Julia Baird of the Australian Broadcasting Corporation, Corbett was asked about his beliefs.

"I'm a committed Christian and ... that is a determining factor in a lot of what I endeavor to do in life and I endeavor to follow the teachings of Jesus Christ and to do unto others as they would have them do unto me and to love my neighbor as myself," he said.

Asked how his faith affected the way he works, he replied, "I believe that I'm a servant and I endeavor to serve the company that employs me to the very very best of my ability."

Baird pressed him on this. She asked Corbett if he had been confronted with ethical decisions that he would not be comfortable making as a

Christian.

"Oh yes indeed. There are instances where I think and on occasions pray very carefully before I act," he said.

He added that he had two guiding principles in those situations. "One—what is the truth and two—in these circumstances, if I was the other person, how would I expect to be treated?"

A year later I would be left wondering how Jack Shewmaker would have answered Baird's question about ethics. I still wonder today.

My students were giddy at the thought of going to Australia. Corbett and Shewmaker said they would try to arrange for our team to visit in August or September, and that SIFE's home office would be in touch to help us with our travel arrangements. Shewmaker, pleased with Corbett's invitation and our reaction, offered another goodie.

"Hey, before y'all sit down to dinner," Shewmaker smiled. "I'd like to introduce you to someone else."

He escorted us backstage to a dressing room. "Say hello to Bill Cosby."

Cosby, the evening's closing act, was as entertaining and friendly off-stage as on. He chatted with us for about ten minutes before we returned to our seats.

"Chico," he said. "Don't they have a prison there?"

We helped him with his California geography, pointing out that he was confusing Chico with Chino, in East Los Angeles. Chico, we said, is home to the *1999 SIFE International Champions*.

Hardly anyone could taste their dinner. Australia. Passports. Bill Cosby. Disney World. Life was good for my students and, for the most part, me, too. But something had been nagging me for a long time, and it was now turning into a real concern.

Alvin Rohrs had not replied to my earlier offer to take a sabbatical with SIFE. He had not replied to my laundry list of concerns from the Branson meetings; and now, neither he nor Bruce Nasby had spent any appreciable time getting to know my SIFE students or me. Other than attending the presentation and collecting business cards as the executives were leaving the meeting, I can only remember one perfunctory comment Rohrs made: "Enjoy Disney World this afternoon. Send Geralyn Mason the receipts for your expenses."

I couldn't help but feel my students and I were being used as SIFE pawns, and Shewmaker was the benign king. Shortly after returning from Orlando, *Discount Store News* printed a feature article about SIFE. The headline for the June 21 article read, SIFE NEARS 25TH ANNIVERSARY OF FUTURE BUSINESS EXECS.[7] Several quotations in the article jumped out at me eliciting my reactions.

The first quote was: "[Students] don't receive any pay for the hours they spend on educational outreach projects such as working in youth entrepreneurship camps or teaching at-risk teenagers in juvenile detention centers how to operate a small business."

My reaction: neither did Walton Fellows, if you consider that most of us gave the $1,000 stipend right back to our teams. And, by now, I knew Rohrs and Nasby were each earning well over $200,000 annually.

The second noteworthy quote was from Rohrs saying, "Almost through sheer accident we have developed a leadership program that fits what business needs these days."

My reaction to this was: sheer accident? Hardly. Satisfying business needs was SIFE's primary goal from the outset. From its very first meeting in 1975, when about a hundred undergraduates were brought to the Inn of the Six Flags in Arlington, students were asked "to discover and discuss what they might do to counteract the stultifying criticism of American business which was flowing from the campus, the press, and elsewhere, seeking to tear down the very system which gave the critics their jobs and their warm, comfortable homes."[8]

The third quote was: "The SIFE program, begun in 1975, has grown to involve teams from more than six hundred colleges around the world."

The key word, once again, *involve*. The total number of teams competing at regionals was actually 379. If a team didn't compete at regionals, its involvement more than likely meant it may have had an active team *up to three years ago but was still being counted as one of the six hundred*. Further, not an inconsequential number of the competing teams had but one or two students make a presentation for only a few minutes, with the faculty member cashing a $1,000 check. SIFE asked no questions because SIFE's senior staff had bonuses dependent on big numbers.[9] Clearly, hyperbole wasn't beyond SIFE's method of accountability.

The next quotes were: "Rohrs said more than two hundred job offers were made at the Expo this year, including ninety from Wal-Mart and forty from Office Depot." And: "Len Roberts, chairman, CEO and president of Tandy, said 'Our company aims each year to hire extensively for our managerial ranks from the graduating class of SIFE.'"

My reaction to these quotes: now we're talking. I believe Wal-Mart, Office Depot, and RadioShack needed SIFE to provide a training ground for more ideological servant leaders. As Nelson Lichtenstein put it, "The story of a Wal-Mart front group, Students in Free Enterprise, demonstrates the potency of such an ideology-cum-theology when coupled with a retail organization seeking to recruit and promote a workforce that shares its missions and values."[10]

The problem that had been brewing between Rohrs and me, I could now see more clearly, was he and I did not share the same values. Also, I sincerely doubted that most of my SIFE leaders would be interested in retail, starting their careers in low-paying management training programs. Most of my SIFE students had their sights on other companies like Hewlett-Packard, Intel, Cisco, and Chevron.

But SIFE's board had given Rohrs a new mission: *go global.* Compared to most powerhouse SIFE teams, which were from predominantly Christian colleges, Chico State was more diversified. We were more liberal, and we were secular.

A fifth quote caught my eye in the *Discount Store News* article. According to a SIFE spokesperson, "About 70 percent of SIFE students receive academic credit for participating in the program. Most participants are business majors, although all students are encouraged to join. The students pretty much work all year long in doing outreach programs. Many of them are targeted toward at-risk youth of the communities, teaching them about budgeting, staying in school and social responsibility."

Yes! This was why I had joined the SIFE network: community service learning. Since I started in 1993, over thirty of my SIFE students had received direct course credit for their service-learning activities, and dozens more had earned "bonus points" as part of my accounting classes.

Finally, there was a sixth item: "Corporate donations are used in part to pay for the teams' travel expenses to the competitions, SIFE programs, prizes and team adviser stipends.ʺ

This made it sound like SIFE was generous. It was not. To be clear, travel expenses to competitions were a huge expense for large teams like ours. The only travel expenses paid by SIFE were three hotel rooms for one night for teams participating in regional competitions. Mileage, airfare, and additional rooms were the team's responsibility. Again, think Tom Sawyer and how he convinced his friends that it was in their best interest to paint Aunt Polly's fence. *Alvin Rohrs was Tom Sawyer, SIFE students and their advisers were Tom's friends, and Aunt Polly—the ultimate benefactor of the painting enterprise—was SIFE's corporate donors.*

As an accounting professor, trained as a PhD to be curious, ask questions, and challenge accepted paradigms, I once again did a cost-benefit analysis. Were the benefits accruing to students—and to me—more than the costs? In spite of the indoctrination efforts to lure my students into servile leadership positions, I still said yes.

And with that, I helped my students launch the second Summer SIFE program, starting on June 9. On June 22, I headed to Bergen, Norway. The trip marked the beginning of my international travels, not as a tourist, but as a service-learning proponent. The next day, I planned to meet incoming Chico State SIFE president Danielle Emis in Bergen. Together, we would be making a presentation at the EDINEB conference. Our paper aligned well with the conference themes. In the end, it was well-received, in no small measure because Danielle was only one of very few student presenters at the conference.

Danielle and I had a marvelous time, mingling with other conference attendees, eating shrimp with mayonnaise on a midnight cruise of the stunningly magnificent fjords, and explaining to the international guests the concept of service learning. It didn't get dark until about 2 a.m., and the sun started rising about 4 a.m. During the conference, I met some new friends from Wuppertal, Germany.

After Bergen, Danielle and I parted ways. Before heading to a second academic business conference in Athens to make a presentation, I took the train from Bergen to Stockholm to see my former college roommate, Bright Ebenezer. Bright and I reminisced for a couple days, and then I caught a train ferry to Cologne, Germany. Originally, I had planned to buy a Eurail pass and tour Holland and France for a few days, then head to Athens, but my plans changed when I was in Norway.

In Bergen I met Professor Ulrich Braukman and his doctoral assistant, Brigitte Halbfast. They invited me to the University of Wuppertal, so instead of touring Holland and France, I gladly accepted their invitation. I asked Bright to help me book a train/ferry combo through southern Sweden, Copenhagen, Hamburg, and down to Cologne. Ulrich picked me up at the train station across the street from Cologne's magnificent cathedral.

After two days in Wuppertal, I caught a train to the Frankfurt airport and flew to Athens. There, I met up with Gail Corbitt, my good friend and colleague from Chico State. Gail was also a presenter at the Athens conference. The day after we made our presentations, we boarded a Blue Ferry out of Piraeus Port to Mykonos.

We spent three days in Mykonos catching sun on the beach, sipping cocktails at Little Italy, and kicking back. After the past few months with SIFE, it was a really good chance to unwind. After Mykonos, we headed for the less popular, but more spectacular, island of Amorgos. Two more days of fun and sun, and it was time for Gail to catch her flight home. I, on the other hand, had four more days all to myself. So I booked a ticket to Paros for two nights, and then ferried back to Athens.

By this time, I was ready to go home, but I had two more nights in Athens. I toured the Acropolis, visited a couple museums, ate some more moussaka and souvlaki, and checked my email the next morning. Suzanne Cozad, who had just graduated and started work with Hewlett-Packard, sent me a message.

"Curt, I just wanted to tell you how much I have enjoyed being on the SIFE team the past two years. Without doubt, winning the SIFE USA competition is one of the absolute highlights of my life." Suzanne had just graduated magna cum laude with a double major in accounting and management information systems.

Anyone who has traveled solo for more than a couple days, especially to foreign countries, has plenty of time to reflect. It was July 16, 1999, a day that I remember vividly. My wife Kris and I had finally split for good in early 1999, and it had been six months since I became a single man. The trip to Europe reinvigorated me. Late that afternoon, when I returned to my hotel in downtown Athens, I turned on the television. The news was not good—John F. Kennedy, Jr. had in all likelihood died in a plane crash, his plane going down with his wife and sister-in-law aboard. I reflected on the fragility of life and how it can be cut short in an instant.

M y dad had died at age fifty-nine, three-and-a-half years earlier. Now, in summer 1999, I was almost forty-four. Though not a religious or prayerful man, I often ended each day with a silent tribute to Dad. I wished desperately to be able to go on more fishing trips with him. His untimely death made me gauge my own mortality. And it made me want to honor my dad by leaving a legacy beyond being "just" an accounting professor. Service learning, I thought, was one way to make a lasting impression. And service learning for business students, in particular, became my rallying cry. From this point on in my life, I vowed to take many more trips to all corners of the globe introducing service learning to other educators and their students. SIFE, for now at least, provided an imperfect vehicle to pursue my passion.

The next day, I boarded a plane for San Francisco.

Butte County's Private Industry Council provided the Chico State SIFE team with a grant for $43,000 to conduct Summer SIFE for the second consecutive year. Led by returning SIFE veteran Ed Person—who is a spitting image of Matthew Fox of TV's *Party of Five* and *Lost* series—the team kicked into high gear. Eight SIFE students delivered the business lessons to sixty-four at-risk youth.

Significantly, one of the new SIFE students was transfer student Reuben Williams who had been team captain on the Butte College SIFE team the previous year. Reuben, a telegenic finance major from Roseville, was a natural leader, and he had his eye on a future political career. Butte College had won the two-year-college division in Kansas City. Butte County was home to both the two- and four-year college SIFE champions in 1999. Reuben, I thought, was a ringer. He knew SIFE, he loved it, and he undoubtedly would be our team's presentation captain this coming year.

Near the end of July, I received a call from Alvin Rohrs' assistant at SIFE Headquarters. "Roger Corbett and Jack Shewmaker want you to come to Sydney on August 10," she said. "Can you get your presenters and one tech student together and submit their details to us? We'll make flight and hotel arrangements for them."

"Sure," I said. But Suzanne Cozad had already taken a job at Hewlett-Packard and Rachel Muzzall couldn't leave her kids for ten days. "Is it okay if Heather Rosdail steps in for Suzanne? And Ed Person can easily take over for Rachel."

"No problem, but get us the information—fast," she said.

By August 5, the Summer SIFE project had come to an end. The Chico State students had helped their protégés create eight mini-businesses—two each at Chico, Paradise, Gridley, and Oroville. The younger students presented their business plans on August 5 to a panel of advisory board members. Incoming dean of the College of Business, Heikki Rinne, was on hand to support and welcome the teams as was the mayor of Chico, Steve Bertagna.

A few days later, I got another call from SIFE. "Your team is all set up. Judy Howard of Woolworths will meet them at the Sydney airport."

"Them?" I asked. "What about us? Judy will meet my students and me, yes?"

"No. Sorry, Dr. DeBerg, but we only have a budget for five presenters and one tech student," she said.

Strange. From the get-go, I had assumed I would be chaperoning the team. It had been pretty clear to me in Orlando that Shewmaker and Corbett not only wanted our SIFE team to strut their stuff in Australia, but that they also wanted me, as faculty adviser, to be on hand.

Rohrs' assistant was telling me this was *not* the case. Naturally, I felt snakebitten—I had done all the legwork to get the team to Orlando and now, just two months later, for Australia. But now I'm being informed that I'm not on the invitation list.

I took a deep breath and shrugged it off. Oh well, I could use the free time to relax a bit and get ready for the fall semester. I had syllabi to update and course schedules to create.

The team was set to depart on August 9, but on August 8 I received another phone call from SIFE.

"There's been a slight misunderstanding," said the assistant, with a hint of panic. "When Mr. Shewmaker found out you weren't going to Australia, he wasn't too happy. He—*we*—really want you to make the trip. Can you go?"

Again, a bit strange. If Shewmaker had been in touch with Rohrs and had leaned on Rohrs to make sure I accompanied the team, why wasn't Rohrs calling me himself? Even now, he couldn't bear the thought of interacting with me. It seemed to me that his assistant was doing work he should have been doing. If the relationship between Rohrs and me wasn't so dysfunctional, he'd tend to this matter—one so near and dear to Shewmaker—personally. After all, Shewmaker was SIFE's unofficial top dog on the SIFE board.

"Give me some time to think about this," I said. "I've made other plans, but I'll see if I can change them," I said.

"Well, please hurry," she said. "If you can make it, book a flight immediately. And don't worry about fare. Book business class if you'd like."

Business class? Sam Walton wouldn't approve of something like this. He made it a point to always fly coach. I found it amusing that, a week earlier, SIFE didn't have the budget to send me to Sydney. Now it had the budget—a real *big* budget. Sending our SIFE team to Australia was Shewmaker's pet project, and he wanted to please Roger Corbett.

Rohrs could be none too happy about Shewmaker's decision to send me. Perhaps I was getting too close to Rohrs' wheelhouse. It seemed Rohrs did not like Sam M. Walton Fellows getting too close to "his" board.

In the end, I made the trip—one day after my students had already departed. I booked a coach ticket on United, departing out of Chico. I couldn't stand the thought of spending $3,500 for a business class ticket when $1,500 would get me there, even though SIFE promised to reimburse me. As I checked into my first leg on regional carrier SkyWest, the young man behind the counter smiled. "Carl Hartman, how are you?" I asked.

Carl was a former student at Chico State who had earned an A in my accounting class. He set me up with boarding passes and checked my luggage. When I connected in San Francisco, I handed my boarding pass to the flight attendant. "Fourth seat on your left. It's a window seat," she said.

Left? That was first class.

Sam Walton wouldn't have paid for a business class ticket, but he wouldn't turn down a *free* upgrade to first class for the fifteen-hour flight to Sydney. To top it off, Carl had booked me for business class coming home. It pays to have friends in high places.

Judy Howard was Roger Corbett's senior assistant. Judy was charged with organizing our agenda. With a friendly smile, she greeted me at the Sydney airport and took me to the hotel. There, my students were shaking off their jet lag.

After a day or two of sightseeing in Sydney, Judy organized an excursion to Wollongong, a coastal town about an hour southwest of Sydney. A beautiful little city, it is nestled between the Pacific Ocean on the east and the Illawarra Escarpment to the west. The hills of the plateau reach over 2,400 feet.

Much like the Chico State presenters had done in Orlando, the team made its twenty-four-minute presentation to over a hundred Woolworths regional managers. Heather did a magnificent job in Suzanne's role, and Ed only looked at his note cards a few times while standing in for Rachel. With the seeds for a future SIFE Australia program firmly planted, our trip back to Sydney went quickly. The team couldn't celebrate too much because the next day we needed to catch an early flight to Melbourne to meet with administrators from several universities, including the University of Melbourne. Another seed planted.

Upon returning to Sydney, we had a couple more days to walk around the Sydney Harbor, taking in spectacular views of the Harbor Bridge and Opera House. We walked the sands of world-famous Bondi Beach and enjoyed Taronga Zoo, feeding a wallaby and taking photos with a koala. The day before our last official event, we took an unforgettable, full-day nature trip to the Blue Mountains. We capped off the day with a boardwalk stroll through the rainforest.

Judy informed us that the next evening, August 19, would be a big one for us. KPMG was planning to host a special reception at its beautiful theatre/conference room at the KPMG Centre, a thirty-floor office building at 45 Clarence Street in downtown Sydney. Corbett had been pressing the flesh hard to arrange a meeting between several business leaders and, notably, university presidents, to let them know about the SIFE program. Bernie Milano and Tom Moser, KPMG brass in the United States, had likely been working the phones, too. Tonight, they would see for themselves why SIFE was such a dynamic youth organization that could provide a direct pipeline to Australia's brightest future leaders.

The title of our program was "How to Start SIFE 'Down Under.'" About thirty of Australia's leading CEOs and university executives attended.

I was asked to introduce the team and explain my role as a faculty adviser. After the presentation, I was bombarded with questions, especially from the university executives: "Why would a faculty member become a SIFE adviser?" "Did faculty members like me receive classroom release time to be an adviser?" "Tell us more about service learning, and how SIFE fosters service learning?" These were questions only I could answer. Shewmaker had pressed Rohrs for me to attend precisely for this reason.

Roger Corbett was ecstatic. He concluded the event by exhorting his fellow private and public sector partners to join him in starting a SIFE program in Australia.

Immediately upon our return, Shewmaker called me. "How did it go, Curt?"

I eagerly shared my ideas and insights with him. "The last meeting at KPMG's office was impactful," I told him. "Roger Corbett brought corporate leaders to the same table as university presidents. If we can get more top-rated American universities to see that their business students can complete service-learning activities as part of SIFE, I think you can grow SIFE here. The key is to be able to speak the language of the academic leaders."

Shewmaker asked if I had any ideas on how this might happen.

"Why not arrange for a future SIFE board meeting to coincide with an academic meeting?" I offered. "Getting some of SIFE's CEOs to sit down with some university presidents in California, or their service-learning coordinators, would be a good place to start."

Shewmaker remembered Chico State president Manuel Esteban winning the SIFE award a couple years earlier. "Would President Esteban be able to join us?"

"I think so," I replied. "The California State University system now has twenty-three campuses, and if he likes the idea he can put the word out to the entire CSU system."

Shewmaker encouraged me to investigate this further. "Let's talk about this in Springfield in a few weeks."

We returned to the United States with heads held high. My students rightfully believed they were changing the world. Though I lost several top students to graduation (Suzanne joined Hewlett-Packard; Kelby signed a generous contract with Chevron; Dawn decided to take a few months off; Rachel took a job, locally, with Safeway), I had more than a few superstars returning to the team—incoming president Danielle Emis, Ed Persons, Heather Rosdail, and Ken Derucher, Jr. And three new dynamos would be taking lead roles: Reuben Williams from Butte College, Jeff Iverson, who had just become Chico State's student body president, and one of the best natural salesmen I have ever met, Jeff Leh.

The first meeting of the 1999–2000 Chico State SIFE team was on September 2. We needed a special room in the student union to hold the group. Danielle laid out the goals for the team for the upcoming year. Among the 212 people in attendance were students, faculty, business advisers, and eleven guests from Russia—Sergei Ravitchev, his wife Tamara, and several students. When our team was celebrating on the stage May 18 in Kansas City, Sergei had asked me if he could visit our campus with several students early in the fall semester.

"We would like to attend the first Chico SIFE meeting to see how your team is organized. To be the best in Russia, we want to learn from the best in the U.S.," he said.

The Berlin Wall had fallen ten years earlier, and the USSR disbanded in 1991. I wasn't the only person who marveled that now, only eight years later, eleven people from Moscow were sitting in Chico State's student union wanting to learn more about American business and free-market capitalism.

Sergei wore many hats in Russia. He was named the new president of SIFE-Russia; he was Russia's director of International Center for Economic and Business Education (ICEBE); and he was a professor of economics at the Moscow University of Physics and Technologies. Tamara was the director of International Projects for ICEBE, and was a former professor of biophysics at Moscow Medical School. She was also a translator of many books on economics.

"The eight students on the trip to Chico earned the right to come to the U.S. by winning a national economics competition at the high school level," Tamara said. "These students already have a competitive spirit, and that is why they can easily pick up on the idea behind SIFE when they enroll at the university."

The Russian guests were intrigued by the notion of service learning. But what made SIFE especially unique is that students *competed* based on their service projects, and the competitions' judges came from the private sector.

For many educators in the service-learning world, competition is antithetical to service. But this was really the beauty behind SIFE, and the reason I wanted to stay with it in spite of its flaws. In my heart, I believed I could make the organization better.

With guidance from faculty, students first had to organize a team and determine its leader. Then, they had to create, implement, and assess the projects. This takes a great deal of cooperation. Then, at the end of the year, students presented the results of their work in front of influential business leaders. The result is remarkably positive—as long as faculty are careful not to indoctrinate their students to their own self-serving ideologies or political beliefs.

Sergei and Tamara were soaking up SIFE, and they had selected Chico State SIFE as their benchmark. They especially liked our high school programs. But Russia had unique challenges.

"One major problem is lack of business support," Tamara said. "Our country needs to learn the free enterprise system, and the best place to start is in the schools and universities. In the U.S., the business support for SIFE is wonderful. Major businesses like RadioShack, KPMG, and Wal-Mart provide many resources. But we don't have this kind of support in our country."

Sergei added, "Russian businesses are not very involved. The economic situation in Russia is such that most businesses wouldn't even consider investing in educational projects. One reason for this is the lack of advantages for them in terms of tax deductions or traditions of promotional and marketing policies. Also, many businesses are corrupt."

What were their plans for SIFE in Russia? I asked.

"We plan to involve about twenty to twenty-five teams in various universities this year, if funds permit," said Tamara. "And thanks to Chico State SIFE, we have many project ideas that we will adapt to our culture."

Ten days after the first SIFE meeting, I was back on a plane to Springfield, Missouri. Walton Fellows on the SIFE Academic Council were invited to participate in a ceremony on September 13, 1999, when SIFE officially dedicated its expanded headquarters. SIFE's board—including Jack Shewmaker, Jack Kahl, and the redoubtable Robert Plaster—eponymously renamed the entire SIFE home office complex as The Jack Shewmaker SIFE World Headquarters. The 11,200 square-foot new addition was called The Robert W. Plaster Free Enterprise Center, and the existing building was named The Jack Kahl Entrepreneurship Center. Each of the three servant leaders made a $250,000 commitment to help kick off the building fund campaign. The expanded headquarters were needed in order to "support SIFE teams in forty-eight states and fifteen countries, provide leadership training for college students in twenty-eight cities, sponsor regional expositions and career opportunity fairs in twenty cities and will award more than $400,000 in cash awards for outstanding educational outreach projects worldwide."[11]

That night, we attended a banquet at a nearby hotel where Shewmaker made some remarks after dinner, and then introduced Al Konuwa and me as the Sam M. Walton Fellows from the 1999 SIFE USA champion teams in the two-year and four-year divisions. Each of us were allowed a minute at the podium. Like me, Al was a service-learning proponent, and our remarks touched on how SIFE was an ideal venue for business faculty to pursue service-learning approaches. I also added, "Someday, I can imagine that SIFE USA regional competitions will take place in large convention halls, much like the SIFE national event now takes place in Kansas City. The SIFE nationals could be like the NCAA Final Four, and that the SIFE World Cup could be like the FIFA World Cup in soccer."

Shewmaker appreciated my enthusiasm, and asked me about the possible meeting between CSU academics and the SIFE board.

"I've talked to President Esteban," I said. "He likes the idea. He put me in touch with the Chancellor's Office to see what kind of interest it has. Let me keep working on this." Notably, Alvin Rohrs and I never exchanged a word that night.

In the next three weeks, a flurry of emails and phone calls were exchanged between CSU executives in Long Beach, along with two CSU campus presidents: Robert Corrigan of San Francisco State and Esteban. Corrigan was considered a service-learning champion among university presidents nationwide. Shewmaker wanted frequent updates, and I obliged.

Tom Payne, SIFE's vice president of university relations, gave me a heads up that Rohrs wasn't pleased that Shewmaker and I seemed to be working behind the scenes without his knowledge. Adhering to protocol, on October 7, I sent Rohrs the following email, with a cc to Tom:

> The purpose of this email is to provide you with a complete set of information regarding the upcoming meeting between Mr. Jack Shewmaker and Dr. David Spence, executive vice chancellor and chief academic officer of the California State University System (see http//www.calstate.edu for details). I spoke briefly with Tom Payne today, and he expressed some concern that I had not included you "in the loop" about this matter. Alvin, at no time did I intend to keep you or anyone else in the dark about this.
>
> As you are aware, Jack was instrumental in sending six members of the SIFE team and me to Australia, where the team made a presentation at the KMPG-Australia office. The presentation was attended by about ten to fifteen CEOs and senior corporate leaders, and about ten to fifteen university presidents and/or their designees. They were delighted to have a reason to meet in the name of "community service for business students."
>
> Jack called me upon our return and asked me to debrief him on our trip. One of my opinions was that it was a good idea to have a meeting among CEOs from industry and academia to discuss how colleges and universities can work together with industry to produce "leaders of tomorrow."
>
> Jack asked what he could do to help. That's when I suggested that I try to set up a preliminary meeting with him and an executive at the Chancellor's Office, preferably Chancellor Charles

Reed. Jack said he was available for an hour on October 22, the day he will be en route to Australia.

Ken Swisher, a spokesperson for Chancellor Reed, was enthused about this when I emailed him a brief description of SIFE and how it related to service learning and business/university partnerships. However, because Dr. Reed will be in Florida on October 22, Ken arranged for Dr. Spence to meet with Jack when he will be in LAX on his stopover. At Dr. Spence's request, only he and Jack will attend the meeting. I will be on hand to introduce them.

Alvin, simply getting the Chancellor's ear is a huge break for SIFE, I think. My goal was simple and straightforward: to get two very important people sitting at the same table to further the service-learning agenda, through SIFE, within the CSU. Once the CSU is on board, I believe the 109 community colleges in California will follow, and perhaps the nine University of California schools will follow, as well.

Our president, Dr. Manuel A. Esteban is thrilled about this meeting, as is the director of Community Service Learning within the CSU.

Thank you, Alvin. Someday, when you're not too busy, perhaps we can have a good long chat. I think it would be beneficial if you and I got to know each other better, because I believe each of us has a vision to make SIFE a household name—worldwide. If we operate from the same page, it would certainly benefit the entire organization (suggestion: having one or two Walton Fellows present at Board meetings?). Thanks, sir.

The next day, Rohrs emailed his terse reply: "Curt, thanks for the e-mail. I appreciate your enthusiasm and the meeting will be very helpful. It would help if you would just keep Tom and me in the loop when working with board members. It avoids the embarrassment of board members assuming we know about the meetings."

This was a bit strange. Why wasn't Shewmaker keeping Rohrs in the loop? By the end of the following week, I had the meeting all set up between Spence and Shewmaker for October 22. I came into my office on Saturday morning, October 16, to grade some papers. There was an angry voicemail message from Rohrs. He said that my actions with *his* board were creating a *powder keg* and that *his and Tom's jobs were at risk*. Obviously, he wanted me to back off on my California agenda.

In my five years with SIFE, I had never gotten this much attention from SIFE's CEO. Rohrs was certainly not accustomed to Walton Fellows getting close to powerful board members. I dashed off the following email reply:

Alvin, I am honored to receive a personal phone call from you. It's a shame that it was prompted by what you apparently believe is inappropriate behavior on my part. It comes as a bit of a surprise, though, as to the harshness of your message … which indicates that we have a communication problem.

To give you a better idea of my perspective, you may want to consider the following.

When Mr. Shewmaker asks for my advice, I will freely give it. When he agrees to meet with the COO of my employer, the CSU, I will vigorously support and help arrange it. When the President of SFSU asks me, through a spokesman for the CSU, if I can arrange a meeting with Mr. Shewmaker, I shall do what I can. Especially when Dr. Corrigan learns that Mr. Shewmaker may be in NYC the week of Feb 7. (Jack's secretary, Deborah Lupardus-Burns, indicated that there are "tentative" plans on his calendar to be in NYC for a possible SIFE board meeting. If Dr. Corrigan can't meet with Jack then, Dr. Corrigan's secretary indicated that he would "go out of his way" to have such a meeting with Jack.)

Alvin, I think this is a great opportunity to further SIFE's presence in California, and also to further the service-learning movement in this state. As a professor within the CSU, and a Walton Fellow, I would hope that you would view me as a valuable "conduit" to further your agenda.

But from the content of your message, I now understand that your agenda may very well be something other than furthering

SIFE's presence in California and other states. All signals I have previously received from SIFE Home Office is that adopting more rookie teams is at the heart of SIFE's strategy ... am I wrong here?

You used terms like "powder keg" and "yours and Tom's jobs being at risk" and my "dealing with 'your' board of directors." I am hoping that the alarming tone of these phrases is a result of your just being angry at me, rather than signaling something more dire and sinister for the whole organization.

In helping to educate my "bosses" (executives within the CSU) about SIFE, and you helping your bosses understand "service learning," how can this create a spark that will blow up a powder keg that threatens anyone's job?

Lots of good things are happening, from my perspective. I am hoping your anger about the latest development with President Corrigan can be mitigated by the end result—more SIFE teams doing community service in the name of free enterprise education.

In closing, my email to you regarding a potential meeting with Dr. Corrigan was my effort to keep you "in the loop." Now, by keeping you in the loop, I get a message from you that makes me feel greatly unappreciated.

Now that I've had a chance to express my feelings, I shall try to enjoy what remains of this weekend.

Do know that I think SIFE is a life-changing organization for students and faculty, and I thank you for all of your efforts. Without you, there would be no SIFE, and I do not want you and I to be on separate pages. I guess that's why we need a good long chat. Respectfully, Curt.

David Spence of the CSU Chancellor's Office met with Shewmaker, as planned, on October 22. I was on hand to introduce them. After their meeting, I saw Shewmaker off at the Admiral's Club of American Airlines' executive lounge at Los Angeles International Airport. He had good news.

"SIFE's Executive Committee has agreed to move our February meeting from New York City to Los Angeles. I want you to work with Dr. Spence and Dr. Esteban to help us get a receptive audience of CSU executives," he said. "The date will February 8 at the LA Hyatt. Do your thing!"

Then he added, "At this point, I suggest you work through Alvin's office regarding hotel and transportation logistics. And it would be great if you could get your SIFE team from last year back together to do its presentation again."

This gave me pause. "Jack, I really don't think Alvin likes working with me. I've made suggestions to him before, and I never hear back. I don't know—he might not like me, or maybe he just doesn't like SIFE advisers interacting with board members."

Shewmaker chuckled. "You know, Curt, you and Alvin are a lot alike. You both have boundless energy and SIFE runs through your blood. Don't worry. This meeting between the CSU folks and the board will work out well for everyone."

With that, we shook hands and off he went to Australia. I headed back to Chico. Little did I know what was in store for me in the year to come. One thing was for certain—Rohrs and I were *not* a lot alike.

The next few months were eventful for the Chico State SIFE team. We had a hundred enrolled members, and Danielle had her hands full trying to manage so many people. I would teach my classes during the week, and on Thursday nights I usually hit the road for a weekend trip to visit new SIFE colleges that I had recruited. Usually, I was accompanied by one or two SIFE students. For example, Danielle and I made a trip to my alma mater in Cedar Falls, Iowa, to help the University of Northern Iowa start a SIFE team. I reminisced with my mentor, Professor Darrell Davis, over dinner. Darrell was planning to retire the following May, and he was happy to learn of my experiences since I had left Cedar Falls in 1979.

Another domestic trip was to Wal-Mart country with Reuben Williams and Jeff Iverson. The three of us traveled to Fayetteville, Arkansas, to help the University of Arkansas rekindle its dormant SIFE team. Another trip was with two rookie SIFE students to Dallas in November to present at the National School Boards Association Technology and Learning Conference.

I phoned David Spence when I got home. He was happy to hear about Shewmaker's decision. Not only would he invite CSU presidents to the meeting, but he was especially pleased to tell me that he would insist on at least one or two representatives from each of the twenty-three campuses' new Office of Service Learning be present. I then contacted President Esteban's assistant, who confirmed his attendance. Finally, I sent an email to the presenters from 1999.

"Gang, are you up to make one last presentation?" Yes, they said—for the last time.

The activity wasn't about to let up. On November 10–14, seven members of last year's team traveled with me to Palm Springs as special guests of NASDAQ and Ernst & Young's prestigious National Entrepreneurs of the Year Award celebration. Bruce Nasby, SIFE's senior vice president for professional development, was sent by Rohrs to tag along with us as SIFE's representative from Springfield. This trip was to be pure fun—no presentations required.

At the conference, we heard Steven Covey make a presentation about leadership, shook hands with Lou Dobbs of CNN, and saw Dick Schultz of Best Buy and Pierre Omidyar of eBay collect the top entrepreneurship awards. We were joined at the final dinner by another finalist for the top award.

Kenneth J. Pasternak, a tall, stately gentleman from Saddle River, New Jersey, was cofounder of the "market maker" firm Knight-Trimark Securities. In fall 1999, Kenny's firm was earning a small commission on every buy and sell transaction that Knight made on NASDAQ. Kenny couldn't deposit his profits fast enough. He took a liking to my students and myself and, later, would become an ardent supporter of my work after I left the SIFE organization in 2005.

Pasternak wasn't the only successful entrepreneur we met in Palm Springs. Many of the award winners were charmed by the precocious SIFE students from Chico State. Dawn Houston, hunting for a job, received two offers. One was for $70,000, but it required moving to Las Vegas. She passed on that one. However, she accepted the other offer from Matthew Stubbs of Regus Instant Offices Worldwide.

As my team socialized with the big crowd of successful entrepreneurs, collecting business cards as they went, Nasby trailed uncomfortably in their wake. Interesting, I thought. Nasby may have been good at raising cash for SIFE when he had Shewmaker and Rohrs doing the blocking for him up front. But on his own? Not so much.

As Thanksgiving approached, the activity level ratcheted up even higher. I had been invited by the dean of United Arab Emirates University in Al Ain to be a guest presenter. UAE University was interested in two things: how Chico State had changed its accounting curriculum, and how service learning could be implemented by its business faculty. I asked the dean if I could bring a SIFE student with me. No problem. Shortly before Ed Person and I left, I sent Shewmaker an email.

> The CSU Chancellor's Office is excited about the SIFE Board meeting in February, and David Spence has asked me to lead a seminar called *SIFE 101* the morning of February 8, before the luncheon. During the luncheon, the CSU, Chico, SIFE students will make its presentation. (By the way, Dr. Robert Corrigan, president of San Francisco State University and CSU Trustee Fred Pierce have already confirmed their attendance!) My question for you … would it be feasible/advisable to arrange some time for the SIFE Board members to meet and interact with the CSU executives? One way to do this would be to arrange seating at the luncheon so there is a nice balance between SIFE Board members and CSU executives. Another thing to consider might be an early evening reception/cocktail hour. I would have put this question directly to Alvin, but I get the sense that he might not want to allow sufficient time for interaction and discourse between both groups.[12]

By this time, Rohrs was refusing to speak to me. All matters were being handled by his assistant, Geralyn Mason. I sent the note to Shewmaker as a precaution—I had been putting so much time and effort into this that I didn't want Rohrs to sabotage it by doing a half-assed job. This was my opportunity to get service-learning academics and socially-responsible free enterprise capitalists at the same table, and I wanted to maximize their time together. Shewmaker, I believed, would make sure my request was honored.

Ed and I had a great trip to the Middle East, with a layover in

Amsterdam. The UAE is one of the wealthiest countries in the world, per capita, as evidenced by the fact that many of the male students and faculty drove BMWs, Lamborghinis, Porsches, or Mercedes. Women students, on the other hand, weren't permitted to drive. And while they attended a beautiful university just like the men, the campuses weren't quite the same. The women's campus had a stone wall topped by barbed wire. Why is this? I asked my hosts. "To keep the men out."

After the semester had ended and I turned in final grades, I prepared to make a solo trip back to Wuppertal, Germany. Professor Ulrich Braukmann wanted me to be a guest lecturer for three weeks at his university. Now that I was a single man with a serious travel bug, I accepted his offer.

The spring 2000 semester started as frenetically as the fall 1999 semester ended. The SIFE team had its first meeting, with Rob Best taking over as the new SIFE president. At six feet, three inches, Rob had been a pure shooting guard on the Chico State basketball team. But he and head coach Puck Smith had a difference of opinion—Rob thought he should have more playing time; the coach disagreed. So Rob, who thrived on competition, said goodbye to basketball and hello to SIFE. He had tremendous organizational and interpersonal skills, making him a good choice to lead the burgeoning SIFE team.

On February 7, 2000, the 1999 Chico State SIFE presenters drove to Los Angeles. That evening we met about thirty SIFE board members at a cocktail reception in the Los Angeles Hyatt Hotel near the airport. Shewmaker was happy to see me. Rohrs—reluctantly—came over to say hello. As the reception hour was coming to an end, Geralyn Mason pulled me aside and told me to take the team to dinner. She, Alvin, and the board would see us in the morning.

What? The dining room was set up for at least sixty people. This was a chance for us to rub elbows with some of SIFE's big dogs. And Mason was shooing us off? As we were about to leave, one of the board members came up and asked where we were going. I told him that Mason wanted us to take off. "No way. We want to get to know you better. Take a seat."

Rohrs, from across the room, couldn't mask a scowl.

The next morning, I learned that Erika Freihage and I would be making a presentation only to CSU folks. SIFE board members, meanwhile, were conducting their own closed-door board meeting. The executives from CSU, including Vice-Chancellor Spence, Trustee Fred Pierce, President Esteban, and a few other CSU presidents and provosts planned to arrive for lunch.

Not good, I thought. No morning interaction. Too stovepiped.

Erika and I made our presentation, "SIFE and Service Learning: A Powerful Formula for University and Business Partnerships through Community Service," to an audience of nearly fifty people, consisting mainly of service-learning coordinators from the twenty-three campuses. Overall, the presentation was well-received, although some of the academics seemed more than a bit concerned that retail companies that supported SIFE, like Wal-Mart, were not big supporters of labor unions, higher wages, or better health benefits. Point well taken.

About ten CSU executives arrived for lunch, joining the service-learning folks and the SIFE board members filing in after their meeting. I was seated at the same table as Shewmaker, Spence, Esteban, and Pierce. No Rohrs. After lunch, Shewmaker introduced Rohrs, who uncharacteristically did *not* get misty-eyed or choked up in his welcoming remarks. He seemed out of his element. This was clearly not the Bible Belt. The CSU audience had never heard of Jack Shewmaker, but all of them most assuredly knew Wal-Mart. And, based on the feedback from the morning meeting with the service-learning coordinators, not all of them were as adoring of Wal-Mart as the folks back in Bentonville or Springfield or Bolivar.

"The Chico State SIFE team won the national SIFE championship last year," Rohrs said by way of introduction. "We would like to involve more campuses in the SIFE program, and that is why we are here today. California is a growth market for us."

Growth market? Not an academic term. Sounds too corporate.

"Like all SIFE teams, they are led by faculty members who we call Sam M. Walton Fellows," he continued, without much enthusiasm. "We give each Walton Fellow a $1,000 stipend to be the adviser to a SIFE team on their campus."

No! It's not about the money. It's about a new teaching strategy called service learning. Why didn't you come to my presentation two hours ago? Nobody on a CSU campus would be interested in a $1,000 stipend to do the mountain of extra work required of a SIFE adviser. Damn, Alvin, this is the wrong approach, I thought. The right approach was to highlight the benefits to students and the community. As for faculty benefits, the ultimate reward should be new publication opportunities or maybe some classroom release time—certainly not the measly $1,000 stipend.

"And Chico State's faculty member, Dr. DeBerg here," he continued, without looking at me, "even collected another $5,000 last year when he was named the Sam M. Walton Fellow of the Year."

No, no! This statement made it sound like I was in this for the money or the recognition. Damn. Damn. Triple damn.

Rohrs then introduced the team. For the last time, they ran through their presentation.

Upon reflection, the event was a lukewarm success. The result, I was certain, was in no small measure due to Rohrs' lack of interest. I couldn't read Rohrs' mind, but I had a pretty good theory. A raging success in California would have been a success for me, too. From that point of view, it's fair to surmise he saw me as a threat to his power base. The fact that Shewmaker moved SIFE's board meeting from New York to California was an ominous signal that he was putting too much faith in me. A huge success in California would have meant that Shewmaker's faith was well-justified. Now, though, Shewmaker might think twice.

From my perspective, the CSU service-learning leaders could now go back to their campuses and invite business faculty to implement service learning in their courses. If the SIFE organization appealed to them, then by all means they could sign on. But I didn't sense nearly the same level of enthusiasm for SIFE by the service-learning academics as the Australian university presidents in Sydney back in August. Opportunity lost? If SIFE wanted to recruit more universities with service learning as its entrée, then yes.

By April 2000, the new Chico State SIFE presenters were ready to roll into regionals. They had another great story to tell, the computer graphics were better than the year before, and the team was as well-prepared as last year. Led by Reuben Williams, the team was stacked with talent. Williams was a natural leader; Jeff Leh had charisma; Jeff Iverson was confident; Heather Rosdail had experience; and Stacie Power was a fighter who would later go on to earn a law degree.

By now, SIFE was a household word in Chico and Butte County, thanks to both Chico State and Al Konuwa's team from Butte College. Chico State's top project, once again, was Summer SIFE. But another project was catching the eye of local schools and funders. The Cal-High SIFE program, started four years ago when we created a SIFE chapter at Chico Senior High School, now included four competing high school teams which, in turn, completed over twenty entrepreneurial and community outreach projects. To top it off, two Silicon Valley companies—Applied Materials and Cadence Design Systems—each contributed $10,000 to our team to further the Cal-High SIFE concept in California's inner cities.

Several other Walton Fellows from the U.S., and now many SIFE leaders from other countries, had been contacting me throughout the year, mainly seeking advice on how to organize and mentor a strong SIFE team. As always, I was happy to oblige. But some of the U.S. SIFE advisers also looked to me to air some grievances, and they looked to me for help. Among their concerns was lack of support from SIFE Headquarters and no voice in SIFE policy making.

In mid-April, Chico State handily won its regional competition for the seventh consecutive year. Over sixty Chico State students and business advisers headed for Kansas City on May 21. The welcome reception, now called the Rally of Champions, boasted more students, more recruiters, and more glitz than ever before. More international guests were on hand. As reigning champion, our team was introduced near the end of the reception, where the entire team carried the traveling gold trophy to the stage. On May 22, our team won its first round league and moved on to the semifinal round the next day.

Many Walton Fellows knew that I had Shewmaker's ear. They asked if I could air their concerns with him. As a result, I arranged a breakfast meeting at the Kansas City Marriott on May 23, the second morning of the SIFE USA 2000 national exposition.

Shewmaker ordered steak and eggs, and I stuck to oatmeal. We had a productive meeting. I shared the concerns of the faculty, and Shewmaker said he'd take them up with the board. Near the end of the one-hour meeting, I mentioned the overtures I had made to Rohrs about my possibly working for SIFE for a year, which had gone unanswered.

"Jack, I would seriously entertain coming to work for SIFE next year, for one year only, to help implement a high school SIFE program modeled after our Cal-High SIFE program. Chico State would grant me a leave of absence," I offered.

I didn't necessarily like the thought of working with, or for, Alvin Rohrs, but if I had Shewmaker's blessing, I could work around him.

Shewmaker thought a moment. "That sounds like a really good idea. But if you come to work for SIFE, I think we'd like you to focus primarily on the global end of things. You like to travel as much as I do, don't you?" he smiled.

Do I? Hell, yes! "Sure, I'd be happy to do that, as long as you'd consider letting me work behind the scenes on the high school project."

Shewmaker replied, "Interesting. Let me run this by Alvin and the board tomorrow. The Executive Committee meets early in the morning."

Uh-oh. Rohrs wasn't going to happy about this, I thought. The board would have to overrule him.

Shewmaker and I shook hands, and off we went. Later that day, Chico State SIFE finished in third place, behind the University of Arizona and the College of the Southwest, in the semifinal round. Damn. I thought we were better than last year, and now we didn't even make it back to the final four. The team was crestfallen.

Shake it off, I advised. "You have done outstanding work for the community. And you have all learned important skills that you didn't have before you joined SIFE. Be strong."

Later that night, before an audience of about two thousand people seated in Bartle Hall's cavernous second-floor exhibit room, La Sierra University was crowned SIFE International Champion 2000. They were back—with a vengeance.

The keynote speaker gave an inspirational speech. He talked about his days as president of one of the world's largest retailers. His associates would ask, "How high can this company go? How far dare we go?"[13]

He responded, "How high is up?"

His point was clear. "As long as you keep trying to do your best … as long as you believe in your mission … as long as you serve the customer and your employees and your shareholders well … then there is no stopping where this company can go," he said.

The speaker was Jack Shewmaker, and the company was Wal-Mart.[14]

Part II

THE FALL

DAWN HOUSTON AND JACK SHEWMAKER
Dawn Houston networks with former SIFE board chairman and Wal-Mart executive, Jack Shewmaker, in Los Angeles, February 2000. Photo courtesy of author.

FORMER WAL-MART PRESIDENT AND CHIEF OPERATING OFFICER, JACK SHEWMAKER, WITH CHICO STATE SIFE PRESENTERS KELBY THORNTON AND SUZANNE COZAD
Shewmaker moved the SIFE Board of Directors meeting from New York to Los Angeles in February 2000, and invited the Chico State SIFE team to make its final presentation to the SIFE board, along with executives from over twenty California State University campuses. Photo courtesy of author.

Chapter 9

How Low Is Low?

———

I had been a Sam Walton Fellow for seven years now, and I had been to SIFE's mountaintop, gaining recognition and accolades for my effort. The Chico State SIFE team had won SIFE's top prize, I was Jack Shewmaker's fair-haired fellow, and Jack Kahl had handed me the award as Sam Walton Fellow of the Year. In the next few months, however, I would plummet back to earth and land with a thud. Neither of the Two Jacks would be there to cushion my landing. As I shook out the cobwebs and regained my senses, I got a much clearer view of what happens when a man of ambition gets close to the inner sanctum of corporate power. Such a man is either welcomed to the club, or he is summarily rejected. Rejection, I can handle. But if it involves deceit, cunning, and malevo-lence—that's another matter.

Immediately after the awards ceremony on May 23, 2000, in Kansas City's Bartle Hall Convention Center, I made my way to the stage to congratulate the winning teams and advisers. I chatted a few moments with Mike Merriman, SIFE chairman of the board. A few minutes later, I joined Barbara Derucher and two of my SIFE students, Shalindar Kour and Tracy McBroom, as they were chatting with Jack Shewmaker, just outside the huge exhibition area on the second floor. Shewmaker was telling them a story about how quickly one of the Wal-Mart stores had re-opened after a fire. He then recounted a touching story of his recovery from a serious motorcycle accident that nearly cost him his life several years earlier.[1]

Saying goodbye to Shewmaker, the Chico State group and I went down the escalator where Judy Sitton was waiting for us. Together, we walked across the central city square to the Marriott. As a group, we waited for the elevator and were joined by Barry Peters, CEO of Yeardisc. We all got on the elevator, chatting amiably. At the sixth floor, all of us got off. Shalindar walked to the Butte College SIFE team's suite to see if they were prepared to accept guests to their party.

She came back and said, "They're not quite ready yet. They're going over their judging sheets and changing clothes."

With that, Barbara and Judy who were sharing a room on the seventh floor, agreed to meet us in the lobby in about ten minutes to walk over to a nearby hotel where several of the Chico State group had gone to set up for our own party. So I went with Shalindar and Tracy to the Chico State student suite in adjoining rooms 625/627. In the suite, I removed my tie and suit coat, dropped off my briefcase, and waited for other students as they were getting ready to walk to the Chico party. Among the students in the suite were three men—Reuben Williams, Jeff Leh, and Jeff Iversen—and four women. After about fifteen minutes, when everyone was ready, we headed to the elevator.

When the first elevator arrived, which was the far one on the right, all the Chico State coeds boarded. One of them said, "Looks like you boys will have to take the next elevator. This one's full."

As the four of us waited for the next elevator, another group arrived. I recognized some of them to be members of SIFE's staff.

What happened in the next sixty seconds or so, between the time we got on the elevator and then exited at the ground floor, is crucial to understanding how SIFE operated under Alvin Rohrs' leadership. I can unequivocally assert that nothing untoward or unusual happened. When we got on the elevator—the last ones to board—I remember Reuben was telling us the story of how his interview with Wal-Mart had gone earlier in the day. He was excited, having accepted a summer internship in Bentonville. That was the extent of it. We were the first ones off the elevator, and we walked to the Chico State party nearby.

Our team flew home to Chico the next morning. As soon as we got home, I hustled to turn in my final grades and pack for a much needed vacation. Every June, since my freshman year in college, I headed to Canada to unwind with a couple books, two fishing poles, and plenty of Labatt's Blue in the cooler. This year, as it had been since the early '90s, my brothers and I, along with a couple more fishing buddies, were headed for the woods of Northwest Ontario, to Sydney Lake.

It was not an easy destination. As usual, we made our ritualisitic ten-hour drive from Minneapolis and then overnighted in Kenora. Early the next morning, we drove another forty miles north to to catch a bush plane to Sydney Lake. After a scenic thirty-five-minute flight, we landed at Sydney Lake's isolated fishing camp with its seven rustic cabins nestled on the rocky shore. In short order, we unpacked our bags, secured our fishing licenses, threw our fishing gear and beer coolers in the sixteen-foot Lunds, and off we went to the honey hole across the bay. Lately, I had been dreaming of landing tasty walleye and fighting slippery, smelly hammerheads, also known as northern pike. I couldn't wait.

The 1999–2000 school year had been filled with so many trips and activities that I really needed a break, not only from teaching duties but also from the daily grind of SIFE. Guiding students as they completed quality outreach projects was exhausting. I let our new dean know that I was planning to take a one- or two-semester leave of absence, and he agreed.

I had two options: the first, of course, would be to work for SIFE, if Shewmaker convinced Rohrs and the board to hire me. If that didn't work, though, my backup plan was to accept an offer to become a consultant for a company in Thousand Oaks, California. The company was Yeardisc Systems, and its CEO, Barry Peters, was a SIFE judge in Kansas City. Barry especially liked our high school project, and he knew that I had an extensive social network of SIFE advisers and high school teachers. Yeardisc was marketing a cool product to high schools where the students could supplement their annual printed yearbook with a multimedia version. This meant that students would include audio, video, and hyperlinks to their photos and clubs, and burn it to a CD. If I didn't get an acceptable offer from SIFE, I thought it would be fun to work for Yeardisc, a company offering a new technology product to high schools.

A day or two before I left for Minneapolis, I received a handwritten, printed note, in blue ink, on stationery with an eagle in the lower left hand corner. The note, dated Monday, May 29, 2000, said:

Dear Curt,

Thank you for all you do for SIFE STUDENTS around the world! Your enthusiasm and commitment is supercatalytic! We need you!

I enjoyed our conversation and will continue to explore the possibilities; please keep me posted, and tell Pres. Esteban, "Hello."

ALL THE BEST!

JACK SHEWMAKER

Between the JACK and the SHEWMAKER, in all caps and with a flourish, he signed his name. Buoyed by Shewmaker's enthusiasm and his offer to "continue to explore the possibilities," I was fairly certain I would be hearing from Rohrs, or someone else at SIFE, as soon as I got home from Canada.

Yes, indeed. After spending a week in Canada, I drove to Sioux Falls, South Dakota, to visit my mom who lived there and my stepmom who lived an hour away in Sibley, Iowa. One day before I was scheduled to return to California, I received a voicemail from Gail Spradlin, SIFE's vice president of administration. She requested that I call her office immediately.

This is good news, I thought. She probably wants to discuss terms of my job offer from SIFE.

I phoned the number. Spradlin answered cautiously, almost hesitantly. Strange.

"Dr. DeBerg, where are you now?" she asked. "I need to overnight express you a letter."

I told her to just send it to my Chico address, since I would be there tomorrow night.

"No, I can't do that; we want you to receive this letter immediately."

We? She and Rohrs? She and Rohrs and Shewmaker?

"Is Alvin there?" I asked. "I'd like to speak to him in person."

"No, he and his wife have already left for a vacation in Italy," she replied. "But it's urgent that you get this letter as soon as possible."

"Okay. Please send it to my brother's address in Sioux Falls," I advised. "But I'm driving back to Minneapolis early in the afternoon to catch an early morning flight to Sacramento. So I need to receive it before noon." I gave her the address.

Sure enough, shortly before I was leaving Sioux Falls, the FedEx parcel arrived. I quickly opened the letter dated June 15, 2000, expecting to see what terms SIFE would be offering. Instead, the letter was a bombshell, and I would spend the better part of the next seven months trying to defuse it. Because of a legal document I eventually signed in late December of 2000, I am precluded from discussing the matter. But I can say that the letter from Rohrs literally turned my stomach. He had used an insidious way to strip me of influence with the SIFE board. Under Shewmaker's leadership, recall, the board had decided to move its February 2000 board meeting from New York to Los Angeles. It had become clear to me that Rohrs was feeling threatened by the warm relationship I had developed with Shewmaker. He knew I was getting close to SIFE's inner power circle. Rohrs needed some way to cool my jets and ground me.

Only three weeks ago, I was flying high. When Shewmaker asked, "How high is up?" I thought, "The sky's the limit." Service learning for business students was my passion, and Shewmaker's personal note of encouragement, "We need you," provided more fuel.

Now, I was asking myself, "How low is low?"

Rattled by the letter, I returned to Chico with two agenda items: one, to call Barry Peters to accept a six-month consulting contract with Yeardisc; and two, to call Shewmaker and explain the situation.

Barry was pleased to have me join his company. However, I couldn't get in touch directly with Shewmaker; instead, I communicated with his assistant, Deborah Barnes. Deborah listened to my side of the story and said that she would convey the information directly to Shewmaker, as his go-between.

This was a new lesson I was learning with SIFE. When conflict occurs that powerbrokers want to avoid, they seldom handle it directly. There is almost always a go-between. In such cases, some servant leaders prefer to delegate sensitive matters to underlings, or attorneys.

My older brother Craig, who had taken a keen interest in the matter, advised me to keep detailed notes of future conversations with Rohrs. Immediately after each conversation, Craig said, send your summary to him, so he can't later claim a different version. Following Craig's advice, I ended future emails to him with, "Mr. Rohrs, the points outlined above are an accurate summary of our telephone conversation. If, after your review of these points, you believe the points above do not reflect the subject matter of our conversation, please respond either by marking up this copy or preparing your own version of our conversation. It is critical that we agree as to what was said and discussed during our conversation."[2]

Chapter 10

Lawyering Up

On July 6, 2000, I hired Jeff Carter to represent me in the matter as described by Alvin Rohrs in his June 15 bombshell letter. Jeff and his wife Kristin had been family friends for almost ten years. Jeff had been practicing law in Chico for over twenty years. He has a great reputation. Tall, slender, and balding, he looks like the singer-songwriter James Taylor. Though quick with a laugh, he was also known to be a fierce litigator—more fire than rain, but he was known to rain on more than a few parades. He earned an undergraduate degree at Georgetown University and his law degree at Santa Clara University. A few years earlier, he had won a big case against the California State University system when its administrators claimed that profits from student-run bookstores should go to the system and not to the students. Jeff, representing the students, prevailed.

Jeff represented me for the next seven months in regard to the June 15 letter from Rohrs. Before publishing this book, I sought Jeff's advice again. He recommended an expert attorney who advised me to delete nineteen pages of chapter 10 and eight pages of chapter 11 of the original manuscript in order to adhere to the terms on which SIFE and I eventually settled. I needed to be careful not to breach the terms of the agreement between SIFE and me.

Those twenty-seven pages have now been deleted. Future references to this matter are referred to as the "alleged incident."

Chapter 11

Attorney Ping Pong

B etween July and December of 2000, Chico attorney Jeff Carter corresponded with SIFE's attorney in Springfield, Missouri, and I communicated with a few members of SIFE's board about what Rohrs wrote in his June 15 letter. Also during that time, I maintained a back-channel dialog with my friend at SIFE, Tom Payne. Tom was now SIFE's vice president of university relations.

By now, Tom and I were on the line with each other frequently. Tom couldn't hide his vitriol for Rohrs on the legal matter. Tom, as a former Walton Fellow, could relate to faculty. Like me, he had taken a SIFE team to a national championship, and he enjoyed working closely with students. Now, working for SIFE and Rohrs, he had a different perspective.

Tom was about the only line of defense for faculty at SIFE headquarters. Over the years, he had to defend a number of faculty from Rohrs' wrath. As a SIFE insider, he could offer some additional insight as to Rohrs' management style. On Monday, July 24, we had another conversation.

I prodded, "Do you think Alvin has a vendetta against me?"

"No, I don't think this is the case," Tom said. "But he's maniacal when it comes to dealing with the board. They're SIFE's bread and butter." Tom continued, "With respect to your case, Alvin is very flustered at me for not buying into this."

Here, Tom was referring to discussions he had with Rohrs in which Tom defended me.

"He's very dictatorial; a very hard man to work for. He has a way of exaggerating things—you know, magnifying the situation."

Tom kept rendering his opinions. "He is not a very good leader. Many of us here just shake our heads. His leadership style is terrible. And Jack Shewmaker, I think, is still upset with me for not being more enthusiastic when he suggested you come to work for us. But I never intimated anything like this to Shewmaker. Alvin did. If Jack were to have asked me, I would have told him the truth that I was not against you working for SIFE on your sabbatical."

The next night, Mike Merriman called. He told me Shewmaker was on the road again and Merriman had tried, but failed, to reach him. Shewmaker informed Merriman that he would be back on August 7. "Curt, I think what we have here is a personality conflict between you and Alvin," Mike said.

Personality conflict? You think?

Then Merriman said something that showed me how serious he was.

"Off the record, SIFE's future is at stake. We want to expedite this and settle this as soon as possible."

By the end of August, I was nearing the end of my rope. Three months had passed and I was beginning to tire of the grind. I had been racking up some pretty big attorney fees. Though my consulting job at Yeardisc was satisfying, the era of easy venture capital for technology startups was rapidly coming to an end. Barry Peters had trimmed his staff from seventeen in May down to just eight people at the end of August. It looked like Yeardisc was sinking fast, and I was happy that I only signed on until the end of the calendar year.

My plan was to go back to Chico State and resume my teaching duties in January 2001. And as crazy as it sounds, I was still considering a return to my duties as a Walton Fellow. When I informed Craig of this, he was incredulous. He thought I should chuck the whole SIFE program out of my life, and sue Rohrs' ass on my way out the door.

But two things weighed against this. First, Chico State SIFE was now a household phrase in our community, and Chico State SIFE alumni would have been terribly disappointed to learn the details of my situation. I didn't want to do this. They were loyal to Chico State, in large part due to their affiliation with SIFE. I didn't want them to find out how dysfunctional the situation had become with Rohrs, SIFE, and me.

The second reason I hesitated was because our high school SIFE project was getting some serious attention. As I've said before, I viewed SIFE as an outlet to showcase how university students, through service learning, could become role models for high school students.

Without the competition and travel opportunities that SIFE offered, I doubted if I would be able to provide enough incentive to continue with a program like Cal-High SIFE. Now that SIFE was truly becoming a global organization, the SIFE network offered me access to like-minded educators around the world.

SIFE and I legally settled our differences just before the year was over. Though I cannot disclose the terms of the settlement, I can disclose one very important item that *wasn't* in the agreement.

After joining the SIFE Academic Council a couple years earlier, I had been corresponding with other Walton Fellows via email. Many of these emails, I knew, were forwarded to Rohrs. As Rohrs continued to ignore us, my emails became more strident and less flattering. No doubt, Rohrs viewed my correspondence with other fellows as meddling in his business.

When Jeff Carter was playing fax tag with John Hammons, SIFE's attorney, hammering out the final agreement terms, one item inserted into the next-to-final draft revealed Rohrs' fear of my influence in SIFE. The clause had nothing to do with the claim described by Rohrs in his June 15, 2000, letter, but had everything to do with Rohrs' underlying rationale to silence me. In effect, the clause said that I would agree to not talk negatively about SIFE or in any manner make disparaging remarks about SIFE or its employees to third parties. Further, the prohibition would include any form of communication, including, but not limited to, email and Internet chat rooms.

Seemingly, this is what Rohrs wanted to begin with—censorship. He didn't want me running to his board of directors any more, and SIFE's claim against me could have been made to keep them from communicating with me. He especially wanted to muzzle me around Shewmaker, Kahl, Merriman, Milano, Moser, and other board members who not only respected the quality projects completed by our team, but also admired how Chico State was helping SIFE grow by recruiting rookie teams. No other SIFE team had recruited more new SIFE teams into other public colleges and universities.

By insisting on this clause, Rohrs showed no shame. Jeff told SIFE's attorney, John Hammons, that we would not agree to this stipulation, and it was removed from the final agreement.

Upon reflection, I was saddened Jack Shewmaker never made contact with me after July. Except for a tight smile and respectful nod at future SIFE events, I would never again interact with him.

Though not likely, there is a remote chance that Rohrs' June 15 letter was simply a case of Rohrs following Shewmaker's directive. To this day, I believe Shewmaker did not authorize Rohrs to send the letter. But when Jeff Carter and I strove to protect my reputation, Shewmaker sat silently. From my perspective, he wasn't practicing leadership.

I believe Alvin Rohrs is a crafty guy. I was bludgeoned with his June 15 letter. However, he didn't foresee the difficulty of my case—I was not an employee. I was a volunteer whose title was named after Sam Walton. In the end, I would not be going to work for SIFE in 2001 or, for that matter, ever. But I would remain a Sam M. Walton Fellow, at least for now.

Chapter 12

Staying the Course

———

The settlement with SIFE brought some closure, to be sure, but even after the lawyers finally agreed to terms, I still felt like I'd been stung by a hornet. The seventh-month long battle left me tired and smarting. My integrity had been questioned, and now many people knew about the allegation: more than a dozen people at SIFE's home office, at least five influential SIFE board members, three Chico State SIFE students, a handful of Chico State's advisory members, a few of my closest friends, and, of course, my family.

I took some comfort in recalling the words of John Wooden, the legendary UCLA basketball coach, who said, "Worry more about your character than your reputation. Character is what you are, reputation is merely what others think you are."[1] My character was built over a lifetime by listening to my parents and trying my hardest to make them proud. I cherished their trust and respect more than anything else. They taught my brothers and me to live by the Golden Rule. Wooden also warned, "I think for every peak there is a valley."[2] If 1999 had been my peak with SIFE, 2000 was the valley.

There had been no lapse in my character on May 23, 2000. But there had been damage to my reputation.

Upon my return to campus, I retook the SIFE reins in late January, the beginning of spring semester. Chico State students, of course, still embraced SIFE, and I would continue to do so. But I would do it at a wary distance from SIFE staff at future competitions.

My brother Craig shook his head in dismay when he learned this. "You should have sued them," he insisted. "They've tarnished the family name. And where's this Jack Shewmaker been lately? I thought he was your friend."

Craig, rightfully, pointed out that I had been very helpful—even useful— to Shewmaker when I guided my team to the 1999 SIFE championship.

After winning the top prize in Kansas City, I had organized the team to make four more trips for SIFE. This was not easy, given that several of my students had graduated and left Chico. Nonetheless, we represented SIFE well in Orlando, Sydney, Palm Springs, and Los Angeles. Each time, we showcased Shewmaker's prized SIFE baby to leading businessmen and entrepreneurs. Unlike Rohrs, who was earning over $220,000 in compensation and benefits from SIFE in 2000,[3] I did all of my work for SIFE on the side—for a $1,000 Sam M. Walton Fellow stipend. But where was Shewmaker, Craig asked, when I needed him in my corner?

As I was writing the first draft of this chapter, the big news story was the Penn State football scandal. I saw an analogy here. Where was Penn State football's legendary coach Joe Paterno when, in 2002, he was told by a graduate assistant that Paterno's senior assistant coach, his pal, had allegedly been seen abusing a ten-year-old boy in Penn State football's shower facilities? In the end, loyalty trumped morality. Paterno came to the side of his pal—the assistant coach—not the victim, and Paterno did nothing to help the victim.

Paterno knew his friend Jerry Sandusky had, in all likelihood, committed an unforgivable wrong against a small boy. On the other hand, what about Shewmaker? What did he know about the charges against me? What should he have done?

At a minimum, I think he should have called to hear my side of the story. Or, he could have asked Mike Merriman to conduct an investigation. Shewmaker had no legal obligation to do either and, as far as I know, did nothing behind the scenes to get to the bottom of the matter.

But what about the moral obligation? This is the part of the sorry episode I still cannot accept. Jack Shewmaker died in 2010 and because of that there will be no closure, at least as far as our relationship is concerned. Shortly after he died, I stumbled on the fall 1995 issue of *SIFElines,* SIFE's newsletter. Shewmaker said, "SIFE's purpose is genuine and good. It benefits not only the people involved, but those around them. SIFE's philosophy is based on treating people right and believing that, by working hard, one should have a better opportunity. That's my definition of free enterprise as well. If students take their better understanding of free enterprise and a strong, moral work ethic and apply it with enthusiasm, they will make the world a better place."[4]

I was saddened. How high is up, really, if getting to the stratosphere means watching someone undeservedly get his wings clipped? Perhaps I was flying too close to the big eagle—Shewmaker—and the big eagle silently watched me fall.

Though it's not likely that public knowledge of my situation could have taken the SIFE organization down, as Mike Merriman feared, it could certainly have slowed SIFE's meteoric rise. In its 2000–2001 handbook, SIFE proudly proclaimed, "SIFE is rapidly expanding as a global program. We are beginning this year expecting at least sixteen countries to hold national competitions. With the rapid growth we are experiencing, that number could expand to more than twenty countries before the end of the academic year. For this reason, in June 2001, we will be holding our first global SIFE World Championship in London, England, where all four-year national champions will compete for the 2001 SIFE World Championship." With typical bluster, it continued, "SIFE Teams are on more than 700 colleges and universities across the U.S. and in thirteen other countries. Annually SIFE Teams reach over 800,000 college students and 1,000,000 school children."[5]

Did I want to be the guy who exposed an organization led by Rohrs—an organization that had given my students so much satisfaction and recognition as part of their collegiate experience? A part of me screamed yes. But I decided not to because my SIFE students and I had achieved a significant amount of goodwill in the Chico community, and also because I saw SIFE as a networking vehicle for my high school initiative. My reasoning involved *social capital.*

Sociologist Robert Putnam authored a book entitled *Bowling Alone* in 2000, where he described the decline in America's social capital in recent decades.[6] According to Putnam, the greater the number of associations one belongs to, the greater the capacity for civic engagement which is essential for the functioning of a modern democracy. Individuals or businesses within a community have strong social capital if they have an influential network of other members who can be trusted to work together for their mutual benefit. Moreover, some of these members have access to additional resources that can help the network accomplish its goals.

Since our SIFE team had won top honors in 1999, I had been besieged with emails from SIFE affiliates in other countries. They were especially curious about our high school program. Whenever I received an inquiry, I happily shared our materials, and often added a blurb about how I offered course credit for student leaders. For example, new students could receive a small bonus in my introductory financial accounting class. With some experience under their belts, they were considered "veteran" SIFE students. These students could then sign up for a one-unit independent study class. After this, the most outstanding SIFE project leaders and presenters could earn three additional units of course credit by enrolling in Technology, Leadership and Teamwork, which was a course team-taught by Rick Vertolli and me.

To spice up my first accounting lecture of the semester and to encourage students to sign up for the bonus, I introduce a little twist to the fundamental accounting equation: Assets - Liabilities = Equity. Another name for Equity is net worth. I abbreviated the equation to be A - L = E.

Then I tell them the real-world equation for net worth: A + B + C = E. The A is for financial ASSETS, B is for human BRAINS, and the C is for social CONNECTIONS. Of course, social connections are the key part of social capital.

It was this line of thinking that provided another reason for me to continue as a SIFE faculty adviser. Early in the 2000–2001 handbook, SIFE proclaimed, "SIFE is dedicated to becoming a global student movement. Many colleges and universities in SIFE have sister relationships or other linkages with colleges and universities outside the U.S. You are strongly encouraged to build upon these relationships and linkages."[7]

I had every intention to do so—I needed the social capital that only SIFE could provide.

There was yet another reason to remain as a Sam M. Walton Fellow, though. My affiliation with SIFE provided me with a means to draw public attention to a powerful formula that didn't really exist in education. The formula involved university students participating in service-learning activities helping teenagers become entrepreneurs—commercial entrepreneurs or social entrepreneurs. This hadn't been done before, and I saw this as a way to make a significant contribution to education reform.

The service learning/social enterprise combination aligned nicely with the Chico State mission and strategic plan. The mission today, much like it was in 2001, states:

> [We are] a comprehensive university principally serving Northern California, our state and nation through excellence in instruction, research, creative activity, and public service. The University is committed to assist students in their search for knowledge and understanding and to prepare them with the attitudes, skills, and habits of lifelong learning in order to assume responsibility in a democratic community and to be useful members of a global society.[8]

Chico State has also adopted a strategic plan for the future. Priorities #1 and #4 related directly to my interests. Priority #1 states: "Believing in the primacy of student learning, we will continue to develop high quality learning environments both in and outside of the classroom.

Priority #4 states: "Believing in the value of service to others, we will continue to serve the educational, cultural, and economic needs of Northern California."[9]

Service learning, therefore, provided me with a teaching approach that allowed me to align the university mission and strategic plan with the Chico State SIFE mission: "To work together with our partners in business, education, and government to help the citizens in our community become business literate, so that everyone has the opportunity to live happy and productive lives."

The service-learning projects undertaken by SIFE students, like the Cal-High SIFE project for high school students and the Wise Kid, Healthy Kid entrepreneurship project for elementary kids, were consistent with the university's mission and strategic plan. SIFE students performed public services; they taught knowledge and skills that connected classroom theory with the practical world; and without doubt, they were inspired to do so, especially when presenting their results to business managers and executives. The competitions, therefore, provided a chance for their work to be publicly scrutinized.

As the spring 2001 semester progressed, the team completed several projects, but the two most substantive projects were Cal-High SIFE and the youth entrepreneurship camp. The camp was designed for children between the ages of nine and fourteen.

At the end of March, eleven high school teams came to campus to present the results of their community service projects. Of these, eight of them were from inner city schools from the San Francisco Bay Area. Thirteen more high schools came to observe.

The champion team was Yreka High School, a small town about three hours north of Chico. There was no doubt—high school students could be just as creative and innovative as their university mentors. The Yreka students had done outstanding work, including restarting a defunct school newspaper. Shortly after the event, I received a note from Yreka's teacher, Margaret Vodicka:

> Thanks so much for providing Cal-High SIFE to enhance my teaching. My students complete so many impressive real projects that support their learning because they like being part of SIFE. Through it they learn the value of giving back to others, planning and organizing, working as a team, using technology and how our free market works. In addition they gain pride and confidence as they steer their project to completion.
>
> We really appreciate the awards. This is the first year you made plaques and they really impress the staff here at our school. The money that comes along with the awards will be used next year to put on some great projects. My kids are already busy planning for next year plus they decided to hold a reception to show off what we accomplished this year. They will invite parents, staff, administrators, advisory members and community members.

Not all high school teachers were as glowing. During the event, I asked some of the observing teachers about their impressions. Surprisingly, I found that many of them were not enthusiastic. Some of them disliked the competitive element. Competition, they argued, compromised the purity of service.

Using the analogy of interscholastic sports, I countered with such questions as: Is it wrong for teams of students from diverse backgrounds to join together for a common cause? Is it wrong for the teams to be scored by the number of points they earn from an independent panel of referees? Is it detrimental for students to observe teams that are judged to be "better" than them?

My argument was that this was an ideal way for students to benchmark, so teams could strive to improve each year. And what could be wrong with community leaders getting a firsthand look at the outcomes of service projects? Nothing, unless perhaps teachers weren't proud of their students' achievements.

By instilling some form of friendly competition into the service-learning area, I believed that the quality of programs would go up from year to year. I witnessed this with Chico State SIFE teams over the years, and had seen it with other outstanding SIFE teams truly committed to service learning. Further, by allowing the students to publicly display the results of their program to a critical panel of unbiased judges, students got the chance to hone their organization, presentation, and communication skills. Academics often refer to such skills as *soft* skills, but there's nothing soft about them. These are *hard* skills—hard skills to learn unless teachers find ways for students to actually get a chance to practice them. Educators pay scant attention to these skills in schools and universities because such skills are hard to measure. A favorite saying of Albert Einstein's applies here: "Not everything that counts can be counted."

One of SIFE's—and now Cal-High SIFE's— main attributes was to provide a public forum to showcase creative activities. Students were putting their projects in the sunshine for public scrutiny. In a way, this was similar to how a free market evaluates the quality of goods and services. Such is the nature of free enterprise.

Not surprisingly, though, I believed there was another reason why many teachers weren't willing to embrace the concept. An educator who employs service learning as a teaching strategy necessarily gives up control. Students working on real-world projects face real-world issues, and they are often messy. Teachers who are attracted to this type of teaching—like me—thrive on solving real-world problems. Some of us enjoy the uncertainty that comes with such problems. The solutions aren't nearly as neat as solving a mathematical proof or learning a new computer program.

In general, high school teachers are risk-averse, certainly not entrepreneurial. They eschew risk and enjoy certainty. Though they are subject matter experts in such areas as math, science, economics, social studies, English, and computer science, many teachers have a hard time applying their theoretical expertise to a practical setting.

Though my crusade for service learning and social enterprise was in its nascent stage with many detractors, I was undeterred. SIFE was my laboratory and also my source of social capital.

One of the Chico State team leaders was a turbocharged young woman from Napa, California. Her name was Allison Steltzner, and her father, Richard Steltzner, had started a family wine business in the 1960s just off Napa's famous Silverado Trail, six miles north of town. The eighty-acre Steltzner Vineyards was well-known for its magnificent cabernet sauvignon and merlot vintages. Richard and his wife Christine had pegged Allison, their oldest child, to become the future CEO of the family business.

Though only twenty-one years old, Allison had an innate business savvy and could easily have foregone a university education altogether and jumped right into the wine industry. But her parents wanted her to develop some hard skills that could only be obtained by moving away from the unique social culture of the wine country and get a university degree.

When she told them she had joined SIFE, her parents were intrigued. Richard and Christine were staunch Republicans, and the SIFE team sounded like a great place for Allison to improve her leadership and teamwork skills. They recognized Allison could be a little brazen, and they believed SIFE could help her get ready to succeed Richard as the next business leader of the family. One story that demonstrates both Allison's leadership and brazenness was widely known among the team members.

Late in her first semester with the team, she politely asked two of the young men—both officers—on the team to post some time-sensitive fliers around campus. They agreed to do so over the weekend. She had every reason to trust they would do the job. After all, they were officers and she had helped them with their projects earlier. Allison expected the favor to be returned. A few days later, after the event was over, she learned that the two guys hadn't done what they promised.

When she found the fliers stacked on the SIFE office desk, she carried them to the next meeting. She walked up to the two men, who were standing at the front of the room. "Do you know what these are?" she asked.

Of course they did. Sheepishly, they looked down.

"Look at me!" Allison demanded. "When you needed me, I had your back, right?" she asked.

The twenty-five other SIFE students looked on in awe and for some of the guys, a bit fearful.

"Uh-huh," they demurred.

"And when I needed you, you had my back, right?"

Silence.

"No!" Allison said firmly. "You didn't. Let's make a deal. Next time you tell me you're going to do something, you'll do it. Right?"

"Right," they mumbled.

"So, if I ask you to do something with these fliers right now, you'll do it, right?"

The men looked at each other, quizzically. The fliers had no value now. The date had passed.

"Right?" she demanded.

The men nodded yes—at which point Allison dropped the stack of fliers at their feet, paper flying.

"Pick 'em up!" she said.

At that moment a new SIFE leader was born. Allison had been project leader for Cal-High SIFE, and she had become the strongest presenter during team tryouts. Joining Allison on the presentation team were young Ken Derucher, the dean's son, along with Shana Alexander, Dave Turner, and a bright young finance major from Colombia, Luis Cardozo.

During the previous several months, I had been active on various listservs related to service learning in higher education. A listserv is a mailing list devoted to a single topic. My posts often described my activities with Cal-High SIFE, which begged the question, "What is SIFE?" As a result, I had begun to receive emails from academics of other countries who were seeking more information.

Alvin Rohrs had assigned Robin Anderson to handle all matters related to SIFE's global expansion, and I wanted to be sure to keep Anderson in the loop with my communications. After all, one of the main reasons I remained with SIFE was to expand my global social network.

Anderson, though, hardly ever answered his email or returned phone calls. Although we had settled our legal problem, I wasn't keen to initiate contact with Rohrs, but I emailed him the following message on March 3.

> Recently I have received inquiries from a couple international universities about SIFE. Because Robin Anderson is very hard to reach directly, I thought I'd ask you this question: If a university is in a country without a National SIFE Competition but would like to send one or two faculty members to observe SIFE in action, what should I tell them? Or should I simply refer them to you or to Robin? (I fear that if I refer them to Robin, they may not receive a timely response.) Thank you.

Fifteen minutes later, Rohrs replied.

"The answer would depend on what countries they are in as to whether they should go to a national competition near them or come to KC," Rohrs emailed back. "Contact Robin directly and copy me. I'll put it on my tickler to keep him on track to contact you and your contacts ASAP."

Opening a direct line of communication with Rohrs was not an easy thing to do because of our strained relationship, but I knew that Jack Shewmaker's top agenda item—as well as the SIFE board's—was global expansion. Though Rohrs would have loved for me to step away from my voluntary role as a Sam M. Walton Fellow, my strategy now was to carry on as though nothing had happened in the past. My plan was to follow SIFE's strategy in taking my high school program global. Where go SIFE, so go Cal-High SIFE.

Once again, Chico State's advisory board members selected the presentation team for spring 2001. Based on the strength of Cal-High SIFE and the youth camp, the Chico State team prepared for the regional SIFE competition in San Francisco, which was set for mid-April. Because I just rejoined the university and I had only been an active adviser for two months, I didn't have the chance to work closely with Rick Vertolli or the presentation team to prepare a high tech seamless presentation, as in prior years.

So we took a shortcut on the technology side. We tried to put the judges at ease by linking our university mascot, the Chico State Wildcat, with the TV video featuring a team of cowboys herding cats. While our regional presentation was good enough to qualify us for the national competition, we flew to Kansas City hoping the quality of our projects would carry the day.

But it didn't. We lost out to a team from Georgia in the first round. Only six judges had been recruited by SIFE. The SIFE scoring system made it possible for just one or two outlier judges to cost a team first place.

Over the years, I had continually asked Tom Payne to change the judging system by tossing out the highest vote and lowest vote for each team. For example, assume there are six judges and six teams competing.

Consider Team A. If four judges rate them first, one judge rates them fifth, and one sixth, their total points are: (4 times 1) + (1 times 5) + (1 times 6) = 15 total points. Now consider Team B. If two judges rate them first and four judges rate them second, their total points are: (2 times 1) + (4 times 2) = 10 total points. The team with the lowest total points is declared the winner. In my example, Team A received twice as many first place votes but still lost by a wide margin. I think this is what happened to us.

The champion SIFE team in 2001 was from Drury University, which had finished in fourth place to Chico State in 1999. Drury is a Christian campus from Springfield, Missouri. Springfield is home to SIFE's home office and lies at the heart of Wal-Mart country. Bentonville, Arkansas, is only a two-hour drive south of Springfield.

One of Drury's most illustrious members of its Board of Trustees was none other than Jack Shewmaker, who joined Drury's board in 1984, almost the exact same time he became the chairman of SIFE's board. In

1989 he made a lead gift in memory of his parents to build the Shew-maker Communication Center.[10] The center, which includes state-of-the art television studios and a student-run radio station, was a fine resource for Drury's SIFE teams.

We felt our projects were superior to the other teams in our assigned league, but even I had to admit our oral presentation wasn't nearly up to par. One of our presenters forgot a few lines, the judges didn't laugh when we expected them to, and the presentation fell flat. The adviser from Georgia could barely contain his giddiness after the results were announced, but he was gracious.

"I don't know how this could have happened," he said. "Your team was superior."

I thanked him for his kind words and went to cheer up my students, who had retreated to their rooms—many in tears.

Allison was especially inconsolable. Her project was Cal-High SIFE, and she had poured her heart into it. I tried to console her. "We're only just beginning. Let's make the project bigger and better next year, and let's get Rick's technology students back on board. I promise you we'll do better next year. Up for the challenge?"

She took a deep breath and stopped crying. Before leaving Kansas City, she was unanimously elected president of the Chico State SIFE team for the upcoming year.

Over the summer, Allison and a few of our returning veterans worked closely with me to develop a strategic plan for the next school year. She was adamant about choosing a theme early on, and then integrating that theme into all the projects. We ultimately settled on a storybook theme for the annual report and presentation with the title of the book, *How to Start a Fire.*

According to SIFE's policies, the written annual report was limited to two 8½ x 11 inch double sided sheets, but nothing prevented a team from turning them sideways and folding the paper in half. By printing back to back, we could produce eight small storybook pages, rather than four regular pages. We wanted Chico State's first impression with judges to evoke Apple's 1997 advertisement: "Think Different."

While some people thought Apple's tagline should be "Think Differently," to be grammatically correct, CEO Steve Jobs insisted that it was meant to be "I want our customers to think: Apple products are different." Along this line of thinking, we wanted the judges' first impression to be Chico State was, indeed, different from the other SIFE teams. And after judges read our eight-page booklet, organized into eight miniature chapters, we wanted to wow them with a dazzling video opening. We envisioned flint on steel, and then a spark turning into a roaring flame.

SIFE teams were beginning to enter into partnerships with teams from other countries, and the Chico State advisory board felt that we needed to add a significant global project to our portfolio. Judy Sitton, chair of the board, put up a few thousand dollars to send Allison and two other students, Siobhan Brennan and Jill Zinke, to Botswana and South Africa. Jill was a member of the 2001 Butte College SIFE team which had won its third of three consecutive national titles in the two-year college division. Though two-year division national champions were not allowed to compete in the SIFE World Cup, they were invited to attend as special guests. At the first SIFE World Cup, held in London July 11–13, 2001, Jill had met several students from the national champion SIFE teams from the University of Botswana in Gaborone, and the University of Orange Free State in Bloemfontein, South Africa. Both teams invited Jill, along with her teammates, to visit their cities to conduct a version of youth entrepreneurship lessons to widows and orphans.

Jill, Siobhan, and Allison made the two-week trip in January 2002. For each of them, it was their first experience in third world countries, and it made a lifelong impression on them. My first trip overseas as an academic had been with Danielle Emis to Norway in 1999, and then Ed Person to the United Arab Emirates in 2000. But this was the first trip made by my SIFE students to developing countries, and, even though I didn't accompany them, I was thrilled to be part of expanding their worldview. Upon their return, they were ready to lead the 2002 SIFE team into the spring semester.

By the end of April, our team had completed twenty-nine projects and traveled thousands of miles *spreading the fire*. Once again, Cal-High SIFE was our top project. Allison and her teammates ingeniously linked two more fantastic projects to the high school project. On the same day the high school students competed, March 16, graduates of the Wise Kid, Healthy Kid youth camp sold their goods at an international trade fair.

At the trade fair, Chico State's SIFE team transformed the CSU, Chico, campus gymnasium into an international marketplace, where six hundred people spent the day shopping at businesses operated by our young students. Bill Gates Avenue and Sam Walton Way led shoppers through sixty booths featuring products from our young entrepreneurs. A Bit of Russia, owned and operated by thirteen-year-old Nikita Schottman, who immigrated to the U.S. at age nine, offered Russian imports. Quality Threads, a partnership of three seventh grade girls, held a fashion show of their custom designed fashions. And it was hard to pass up Adrian's Tamale Stand.

We received outstanding press coverage: four network TV broadcasts, a front page feature in the daily *Chico Enterprise-Record*, coverage in the *Oakland Tribune*, live radio broadcasts from the fair, four billboards placed prominently around Chico, and the coup de grace—a sixteen-page trade fair guide inserted into twenty thousand copies of our daily paper.

I was especially pleased to see the growth in size and quality of Cal-High SIFE. In all, twenty-three high schools competed, with an additional eight teams observing. Applied Materials, a semiconductor equipment manufacturer in Silicon Valley, provided us with a grant of $22,500. Eighty-two judges from the business, civic and education communities were on-hand to evaluate the quality of the high school projects.

Four Cal-High SIFE finalists were announced at the close of the trade fair. Then, like university SIFE teams, the high school teams presented in front of an audience of over two hundred judges and visitors. The suspense mounted, but the results wouldn't be known until that evening's banquet.

At precisely 8:15 p.m., the Student Union auditorium was filled with four hundred people anxiously waiting to find out who would be this year's Cal-High SIFE champion. The climactic moment arrived as the announcer boomed, "And the 2002 Cal-High SIFE champion is the team from Oakland's Fremont Business Academy." Forty Oakland teenagers went absolutely crazy.

One of SIFE's national board members, Rieva Lesonsky, had flown in from Southern California. She accepted our invitation to be an honorary judge, and we ended up using her quote in our annual report: "As an active SIFE supporter I want to issue a challenge. If California State University, Chico, can create the hugely successful Cal-High SIFE in northern California, why can't someone recreate it in southern California? While I'm at it, why can't this happen in Arizona, Texas, Utah, or Nebraska? Why can't there be a nationwide high school SIFE competition?"

Rieva was speaking my kind of language, but I was thinking *global,* not national. Another SIFE national board member, Joe Pedott, also drove to Chico from the Bay Area to judge. He judged the Chico State SIFE team at the regional competition in San Francisco the year before, and was impressed with the talented Chico State students. Pedott is best known as the man who made the Chia pet a household name in America. Clearly, many of SIFE's board members, when they saw we were making an impact with high school students, began asking the same questions as Rieva's.

Riding high from the March event, the Chico State SIFE team turned its focus on its own competitions. Under Allison's leadership, the presenters cakewalked through regionals and turned their sights back to Kansas City. In Kansas City, May 12–14, Courtney Kimball, Jill Zinke, Siobhan Brennan, and Greg Yatman nailed their first presentation and sailed through the first round at the Bartle Center.

Ditto for the second round. Judges loved our projects, especially Cal-High SIFE. Among the final round judges was Tom Coughlin, then president and CEO of Wal-Mart Stores & Supercenters. Coughlin would become SIFE's new chairman of the board later that year, in October 2002.

As for the final round, the presentations were moved to the huge second floor exhibit area and, fortunately, the team did a microphone check. Courtney's mike was dead and we quickly fixed the problem. The room had about two thousand audience members. I was so nervous I stood at the far back next to the wall. The team, once again, was flawless. We believed we had a chance to win it all again. And if we won, two more things would be ours: a team photo adorning two million Kellogg's Frosted Flakes and Corn Pops cereal boxes, and a trip to represent the USA at September's SIFE World Cup in Amsterdam.

In the end, though, La Sierra University came storming back. Again, they put on another incredible show. One of their students, I learned, was an intern for a movie studio's animation department, and the team graphics were dazzling. La Sierra claimed to have over a hundred team members, many of whom completed SIFE projects overseas. With SIFE's global push, it was hard for judges not to rate these projects favorably.

No sour grapes on our part, though. Hats off again to Johnny Thomas, who was now La Sierra's dean, and their new SIFE adviser, Heather Miller. Flagler College of St. Augustine, Florida, came in second, Chico State third, and fourth place went to Valdosta State University in Georgia.

Our team was happy. We made it to the final stage, and earned $9,000 in total prize money, including our third place finish and special competitions. We also captured first place honors in two special competitions. One competition—Best Use of Mass Media—was sponsored by *Business Week*. Our media coverage included local television, San Francisco Bay Area television and newspapers, one national magazine, local and national radio, and four prominent local billboards.

We also won first place prize in the Best Entrepreneurship Assistance Project, sponsored by the Kauffman Foundation in Kansas City. The objective of this competition was to encourage SIFE teams to educate entrepreneurs on how to manage and develop their businesses more successfully. One component of Cal-High SIFE was to reward the best high school teams that had started entrepreneurial ventures by encouraging them to enter our own special competitions.

Again, I was copying and improving upon the collegiate SIFE model to advance our own high school project. I had no problems with this. Sam Walton was a master at copying successful techniques of his competitors. Though I hadn't yet begun to think of SIFE as a competitor—rather, I viewed SIFE then as more of an enabler—I couldn't help but think of Steve Jobs when he said in a 1994 interview, "Picasso had a saying, 'Good artists copy, great artists steal.' We have always been shameless about stealing great ideas."[11]

Though I was using SIFE to enable exposure to service learning and social enterprise, and to make new contacts overseas, Alvin Rohrs saw things differently. Once again, it appeared he viewed me as a threat. Not so much for his job, now, but for the allegiance of SIFE's board of directors.

SIFE's national board of directors continued to grow, but the fifteen-member Executive Committee remained essentially the same. Mike Merriman's term as SIFE chairman ended May 2001 when Tom Moser, KMPG's vice chairman, assumed the title. Moser would serve until October 2002. While Moser was chair, SIFE's board grew to more than 170 members strong. In its 2001–2002 annual report, SIFE reported total revenues of $7,968,879 and unrestricted net assets of $1,793,969. The previous year, revenues were about $6.5 million and, according to GuideStar, a website devoted to nonprofit accountability and reporting, SIFE received no government funding.

Since I joined SIFE in 1993, SIFE had discouraged teams from seeking grants from the public sector. They encouraged teams to teach about the bane of deficit spending and national debt. That would soon change, however. Very soon.

Moser and his colleague at KPMG, Bernie Milano, who was president of the KPMG Foundation, were both keen on the idea of service learning. As a firm, KPMG had its sights set on becoming one of SIFE's greatest global supporters. Though Milano would claim KPMG "does not become involved in encouraging community service for business development," at least for KPMG's junior staff members—he certainly recognized the business benefits when senior executives like him and Moser became involved at the highest levels. "Our partners' activities might have a business development side, but they get that through serving on boards of hospitals or boards of trustees, that is, board-level positions."[12]

No doubt Moser and Milano saw Wal-Mart and its army of retail vendors made for an attractive potential client list. Also, it didn't hurt that KPMG could recruit from some of SIFE's few accounting majors to the public accounting profession.

Moser had risen to KPMG's vice chairmanship in 1998. Later in his career he became a director at the National Retail Foundation. Milano, short in stature, dressed like a powerful executive but carried himself like an erudite professor. Wearing tailored suits and sporting perfectly-coiffed silver hair, he was always friendly, though circumspect. He wasn't a fan of small talk, but when he did offer a word, it was wise to listen. Prior to leading the foundation, he was KPMG's national partner in charge of university relations and national partner in charge of human resources.

Milano and I first met in 1997 in Kansas City. He took a liking to the Chico State team. "If your students would focus a bit more on outcomes and impact, I think you will fare better at competition." Good advice.

In spring of 2000, Milano and I, along with three other accounting professors, began to coauthor a manuscript linking service learning and SIFE. The paper, "Developing Personal Competencies through Service-Learning: A Role for Student Organizations," was published in an academic journal in 2003.[13]

At the end of May 2002, after easing my way back into the SIFE saddle, I didn't know I would soon be knowing Moser and Milano much better—and that my attorney, Jeff Carter, would need to be called back into action.

Chapter 13

SAGE Baby

===========

Tom Payne, like Mike Merriman and me, was a CPA. Tom had become SIFE's vice president of university operations back in the summer of 1995. SIFE's meteoric rise since 1995 was due in no small part to his leadership in university relations. Since then, he had become a good friend of mine, especially after the alleged incident in May 2000.

"I was one of your few supporters here at headquarters," Tom said. "I'm sure Alvin thought you'd walk away quietly after that."

I didn't leave the SIFE organization—yet.

During Chico State's May 2002 performance at the SIFE USA national competition in Kansas City, over 2,000 people could see our projects were more steak than sizzle. We were now completing a few more substantial outreach projects than our prior years' teams and we had a large roster of enthusiastic team members. I took care, though, to limit my students to very few "one-pop" projects with cute names and storefront appeal. Instead, we continued to focus on our best projects. Cal-High SIFE was at the top of the list.

In the three rounds of the 2002 Kansas City competition, over 150 business leaders, including many of SIFE's board members, had judged our team. I kept all the scoring sheets, and we received rave reviews from the judges. Among them:

- Have you considered forming a partnership with other SIFE teams in the U.S. even though you compete yearly? It would help spread the fire, especially dealing with the high school teams.
- The Cal-High SIFE program is really awesome—what a neat idea to drive down (up) to the younger students.
- High school is your lifeblood—great job getting them in-

170

volved—do more!!

- Honesty! Your facts were clearly stated and believable. You stayed away from theatrics which aided greatly in grasping what you said.
- The teaming with other SIFE chapters shows how business is really done! Spreading the word to the high school level with a competition was awesome.

Indeed, our Chico State SIFE team had started a fire. We finished third place in Kansas City, and now I wanted to focus on Cal-High SIFE. Less than a week later I emailed Milano. I wanted to let him know I had a potential Cal-High SIFE supporter at Cisco Systems in Silicon Valley, and I also asked if the KPMG Foundation might want to provide financial support. Given that Milano was a fellow CPA and his foundation supported SIFE, I thought he might want to see a proposal.

Bernie replied on May 16 with a carbon copy to Tom Moser, "Great seeing you in K.C. and congratulations on making it to the Sensational Sixteen. KPMG Foundation is fully committed. Hopefully, Cisco will pick up on this. Also, the Kauffman Foundation might be a good prospect. Suggest you engage Bruce Nasby ASAP so we don't lose opportunities to get funding on this terrific idea." The idea: expansion of Cal-High SIFE and possibly having it officially endorsed by SIFE.

Bruce Nasby? I knew Nasby had full knowledge of the May 2000 alleged incident. Now, Bernie Milano, a SIFE board member, was pushing my request down to SIFE staff. This wasn't good news. I hoped Milano would be excited enough to take the Cal-High SIFE program to the KPMG Foundation or to other SIFE board members. Nasby was Rohrs' right-hand man, especially in the fundraising area. Based on my personal interaction with him in Orlando and Palm Springs, he wasn't very friendly or approachable.

The Cisco lead could be a dead end, but nonetheless, I followed protocol. I immediately sent Nasby an email.

"Bruce, first, thanks for all the work you and the SIFE staff have put into making this year's expo a big success," I wrote. "Second, note Bernie's message below. Will you help us follow up on the potential funding of the high school mentoring idea?"

Three days later, Nasby replied, with a carbon copy to Milano, Rohrs, and Mat Burton, a senior member of SIFE's staff.

"Thanks for your e-mail. I have forwarded it to Mat Burton," Nasby wrote. "He is working very closely with Kauffman Foundation and should be your contact. I am sure he will give you a call."

With this email, I learned three things. First, Rohrs was in the loop on this conversation, which was good. In matters related to the SIFE board and funding, I had no qualms with Rohrs knowing my every step. Cal-High SIFE was a great project, and I knew from my earlier experience with the accounting FIPSE grants from 1992–1997, good projects deserved to be disseminated far and wide. Second, Mat Burton was now part of the discussion. Tom Payne had hired Burton as director of university relations in July 1999. Burton had been promoted to vice president of USA programs, and he was now assigned to be my main point of contact in Springfield. Third, Burton was working with the Kauffman Foundation, which provided funding to sponsor one of SIFE's special competitions. Chico State had won $3,000 for first place in one of the Kauffman competitions in 2002.

Burton called me. Like Nasby and about half the rest of SIFE's entire staff in Springfield, he knew about information contained in Alvin Rohrs' June 15, 2000, letter to me. As one of Rohrs' up-and-rising acolytes, Burton sounded a bit cool, as though he had been instructed to keep a comfortable distance from me. Tom kept me posted on what was happening internally at SIFE's home office—he believed that Burton had been instructed to keep me on a tight leash.

Rohrs was unhappy about the Cal-High SIFE program. He saw it as creeping into the university SIFE brand. Naturally, I saw things differently. I viewed the high school program as a training ground for future SIFE students, which could only help the brand. I hadn't thought of SIFE as a *brand*, like Coke or Apple or McDonald's, except for the fact that SIFE might be branded as a new form of experiential education. Like many of the SIFE teams, we had included the SIFE name in our main projects. One of SIFE's judging criteria at the time was based on how well teams used the media for its outreach projects.

So what was different about Chico State's high school project? One, I was the faculty adviser. Two, Chico State was in California, far away from the control center of Springfield and Bentonville. If SIFE's board were to direct Rohrs to expand SIFE to the high school level, it would likely ask him to work closely with me to make this happen. There is no way Rohrs would want this to happen, given our stormy history together.

I could only surmise that there was yet another reason why Rohrs was unhappy with Cal-High SIFE, and this involved money. If Cal-High SIFE continued to grow, some board members might ask why this wasn't part of the existing SIFE infrastructure. Certainly, judges' comments at SIFE competitions were glowing about the high school program, and encouraged by its growth. Where there is board interest, there is board money, and Rohrs, in all likelihood, would be very reluctant to relinquish even a little bit of control over his burgeoning budgets.

I was on a first-name basis with several other board members including Rieva Lesonsky and Joe Pedott. They knew me and Cal-High SIFE well. They also were aware other board members had commented favorably about Cal-High SIFE. While Rohrs may have been quietly trying to downplay our program, many of his board members wanted to see it grow.

The Chico State SIFE student leaders knew I had some personal issues with SIFE's management. They weren't concerned, as long as it didn't interfere with how they might fare at competition. Now, though, Tom Payne had clued me that Rohrs was going on the offensive *against* Cal-High SIFE. He kept referring to it as a "junior" SIFE program. I decided it would be best to rename Cal-High SIFE for the sake of my students, and for the program.

Soon after returning to Chico from Kansas City in late May 2002, six SIFE students and I met at Charles Brooks' home. Also sitting at Charles' kitchen table were Jeff Leh, Melissa Houston, Tina Renot, Bob Zinke, and Bob's wife Jill. After a couple hours of brainstorming, we agreed that we needed to change the name. Cal-High SIFE would no longer do.

Without doubt, the primary audience for the program were high school students, under mentorship from college students. Bob jotted the word *students* on his notepad.

Next, we all agreed the main goal of the high school teams should be risk taking—starting an entrepreneurial venture. Bob added *entrepreneurship* to his pad.

Our next question dealt with scope. The students knew I had my sights on a worldwide outreach, so we settled on *global*. Bob added it to the list. Students. Entrepreneurship. Global.

Bob smiled. "Aren't we really all about helping students *advance* entrepreneurship around the world?" Voila! Thanks, Bob—Students for the Advancement of Global Entrepreneurship. The SAGE baby was born.

SAGE, we decided, would continue to use SIFE's tournament structure and, using Rohrs' parlance, we would begin to *brand* ourselves differently. First, high school SAGE teams would focus on entrepreneurship rather than corporate careers as one of their main goals. Instead of "teaching others how free markets work in a global economy," or "teaching others how entrepreneurs succeed" (about which, quite frankly, most undergraduate students don't have the knowledge or skills), we wanted high school students to actually do something entrepreneurial while also giving back to their communities.

Second, we wanted to engineer a more holistic set of judging criteria that included a component on civic engagement, environmental awareness, and community service. Our philosophy was grounded on that of businessman and author Paul Hawken. In his 1993 book, *The Ecology of Commerce*, Hawken said, "The ultimate purpose of business is not, or should not be, simply to make money. Nor is it merely a system of making and selling things. The promise of business is to increase the general well-being of humankind through service, a creative invention and ethical philosophy."[1]

A third reason that would set SAGE apart from SIFE was the name itself. Sage is defined in *Webster's Dictionary* as "wise; proceeding from wisdom; well-judged; grave; serious."[2] This definition, we believed, more appropriately captured our vision of creating better futures through entrepreneurship and community service, with teenagers working collaboratively with older, more experienced consultants from nearby universities and the private sector.

Based on the positive feedback of our presentation in the Kansas City 2002 competition, and now with a new name and focus, I was determined to circulate the SAGE name far and wide. Jack Shewmaker was a wildly successful retailer, and he had adopted SIFE as his baby. I was just an accounting professor. Compared to Shewmaker, I was a piker. But SAGE was my baby. The Chico State students began drafting a 2002–2003 SAGE information handbook. It contained examples of outstanding businesses started in prior years under Cal-High SIFE. We also gave students pointers on how to obtain startup capital from nearby companies—like Walgreens and RadioShack. And we scheduled the first annual SAGE World Cup to take place in Kansas City on May 11, 2003, immediately before the May 12–14 Kansas City SIFE USA tournament.

I worked furiously to update my global contact list. Many of the contacts included international guests I met at SIFE expositions through the years. The list was diverse. It included Robert Galindez of the Philippines, John Thornton of Australia, Magdiel Unglaub of Brazil, Sergei Ravitichev of Russia, Yusuf Majidov of Tajikistan, Raisa Kaziyeva of Kazakhstan, and Volodymyr Melynk of Ukraine.

I met other contacts through various service-learning listservs and international business conferences, including Ulrich Braukmann of Germany, Isabelle Sequeira of France, and Tienie Crous of South Africa. Fortuitously, Tienie was the business dean at the University of the Orange Free State in Bloemfontein, and he was well aware of the SIFE program. He had met Jill Zinke, Allison Steltzner, and Siobhan Brennan on their visit to South Africa the previous January.

A year earlier, at the 2001 SIFE USA competition, I met a dapper gentleman, Mr. Denis Neveux. Denis was a senior partner with KPMG in Paris. He had seen the final four presentations and was most impressed by Chico State. He came to the annual Chico State party afterwards in the Hyatt. At the party he said, "I'd like to invite you to Paris on June 29–30 to be one of our featured speakers at the inaugural SIFE France competition."

Because I was planning to go to Europe to see my college roommate Bright Ebenezer in Sweden, and then go on to Wuppertal, Germany, to visit Ulrich, I said *mais oui* to Denis' kind invitation.

I knew SIFE headquarters was keeping an eye on my every move. Once Rohrs and Nasby discovered I was going to be a featured presenter at a SIFE event in France, they let Neveux know, in no uncertain terms, that I was traveling in my own capacity as a Sam M. Walton Fellow, rather than as an official representative of SIFE's home office. Denis knew I had been the Walton Fellow of the Year in 1999, and Chico State had finished in the top three spots in two of the last four years. My credentials were worthy of Denis' invitation.

The trip went off without a hitch. Denis was so appreciative he took me out to dinner after the presentations and splurged on an elaborate meal, including a fine Bordeaux and exquisite French cuisine. Among other things, we talked about how we might start SAGE in France in the future. Afterwards, we took a long walk east to the Notre Dame Cathedral and then crossed the bridge over the Seine to the South Bank. On the way back to my metro stop, we had a clear view of the Eiffel Tower to the east. Denis, quite the historian, was an excellent tour guide. *C'est magnifique.*

Returning to the U.S., I was delighted to learn the returning SIFE veterans were hungry. Jill was elected as Chico State SIFE team president, and Greg Yatman quickly assumed the role of presentation team leader. He and his girlfriend Carrie Yatman were both from Yuba City, forty miles south of Chico. Greg was an MBA student and Carrie a public relations major.

Joining Greg and Carrie were three other women on the presentation team. Melissa Houston from Roseville was an excellent student, sporting a 3.8 GPA. Casey Hatcher, a veteran SIFE student who had transferred from Butte College, was from Chico. Casey was a Dean's List student and a confident public speaker with dramatic flair. Sarah Robbins was a sophomore management major from Walnut Creek, near Oakland. Although the youngest presenter, Sarah, was poised and determined.

We all got together to discuss our plans for next year's competition. The SIFE students knew they had meaty projects in their portfolio. The question was: how best to package the presentation? With input from Judy Sitton, Ken and Barbara Derucher, Tim Colbie, and other business advisers, we settled on a theme entitled, "Making the Case."

With the legal theme, we could cleverly ask "leading questions" that we believed SIFE judges often failed to ask. By asking and then answering our own tough questions, we felt we could prompt judges to ask the competing teams in our league the same tough questions.

Rick Vertolli's student computer animators adapted the theme from television's *Law and Order* show to make snappy transitions from one major topic to another. Greg played the role of defense attorney, Sarah was the prosecuting attorney, and the other three women were star witnesses for the Chico State defense. Together, they would make the case that Chico State deserved to be the best-rated SIFE team in the USA.

Before the 2002–2003 school year started in late August, I packed my bags and headed to South Africa for a two-week visit beginning in Cape Town, August 6. In South Africa I was invited to make three presentations describing my work in the service-learning field. Of course, SIFE and SAGE were part of each presentation. The first was at the University of the Western Cape near Cape Town, followed by Stellenbosch University in the wine country, and then up to University of the Orange Free State in Bloemfontein. Stellenbosch, one of South Africa's elite universities, did not have a SIFE team. The other two, however, had active SIFE chapters.

Upon arriving in Bloemfontein, I was pleased to learn the University of the Orange Free State had recently created an office dedicated to service learning. Further, their SIFE team had been selected to represent South Africa at the upcoming SIFE World Cup event in Amsterdam. The business dean, Tienie Crous, asked if I might offer the team some coaching tips, and I was more than happy to oblige. I also encouraged them to consider starting a SAGE program next year.

Business completed. I flew to Johannesburg for a night and then headed for Kruger National Park for a five-day tent safari. Getting an up-close and personal look at the park's "Big 5"—the lion, elephant, Cape buffalo, leopard, and rhinoceros—was thrilling. I was only forty-five years old, and as I hiked the trails of one of Africa's largest game reserves, I reflected on life's pleasures. I also recalled a conversation between Jack Shewmaker and myself in Orlando two years earlier. Shewmaker told me that one reason he left Wal-Mart in 1988 was so he and his wife would have more time to travel the world.

I had been a Sam M. Walton Fellow since 1993, and now, ten years later, I was traveling the world. For this, I owed SIFE and Shewmaker—if not Alvin Rohrs—a debt of gratitude.

Had I gone to work for SIFE for a year as Shewmaker and I discussed,

I would have been a SIFE global ambassador and a proponent for a "junior" SIFE program. As fortune would have it, though, I was beginning to achieve both goals. But instead of trumpeting SIFE's virtues on my travels, I was now a global ambassador for SAGE. This was the beginning of a dream come true.[3]

A few days after my return to Chico, about two dozen students and I carpooled to Napa where we held our official SIFE new-school-year kickoff meeting and retreat on August 24, 2002, at the Steltzner Vineyards on Silverado Trail. At the retreat, we devised a plan to recruit more high schools to SAGE, to encourage other SIFE teams to start their own high school mentoring programs, and to enlist the support of business sponsors on the West Coast.[4] We had a good start. Walgreens, Gallo, Pepsi Bottling Group, and Sprint PCS had all committed financial support for our inaugural SAGE program year.

The Chico State SIFE team operated like clockwork working on projects as the new fall semester got underway. I enthusiastically accepted Rohrs' blanket offer to all Walton Fellows to attend (as observers, and at our own expense, of course) the second SIFE World Cup in Amsterdam. It was slated for the next month, September 22–24, 2002.

I had three main reasons to attend. First, I wanted to see how well Tienie Crous' SIFE team from Bloemfontein had implemented my coaching tips. Second, I wanted to conduct a training workshop on September 22, the first day of the SIFE competition, for SIFE teams that wanted to learn how to implement the Chico State SAGE program. Third, one of the Chico State project leaders for SAGE was Tina Renot, who had assumed a new position with the SIFE team as director of global programs. Tina, like Jill and Casey, was another Butte College SIFE alumnus who had transferred to Chico State. Tina asked to go and lead the SAGE workshop in Amsterdam. "We can call it Project Amsterdam, and include it as a SIFE project," Tina said. Brilliant suggestion.

To be sure, conducting a SAGE workshop the day before the official SIFE World Cup was not going to please SIFE's executives. The best thing to do, I thought, was to at least keep Rohrs and Nasby informed. They couldn't prevent it—after all, I was still a Sam Walton Fellow. Though unofficially not in good standing with Springfield, I had valuable social capital with certain board members.

On September 3, I had Tina forward an invitation to Nasby, which included a copy of the original workshop invitation to SIFE country coordinators, and individual SIFE teams. Nasby tersely replied the next day: "I wasn't aware of this meeting being scheduled. Please, in the future, communicate with us beforehand. I will try to stop by your meeting for a few minutes."

I immediately replied, reminding Nasby of a prior communication with him. "You may recall that I inquired, on at least two occasions, what SIFE planned to do on Sunday afternoon, September 22. I wanted to be sure that whatever session my SIFE students decided to organize would *not* conflict with any of SIFE's plans. We look forward to seeing you in Amsterdam."

Nasby hadn't replied to my inquiries. Not surprisingly, he didn't attend the workshop, either. But other people did.

When the Chico State advisory board learned Tina and I planned the trip to Amsterdam, three of its leading members asked to accompany us—the more the merrier, I thought. Judy Sitton, Tom Dwyer, and Barbara Derucher booked their flights. Tom, a good friend, was a financial adviser for Merrill Lynch. Both he and Judy would actually participate in the SIFE World Cup as first round judges. We arrived late evening on September 21. With the nine-hour time difference, we stayed up most of the night in the hotel lounge. Late the next afternoon, we were scheduled to conduct the SAGE workshop with Tina leading.

Before the workshop, Tom and I were milling around the hotel lobby when I saw a bear-of-a-man checking in at the front desk. It was Tom Coughlin, who had become chairman of SIFE's board of directors a month earlier, replacing Tom Moser. A personal hunting buddy of Sam Walton and Jack Shewmaker, Coughlin joined Wal-Mart in 1978. He was recruited by his mentor, Shewmaker, to reduce customer and employee theft.

Coughlin rose through the ranks of Wal-Mart, starting in the company's security division. He moved up to vice president of loss prevention, and then on to vice president of human resources. As Coughlin climbed the organization chart, he earned the reputation of being an Ozark cowboy, a "tough talking, self-described bubba with a temper that exploded if he found a store in poor shape or a vendor seeking a price hike. He started wearing a Stetson, listening to country music, and raising bulls on a twelve-hundred-acre ranch outside of Bentonville."[5]

In addition to chairing SIFE's board, Coughlin, who was now CEO of Sam's Club and a member of Wal-Mart's board of directors, would soon become vice chairman of Wal-Mart's entire operation, making him the second most powerful person of America's largest corporation. For fiscal year ended January 31, 2002, Wal-Mart had revenues of $218 billion and profits of $6.67 billion.[6] In the late 1900s, he was executive vice president and COO of the Wal-Mart Stores Division—the company flagship.[7]

The previous year, he was a final round judge at the 2002 SIFE USA competition. "Mr. Coughlin, it's a pleasure to see you," I said. "I'm the faculty adviser from Chico State."

"Ah, yes, California," he replied. "That's where all the whackos are!"

What? What is he talking about?

"Excuse me?" I said. I knew Coughlin had graduated from California State University, Hayward, with a degree in political science—California was not foreign to him. At six feet, four inches and hovering around three hundred pounds, he had played defensive lineman for the university.

"I mean, Wal-Mart is having a devil of a time getting some of your cities to let us build new stores and supercenters," he continued. "What's wrong with you guys?" He said this with a half-grin, which I took to mean that he was half-serious.

"Well, there's a Wal-Mart in my home town of Chico, so you don't have anything to worry about there," I said. Little did I know that in two years, Wal-Mart would start a six-year battle with the Chico City Council in an effort to expand its big box discount store to a supercenter in the south part of Chico. Wal-Mart would eventually lose this one.

To accommodate Wal-Mart's expansion plans, both domestically and globally, Wal-Mart needed more people, and such was the main reason Coughlin was in Amsterdam. SIFE was a management pipeline. This fact was highlighted a year later in an October 6, 2003, cover story in *Business Week:*

This year alone, Wal-Mart hopes to open as many as 335 new stores in the U.S.: 55 discount stores, 210 supercenters, 45 Sam's Clubs, and 25 neighborhood markets. An additional 130 new stores are on the boards for foreign markets. Wal-Mart currently operates 1,309 stores in 10 countries, ranking as the largest retailer in Mexico and Canada. If the company can maintain its current 15% growth rate, it will double its revenues over the next five years and top $600 billion in 2011.

That's a very big if—even for Wal-Mart. Vice-Chairman Coughlin's biggest worry is finding enough warm bodies to staff all those new stores. By Wal-Mart's own estimate, about 44% of its 1.4 million employees will leave in 2003, meaning the company will need to hire 616,000 workers just to stay even. In addition, from 2004 to 2008, the company wants to add 800,000 new positions, including 47,000 management slots. "That's what causes me the most sleepless nights," Coughlin says.

At the same time, Wal-Mart will have to cope with intensifying grassroots opposition. The company's hugely ambitious expansion plans hinge on continuing its move out of its stronghold in the rural South and Midwest into urban America. This year, the company opened what it describes as "one of its first truly urban stores" in Los Angeles, not far from Watts. Everyday low prices no doubt appeal to city dwellers no less than to their country cousins. But Wal-Mart's sense of itself as definitively American ("Wal-Mart is America," boasts one top executive) is likely to be severely tested by the metropolis' high land costs, restrictive zoning codes, and combative labor unions—not to mention its greater economic and cultural diversity.[8]

Like all of Wal-Mart's top brass, Coughlin was a staunch anti-unionist.

Later that afternoon, Tina made an excellent presentation in one of the hotel's conference rooms, outlining the SAGE program with me acting as her copilot. In the audience were about twenty people from six countries including two recent graduates from the Poznan School of Management and Banking in Poland. Under the leadership of Gosia Smigielska and Ewelina Marcinkowska, Poland would become the first country to sign up for SAGE. Also signing up were Mexico and Tajikistan.

Tina and I explained how they could organize a SAGE competition in their country. We also offered advice on how to raise travel funds. Unlike SIFE, though, we would pay all hotel and food if they sent their winning team to compete in the inaugural SAGE World Cup in Kansas City the following May.

After the SAGE workshop we enjoyed the SIFE festivities. In all, twenty-three countries competed in Amsterdam for the World Crown. Not surprisingly, La Sierra won the gold medal, followed by Ghana, South Africa, and Russia.

I was extremely proud of the Free State team from South Africa. They implemented almost all the suggestions from my coaching a month earlier. They followed my advice to begin their presentation with a more personal introduction to Bloemfontein. Few of the judges knew Bloemfontein is the birthplace of great author J.R.R. Tolkien and hometown of barefoot distance runner, Zola Budd. Also, I insisted they give a bit more background of apartheid and its official end in 1991. SIFE students, I suggested, could make the transition from apartheid easier by completing innovative outreach projects designed to ease racial divides. After their third place finish, the entire team sought me out to say thank you. Doris Sebala, their adviser, presented me with an African drum used in their presentation.

Before flying home, our crew enjoyed Dutch pastries and chocolate, toured a couple museums, took a boat ride on some of Amsterdam's 165 canals, and dined in Old Amsterdam. Tom and I even ducked into a specialty coffee shop that sold more than coffee. A sign on the wall said, THANK YOU FOR NOT SMOKING, but the N in NOT was crossed out and replaced with a P for POT. We stuck to coffee. All told, we packed a lot into four days in Amsterdam, and Tina and I made it back to Chico in time for our Tuesday classes.

As the fall semester ended, the Chico SIFE team had completed about ten projects. Four students—Jill, Greg, Carrie, and Casey—travelled to Africa in January 2003 to replicate the Botswana and South Africa programs from the previous year.

Though apartheid officially ended in South Africa twelve years earlier, the four Chico students had seen a society still living in silent segregation. Upon her return from South Africa, Casey said, "Whites and blacks do not commonly intermingle, especially at a personal level. I had the privilege to share a message of opportunity with these children that most had never heard from the white community."

The power of travel to expand one's worldview cannot be overstated. One of my favorite quotes was by Mark Twain: "Travel is fatal to prejudice, bigotry, and narrow-mindedness," and the Chico SIFE students were learning this firsthand.

On December 31, 2002, Nasby emailed a lengthy missive to all SIFE country coordinators. Prominently included was a note about SAGE.

Some of you may have received information about an organization called "SAGE." I would like to point out that SAGE is not an official part of the SIFE organization operating out of Springfield, Missouri. Rather, SAGE is a project conceived by the Chico State SIFE team under the leadership of Dr. Curt DeBerg. SAGE is a program which works with high school student organizations to develop projects in their communities. There has been some confusion from some country coordinators that this program is working under the direction or support from the SIFE World Headquarters. Your decision to be involved with this particular program is up to each of your university teams within your country. One caution I would give you is the confusing message that you may be giving your donor and university officials about SIFE. As you know, Students in Free Enterprise is difficult enough to explain. If your SIFE organization starts blending university students with high school students in similar programs, your donor or university officials may assume that your program focus has been refocused to this lower grade level.

When Tina had contacted SIFE teams and SIFE national coordinators about our Amsterdam workshop, she carefully explained she was the

Chico State SIFE team's director of our global programs, and that Chico State was introducing one of our new global SIFE projects. Now, Rohrs, through Nasby, was cautioning them: if they pursued SAGE, it might confuse university officials or potential donors.

SIFE feared that *blending* its program would lead to confusion. I believed, as did many of SIFE's judges, that university students could be outstanding role models for their younger protégés. Nasby had now made it clear—SAGE should be avoided, not embraced as a successful program to be replicated.

Though the dot-com economic bubble had burst, Chico State SIFE had no problems securing funding. We received a $50,000 grant from a local foundation, the Earl Foor Foundation, along with a $25,000 grant from Pacific Gas & Electric. Melissa Houston was the project leader for SAGE. Under her direction, the Chico State SIFE team mentored over three hundred high school students from thirty-two high schools.

Alvin Rohrs wasn't having any trouble raising money for SIFE, either, and he was getting some help from his congressman, Roy D. Blunt. Blunt has served as the U.S. representative in Missouri's seventh congressional district since 1997.[9] The seventh district contains most of southwest Missouri including Springfield and the Ozarks and is considered one of the most conservative parts of the state. In a few years, Blunt would serve as interim House Majority Leader following House Majority Leader Tom DeLay, who was criminally indicted in 2005 and subsequently convicted for money laundering.

Blunt knew Rohrs well, having served as president of Rohrs' alma mater, Southwest Baptist University, from 1993–96. On February 11, 2003, Blunt submitted a resolution to Congress honoring SIFE. As part of the resolution written into the *Congressional Record* of the 108th Congress, Blunt said, "Mr. Speaker, I'm proud of the investment SIFE continues to make in young people, and I'm proud they join me in calling Missouri's Seventh Congressional District home."[10] Less than a year earlier, SIFE had begun using its political connections to chase federal government grants, in addition to adding new board member companies at $25,000 a shot.

For fiscal year ended August 31, 2002, SIFE's revenues were $7,769,000. A year later, its revenues would jump almost 16 percent to $9,202,000.

The board continued to treat its two main officers, Rohrs and Nasby, well. In 2002, Rohrs earned $155,000 in compensation and $112,000 in employee benefits and deferred compensation. Nasby earned $137,000 and $75,000, respectively.[11]

The board gave each of them a raise in 2003, with Rohrs taking in $159,000 in compensation and $119,000 in employee benefits and deferred compensation. Nasby earned $140,000 and $79,000, respectively. Notably, Sam M. Walton faculty stipends remained at $1,000, and SIFE teams still paid for their own hotels and most of the meals at national competition.

In early March, I received a call from Ken Ellis, director of the George Lucas Educational Foundation. His foundation had learned about the success of our high school SAGE team from Oakland. He was interested in filming a documentary about the Fremont Business Academy and wanted to send a film crew to Chico on March 29 to capture footage of the Oakland teens in action. The ultimate goal was to air the documentary on KRON, one of the Bay Area's leading television stations.[12]

Ellen Langas-Campbell was SIFE's media consultant. She and I had gotten to know each other well over the years. She really liked the Chico State projects, so I sent her an email on March 4. "If SIFE plans to highlight any U.S. projects for future promotional purposes, this is our best event," I told her. "Any chance of getting any of your PR people to come check it out?"

Ellen replied that she would be doing some press work for the SIFE regionals in Los Angeles, and asked if our team would be going there. No, I said. We're going to Seattle this year, on April 3.

But, I said, the winning high school team from California would be joining us in Kansas City to compete for the SAGE USA title against teams from Arizona and Michigan. The USA winner would go head-to-head with Mexico, Poland, and Tajikistan the day before the SIFE USA competition. I also let her know I invited Alvin Rohrs to attend our inaugural SAGE World Cup and make some inspirational remarks. I knew Rohrs well enough by now to know that he wouldn't bother to reply.

Rohrs was so angry I had contacted Ellen that he called me an asshole in an Executive Council meeting in Springfield. Knowing he had crossed the line, Rohrs started the next day's council meeting by apologizing to his Springfield colleagues for his colorful language.

I already knew how Rohrs felt about me. But when I heard he actually said this, I was ambivalent though slightly amused. If he and I could actually work together, we could do some incredible good for both of our programs.

My main role for the Chico SIFE team in the spring semester of 2003 was to help recruit judges for the first SAGE California competition. Nearly 140 business leaders came to Chico on March 28–29 to see the Fremont Business Academy from Oakland take first place. The film crew from the George Lucas Foundation now had an even better story, having shadowed the Fremont teens the past couple months.

As in previous years, SIFE offered several special competitions with prize money attached. SIFE teams were encouraged to write two-page summaries of their special competition entries. The summaries, along with supporting documentation, were to be submitted to SIFE before the stated deadline. Four of these competitions, called "Special Topics" competitions, had specific sponsors. Two of the special topics were sponsored by AT&T, one was sponsored by Kansas City philanthropist Norman Polsky, and one was sponsored by the Kauffman Center for Entrepreneurial Leadership.

AT&T's special topics competition was designed to encourage SIFE teams to teach students in grades K–12 how to use the Internet. This was in the earlier days of the Internet when fewer people had access than today. Their second topic was to teach business owners how to take advantage of the Internet. The Polsky competition encouraged SIFE teams to develop programs to teach about personal investing, and the Kauffman special topics competition rewarded SIFE teams for developing educational entrepreneurship programs.

Chico State had excelled in these competitions previously. In fact, last year (2002), we won first place in a special competition sponsored by *Business Week*, and first place in the Kauffman competition. Prize money payout was $3,000, $2,000, and $1,000 for the top three schools, with twelve additional finalists each receiving $500 for the Kauffman and Polsky competitions.

In addition to the four special *topics* competitions sponsored by AT&T,

Polsky, and the Kaufman Center, SIFE itself had four special *events* competitions—none of which had sponsors. It is important to distinguish the difference between a *topic* versus an *event* special competition.

The four SIFE special *event* categories were organized around projects teams were to complete during *specific months*. For example, SIFE teams were encouraged to focus on business ethics in October. November's focus was financial independence. February's was educational outreach projects teaching others how entrepreneurs succeed. March's was free market economics. Just as it was with sponsored special topics competition, SIFE's special events prize money paid the same: $3,000, $2,000, $1,000 for the top three winners, along with $500 for each of the twelve additional finalists. Between SIFE and the sponsors there were eight special written competitions offered during the year to SIFE teams in addition to the regional, national, and world competitions held for personal presentations.

This sounds pedantic, but hang in there. SIFE was about to make a big error. As it turned out, a better term for error might be *snafu*, a word that is believed to have originated in the U.S. Army during World War II as an acronym for *situation normal: all fucked up*. But to understand the significance of this blunder, one must first understand the special competition process and Chico State's history in special competitions.

In spring 2003, Chico State planned to enter six of the eight written special competitions. The only two that we decided not to enter were sponsored special topics: the Polsky competition and the second AT&T competition—the one that teaches business owners how to use the Internet. Based on our historical success, we fully expected to become finalists in all six of the competitions with hopes that we might finish in the top three in some of them. We had come to depend on the prize money to defray our big travel bills.

Entries for the entrepreneurship competition, sponsored by Kauffman, and the AT&T K-12 competition had March 7 deadlines. I sent Mat Burton and Tom Payne an email on February 15 requesting an extension to March 11 because we were finishing some of our high school SAGE activities on March 10. That way, we would have a more complete entry by including the SAGE results. As SIFE had done in previous years, if a SIFE team requested a couple-days' extension with a justifiable reason, the request was granted.

Dawn Peters, a staff member on SIFE's university relations team, emailed me back giving us a one-week extension on the Kauffman and AT&T entries. On March 11, I emailed Dawn with a carbon copy to Judy Rogers, letting her know a box had been shipped that day.

On March 12, SIFE received the fourteen-pound box via FedEx. It contained three items: (1) the Kauffman entry with a fat three-ring binder of supporting documentation; (2) the AT&T entry, with another three-ring binder; and (3) a spiral-bound packet containing Judy Sitton's nomination for SIFE Business Adviser of the Year. A significant part of each of the two entries contained details about our high school mentoring program, which during our transition to SAGE was still called Cal-High SIFE in California but SAGE everywhere else.

Importantly, the deadline for another competition—SIFE's *special events* competition for projects completed during specific months—was due one week after the Kaufman *special topics* competition, on March 14. On March 13, the day after the big box for special topics competition arrived, SIFE received a second package from us containing the entry for the SIFE *special events* competition—a day before its deadline.

The next month, SIFE announced the top fifteen finalists in all of the competitions. Shockingly, Chico State wasn't a finalist in *any* of the six contests we entered. My students were flabbergasted, especially Jill Zinke. As president of the team, she was distraught. On April 24, she sent Burton a thoughtful email.

I have been on two very successful SIFE teams who, in the past, have fared very well in the Special Competitions. Although we have tried to use what had worked in the past, we did not even place in any of the special comps this year, despite the fact that we put much more time in planning and implementing quality projects. The format and competitions offered have changed and I was wondering a few things: (1) Who judges the competitions (are they from the pool of judges that SIFE uses for regional and/or national SIFE competitions, alumni, SIFE executives and/or staff, or judges who only judge special comps and nothing else?); (2) Will the special competitions be showcased for other teams to see how the winning teams prepared their projects and their binders? and (3) Will there be judges' comments available for our entries so that we can use this to improve our entries in upcoming years. In other words, what constructive feedback will SIFE provide? Many successful companies today know that the key to excellence is understanding your competition and using the best of the best as your benchmark to improve upon. We are always trying to improve and strive for excellence. I am hoping that feedback will be provided so that we and other teams can gain insight to raise the bar again!

Burton did not reply.

Despite not faring well in special competitions, the 2003 Chico State SIFE team traveled to Seattle for the regional SIFE competition and sailed through with flying colors. Next stop: Kansas City.

The day before the SIFE Kansas City competition, May 11, our Chico State SIFE team conducted the first SAGE USA national tournament, with the California SAGE team from Oakland nudging out the Arizona team for first place honors. That afternoon in Kansas City, Oakland's team went on to narrowly defeat Poland and became the first SAGE World Cup Champions. We celebrated by taking all the participants to a Royals baseball game. The American kids had fun discussing baseball with the teens from Poland, Tajikistan, and Mexico.

The next day, on May 12, our SIFE team was assigned to the Kraft Foods first round league. The league looked competitive—we drew the University of Nebraska, Lincoln, and a strong team from Lamoni, Iowa, called Graceland University. The Chico State presentation was flawless, and unlike the first round last year when we had only six judges, this time we had nineteen judges—fourteen men and five women. They all seemed to love our *Law and Order* courtroom theme, and we prevailed.

That night, league assignments were made to determine what four teams would face each other in the next round. Our league consisted of

2001 SIFE USA champion Drury University and Southwest Texas State University, the 2000 SIFE USA champion. The third team we were to compete against in our league was another hometown favorite—the University of the Ozarks.

No one on our team was happy because Drury was glitzy, like La Sierra. I, too, was worried about them. Their team had access to the technology resources at the state-of-the-art Shewmaker Communications Center in SIFE's hometown of Springfield. Like Wal-Mart and many of its senior executives, the small Christian college espoused a management philosophy of servant leadership.[13]

Vicki West was the Sam Walton Fellow at Southwest Texas State. She was a SIFE fanatic wearing flashy dresses and carrying designer handbags. SIFE staff in Springfield affectionately referred to her as the "mouth from the South." She, as a spirited competitor, would do whatever it took to see that her students came out on top.

Before the drawing for league assignments that night, the top three winners of the special competitions were announced. We already knew we hadn't placed in a single one of them—not even the top fifteen of any of the six we entered. This total loss defied probability. We could accept not winning, but we couldn't figure out why. My students had every right to know. One thing that I had harped on when I was a member of the SIFE Academic Advisory Board a few years earlier, and it still held true now—SIFE never provided any judging feedback on the written *special competition* entries, although they did with the staged presentations.

There was a good omen, though. We had nominated Judy Sitton for the most supportive business advisory board member of the year. Judy had contributed her time, talent, and treasure to Chico State SIFE, and my students will never forget the many practice sessions they had at the Sitton residence in the foothills off Honey Run Road just east of Chico. Judy had no idea we had nominated her. Her husband and daughter were in the audience to watch her accept the award.

A couple other noteworthy things happened that night. A ten-minute video tribute was made to Alvin Rohrs for his twenty years of service to SIFE. The tribute came with a personal letter of congratulations from former President George H.W. Bush.[14] Furthermore, he and KPMG's Tom Moser were inducted into the SIFE Hall of Fame, and Tom Coughlin was presented with America's Free Enterprise Legend Award. This award was made for his "significant contributions to the prosperity of the nation in a way that ensures that their accomplishments will serve as an inspiration to America's youth, now and for future generations."[15]

Especially galling to many SIFE observers, including Walton Fellows Lisa Borstadt of Northern Arizona, Diane Welsh of John Corrall University, and Al Konuwa of Butte College, was the presentation of a Chevy Tahoe to Rohrs. SIFE advisers like us worked our tails off to provide startup funds for disadvantaged youth and widows. In return, we received $1,000 fellowships and turned them over to our SIFE teams. What did Rohrs get? An ostentatious gift from the board. The vehicle was tailored especially for Rohrs, and funded by private gifts from the Executive Committee.

In addition, more than fifty board members contributed $65,000 to fund a SIFE scholarship in Rohrs' name. The $5,000 annual scholarship would start to be offered next year, and it would be called the "Alvin Rohrs Servant Leadership Scholarship."[16] Lisa, Diane, and Al chatted with me later. Our SIFE teams all could use more financial support. I couldn't help but wonder how many widows and orphans in Botswana could be helped with this kind of money.

After the four teams in each of the four semi-final leagues made their presentations the next morning, the Chico State team was further heartbroken when it learned Drury had come in first. We placed second, followed by Ozarks and Southwest Texas. Along with Drury, the final four teams included the University of Arizona, John Brown University, and the University of Texas-Pan American. That night, we found little consolation when Drury, the team that beat us in semi-finals, was crowned champion, earning their photo on Kellogg's cereal boxes and an October trip to Mainz, Germany, for the 2003 SIFE World Cup.

At this point in SIFE's history, there were four main judging criteria, worth twenty points each, and four more criteria, worth five points each. Criterion number six required students to demonstrate effectiveness at utilizing mass media and the Internet. Over the years, my team and I had become extremely adept at using the mass media. Before traveling to

Kansas City, we sent a press release to the *Kansas City Star* about the SAGE USA event scheduled for May 11, a day before SIFE's USA competition.

On May 9, Rick Alm, a senior *Star* writer who had covered the SIFE event over the years, wrote a lengthy article about SIFE. A good part of the article, however, was dedicated to SAGE. Alm quoted me saying, "For seven years this was a nice little project in Chico for local high school students." Alm went on to report SAGE events are not formally affiliated with SIFE, and that all I got was a lukewarm reaction from SIFE headquarters.

Rohrs was quoted as saying, "Creating a new SIFE-type, high-school-level organization is not part of our strategic plan." Rohrs continued, "We don't want to start a competitive group with other (high school business) groups, or give our SIFE teams a model of how they have to work with high school groups."[17]

I was amused when I read this. Up until a year or two ago, *Business Week* had sponsored a special SIFE competition called the "Best In-Depth Education Project." The overall purpose of the competition was "to reward SIFE Teams who develop outstanding business-related educational projects which have potential for application nationally." I certainly was not asking Rohrs to mandate that SIFE teams adopt SAGE; instead, I was demonstrating that one of our projects did, indeed, have the potential for national—and even international—application.

The day after the SIFE USA event, Alm wrote a follow-up article. Four prominent paragraphs explaining the SAGE results were included near the end. It cited Oakland's thriving sales in the business card printing operations and its creation of an alternative lunchroom at school.[18]

Once again, the feedback we received from judges was encouraging. Other Walton Fellows started asking me more about our SAGE project, which included our inaugural SAGE USA event a few days earlier and was part of our presentation. One international guest was Dr. Robert Galindez, the SIFE country coordinator from Iloilo City, Philippines. I received the following email a few days after we returned to Chico:

> Congratulations for your team's splendid presentation and the
> growing potential of your SAGE project. I have always admired
> you and your team thus, excited about partnering with you in

establishing SAGE in the Philippines. Do you know that my program in the Philippines is the second biggest country SIFE operations having 272 member schools in affiliation? This year, 75 colleges and universities competed. With my three-year experience in running SIFE and the network that I have established, I am confident that SAGE can easily grow in the Philippines and will surely enrich the high school curriculum. You are welcome to visit my country and will be happy to organize the schools to listen to you and learn from you. Just let me know when and how. I will be in Springfield until June 15, 2003 and be back to the Philippines on the 17th. Regards.

Jill Zinke, the 2003 Chico State SIFE team president, recall, had asked Mat Burton several questions about the special competitions. On May 16, I sent Mat a note asking him for answers. I told him that I was not the only SIFE adviser who had the same concerns as Jill.

"Jill's concerns are not unique to Chico State," I said. "All Walton Fellows who helped their teams submit entries want, need, and deserve feedback."

The same day, I sent Bernie Milano and Tom Moser a brief email expressing my frustration with SIFE. "Many Walton Fellows have expressed great dissatisfaction at not having any voice when it comes to policy and procedures that directly affect us."

Then I added the following about SAGE, "I am passionate about pursuing SAGE, preferably with SIFE's endorsement. I spoke with several country coordinators who are hungry for this program, and a word of encouragement from SIFE HQ would go a long way in helping them start such a program."

I attached a file responding to Rohrs' concerns, as he had expressed them in the *Kansas City Star* article by Rick Alm.

Milano, a process-oriented and cautious accountant, replied a few moments later. "We'll have to let some time pass after the (Kansas City) Expo and then pursue resolution of this with all interested parties weighing in. When SIFE truly went global it was only after many discussions and reviewing the challenges and opportunities. We ultimately made a good decision there and I'm certain the same process will deliver the right answer on this issue."

Four days later, on May 20, Burton finally replied to Jill and me. I read the first part. "Your questions about the need for feedback are very appropriate and you are not alone in your frustration. The challenge in providing this feedback is in the number of entries received in each competition. Unlike at regionals where the judges only have to review the programs of six or seven teams and then are given plenty of time to make comments, we often receive more than 100 entries in each special competition. The judges put in close to a full day reviewing these and making their decisions. Because of the volume of entries, it would be an overwhelming task for them to also complete a written critique for each team—even if each judge spent only five minutes on this task, it would take them more than eight hours, in addition to time they already contribute, to complete written reviews."

I let this sink in. Hmm? More than a hundred entries in each competition? That didn't seem realistic. Also, every team merited feedback, and it could be done easily. For example, we encouraged our SAGE teams to enter special competitions, and as our Chico State SIFE students evaluated each SAGE team entry, they completed a simple judging rubric. The rubric was given to each teacher. I went back to Burton's email.

"With that said," he empathized, "I certainly understand the need for this feedback—I can promise you that we are working on some ideas to reformat these competitions and the proposals that we have developed would not only provide more prize money but also the type of evaluation you are asking for. We are working hard to find sponsors for these competitions and I would hope we can introduce the new concepts next year or the following year."

Strange? Burton didn't even address the question of who served as special competition judges. I wanted to know who served on the "independent panel of business executives," as promised on page five of the *SIFE Information Handbook.*

Again, we had received positive feedback from judges of the overall competition in Kansas City. I came into my office on Wednesday morning, May 21, to find a voicemail message from Rohrs. It was about four minutes long, and he requested that I author a white paper for SIFE's Executive Committee.

Whoa! This was good news. Obviously, many of SIFE's board members had seen our team present, and certainly many of them had seen the articles by Rick Alm. They must have been leaning on Rohrs to learn more about the "junior-SIFE program" from Chico. Maybe Bernie Milano or Tom Moser had been whispering in his ear.

The white paper, Rohrs said, should provide a description of SAGE, including our progress to date, goals, my vision for its future, how I intended to provide financial support, and my overall feeling about why this is the direction I think SIFE should be going.

I was wary.

Rohrs had made his feelings publicly known in the article, and Nasby's email about SAGE to country coordinators said basically the same thing. But the voicemail made it clear to me that he was getting pressure from above. Some heavy hitters must have liked the SAGE idea. Was Jack Shewmaker back in the picture? Certainly, the last thing Rohrs wanted to do was support SAGE, but he couldn't refuse his patron saint.

"This is an opportunity to put together your views to the group," he said.

Group? Executive Committee members? SIFE staff?

"I know who the group consists of, but I can't say more until I find out who the chair will be," his voicemail message said. "I want to make sure that we take a very serious look at the opportunities that are in front of us and that we don't shut the door when the door should not be shut."

He went to say that the purpose of my paper would be for the group to sit, read, and think about my views. Further, he had asked Mat Burton to research all the SIFE teams by going through their annual reports so that SIFE could determine which teams were working with high schools and how they are doing it. Burton would find out what models were being used, which ones SIFE should endorse, and which ones should SIFE discourage.

In the next two days, we exchanged emails. I told Rohrs that I would be happy to author a white paper and present it to the Executive Committee in person. No, he said, the paper would be enough—my presence wouldn't be needed. We agreed he'd phone at 9 a.m., Friday, May 23.

The conversation started with about five minutes of chit-chat about Alvin's son, Ben. Small things, like Ben's high school graduation and his college plans to attend Biola University, a private Christian university in La Mirada, California. I could see why Rohrs was effective in raising money for SIFE. He was a good-old-boy conversationalist, and he acted as though we hadn't any history between us.

I finally got down to business. "Your voicemail was interesting. I am curious about what you and the executive board have in mind with SAGE."

"Well, I have several issues," he began. "First, it was awkward with your event in Kansas City with the media and all. Also, I have some branding issues. Using the name "Cal-High SIFE" or "Junior SIFE" for high school mentoring programs is confusing. There are beginning to be some problems with teams making "SIFE Beer" and "SIFE Wine." There might be some potential liability issues. Historically, SIFE teams have been given wide latitude, which has been healthy. Lots of good models have resulted. Now, we want to know if there is a commonality with SIFE teams working with high school groups, like DECA, FBLA, and FFA."

As he was talking, I had to stop from interrupting. Except for our California program, we weren't using SIFE in our name anymore, and he knew it. It was SAGE. And I never referred to it as Junior SIFE. And, to my knowledge, no SIFE teams were making or promoting alcoholic beverages. The only one promoting alcohol (and tobacco) was SIFE itself, given that three of SIFE's longtime sponsors were Coors, Philip Morris, and British American Tobacco.[19]

Rohrs *now* wanted to know if there was some commonality with high school groups? Some board members, no doubt, were wondering why he hadn't explored this long ago. Strategic alliances are an integral part of any CEO's job. But I continued to listen.

"Mat is researching all SIFE teams. The big question is, should we encourage more structure for this? Should we say, 'Here's a handful of models you ought to use?' or should we create a venue where we say, 'Here are the models; here's who to work with if you want to use these models.'"

I interjected, "Whenever high school groups learn about SAGE, it's an opportunity for them to join SIFE when they get to college, or to put pressure to start SIFE teams." More SIFE teams, the board knew, meant more interest from the private sector.

But Rohrs was just following the board's marching orders on the high school issue. He still had a bone to pick with me about my correspondence with some of SIFE's board members and the *Kansas City Star* articles. He couldn't refrain from giving me a little lecture.

"Some of our donors are getting emails from you and others asking for funding; do we need tighter rules about this? Also, there are concerns about protecting our event so that there aren't a lot of conflicts?"

Money and control. True, I had approached everyone in my social network, including some of SIFE's board members, who I thought might support the SAGE concept. That's what entrepreneurs do.

I took the high ground. "My intent has never been to conflict with SIFE. I wish that all the country coordinators who were in Kansas City last week could have watched the high school teams. They could have seen the power of the high school SAGE system, modeled after collegiate SIFE. The incredible high of SIFE students can be bottled at the high school level."

I continued. "When business people who call me and ask, 'Where is SAGE going?' I tell them it's a Chico State project that other teams have chosen to adopt. I would love to be able to provide financial support for high school teams. High school teachers believe they are helping create something."

Several of SIFE's country coordinators had been asking about SAGE, I told him.

Aside from possibly feeling personal vitriol for me, Rohrs was mostly concerned with money, and he saw this as a zero sums game. "These same country coordinators need to figure out how to raise money," Rohrs said. "We try to get resources to get a team from their countries to the SIFE World Cup. The question is where to use scarce resources. Will SAGE complement or compete with SIFE for dollars and that kind of stuff?"

I saw it differently. The more people who learned about SIFE, I reasoned, the more funds would become available, including possible funding from the public sector.

Rohrs then expressed his belief that SIFE's support for SAGE would be viewed as favoring Chico State.

"If we push SAGE to country coordinators and U.S. Sam Walton Fellows, then we hear it that we are favoring CSU, Chico," Rohrs said. "We have to bend over backwards to make sure everybody knows we don't play favorites."

Then he turned to the difficulties he would have if, in fact, SIFE officially sanctioned SAGE, and his office had to administer it. "Our CEOs
on our board don't understand that Sam Walton Fellows are volunteers.
SIFE cannot mandate how teams should go about this. Tom Coughlin and
Len Roberts can issue a directive to all of their employees to use the same
light bulb in every store, but if SIFE tried to mandate a certain program
with Walton Fellows, there'd be a huge uproar."

I bit my tongue. The cynic in me thought that if maybe Rohrs and
Nasby gave up a little of their fat salaries and redirected some of it to Walton
Fellows or their students, then SIFE's executives would have more authority.
You know, the more you give, the more you get. True servant leadership.

In any case, Rohrs had no idea how Walton Fellows would react. He
never interacted with us. Then, using his analogy, I countered, "What if
Tom and Len issued a directive like this: 'We currently offer a commu-
nity matching grants program. Within this program, let's have each store
allocate some funds for any high school to work on a project with a local
SIFE college team.' This way, SIFE wouldn't have to mandate anything.
Any group of high school students could apply for local funding, and
SAGE would just be among one of the many SIFE-endorsed programs."

Rohrs sighed. He said that the board had already discussed these kinds
of issues, and he didn't want to go down that path again.

But I was quite sure of his endgame. Though he hadn't succeeded in
ousting me, he would do whatever it took to convince the board that SAGE
was bad for SIFE's "brand." Some members of the board, though, really
wanted to know if I had thought deeply about the prospect of SAGE and
SIFE teaming up. Rohrs may have feared that if I had a good case, the
board might require us to work together.

When hell freezes over.

I wasn't crazy about the thought of working with Rohrs, so if the board
ended up mandating an alliance between SIFE and SAGE, I would insist
on autonomy and report directly to the board. Rohrs turned the conversation back to SAGE and the white paper.

"The task force is looking for structure," he said.

But then he returned to the issue of SAGE conducting our event just
before the SIFE event. "We just can't have SIFE teams doing projects at

SIFE events that everybody can't get access to."

Point well taken. I informed him that the Chico State advisory board had advised me to pull the SAGE event out of Kansas City the next year. He didn't seem to hear.

"We want a brand to create a real clear understanding of what SIFE is," he said. "We don't want confusion with judges and schools. In whatever city we are doing our SIFE competitions, we are going to do a hard core press to get media, and it needs to be directed from us."

Then, back to the beer. "If we let SAGE do something this year, then next year, we have Junior SIFE and the SIFE Beer Truck."

"Alvin, clearly, you must have a policy that everyone abides by," I agreed. "One of my goals is to introduce high school students from other countries into the SIFE family so that they will go to college and start a SIFE program. This is a bubble-up philosophy."

This seemed to pique his interest. He asked if the international SAGE teams competing this year had been mentored by universities with SIFE teams. I informed him that the Poland team was mentored by the Poznan SIFE team that placed second in the SIFE Poland National Competition, and the SAGE project was entered by them for special recognition. SAGE, in fact, had helped the Poznan SIFE team win first place in the Best Entrepreneurship Project Special Competition in Poland. I also let him know that the Mexico students were mentored by a SIFE team from Guadalajara.

"Right now, the mentoring is coming from SIFE teams, but it wouldn't have to," I continued. "Any college or university can mentor a group of entrepreneurial students. They can come from Marketing Associations, Beta Alpha Psi, Delta Sigma Pi. The intent right now, though, lies mostly with SIFE. The SIFE criteria make it perfect for a high school mentoring program."

Once again, I tried to hit Rohrs in his sweet spot. "If packaged the way you and the board want it, and in a way that I could live with, I think you could generate a lot more revenue for SIFE."

After all, we raised $75,000 from two non-SIFE sources this year.

But that didn't seem to sway him. He already had his mind made up, and I could almost hear him countering my every move with a move of his own. Chess.

"Let's wrap this up," he said. "Once you put the paper together, I'll let you know who to send it to." We hung up.

Whew. If the board could be convinced that SAGE should be part of SIFE, my service-learning agenda could really make a splash. I decided to put every ounce of energy into the white paper. After I spoke to Rohrs on May 23, I called my friend, Tom Payne, and asked if he could send our judging sheets for the Kauffman Foundation special topics competition, since we had not received any feedback from Burton. He said he would ask Judy Rogers to mail the green evaluation sheets to me.

On May 25, Tom called back. "We have no records of your having competed in the Kauffman-sponsored event," he said. "Are you sure you entered this special competition?"

What? I was stunned. I told him we had absolutely sent an overnight package to SIFE containing this particular entry.

"It's no wonder Chico State didn't win anything here," I said.

Tom repeated, "You're positive you entered Kauffman?"

"Yes, absolutely," I said.

After a long pause, Tom hit me with another bombshell.

"Curt, there were some teams who won prize money in one of the special competitions that they hadn't even entered," he alleged.

It wouldn't be long before I would learn that "irregularities" involving both the Kauffman special competition and the special events competition were a ticking time bomb at SIFE world headquarters.

If I hadn't had such a history with SIFE, this would be completely unbelievable. The SAGE program was an integral part of the Kauffman entry. I couldn't help but think of grunge rock band singer Kurt Cobain, who said, "Just because you're paranoid doesn't mean they aren't after you." Would SIFE stoop this low?

I had to do some digging. If it was really true that some teams had won prize money without entering the competition, while others—like Chico State's—had entered the competition, but didn't even get judged, then it might be time to give attorney Jeff Carter another call.

Rohrs wasn't the most ethical guy around, I already felt, but if he was aware that there was intentional manipulation of special competition results, this was reprehensible. Consider the irony. Two days earlier Rohrs told me that SIFE bent over backwards to make sure no teams received favorable treatment.

If results could be manipulated in special competitions, couldn't the results from the overall competition be tampered with?

I thought of Kurt Cobain again.

Chapter 14

Lower

Tom Payne's May 25, 2003, phone call about the special competition improprieties had my head spinning. Since the summer of 2000, I had done my best not to be consumed by resentment for SIFE—and Alvin Rohrs. To me, there was a an almost sinister side to SIFE now, and to make matters worse, SIFE held itself out as an organization that considered ethics as the flagship of its guiding values.[1]

Just like the letter I received from Rohrs three years earlier, Tom's call set into motion a whole chain of events that would last until the end of the year. After it was over, Tom would eventually accept a buyout from SIFE's board of directors and go quietly on his way in November 2003. Gail Spradlin (who now went by Gail Beutler), SIFE's vice president of administration, turned in her resignation the first week of June, agreeing to stay until August to help with the transition. She had resigned from SIFE in disgust, telling Tom Payne she simply couldn't work for Mat Burton anymore. Also resigning soon thereafter were vice presidents Dick Laird and Kay Volkema, along with long-term director Theresa Skidmore.

Beutler had been aware of the alleged incident in 2000, acting as Rohrs' go-between, and it made her uncomfortable working with Rohrs. Tom let me know that she was also upset by the special competition mix-up. By summer 2003, she had enough.

As she would write Tom in an email two years later, "You and I paid our price. It's not easy quitting a secure position and throwing yourself out into the cold cruel world. Certainly no one stepped up to help us! I think you are lucky to be out of there, as am I."[2]

When Tom called me on May 25, five months before his eventual departure, he was livid. He couldn't give me all the details and played it a bit coy. The main purpose of the call was to give me enough leads to start asking the right questions. He knew that if there was any Walton Fellow who'd look into teams winning prize money in competitions they didn't enter, it would be me. He started the conversation by expressing his frustration that Sam Walton Fellows and, more importantly, SIFE students, weren't getting a fair shake.

"Whenever SIFE advisers have concerns, they are blown off by Mat Burton," he said.

By now, Tom was pretty much in charge of recruiting major universities into SIFE, a point of emphasis of SIFE's board of directors. The day-to-day operations involving Walton Fellows were Mat's responsibility. "I'm calling you because I have always had great respect for you and the way Chico State SIFE conducts itself, win or lose," Tom said. "Plus your team always kicks ass in the special competitions."

Tom provided more details. "Fraud has occurred in at least one SIFE special competition. At least one SIFE team that either placed in the top fifteen finalists (winning $500 each) and one team that had finished first, second, or third (winning a total of $3,000, $2,000, and $1,000 prize money) in this competition did not enter this special competition."

What did Tom want to accomplish by telling me this? If he wanted me to do anything, I'd need more facts.

"I don't want anyone to lose their jobs over this," he said.

"If this is true, somebody deserves to lose their job," I said. "SIFE is an organization that preaches ethics. This is a serious ethical breach and the person committing it needs to be fired. And if anyone treats this matter as a minor incident, they might need to be fired, too."

Before hanging up, we chatted about SAGE and my conversation with Rohrs just two days earlier about the SAGE white paper.

"Be very careful," he cautioned. "I'm about your only friend in Springfield. The [alleged incident as described in Rohrs' letter to you on June 15, 2000] was terrible management on Alvin's part. And he hated the fact that you went over his head in arranging the Executive Committee meeting in Los Angeles, when the Chico State team made its presentation to the CSU folks. He hasn't forgiven you for that."

I couldn't sit tight. The next day, I sent an email to all Walton Fellows whose teams were a finalist or a top three finisher in the Kauffman sponsored special topics competition. Having no proof of wrongdoing, I simply asked if they would send me their executive summaries in order to learn how our team might improve next year.

Ohio State's SIFE adviser, Cindy Collier, was an adjunct professor of finance. She immediately replied, with a carbon copy to Nicholas Lingen-felter, one of her SIFE leaders. Nicholas sent me an email later that day, May 26, that read, in part, "I also think it is important to let you know that this entry was originally written and submitted for national entre-preneurship month and not the Kauffman award. When we submitted it they put it in the Kauffman for some reason."

Okay, now we're getting somewhere. This was the first piece of hard evidence of SIFE wrongdoing in the Kauffman competition. Tom said at least two teams had been involved. One more to go.

On Thursday, May 29, Tom called back and he was now more outraged. According to Judy Rogers (Mat Burton's assistant) and Harriet Rodriquez (Tom's assistant), at least two more teams had won prize money for this competition without entering it. Further, he had gone back to the records to verify Chico State's entry hadn't been judged.

"Chico State's entry never made it into the Kauffman competition. Can you prove that it got to SIFE's headquarters on time?" Tom asked.

"Hell, yes. I have the documentation from FedEx," I replied. I then told him about Ohio State.

I had lots of questions for Tom. Who was directly responsible for this? My guess was that it was Mat Burton, or maybe even Rohrs. Why? How? And was the Chico State entry intentionally *lost*?

Tom said that it was Mat Burton's fuck-up about the undeserved awards. He also told me that Judy Rogers and Harriet Rodriguez both knew about this, and that they were livid.

"What about Alvin? Does he know?" I asked.

"Yes, but he doesn't think that what Mat has done is egregious," he claimed.

To call attention to this matter, especially to the SIFE board, would signal that everything wasn't running smoothly in Springfield. Tom commented that everything else was going well for SIFE, saying that future prospects for SIFE were looking terrific, with new donors and more colleges coming on board every month.

Tom asked me to keep digging. He indicated that he would be calling Bernie Milano. Milano, recall, was the director of the KPMG Foundation and a member of the SIFE board's Executive Committee—whom Tom had been working with on the recruitment of larger universities. Tom indicated that he did not want Walton Fellows and SIFE students to get shafted and thought Bernie would be a fair and impartial arbiter. He also let me know that the next board meeting was set for August. "Be patient," he said. "And one more thing. Don't send any more emails to my SIFE address—send it to my personal address. The computer boys downstairs can retrieve this if they really want to."

If Mat Burton was responsible for this, why and how did he do it? To understand this, one has to know how SIFE organized its special competitions. I touched on this last chapter.

Each year, SIFE would encourage teams to target its projects to address certain topical areas that were of special interest to donor-sponsors. Therefore, each of the *special topics* competitions had a sponsor, who usually put up $50,000, explicitly for the competition. The competition was structured according to the sponsor's specifications. For example, entries for the *Kauffman Entrepreneurship Assistance* (KEA) Special Topics Competition were due on *March 7*. The specific purpose of this competition was for SIFE teams to educate entrepreneurs on how to manage and develop their business more successfully. Teams could enter projects that occurred throughout the year. In other words, teams didn't have to complete these projects during a specific time period, such as those projects completed only in February.

As usual, SIFE never solicited any input on the details of these competitions from Walton Fellows—the competition details simply appeared in each fall's new handbook.

Compare this with *National Entrepreneurship Month* (NEM) Special Events Competition, which was not sponsored. The specific purpose of this *special events* competition was for SIFE teams to develop educational outreach projects that teach others how entrepreneurs succeed. Teams entering this competition were required to enter projects that occurred during the month of February. Entries for this competition were due *March 14.*

Without further information, one could guess at what might have gone wrong at SIFE headquarters. In the case of four SIFE teams that won prize money from a competition they didn't enter, two possible situations were likely.

First, if a SIFE team like Ohio State entered the second competition (the NEM), SIFE could have inadvertently placed it in the first stack—the KEA—and the judges mistakenly judged it as a Kauffman entry. This would not lead to any problems, as long as the team didn't place in the top fifteen teams.

This situation wasn't plausible, though. Entries postmarked on or before March 7 would be intended for KEA. If the team wasn't clear about what competition it was entering based on the cover letter, the executive summary, or the supporting documentation, it rightfully should have been eliminated. Barring that, however, a quick call to the Walton Fellow would have cleared up any confusion.

A second situation is much more likely. If a SIFE team entered the second competition, it could have been placed in the first stack—KEA—*on purpose.* The incentive here could be for SIFE to curry favor with Kauffman—demonstrating that Kauffman's sponsored topic was more popular than it actually was. This, in turn, would provide stronger justification for future funding. At the same time, it would mean Mat Burton was currying favor with his boss, Rohrs. The more entries, the better both of them would look when they went hat in hand back to Kaufman for next year's funding.

Prize money for each of the two competitions was the same: $3,000, $2,000, and $1,000 for the top three teams, and $500 for each of twelve additional finalists. Total prize money payout, therefore, was $12,000. Keep in mind, however, that Kauffman had kicked in $50,000 to sponsor its competition.[3] At this sponsorship amount, SIFE would presumably net a cool $38,000 *administrative fee.* In other words, special competitions that were *sponsored* were a real money maker for SIFE. Unsponsored competitions were not—instead of making SIFE money, these competitions cost SIFE money. For this reason, it was extremely important to keep Kauffman and other sponsors happy.

Again, this would cause SIFE no problems, as long as the team didn't make it to the Top 15. Unfortunately for SIFE, Rohrs, and Burton, four teams won prize money for the KEA competition even though they didn't enter. But this begs the question—weren't Kauffman executives or other senior executives judging the competition, as SIFE led us all to believe? How could *they* get this wrong?

According to page five of SIFE's handbook, the eight special competitions were to be "reviewed by a panel of business executives" and on pages 22–28, "an independent panel of business leaders will judge the entries in this special competition."

It had to be pretty obvious to the judges, especially if they were business leaders, as to what competition was being judged: did the projects teaching *others* how entrepreneurs succeed occur only in February, which would make them an entry for the unsponsored entrepreneurship month competition? Or did projects educating *existing entrepreneurs* occur throughout the year?

Equally as interesting was the case of the Chico State KEA entry *not* being judged. From SIFE's perspective, four possible situations could have led to this: (1) I never submitted an entry, (2) I submitted a large package to SIFE via FedEx, but forgot to include the Kauffman entry, (3) SIFE received the entire package, but lost the KEA, or (4) SIFE received the entry and pulled it.

People make mistakes. But I had taken great pains to work with Jill Zinke to submit the KEA entry in time and, after all, I had been doing this since 1994. Included in the heavy FedEx package were three items: (1) an entry for the Kauffman competition, (2) an entry for the AT&T Internet competition for K-12 students, and (3) Judy Sitton's nomination packet for SIFE's most supportive business adviser of the year. SIFE received the package and its contents which ruled out (1) and (2). That meant SIFE either lost it, inadvertently, or pulled it, *on purpose.*

If SIFE lost the entry, then this was further evidence that internal controls at SIFE were horrible. Given that two of KPMG's top executives served on the board, this would be embarrassing for the entire organization. The Sarbanes-Oxley Act of 2002 was passed after Enron collapsed, and along with it, Enron's accounting firm, Arthur Andersen. Sarbanes-Oxley required that top management take full responsibility for its internal control system. Though the act applied to publicly traded companies, the same was expected from CEOs of nonprofits.

In my May 29 conversation with Tom, he said Rohrs was well aware of the special competition snafu but was planning to keep it quiet. "I told him about this problem five or six weeks ago," Tom said, "and he hasn't yet realized the scope or potential consequences. I told him that if the specifics get out, SIFE runs the risk of losing half its schools."

I asked Tom how he would have handled this if he were Rohrs. Tom opined that Rohrs should have announced to all SIFE teams mistakes were made, and that he was taking measures to rectify it. He also should have assured the advisers that it wouldn't happen again, and Rohrs should have told them the person who made the mistake had been reprimanded.

I reminded Tom that SIFE advisers had been seeking feedback on special competitions for years, and we'd never gotten any. If this year was any indication of how seriously SIFE treated special competitions, we now had a pretty good idea why—they were terribly mismanaged. Without transparency or accountability, the only work SIFE had to do basically was deposit $50,000 and write checks totaling $12,000.

From SIFE's vantage point, the key stakeholder had always been sponsors and the board who, for the most part, were one and the same. Keep the sponsors and the board happy, SIFE makes money, and Rohrs' salary grows with his waistline. But invest the sponsors' money in running a clean, comprehensive program befitting an international, nonprofit education organization? Nah.

Rohrs ignored Tom's request to set the record straight. Rohrs told Tom, "This matter has been taken care of. Letters have been sent to the relevant people explaining that an error occurred."

No action would be taken against anyone who caused the error.

"I stand by my decision to back my employees," he said, nobly. Again, Rohrs was playing the white knight, taking the high road with employees.

"If I were Alvin," Tom added, "and if I saw what happened, I would be disgusted. Those of us that know about this realize that this is going to come out. Both Gail Beutler, who also knows about this, and I are battle worn. Gail may not be around much longer, and if she goes I won't be far behind." Tom said that he had great admiration for Beutler and her courage under fire.

The only thing I could conclude was that SIFE either had a cluster-fucked system of internal controls, which amounted to gross negligence, or it intentionally manipulated the results of the special competitions, which some would see as fraud. Both were reasons for me to pay a return visit to the office of my attorney, Jeff Carter.

After explaining the situation to Jeff, he said, "There appears to be some incredibly arrogant and egotistical people at SIFE's home office." Jeff started drafting a letter to Rohrs. Attorney battle Round 1 started in June 2000. Round 2 was now beginning in May 2003.

As Jeff keyboarded the letter, I learned the identity of the other three teams in addition to Ohio State that unjustifiably won prize money. They were North Dakota State (NDSU) in Fargo; Bethune-Cookman College from Daytona Beach, Florida; and Montgomery College in Rockville, Maryland, just northwest of Washington, D.C.

Chuck Harter of NDSU called me in response to my email a few days earlier. I asked him if I could get the details of his team's KEA project, which he said he would gladly send. Then I asked him if he might know about any mix up in the judging of the competition.

Long silence. Then, "What do you mean?" Harter asked.

"Well," I said, "I know of at least one other team whose entry somehow got mixed up. They entered one competition but got judged in another, and ended up being a finalist."

Harter took a deep breath.

"Actually, you know, that's the same thing that happened to us," he said. "We got a call from Mat Burton saying that our Best Entrepreneurship Month entry was really better suited for the Kauffman competition, and that he took the liberty of shifting it to the Kauffman stack. He also wrote us an email saying something to the same effect. At regionals in early April, my kids were shocked to be a Final 15 contestant in Kauffman, because we believed that if Mat didn't think we met the criteria under the E-Month competition, it was kind of odd that we would make the finals in a competition we didn't directly shoot for."

He sounded relieved to get this off his chest.

"I'd be shocked, too," I offered. "And it's really not right that other schools that entered Kauffman didn't have a chance to make the Top 15 because several other schools were counseled into the Kauffman after entering the E-Month."

Then the kicker. I said, "To top it off, in Chico State's case, I have reason to believe our entry this year didn't even make it into the Kauffman pile—and we took first place last year in the Kauffman competition."

"Whoa!" said Chuck, "That'd really be wrong." He went on to say that he'd had some real concerns with the way the competitions had been judged, citing lack of input from faculty and lack of feedback. He was preaching to the choir.

Before saying goodbye, he offered to dig up some correspondence on the matter between his team's leader, Joel Hansen, and the rest of the NDSU SIFE team. As we were talking, he sent me the following:

Date: Wed, 26 Mar 2003 17:47:58 -0600
From: Joel Hanson
Subject: NDSU SIFE TEAM - Top 15 finalist for Kauffman Center For Entrepreneurial Leadership Entrepreneurship Award
All,

Just received a call from Tim Clow with SIFE and he wanted me to let everyone know that we made the top 15 for the Kauffman Award which means we won $500 and a trophy. We are now in the running for up to $3000. Although we had not originally submitted the paper work for this award, Mat Burton did so on our behalf after reading the submission for the National Entrepreneurship Month. So we owe Mat a big thank you for doing that for us. Pretty awesome! Congrats team. Nice work. Joel

Yes, awesome, Mat Burton. And who could blame Joel and his NDSU team from being excited? After all, the benevolent folks at SIFE HQ believed that their entry was so meritorious that they unilaterally decided to enter them into another competition. What Mat didn't count on, of course, was that NDSU ended up winning second place in the Kauffman competition.

Joel's team won $2,000 for a competition it hadn't even entered.

How was Burton being advised to handle this from his CEO, Alvin Rohrs? Didn't the *true* second and third place teams deserve more prize money? What about all the teams that entered KEA that didn't win anything?

Rohrs had Burton move up the two teams immediately below NDSU. Graceland University moved from third to a tie as second place winner, and Northeastern State University of Tahlequah, Oklahoma, which had come in fourth, was moved up to third. The SIFE adviser from Northeastern, Grant Alexander, obviously shared the same gratitude toward Mat Burton as Joel Hanson. Alexander gladly cashed the $1,000 check that came in the mail a week later. He didn't think to ask Mat Burton too many details about what might have happened.

SIFE error in your favor, collect $200—no, make that $1,000. Just like *Monopoly*, practiced ethically and correctly, with honesty and integrity.[4]

I really didn't think I needed to dig any further. But before I knew it, I was on the phone with William Ziegler, adviser for the Bethune-Cookman team. Like Ohio State, Bethune-Cookman had received a $500 prize as a Top 15 finalist for the KEA competition.

There was an interesting twist here. Ziegler's team also won second place, and $2,000, in the NEM Special Events competition *with the same entry*. After being judged a silver medal winner in the unsponsored category, the same entry was judged to be a finalist in the Kaufman category. Ziegler, who was truly living up to the SIFE's guiding values, went on the offensive.

Knowing that some deserving teams got jobbed, Ziegler was so upset that he refused to cash the check. "When Dick Laird of SIFE called and told me we were a finalist in the Kauffman competition," Ziegler told me, "I said that there's a mess-up. Our entry was entered for the other competition. Some other team is entitled to this prize."

Later, I would learn the following facts. SIFE would list a total of eighty-one teams as being entered into the unsponsored NEM competition. The deadline for the entries for this special events competition, remember, was March 14. SIFE staff member Jared Boyd was assigned to handle the NEM entries and, in this role, he recruited three people to judge. Tellingly, all three judges were *young SIFE alumni*, and the entries were judged on March 22. The young judges may have been leaders on their respective SIFE teams a few years earlier, but they were certainly not *business executives* as promised in SIFE's handbook.

For the Kauffman competition, SIFE would list a total of thirty-five teams as being entered into the KEA competition. Though the entries deadline for this special topics competition, remember, was March 7, it was judged after the NEM competition, on March 26. Mat Burton was assigned to handle the judging of this competition, and in this role, he recruited two judges: Professor Tom Lyon of Rockhurst College in Kansas City, and Bev White, a retired staff member of the Kauffman Foundation. Lyon was a lifelong academic who did some consulting for the Kauffman Foundation on the side.

Tom Payne informed me that the profile of special competition judging panels in prior years was similar to the 2003 panels. This upset me. Chico State had won some of these competitions, and now I learned that some of them, at least, had not been taken seriously. Once, in fact, Tom's father, a retired government official, and other retirees, had been recruited at the last minute to be special competition judges. Tom didn't approve of handling special competitions this way, but Rohrs desperately needed judges for the main competition and as a result several special competitions were judged individually by totally unqualified judges.

If Walton Fellows had known about this, there would have been an uproar—and that would have reflected on Alvin Rohrs' executive skills. SIFE was being deceitful with us. No transparency meant no accountability. Rohrs was the man who had been leading SIFE since 1982. When SIFE's board discovered this wrongdoing, would they fire him?

On Friday, May 30, I received a return call from Maggie Kenafake of the Kauffman Foundation. I told her I was the SIFE faculty adviser for the winning team in the Kauffman event last year, and I had a few questions about Kauffman's involvement. She said she'd be happy to answer my questions. She explained Kauffman now only provided facilities to judge the SIFE Special Competition. "SIFE provides its own judges and keeps its own records. We basically support them with the sponsorship money, and provide some judges at the SIFE USA expo, but that's about all."

She told me she could give me more information later. "Let me get in touch with our main contact, Mat Burton, in the next few weeks. Mat handles everything." Once Kenafake called Mat and dropped my name, I was quite sure that he would shit a brick.

A couple days later, on June 2, Jeff Carter sent an email and FedEx package to Rohrs. The email was carbon copied to the thirteen members of SIFE's Executive Committee, including Tom Coughlin, Tom Moser, Bernie Milano, Mike Merriman, Jack Shewmaker, and Jack Kahl. Ken Derucher, our dean of engineering, was also copied. Now that we had proof SIFE mishandled special competition judging, we were obliged to question SIFE's overall judging process. Excerpts of the letter are presented below.

Re: 2002/2003 SIFE Competition Irregularities
Dear Mr. Rohrs:

My client, the CSU, Chico SIFE Program, has asked that I write with respect to its concerns over possible irregularities that may have occurred in this year's special competitions and the SIFE USA National Exposition. Dr. Kenneth N. Derucher, Dean of Chico State's College of Engineering, Computer Science and Technology and former nominee for SIFE's "Dean of the Year," and Dr. Curtis L. DeBerg, Chico State faculty member and director of Chico State's SIFE program, firmly believe that if true and if not addressed immediately and substantially, these competition irregularities will besmirch not only the results of past and future competitions, but also SIFE itself, thus affecting negatively the success and support it has gained in recent years.

There may be a tendency to discount Chico State's concerns as nothing more than "sour grapes," its team having lost to eventual champion Drury University by a very slim margin in the second round at the SIFE USA National Exposition, and not placing in any of the six special competitions in which Chico State entered. Given the Chico team's huge successes in placing first, second or third place nationally in many of SIFE's special competitions since 1994, winning over $50,000.00 in award monies, Chico State would be justified, absent any suggestion of irregularities, in questioning its failure to place in the Top 15 in any of this year's competitions. More will be discussed on this below. However, the possibility that irregularities occurred tainting the results cannot be diminished by the fact that Chico State is the messenger of this information.

Independent of anyone currently employed by SIFE, Chico State has learned that award winners in one certain special competition did not even enter the competition for which they won awards, while at least one other team which had entered was not even considered. I refer to the Kauffman Center Entrepreneurship Assistance competition, in which, Chico State has learned, teams that had not even entered such competition were recipients of awards in the competition. On the other hand, Chico State's SIFE team, which in fact did enter the competition on a timely basis, was not even considered. Obviously, one must question how this occurred and if it did, what effect it had on the entire competition. And, more importantly, did similar irregularities occur in other competitions such as the National Entrepreneurship Month competition? ...

As intimated above, Chico State is concerned that its not being considered in the Kauffman Center Entrepreneurship Assistance competition may have been an intentional slight, and not just a procedural irregularity. It is concerned that friction that has existed and continues to exist between you and its program's director Dr. DeBerg, may have resulted in its being singled out for punitive treatment. Dr. DeBerg has shared with me the difference in opinion between SIFE management and him concerning Chico State's SAGE program that was made public in a Kansas City Star article preceding this year's National Exposition and the fact that despite management's prior lack of interest in the program, it now apparently wishes to explore the possibility of incorporating Chico State's program within the SIFE organization. He also has advised about past conflicts with management over SAGE, including a dispute involving SIFE's public relations campaign and his involvement therein. Coupling these matters with the (summer of 2000 incident) for which I previously communicated with

SIFE, one might reasonably opine that the disparate treatment accorded Chico State's SIFE team in this year's special competition may have resulted from management's differences with Dr. DeBerg.

Chico State is concerned enough about competition irregularities and the possibility of disparate treatment for reasons unrelated to procedural irregularities that Dean Derucher, Dr. DeBerg, and I wish a meeting immediately with you and the chair, vice chair and executive director of the Executive Committee. We are prepared to make arrangements to fly to Springfield at the earliest time such a meeting can be arranged in order to discuss the above with you and the Executive Committee members. It is hoped that with such discussions, Chico State may be assured that immediate and substantial steps will be taken to assure that competition irregularities do not occur in the future and that all competition entrants are treated fairly and accorded the same judging criteria.

Dean Derucher and Dr. DeBerg strongly support SIFE, a fact apparent from Chico State's participation in the SIFE program over past years. They are heartened by SIFE's newfound interest in Chico State's SAGE program and would be more than happy to share the formula for such with SIFE, but only after they can be assured that fundamental principles of due process and fair play are in place for the protection of all SIFE competition entrants in the future. Please let us hear from you immediately with respect to when such a meeting may be scheduled.

Jeff's letter demanded action from SIFE's new board chairman and Wal-Mart heavyweight, Tom Coughlin.

Coughlin jumped into action, with three items at the top of his agenda. First, he hired a special investigator from Tulsa, Oklahoma, Larry Pinkerton, to look into the matter. Second, he asked KPMG's Bernie Milano to head up a special task force to look into SIFE's internal controls. The task force, eventually consisting of seven business leaders from seven board member companies and five Walton fellows, had one primary goal:

to make recommendations to SIFE's management about how to improve internal controls. Third, he insisted that Rohrs obtain a written statement from Mat Burton summarizing his side of the story.

Unlike the incident a few years ago, where I was the only person directly affected by Rohrs' decisions, the special competition fiasco directly involved my students. That made my blood boil even hotter. Furthermore, at the same time he was apparently helping Mat Burton cover up the Kauffman fiasco, Rohrs was going through the motions of asking me to submit a white paper to SIFE's board of directors. As such, he was being forced to *pretend* to be interested in SAGE. Working with an asshole like me on junior SIFE wasn't going to happen, at least if he had anything to say about it.

Two days after Jeff's letter landed in Rohrs' inbox on June 4, Burton penned a one-page, six-paragraph memorandum to Rohrs on SIFE letterhead, explaining what happened. I was able to retrieve this memorandum in September.[5] Given what I already knew about Ohio State, NDSU, and Bethune-Cookman, I read each paragraph very carefully. It proved very insightful, both as to Mat's version of the incident, and to Rohrs' executive management style. Below is the memorandum, with my comments, to each paragraph.

Paragraph 1. "Following is a review of how the entries for the Kauffman Foundation's Entrepreneurship Assistance Special Competition were processed and the mistake that was made. Entries for the Kauffman Competition were due at SIFE World Headquarters on March 7, 2003. As with any special competition, we begin receiving entries a few days before the deadline and usually continue to receive a few for a day or to [sic] after the deadline."

According to the SIFE USA 2002–2003 handbook, "all entries must be received (not postmarked) at SIFE World Headquarters by March 7, 2003." Unless special permission had been granted for extenuating circumstances, any entry received after March 7 was ineligible for Kauffman.

Paragraph 2. "In addition to Kauffman Competition, which rewards teams who did the best job of 'business consulting', we added the SIFE Entrepreneurship Month Special Competition this year. The criteria for this competition are much broader in scope and simply ask the team to develop educational outreach programs that teach others how entrepreneurs succeed. Entries for this competition were due at SIFE World Headquarters on March 14, 2003."

This is factually incorrect, and Burton knew it. The SIFE handbook clearly explained the purpose and criteria for both competitions. Kauffman's purpose was to "educate *entrepreneurs* on how to manage and develop their business more successfully." The other competition was "develop educational outreach projects that teach *others* how entrepreneurs succeed." The projects for Kauffman—targeting existing entrepreneurs—could take place any time during the year; projects for the second competition—targeting others like children, teenagers, other college students—had to be completed during the month of February.

Paragraph 3. "Unfortunately, because of the similarity between the criteria for the two competitions, the close proximity of due dates and the manner in which many of the entries were labeled, a great deal of confusion arose as we began to receive the entries and process them. Many of the competition entries arrived with no cover—in other words, the team did not indicate which competition they entered. In these cases, we had to review each entry to determine which competition criteria the project fit in. In other instances, there was no cover to the entry, but the team referenced the official name of the competition in the body of their written executive summary."

Poor labeling on the part of any entry should have justified elimination; by no means should SIFE staff have had to *guess* at which competition a team was entering. Poor labeling meant a poor entry; the only reasonable thing to do would have been to eliminate the entry. Instead, four SIFE teams managed to get two shots at winning two different competitions with only one entry. In fact, NDSU and Bethune-Cookman, much to Burton's surprise, ended up killing two birds with one stone.

> Paragraph 4. "After spending a great deal of time reviewing the content of so many entries, and given the specific nature of the criteria for the Kauffman Competition (business consulting projects) we noticed that several entries clearly fit the criteria for this competition but were not labeled or were labeled for the National Entrepreneurship Month Competition. Therefore, our initial questions were 'what competition is the team entering', and 'Are they really intending for this entry to be submitted in both competitions?' Initially, our action was limited to simply placing the unlabeled entries that were clearly consulting projects at that we received [*sic*] on or for March 7th in the Kauffman competition."

Other than being a mangled piece of writing, this paragraph indicates that Burton and his staff were making judgments that were harmful to teams that had clearly entered their intended competition, on time. Entries received before March 7 should have gone in the Kauffman stack, and entries received after March 7 should have gone in the other stack or, if poorly labeled, tossed out. If Burton wanted to stretch the rules a bit and remove the ambiguity, a phone call to the Walton Fellow should have been made.

Instead, Burton and his staff "spent a great deal of time reviewing the content of the entries" rather than make three or four calls. Then, after expending such great amounts of time, they *noticed* that several entries *clearly* fit the Kauffman criteria, even though they were labeled for other one, or they were unlabeled. In paragraph two, Burton claims great *confusion* because of *similarity of criteria for the two competitions.* Burton's statement is contradictory. Earlier, he said the criteria are too similar to distinguish, causing him to be confused. But then, after reading the content of the entries, it was clear that the entry was meant for one competition and not the other.

Huh?

Without reading between the lines, it is apparent that Burton was trying to cover up a major mistake—at best—or to make up a story to justify intentional wrongdoing. I had documented proof that Ohio State, NDSU, and Bethune-Cookman specifically state they did not enter Kauffman; rather, they only entered the other one, whose deadline was March 14. Like most teams, the three teams submitted their entries after March 7, but before March 14, making them ineligible for the Kauffman competition. This likely was neither a small inadvertent mistake, nor was it a major fuckup—as Tom Payne told me, it was "a fraud perpetrated on all teams who had legitimately entered the Kauffman competition."

> Paragraph 5. "On the day we were preparing the Kauffman entries to be judged, I was presented with a fresh batch of entries by a staff person who was unsure what competition they belonged to? After addressing this, I decided to revisit the questions and made a quick scan of the executive summaries for the National Entrepreneurship Month Special Competition. I quickly noticed that there were four teams, in which the projects they described were clearly 'business consulting activities.' I added these entries to the others being prepared for judging by the Kauffman Foundation."

What? Somebody presented Burton with a fresh batch of entries? And they are about to be shipped out to the illustrious business leaders on the judge's panel? Did the entries arrive after March 14? Look at the postmark. If so, that would make them ineligible for either competition. If they made it prior to March 14, and now had been suddenly discovered, who found them? Were they hiding under a desk somewhere? If what Burton says is true, we would now see he hired incompetent staff who presented him with a whole new batch of entries long after the deadline. At least he can blame the staff for this mistake.

So what does Burton do after he learns of this new dilemma? He, himself, now steps in to address it. Perhaps he revisited the "questions" (judging criteria?) and made a quick scan of the executive summaries for the other entrepreneurship competition. The clock is ticking. Executives on the judging panel—who we now know are a professor and a retired staff member at Kauffman—are waiting for Burton to deliver the complete batch of entries. Quickly he notices there are four teams that might better qualify for the Kauffman competition. Ever the good guy—he makes an executive decision and saves the day for his harried and beleaguered staff—he adds these entries to Kauffman stack. And off to the Kauffman offices they go!

As they say in Great Britain, this is complete bullocks.

Here is the likely story. Burton sees that there are eighty-one entries for NEM. Not a bad number, he thinks. Too bad this competition isn't sponsored. The NEM entries had been judged four days earlier, on March 22, under Jared Boyd's stewardship.

For each special competition, a SIFE team had to submit *six copies* of a two-page executive summary, along with one bound copy of all relevant documentation. Given that there were only *three judges* for the unsponsored competition, there were three more executive summaries still lying around. Let me see, Burton may have thought, how many entries are there for Kauffman—ah, thirty-one.

Maybe we can just put a few more entries into the Kauffman stack? The final report to Kauffman would look a whole lot better if there were more entries. Well, why not just take a quick look at the executive summaries of the unsponsored NEM competition, and see if they might fit the KEA competition? It would really be nice if they didn't refer to the NEM in the executive summary. Ah, this one looks pretty good. And there's another. Here's two more. Let's just put them in the Kauffman stack. No one will ever have to know that these entries have been handpicked and put in the Kauffman pile. The two KEA judges—the good professor from Rockhurst College and the kind retiree from Kauffman—won't know the difference. Educating entrepreneurs, or educating others—same thing.

If my scenario is correct, one thing Burton didn't think of, though, was, what if any of these teams win and the Sam M. Walton Fellow tells Tom Payne about it? And what if Tom does his own little investigation?

Shortly after Tom learned there was something awry, he sent Gail Beutler a lengthy email on April 12 describing the issue. He suggested that she help arrange a meeting with Rohrs so a proactive course of action could be taken. Rohrs agreed to meet with Tom a few days later, where Rohrs assured him that corrective action would be taken before the SIFE USA national competition on May 11–13, 2003, to be held a few months after the special competitions ended. Tom suggested that Rohrs acknowledge the problem and admit the error to all affected teams.

The only corrective action that I know of was to award Northeastern State University an additional $1,000. Later, SIFE would claim that an additional four schools were awarded $500 for the KEA competition. I don't know if Graceland ever got its extra $1,000, moving up from third to second place. Tom would say later, "I was literally stunned that no other action was contemplated."

But back to Mat Burton. If Tom was unhappy with the way SIFE treated the situation, what would happen if Tom called his buddy from Chico? And what if Chico's adviser discovered that his team's entry never got judged, even when it played by the rules? Burton probably didn't think of that.

Two questions nagged at me now. First, if SIFE—Mat Burton and Alvin Rohrs, in particular—believed they could make a decision to enter a team for a competition it hadn't intended to enter, how unreasonable was it for me to believe they could have reviewed the content of an entry, like ours, and decided that it shouldn't be judged? Our SAGE project was a significant part of our Kauffman entry. We were assisting teenage entrepreneurs with how to manage and develop their businesses successfully, and our entry was a perfect fit for this competition.

Second, now that I knew Burton had reviewed the content of specific entries and decided to enter some teams in two competitions, this cast a shadow over the entire judging process—not just the special competitions, but the overall competition, too. To what lengths would SIFE go to justify rewarding one team at the expense of another, especially if the penalized team was led by an asshole from California?

Chapter 15

Lawyering Up, Encore

The same day Alvin Rohrs had called me about SAGE and asked me to write a white paper describing how I thought SIFE could benefit by endorsing SAGE as an official SIFE initiative, he was featured in the May 23, 2003, *Springfield News-Leader*. Karen Culp's column, "Ozarks Influential," spotlighted local community leaders. One of the questions she asked Rohrs was what he would do with an extra hour each day. Rohrs replied, "I'd focus more on writing thank-you notes. I'm way behind on my thank-you notes."[1]

After Jeff Carter's June 2 letter, Rohrs wouldn't be finding much time to catch up on his thank-you notes for a while. Instead, he'd be cleaning up Mat Burton's mess and doing his best to keep Tom Coughlin happy. Coughlin, second in command at Wal-Mart, was now the chairman of SIFE's board of directors. Bethany Moreton, author of *To Serve God and Wal-Mart*, reported that by 2003, Wal-Mart "hired 35 percent of its management trainees out of SIFE."[2]

On June 3, Tom Payne and I had another conversation. He told me SIFE had found the FedEx documentation that I had sent. SIFE received two packages from me. The first one was a big one, received by SIFE on March 12. The package contained the Kauffman Entrepreneurship Assistance entry, the AT&T entry, and the Judy Sitton nomination. The second one was received by SIFE on March 14, and it contained the unsponsored National Entrepreneurship Month entry.

Tom said, "The burden of proof will be on you to prove that the Kauffman entry was in one of the packages." If I couldn't prove this, SIFE could simply claim that I hadn't included the entry, or that mistakes may have been made on their part, but with no admission of fraud or dishonesty.

Tom told me he had been up all night pulling material from old emails. Having notified me about the special competition mess, he was clearly afraid of losing his job, and he wanted to collect as much evidence to support his cause. "I may need to bring Bernie Milano in on this to get some audits done," he said. Milano was a member of SIFE's board and was also the director of the KPMG Foundation.

"How are Rohrs and Burton reacting to this?" I asked.

"Alvin's smug, and Mat is cock-sure and confident that everything's going to be okay," he replied.

The next day, Burton wrote his June 4 memorandum explaining his version of the special competition judging fiasco. Coughlin was making arrangements for a hotshot litigation attorney from Tulsa, Oklahoma, to conduct a special investigation. If Chico State's claims could be proven, SIFE might find itself on the defendant's end of a big lawsuit.

Coughlin was an expert in security, having been Wal-Mart's director of loss prevention when he first joined the company, long before he had been promoted to his current position as vice chairman of the entire Wal-Mart organization. No matter what the investigation might yield, however, it was clear that the SIFE board had to become more involved in making sure Rohrs did some housecleaning.

On June 12, Jeff Carter received an email from Janet Rusch, Tom Coughlin's assistant. She informed Carter that Coughlin "felt it wise to hire an independent look at the concerns you've expressed. He is hiring someone outside the organization to review the concerns and allegations and will get back to you as soon as possible."

Coughlin hired Laurence L. "Larry" Pinkerton, who received his law degree in 1976 from Columbia Law School. One of his claims to fame at Columbia was to win the Greenbaum Prize in 1976. The prize is awarded annually to the student who has made the best oral presentation in the final argument of a moot court competition. The chairman of the panel of judges making the award to Pinkerton was Thurgood Marshall, associate justice of the U.S. Supreme Court.[3]

Pinkerton and his partner in Tulsa, Judith A. Finn, specialized in litigation services. According to their website, Pinkerton & Finn "are referred by other attorneys when it becomes clear that the case requires resolution through litigation. Through years of experience, Pinkerton & Finn, P.C.

is familiar with the many reasons, both legal and practical, that compel attorneys to refer cases that are headed to trial." Coughlin saw that Jeff's letter might well lead to litigation, so he hired Pinkerton to conduct a special investigation.

As Pinkerton was beginning his investigation and preparing to make a trip to Springfield, I was continuing with my own investigation. On June 11, I had a phone conversation with Grant Alexander, the first-year Walton Fellow at Northeastern Oklahoma State University. Recall that his team had originally been among the fifteen finalists in the Kauffman competition, but hadn't made the top three. Among the top three was the team from North Dakota State, whose entry Mat Burton had graciously included in the Kauffman pool, though it had entered the other competition.

After a bit of chit-chat, I asked, "Has SIFE been in touch with you at all about the Kauffman competition?"

"Ah, yeah," Alexander said. "Where you goin' on this?"

I told him that I was aware of some irregularities with the Kauffman contest.

"There apparently was some confusion about who entered which competition," he said. "According to Mat Burton, there were eighteen finalists instead of fifteen. Mat called me up after the Kansas City expo and explained that there were the 'original' fifteen finalists, but he added three more finalists. And somehow one of these three special finalists made it in the top three, so SIFE took it upon themselves to set matters right by awarding our team a third place finish."

I asked him if he was happy with this explanation.

"My kids are happy they were in the top three, so I guess, yeah, we were pretty happy with the fact that we won," he replied.

Then I asked if he would be troubled by the fact that some teams entered one competition, but were given prize money for another.

"Curt, I think SIFE has quite adequately explained the situation," Alexander said, a bit defensively. "Mat indicated that SIFE would make sure the three original finalists who were bumped by the three added finalists would be taken care of."

I then informed him that I was certain there were more than three additional finalists added by Mat.

Alexander took a deep breath. "Are you sure?"

No doubt about it.

Burton hadn't been honest again—stretching the truth was becoming a habit. He had included *at least* four entries, not three, from the non-sponsored entrepreneurship competition. There was no telling how many more entries he added that didn't make it into the Top 15 finalists. Also, he had told me in a May 20, 2003, email that "we often receive more than one hundred entries in each special competition."

This was stretching it, too. Later, I obtained a complete list of entrants to every competition. Only two special competitions had over a hundred entries—117 entries were received for the National Ethics Month Competition and 101 for the National Financial Independence Month. Neither of these was sponsored.

Only thirty-six entries were received for the National Free Markets Month, eighteen for AT&T Best Use of Internet (Teaching students in grades K-12), fifteen for the Polsky investing competition, and nine for the AT&T Best Use of Internet (Teaching business owners e-Commerce). A total of eighty-one entries were submitted for the National Entrepreneurship Month and only thirty-five for the Kauffman contest, if one counts the four entries submitted to the other competition.

Soon after he hired Pinkerton, Coughlin commissioned fellow board member Bernie Milano to serve as chair of a special task force. Milano already had a heads-up that something was awry at SIFE headquarters, because Tom Payne had contacted him a week or so earlier and let him know about the special competition problems. Milano called me on June 14 to let me know he was heading up the task force to investigate SIFE's internal controls. This task force was prompted by Chico State's allegation of improprieties.

On a separate note, Milano told me that he would also be serving on a "steering committee" of SIFE board members looking into SIFE's possible collaborations with high school organizations, including SAGE. Six board members would serve on this committee, he said, and they were planning to meet in Cleveland on June 25. Mike Merriman, he said, would be the chairman.

Shit, things were getting complicated. Three things were happening simultaneously: the Pinkerton investigation, the Milano task force, and the Merriman steering committee. Before I learned about the special competition mess, Rohrs was getting pressure from his board to look into SAGE. Now that SIFE's Executive Committee had been put on notice that there were serious problems with the special competitions, the board had no choice but to be extra nice to me.

A potential lawsuit was hovering. On one hand, I was viewed by some board members as an innovative maverick. On the other, I was viewed as someone who could sue SIFE for big money. But there's no doubt how I was viewed by Rohrs as the non-eating end of a horse.

Milano quickly got to work and created a twelve-member force, which included seven business executives and five Sam M. Walton Fellows. One of the Walton Fellows was my good friend, Al Konuwa, of Butte College. The task force was formally named The Rules, Policies and Procedures Task Force.

On June 26, Milano sent the following email to 960 Sam Walton Fellows acknowledging a SIFE "glitch."

> The Executive Committee of SIFE is forming an independent task force to take a fresh look at all competition policies, rules, and procedures. I have been asked to chair the task force and am reaching out to you for your input. Members of the Task Force will include members of the SIFE Board of Directors and Sam Walton Fellows to be identified by the board members on the Task Force
>
> Why are we doing this? SIFE has experienced incredible growth and with that growth has become increased complexity caused by more regional competitions, more teams and therefore more leagues per region, more teams in Kansas City, more special competitions with more submissions for each, and of course, the World Cup.
>
> Why are we doing this now? As some of you know, we had a "glitch" in one of our special competition's judging this year and while we subsequently resolved the problem, it caused some

concern about our processes. We were able to overcome this one but we want to be certain we take steps to try to avoid problems going forward.

This is where we need your help. Please take a look at the *SIFE Handbook* from this past year and, if you identify areas you believe need to be addressed, please highlight those and your recommended changes/additions in an email to me. I will acknowledge your email and include your input into the task force deliberations.

SIFE is an incredible organization thanks in large part to your leadership. I hope you will take the time to help us in this Task Force effort.

Glitch? To me, a glitch is a quirk, or a bug, or a slight imperfection. What had been done was certainly not a glitch. At least four teams had gotten screwed out of prize money and recognition, while three teams accepted an award rightfully belonging to someone else (the team from Bethune-Cookman did not cash the check, on principle). And now Milano told the Walton Fellows that the problem had been overcome? Maybe all was well with Milano, but the matter was far from settled with Jeff Carter and me.

Milano was a perfect candidate to lead the task force—KPMG was among the Big 4 international accounting firms. Milano's selection of seven SIFE board members to serve on his committee included heavy hitters in the retail industry.[4] In appointing Milano to head the task force and hiring Pinkerton to conduct an independent investigation, Tom Coughlin appeared to be taking Chico State's charges very seriously. Like it or not, Rohrs would have some explaining to do at the next board meeting in August.

Milano had been the former chairman of a student organization called the Golden Key International Honor Society, and he must have seen some similarities between Golden Key's and SIFE's management. Golden Key's former CEO, James W. Lewis, had been fired two years earlier for a long list of improprieties. Included among them were padding the profits and size of the organization by accepting ineligible students, improper sexual relationships with students and interns, and creating a culture of intimidation that pervaded Golden Key's headquarters in Atlanta. On July 17, 2003, Milano sent his task force an email containing a March 22, 2002, article detailing Lewis' story. At the top of the email, Milano wrote, "A few years ago this story made the front page of the *Chronicle of Higher Education* with a picture of a student in a cap and gown with DISHONOR SOCIETY as the headline. I hope you'll take the time to read it."[5]

Golden Key was remarkably similar to SIFE in many ways—its budget in 2002 was $10.9 million. Founded in the mid-'70s, Golden Key received much of its revenue from corporations who paid at least $50,000 to serve on its board. In turn, the companies gained unique access to outstanding students.

Similarly, a seat on SIFE's board cost $25,000, and SIFE's revenues were generated almost entirely from corporate donations, totaling just under $4 million in 1998 to over $9 million in 2003. CEO pay was similar, too. In 1999, Lewis earned nearly $300,000 in compensation, a salary almost unheard of in the nonprofit world. Rohrs, by comparison, earned $238,000 in compensation plus $48,000 in benefits in 1999.

It was obvious why Milano wanted to share the Golden Key story with the task force. First, Lewis' ego apparently got the best of him. The article said, "But what's not visible on the Golden Key Web site is that Mr. Lewis has been forced out, amid criticism that the business he started in his parents' house was becoming a nonprofit empire in his own image."

One former board member, who had been president of Tufts University, said, "The leadership had been in place since its inception and had become comfortable. They were engaged in things to perpetuate themselves. People thought they were building an empire."

Another detail involved conferences conducted by Golden Key—they sounded a lot like SIFE's expositions. The article reported, "Students flocked to regional and international conferences—lavish affairs that combined elements of a Tom Peters leadership seminar with a heavy dose of corporate schmoozing and production values worthy of the MTV generation."

Milano himself was quoted in the article as saying, "They were among the best conferences I've seen anywhere, and I've been to many. They had everything just right: the lighting, the balloons, the pomp as each chapter was announced, school by school." This sounded exactly like the SIFE expositions I had seen in Kansas City the past ten years.

The Golden Key story, like SIFE's situation now with Tom Payne, also involved a whistleblower. A Golden Key insider had sent several board members an anonymous letter in 1998 warning them that Lewis had been fudging numbers in order to raise more money. One former director said, "Even though it was a nonprofit, there was a lot of emphasis on making money, on getting more and more people to join. The attitude was, 'Let's see how far we can push this without driving people up the wall.'"

Amid growing criticism, Lewis ended up stepping down as chairman of his own board in January 2000 but remained as executive director. The new chairman ordered an investigation into Lewis' history, with interviews of current and former employees. Finally, in summer of 2001, Lewis was completely ousted. Near the end of the *Chronicle* article, Milano was quoted again, "Jim poured 100 percent of his heart into the place. But at some point, the ego got bigger than the organization."

By sending the SIFE task force this email, it appeared that Milano was preparing its members—and SIFE's board—for the possibility that Rohrs might have to go.

As Milano was organizing the rules task force in late June, Larry Pinkerton made a trip to Springfield to interview everyone involved in the special competition snafu. Among those interviewed, of course, was Tom Payne. After the interview, Tom submitted a written memo to Pinkerton on July 3, under the subject: "Rebuttal of arguments of Mat Burton & Alvin Rohrs."

The rebuttal included Tom's assertion—supported by evidence—that five of the eight special competitions had not been judged by business leaders; instead, they had been judged by a combination of young SIFE alumni, non-SIFE faculty, and retired staff members of sponsoring organizations.

Tom also blasted Burton in the rebuttal. "By taking entries clearly labeled for one competition and submitting them to both the Kauffman and National Entrepreneurship Month competitions, Mat acted unprofessionally, unethically, and committed fraud on our stakeholders (specifically students, faculty, and the Kauffman Foundation). ... Mat's action has tarnished and put SIFE in jeopardy. A mass email from an affected faculty member or, worse, an administrator, could prove catastrophic."

Why didn't Rohrs simply fire Tom Payne? After all, Tom had supported me in the summer of 2000, and now he stood in my corner with the special competitions. The answer: Rohrs simply could not do so at this point. First of all, Tom was well thought of with the key players on the board, including Shewmaker, Kahl, Milano, Tom Moser, and Gene Bicknell, a successful entrepreneur from Pittsburg, Kansas. Bicknell made it big in the pizza business. Also, Tom Payne had recruited quite a few influential board members, including Tom Hopkins, senior vice president of Sherwin-Williams and Tom Kroeger, executive vice president at Office Depot. Plus, many of Tom's former students at Pittsburg State were making a name for themselves with board level companies, including Kahl's duct-tape company in Cleveland, Manco, and Wal-Mart. These students were loyal to Tom.

Only after our letter—the one Jeff Carter mailed to Alvin Rohrs on June 2—did SIFE select a corrective course of action by agreeing to pay an additional three colleges a $500 finalist prize for the Kauffman competition. The official reason given to these schools for the unexpected prize money was that SIFE had made an inadvertent mistake. This mistake was now referred to by Milano's task force as a "glitch."

As for the Chico State entry into the Kauffman competition, Tom told Pinkerton, "I don't know how to read Cal-Chico's SAGE Kauffman entry. Based on the weight of the overnight packages (FedEx) per Dr. DeBerg—I believe that it is entirely possible that (a) Cal-Chico's entry was lost or (b) sabotaged. Alvin and Mat have been vocal opponents of SAGE and Curt DeBerg. The personal animosity between Alvin and Curt has become very dangerous—to SIFE. Judgments have become clouded on both sides. I believe the Executive Committee must mediate this dispute."

Soon after Pinkerton interviewed the SIFE associates in Springfield, he flew to California to meet with Jeff, Ken Derucher, and me at Jeff's office in downtown Chico. Now in his mid-fifties, Pinkerton was impeccably dressed and professional. We spent about three hours in Jeff's conference room. Of special interest to him were the specific contents of the box that had been overnight-mailed to SIFE on March 11.

Also of interest to him was our claim that some SIFE teams appeared to have been improperly coached during question and answer periods during the regular competitions, violating competition rules. Since we were on the offensive with SIFE with respect to special competitions, we figured we might as well air some criticisms with respect to the overall competition judging process. Kurt Cobain again.

There was no doubt SIFE had received the box. I retrieved the tracking slip and invoice number showing it was picked up by FedEx on March 11, and delivered to SIFE at 9:51 a.m. on March 12, signed by M. Sparkman of SIFE. The box weighed exactly 14 pounds.

"Did you have backup copies of the entire contents?" Pinkerton asked.

"No, sorry, I only have copies of the executive summaries of the two entries," I said. "But I can do my best to recreate the contents of the two three-ring binders, along with Judy Sitton's nomination."

I sent him a big box a couple days after he returned to Tulsa.

A few days later, Pinkerton called and asked me what actions Chico State would like to see taken by SIFE if his investigation established that, in fact, irregularities existed in the 2002/2003 special and overall competitions. Ken Derucher and I met with Jeff on July 24, and Jeff sent Pinkerton a letter the next day with a long list.

First, we insisted that there be no retaliation against Tom. Second, we insisted that SIFE implement a new set of internal controls and safeguards, including rules and regulations for the various competitions. The Milano task force addressed this. Third, we informed that Walton Fellows had long been treated as far-removed relatives of SIFE, despite their being on the ground where the rubber meets the road in the interface between SIFE and the colleges and universities which participate in its programs and competitions. To this end, we asked that two voting memberships on the Executive Committee of the board of directors of SIFE be provided to two Walton Fellows, to serve in staggered two-year terms.

The fourth request was for SIFE to write a letter, approved by the Executive Committee of the board of directors of SIFE, and send it to all college and university teams which participated in the special and USA National Exposition competitions advising them that irregularities occurred in the competitions that may have affected the outcomes of the competitions.

The fifth said, "Chico State believes that by act or omission it was subjected to unfair treatment in the 2002/2003 special and USA National Exposition competitions. These competitions mark the culmination of the Chico State SIFE team's program for the year, and its success or failure in them serves as a gauge of the success, or failure, of the entire program. If Chico State was treated unfairly, as we think it was, Chico State asks that it be reimbursed its 2002/2003 program costs and expenditures totaling approximately $115,000, thus restoring it to the position it was in before participating in the 2002/2003 SIFE program, flawed as it was by the competition irregularities." We also asked that we be reimbursed for our attorney's fees.

The letter was great, I thought, but Jeff warned me that it was unfortunate I hadn't kept exact replicas of the package that I had sent to SIFE on March 11. My failure to do that would likely lead SIFE to claim that I couldn't prove that they had intentionally removed our Kauffman entry. Further, Jeff said, they would likely argue that Mat Burton's handling of the special competition entries was not intentional but, rather, a serious lack of judgment.

Pinkerton told us he would be meeting with SIFE's Executive Committee in late August, and that he would get back in touch with us then.

In the meantime, Mike Merriman, former chairman of SIFE's board of directors, and current CEO of Royal Appliance/Dirt Devil, had begun his work as chair of the special task force dealing with high schools. This is the task force Rohrs referred to when we had last spoken at the end of May.

My hunch was that even though Tom Coughlin, as current SIFE board chairman, was busy appointing Milano's task force and overseeing the Pinkerton investigation, another board member was silently watching from his perch far above the fray. I wondered how much Jack Shewmaker might have been involved, maybe even calling the shots. Merriman, recall, had been the board chair during the alleged incident three years earlier, and Shewmaker knew that Merriman and I respected each other. No matter what Shewmaker thought about SAGE now, he had to mollify me as a potential litigant against SIFE.

Joining Merriman on the steering committee looking into possible high school partnerships were Milano and Tom Moser. As with Merriman, I had a good relationship with the two KPMG executives. Also serving on the committee were duct tape maestro, Jack Kahl of Manco; Ron LeMay, CEO of Sprint; and Joel Connor, CEO of Michelina's.

Everyone on SIFE's board knew SIFE was Jack Shewmaker's baby, and he and Rohrs had known each other for almost twenty years. The high school task force was an extremely delicate matter. Its members were now having to deal with me—and SAGE—at the same time that I was threatening a lawsuit against Rohrs and SIFE. By extension, the lawsuit could ultimately, and quite possibly, be aimed at them.

All six members of the high school task force were members of the inner circle of SIFE's Executive Committee. Each of them had received Jeff Carter's letter. The letter, in turn, prompted Coughlin to hire a special investigator and to appoint Milano to head up the rules special task force. And now, with Jeff's letter to Pinkerton on July 24, members of the high school task force knew that litigation was a real possibility.

If Tom Payne hadn't been in touch a couple months earlier, Alvin Rohrs could easily have swept the incident with Mat Burton quietly under the rug. But damn! Tom had blown the whistle, and now the shit was hitting the fan. Up until now, Shewmaker and the board had let Rohrs call pretty much all the shots at SIFE. As long as he continued to expand the program domestically and globally, the board was happy. But now, with the threat of pending litigation, things were different.

Just a few weeks ago, Rohrs was flying high. He, along with his sidekick Bruce Nasby, were raking in the cash for SIFE with very little accountability to board members and zero accountability with Walton Fellows. They were easily recruiting new donor companies to write $25,000 checks, and plans were well under way to host the third annual SIFE World Cup in Mainz, Germany. Everything was going swimmingly well until June 2, when Rohrs received the email letter from Jeff.

Ever since the 2000 legal incident was settled three years ago, my influence with SIFE's board had been neutralized. But SAGE's success had kept me on the board's radar, and as much as Rohrs wished I would go away, I remained a pesky little pain in the ass, and before Tom blew the whistle, SAGE was a pesky little sideshow.

Rohrs was confident his argument—SAGE might harm the SIFE

brand—would hold up with the board's most powerful members. Rohrs' request for my SAGE white paper was merely a formality to appease a few other board members, like Mike Merriman. So, between July 25 and August 12, I turned my attention to writing the SAGE white paper presenting my argument for why SIFE should embrace SAGE. Merriman invited me to come to Cleveland on August 13 to present my case to his steering committee, with SIFE picking up the tab. I doubted the trip would have any value, but with Jeff's letter sitting on the desk of every one of SIFE's Executive Committee members, the invitation to Cleveland was just one way for them to try to placate me.

On Wednesday, August 13, I boarded a plane for Cleveland. That night, I had a pleasant dinner at the hotel and reviewed my notes. The next day, I woke up refreshed and ready.

I gave each task force member a small three-ring binder and worked from a one-page summary entitled, "Why SIFE Should Endorse SAGE." Service learning and mentoring were at the top of the list. Included in the binder were emails from countries like Poland, Brazil, Philippines, Chile, South Africa, and Australia, all putting in a good word for SAGE. For example, John Thornton, SIFE Australia's country coordinator, said, "I admire your initiative and would be very glad to take an active role in running a 'pilot' Australia SAGE program."

The steering committee was kind. Joel Conner said, "You've obviously put a lot of thought into this." Jack Kahl added, "SAGE is really like a farm team in baseball. As the students get older, they can move up to the SIFE big leagues."

I had a good feeling about the meeting. As I was leaving, Mike Merriman said someone from the committee would be in touch soon.

Right after my scheduled time slot, the committee had asked Burton and Rohrs to make their own presentation, explaining why SIFE should *not* enter into a formal relationship with any high school organization. As I was leaving, Rohrs and Burton were waiting outside. Shaking hands with them was not easy, but it had to be done. Board members were present, and I was determined to remain professional.

Later that afternoon, about four o'clock, I was about to board my plane for home. That's when the famous Northeast blackout of 2003 hit Northeastern and Midwestern states and Ontario, Canada. It was the second most widespread blackout in history. I checked into my hotel just about 7 p.m., and a couple hours later, as the sun set, everything became eerily dark and quiet. The hotel had already given out all of its spare flashlights, and before long my room was totally dark.

With no light, TV, or air conditioning, I found it hard to sleep. The room was stuffy, so I went for a little walk around the hotel, able to see only by the faint emergency lights powered by backup generators.

Serendipitously, the next morning I bumped into Burton in the lobby as Rohrs was sawing logs on a lobby couch. "Fancy meeting you here," I said.

"Hey, Curt, I just want to tell you that the special competition mix-up was just that. It was a simple mistake. There was never any intention on our part to manipulate the results," he said, somewhat pleadingly.

Giving no ground, I looked him straight in the eye. "I know the story, Mat," I said. "And I know that what you're saying isn't true. There was intentional manipulation of special competition results."

Unaccustomed to such directness, he was caught off guard. Then, he sputtered, "You're wrong. You are dead wrong!" Then, raising his voice, "And if you keep spreading the word that SIFE somehow cheated, I will bring you down. You don't know how much influence I have. I can put your career in jeopardy."

True colors coming out?

"You don't scare me, buddy," I said. "Where I work, I'm encouraged to express my views."

He skittered away.

A little while later, as I was leaving the hotel to catch a cab, I veered over to the couch where Rohrs was sleeping. He was still snoring like a baby. I fought the urge to wake him up and tell him what I had told Burton. No worries, though; Burton would probably relay our conversation to the boss.

Milano and Moser set up a conference call with me a few weeks later. At the outset of the conversation, Moser commented that the formation of a high school task force was a huge positive step, and that SIFE's Executive Committee had made this a strategic priority. He then brought up the upcoming World Cup, to take place the next month in Mainz, Germany. Like Amsterdam last year, I was planning to bring a Chico State SIFE group to conduct another SAGE workshop.

Milano advised me not to aggressively promote SAGE in Germany. He said that it wouldn't be advisable for any high school organization, like Junior Achievement, to be promoting its program at another organization's event. Instead, he suggested I try to take part in the SIFE country coordinators' meeting immediately before or after the event.

Knowing how Bruce Nasby felt about SAGE, I knew there was no way that he'd allow me to participate in such a meeting.

"I think we are going to go ahead to do a workshop," I told them. "Rest assured, though, it won't take place during the World Cup nor will it take place at the competition hotel. A lot of countries have expressed interest in learning more about SAGE, and they want us to go forward with this."

Milano had made an analogy to Junior Achievement, so I countered with an analogy to a typical academic conference. "It's very common at such conferences to hold preliminary programs for registrants to learn more about best practices or to attend continuing education classes," I said. "In a similar vein, our workshop makes perfect sense."

Moser then chimed in. He asked that I put aside issues regarding my relationship with Alvin Rohrs, and that it would be in everyone's best interest if we could keep the "tension down."

"The differences between Alvin and me cannot simply be chalked up to personality differences," I countered. "It's a matter of ethics. SIFE's own code of conduct indicates that all participants should demonstrate honesty and integrity. Based on our own findings and, we believe, corroborated by the Pinkerton investigation, we have evidence that SIFE has failed to live up to this standard."

I told Milano and Moser that I, for one, had a difficult time serving in an organization that is led—front and center—by a CEO who has attempted to cover up a situation that unfairly gives preference to some teams, and by intention or omission, punishes others.

"Other Walton Fellows would find this very difficult to accept," I concluded. "As would SIFE students, board members, and others who insist on teaching our students that ethical behavior is always expected without compromise."

Four days later, on September 15, Pinkerton sent us a letter. Jeff's prediction was dead-on. Bad news.

As for the Chico State entry into the Kauffman competition, he wrote, "I have not found a 'smoking gun' that points to individual or group of individuals intentionally removing an entry. While Alvin Rohrs has personally indicated in the past that SAGE was not a direction that SIFE wished to go, his long period of service and other personal attributes, do not lead the Executive Committee to conclude that Alvin personally, or with others, acted to remove an entry from Chico State."

Okay, so the board let Rohrs off the hook here.

Pinkerton continued, "The Executive Committee has asked me to express to you its deepest regret that any entry received was apparently misplaced. A similar occurrence has not been reported, but errors can happen, and that appears to be the case in this circumstance. To avert future occurrences of this kind, new procedures will be implemented at SIFE."

He then referred to Milano's task force on internal controls, and said that the task force had developed draft recommendations, soon to be reviewed by the Executive Committee. Nowhere in his letter did Pinkerton mention Burton's placement of North Dakota State, Ohio State, or Montgomery College entries into the Kauffman competition.

However, Bethune-Cookman was mentioned as "one school entered erroneously by Burton" in the Kauffman competition. Pinkerton had contacted William Ziegler, who reported to him that, in the prior year, his school had won a prize and trophy but SIFE had not sent him any money or a trophy. But Burton had proven to Pinkerton that Ziegler was wrong about last year, which led Pinkerton to conclude, "I spoke to Ziegler and other than this possible issue, he was very pleased with SIFE."

Again, Pinkerton let Rohrs off the hook here, and Burton, too. Burton had made an "error."

As for SAGE, Pinkerton referred to the high school task force. He noted that Merriman had invited me to make a presentation about SAGE at the task force's meeting in Cleveland. The Executive Committee, he said, had discussed preliminary recommendations of the task force at its meeting.

They would extend an invitation to me to participate in the on-going process of developing SIFE's approach.

What? This was clearly SIFE's blow-off to SAGE. How could I participate in the on-going process now? I doubted Bruce Nasby would let me near his SIFE country coordinators at any SIFE events. And unless the Executive Committee mandated that Rohrs work with me, Rohrs was certain to quash it.

Pinkerton's letter was like a stick in the eye, and it concluded with kick to the groin.

Pinkerton ended by writing, "I hope the above resolves the questions that have been raised, and presents a satisfactory solution so that the SIFE team at Chico can move forward with the same great vigor and enthusiasm that it has had in the past."

Deflated, Ken Derucher and I asked Jeff how we might proceed. "Well, let's sit on this for a little while, and then we'll send him a letter." Jeff didn't look too optimistic.

Two weeks later, on September 30, we wrote back:

Dear Larry:

Dean Kenneth Derucher, Curt DeBerg and I have reviewed and discussed your September 15, 2003 letter in which you summarize the results of your investigation. We are saddened.

We feel that your investigation clearly established the programmatic deficiencies that we called to your attention last spring. Indeed, we have independently verified that an employee of SIFE took at least four submittals clearly labeled National Entrepreneurship Month Special Competition and despite their labeling, submitted these to the Kauffman Entrepreneurial Assistance Special Competition. In reporting to his or her superior, the employee justified his or her action claiming that because of the similarities in the competitions and the close proximity of their respective due dates, the employee justified his or her action claiming that because of the similarities in the competitions and the close proximity of their respective due dates, the employee was confused and made a mistake in processing them. The employee then admits that "I made a mistake in judgment," not in submitting the NEM applications to the KEA competition, but in failing to call the Sam Walton Fellows and the institutions involved in explaining the situation."

We find it hard to believe that the employee, an upper level manager of SIFE, could be so disingenuous in seeking to justify his or her actions in submitting applications clearly for one competition not only in the competition for which they were intended but in another, completely different competition. The two competitions were not similar. The NEM competition judges outreach projects intended to teach how entrepreneurs succeed. The KEA competition judges programs intended to teach how to better manage and develop businesses.

Assuming arguendo that a SIFE employee could be confused as to which competition an application was being submitted, the filing deadlines for the applications should have been the end of the argument. KEA applications were due March 7, 2003 and unless an extension had been granted to a particular applicant, applications received after March 7, 2003 were not timely. The NEM competition deadline was March 14, 2003, and applications received after March 7, 2003 but on or before March 14, 2003, logically could have been presumed to have been submitted to NEM, and not KEA.

We felt, and hoped, that SIFE, a body educating the next generation of business leaders in the world, would exemplify its Code of Ethics, so much that it would have endeavored to avoid even the appearance of impropriety. Instead, it appears from your letter that SIFE not only accepts the appearance of impropriety, but the actual impropriety, justifying in at least two instances on the basis that the affected institutions are "pleased with SIFE." One would be hard pressed, we presume, to find an institution that was not "pleased" with winning an award in a competition it did not enter. What lesson is SIFE teaching our future business leaders about corporate responsibility?

Chico State is at least heartened that SIFE has taken some

steps to cure the programmatic deficiencies. We wonder, however, if these are not "too little, too late." Chico State is now considering its options in light of SIFE's surprisingly tepid response to gross negligence, if not willful wrongdoing, of its staff.

After faxing the letter to Pinkerton, Jeff asked me how much longer I wanted to fight. Deep sigh.

Three years ago, Alvin Rohrs tried to get me to leave SIFE or, at the very least, to neuter my growing influence with board members like Jack Shewmaker. And now, three years later, he had stood by silently as Mat Burton's "glitch" screwed over SIFE teams that believed they were getting a fair shake in the Kauffman special competition.

I was angry. Hell, by error or intention, Chico State's entry never even made into the hopper! And to top it all off, the majority of these competitions were judged primarily by recent SIFE alumni—certainly not by a panel of business leaders.

All told, such deceit should have been enough to get Burton fired, at a minimum, with Rohrs collecting the next pink slip. But Jack Shewmaker and Alvin Rohrs went back a long way, and Shewmaker's silence was deafening.

Al Konuwa told me Bernie Milano's internal control task force was going to issue its final report after Rohrs and SIFE had a chance to respond to its recommendations. Al said that he would send me a copy when it was finished, which was likely to be in December. I fully expected Chico State's influence to be alive and well in the finished document.

By now, the fall 2003 semester was under way, and once again I had another outstanding group of Chico State SIFE students. It would have been easy for me to throw in the towel with SIFE; in fact, some people, like Craig, thought I was crazy for staying with SIFE.

Fool me once, shame on you. Fool me twice, shame on me. So did I quit?

Nope. I booked a flight to Mainz, Germany, to conduct another workshop.

This time, I would be bringing three Chico State SIFE students with me. My SIFE team loved SAGE, and by God and Allah and the Great Wise One, we were going to expand our SAGE social network on the river Rhine.

Chapter 16

Love on the Rhine River

===============

Almost all Chico State students who have participated in SIFE over the years have genuinely valued—and benefited from—their experience. And most of our community outreach activities have been successful, too. I knew this from the appreciation I received from local schools, the juvenile hall, President Manuel Esteban, and the Chico Chamber of Commerce. In SIFE, my Chico State students found an organization that welcomed them, no matter their major, GPA, ethnicity, religion, or age. Students increased their project management, leadership, teamwork, and communication skills. SIFE's mission was noble, but some of the people who ran the home office in Springfield were—less so. Servant leaders? More like self-servant leaders. Pardon my cynicism.

The special competition ordeal put me in a whole new frame of mind. My run as a Walton Fellow was coming to an end. For the short term, though, I decided to stay a little while longer. Returning Chico State SIFE students knew I had issues with SIFE management, but they asked me to please remain as their adviser. Together, they said, we could continue to grow SAGE. So I agreed to stay. I would never trust the SIFE organization to do the right thing—at least while Alvin Rohrs remained as Jack Shewmaker's anointed one. I still saw it as a tool to promote service learning for university students and to promote commercial as well as social entrepreneurship. Social entrepreneurship was gaining popularity in leading business schools throughout the U.S., and SAGE was one of the first programs to introduce this at the high school level. In short, I could still use SIFE as a lever to advance SAGE.

I had a bitter taste from my direct personal experiences with Alvin Rohrs, Bruce Nasby, and now, Mat Burton. After reading Larry Pinkerton's final report informing us that we had no smoking gun to sue SIFE for the special competition *glitch*, I didn't have much faith in Bernie Milano, Tom

Coughlin, or the rest of the SIFE board, either. In my view, the board's refusal to do anything but slap Rohrs and Burton on the hand made the board complicit, too. Substituting special competition entries from one category to another was not a simple mistake, or a glitch; rather, it was another example of the opaque, freewheeling actions of SIFE's senior staff. Though Burton argued that it was a minor contretemps, I saw it as an intentional attempt to curry favor with the Kauffman Foundation, which had paid $50,000 to SIFE to sponsor a competition which paid out only $12,000 in prize money.

Knowing that some SIFE teams had won money for a competition they hadn't entered, it was not unreasonable for me to believe that Burton had intentionally *lost* the Chico State Kauffman entry. He knew his boss was anti-SAGE and that our entry in the Kauffman competition described our nascent SAGE program. By pulling our entry, he could curry favor with Rohrs and deny our SAGE its due recognition. Two birds, one stone.

Though it wasn't easy, I did my best to maintain an upbeat attitude going into the fall 2003 semester. I could no longer look at the SIFE organization the same way anymore. On the surface, SIFE was a feel-good education organization with a strong mission. Below the surface, though, I thought it was oily. My earlier intuition had become conviction—I was now convinced that SIFE was using its Walton Fellows and students as pawns to promote a global, conservative, free enterprise ideology. Though the Christian-based, servant-leadership philosophy was downplayed globally—no prayers during opening or closing sessions, no prayers before meals—the underlying current of the Christian faith permeated the national event in Kansas City. I cringed when the $5,000 Alvin Rohrs Servant Leadership Scholarship was ceremoniously handed out in honor of SIFE's leading servant. I cringed even more when Rohrs continued his habit of choking up when setting the table for Nasby to collect checks from new donors. To many, Rohrs may have been a servant leader. But to me, he was a cunning, surreptitious, disingenuous, avaricious, deceitful crybaby. If America's CEO leaders like Jack Shewmaker, Jack Kahl, David Bernauer, Len Roberts, Tom Coughlin, and Bernie Milano were putting their faith in Alvin Rohrs to teach youth about American business ethics, then their collective judgment represented the *worst* in corporate America.

Early Friday morning, October 10, 2003, three Chico State students and I boarded a plane from San Francisco to Frankfurt. Our final destination was Mainz, Germany, host city of the 2003 SIFE World Cup. Two years earlier in 2001, SIFE staged its first overseas tournament in London. Europe was high on the priority list of Wal-Mart's international growth strategy. Only two years earlier, Wal-Mart had acquired the UK's second largest retail chain, Asda. The next year, 2002, SIFE chose Amsterdam and now in 2003, the host city was Mainz.

Germany was also a hot spot for Wal-Mart, having moved into Germany in 1998. But Wal-Mart was struggling there. High labor costs, German labor law, and tradition made it difficult to implement its everyday low price strategy. Showcasing SIFE—and indirectly Wal-Mart—in Mainz was part of Wal-Mart's strategy to resuscitate lagging sales in Germany.[1]

The three students joining me in Mainz were senior Mollie Perlman, a petite marketing major from Southern California; Allison Smith, a junior management major from Chico; and Becky Monmaney, senior accounting major from Foresthill, near Sacramento. A month earlier, I promised KPMG's Bernie Milano and Tom Moser that we would not hold a SAGE workshop at the SIFE venue. True to my word, I instead booked a suite at a nearby Hyatt, and invited our global contacts to an afternoon meeting on Saturday, October 11.

The meeting was marvelous. Representatives from nine countries were on hand to learn about a grant program from the U.S. Department of Education's "Business and International Education" program. Educators from Russia, Tajikistan, Ukraine, Brazil, Chile, Poland, China, South Africa, and the Philippines joined us for the meeting. The grant program encouraged U.S. universities to work with international organizations to promote an understanding of economic education for K-12 educators, especially targeting Russia, the Independent States of the former Soviet Union, and Africa. We also made a PowerPoint presentation explaining how their SIFE teams could champion SAGE.

Late the next afternoon, I hired a Mainz riverboat to take our diverse group upstream on a three-hour tour of the Rhine River. As the guests boarded, Molly, Becky, and Allison handed out SAGE baseball caps to our sixty guests. The Chico State SIFE students were having a great time. None of them had any international travel experience, except for Molly who had been to France on a one-semester student exchange. The women saw, firsthand, that youth entrepreneurship was in high demand.

Before boarding, the Filipino delegation, led by Robert "Bob" Galindez, met us in the lobby at the Hyatt. He was joined by about a dozen others, and as each of them introduced themselves, I couldn't help but notice a beautiful, somewhat shy woman wearing stylish brown boots, designer blue jeans, and a brown derby.

Her eyes twinkled, and when she smiled, her brilliant white teeth contrasted against her jet-black hair and mocha skin. As she said hello, she tipped her hat and did a little curtsy. "Pleasure to meet you, sir," she said. "My name is Tricia Mendoza." My heart skipped a beat.

Tricia was a star engineer for F.F. Cruz and Company, one of Manila's oldest and most successful engineering firms. Bob had recruited Tricia's colleague at F.F. Cruz, Bernadette Rosales, to serve as a SIFE Philippines business adviser. Bernadette and Tricia were close friends, and she invited Tricia along to Europe as a bonus.

Tricia no longer did straight civil engineering work for her company because Eric Cruz, the founder's son and now CEO, discovered she was more valuable in another capacity. Cruz saw Tricia had a razor-sharp legal mind and outstanding negotiating skills, and she had risen quickly in the company to become its contracts manager.

Bernadette and Bob were close friends, sharing the same hometown of Iloilo [ee-low ee-low] City in the Western Visayas. I had met them in Iloilo City only a few weeks earlier when I made a brief visit to various schools in the Western Visayas and Manila, laying the groundwork for SAGE Philippines. While there, I learned that Filipinos are some of the friendliest, smartest people in the world. And now, having met Tricia, I believed the Philippines was home to one of the world's most beautiful women.

The cruise included a light buffet and a three-piece orchestra. Everyone seemed pleased to learn more about SAGE. As the host, I made sure to mingle with as many people as I could. Secretly, though, I kept an eye out to see where Tricia was. Near the end of the tour I found a chance to chat with her on the upper deck and was smitten. I had been a single man for nearly five years, and while I had dated here and there, nobody had the effect on me that Tricia did.

Yes, it's true—I fell in love on the river Rhine. Though we only had a few more chances to chat with one another in the next couple days, we exchanged phone numbers and email addresses. I promised to return to the Philippines the following February, for Valentine's Day.

Drury University of Springfield, Missouri, prevailed as the SIFE World Cup 2003 Champion Team. Drury, as you recall, was the team that knocked Chico State out in the semi-final round at the May 2003 USA qualification event that determined which team would advance to the world championship. I wasn't happy Drury University won the SIFE World Cup. La Sierra University, from Riverside, California, had won in 2002, and Drury the year before that in 2001. I wondered how long SIFE teams from other countries would put up with the USA always winning the world title.

The last night I was in Mainz, Tom Payne invited me to stay with him at the competition hotel. He had a room with two beds, and he knew it would save me a couple hundred bucks. Tom and I had become close over the past three years. He told me his position with SIFE may soon be coming to an end and that he was working on an exit strategy. He wanted what was best for the organization and felt he could no longer be effective in the organization. He also volunteered that at least two members of SIFE's Executive Committee encouraged him not to leave but I knew that his days were numbered. I also knew he was probably in a strong bargaining position and that SIFE would probably pony up.

Tom had scheduled a breakfast meeting with Jack Shewmaker for the next morning. As I was checking out, I caught a glimpse of Shewmaker and Tom in the restaurant. Sad. For nearly two years, Shewmaker was my mentor, and he valued my input. Now, all communication was severed. At this point, I was so disgusted with how he and the board had handled the special competition fiasco that I was happy to avoid a conversation with him. Later, Tom let me know one of the main topics he and Shewmaker discussed was "what Tom thought really happened with Chico State's

Kauffman entry."

On my flight home, I reflected on the trip. We had solidified our relationship with several people who were planning to head up SAGE. I was especially happy to make the acquaintance of Lili Qu, an undergraduate business major from a prestigious university in Shanghai. She pledged to launch a SAGE program in China.

Upon our return, the Chico State team was excited to hear about their classmates' adventures. The team dove into its fall projects, and the Chico SIFE machine was up and running. Tom Payne called me a week or two later. "Curt, my last day with SIFE is November 5."

In fall 2003, I applied for a sabbatical leave of absence for the 2004–2005 school year. In my request to the leaves committee, I wrote, "The objective of the sabbatical is to pursue my interest in community service learning on an international scale. I want to combine my knowledge in the service-learning area with the international perspective gained through extensive travel the past five years (e.g., I have studied community service learning in Germany, Poland, France, Australia, South Africa, the United Arab Emirates, and soon I will be returning to the Philippines). Community service learning is an area in which I have some experience, and I want to obtain a greater expertise in this pedagogy."

As a tenured professor, I was eligible for a full semester's paid leave of absence, or a year at half-pay. Since coming to Chico in fall 1990, I had taken just a one-semester, *unpaid* leave of absence in fall 2000 to go to work for Barry Peters and Yeardisc. I was due for a paid leave.

I submitted a request for the full year, and the dean and provost approved it. Earlier in the year, in April, the accrediting body for university business programs, the Association to Advance Collegiate Schools of Business (AA-CSB), passed its new accreditation standards for business accreditation. The standards emphasized a global worldview. The experiences I was providing students like Becky, Molly, and Allison were right down the AACSB's alley. For example, one standard read: "Every graduate should be prepared to pursue a business or management career in a global context. That is, students should be exposed to cultural practices different from their own. The learning experiences should foster sensitivity and flexibility toward cultural differences. For the benefit of all, active support of a number of perspectives is desirable."[2] Fortunately, the dean and provost saw how my work with SIFE and SAGE could help us maintain our accreditation. Starting June 1, 2004, I would have one full year to devote to SAGE.

Just before the Christmas holiday, on December 15, 2003, I received an email from Al Konuwa of Butte College. Al had received the final draft of the Milano task force's memorandum to the SIFE board, and he knew I'd want to see it. The report, dated December 11, was entitled, "Report to the Executive Committee of Students in Free Enterprise from The Rules, Policies, and Procedures Task Force." The introductory paragraph stated:

> At the direction of the past, current, and elect Chairmen of the Students in Free Enterprise (SIFE) Board of Directors, a task force was commissioned to review the rules, policies, and procedures, pertaining to the Special and Regular SIFE Regional, National, and World Cup competitions. This action was taken following concern expressed by certain Sam Walton Fellows as to the handling of Special Competitions in 2003.[3]

The memo went on to list the original twelve members of the task force and one new member, a Sam Walton Fellow from John Carroll University of Cleveland. I quickly read through the twenty-page report, starting with the executive summary:

> The Task Force identified two general areas and twenty-two issues to be addressed. We also identified nine other items which we believe to be beyond our scope but on some we have provided recommendations.
> One issue we have not fully addressed but believe deserves serious consideration by SIFE leadership is the engagement of Sam Walton Fellows in SIFE. Apparently, in previous years, SWFs were assembled at the Kansas City event and on a regional basis. As the number of SWFs increased those events were discontinued. Certain SWFs have recommended that a SWF Advisory Board be

established to represent the SWF network and provide input both on an unsolicited basis and on issues being considered by leadership, before they are enacted.

This report, in draft form, was provided to Alvin Rohrs for his and his team's responses to our recommendations. All of the above and the SIFE responses are reported in detail below. SIFE has agreed with all of our recommendations allowing for certain modifications which we find acceptable.

The most important theme is the objectivity of the judging process and within that, the use of SIFE alumni as judges. We recognize and applaud that keeping SIFE alumni engaged is an important objective but the credibility of the judging process trumps all other considerations.

It is our view that the signing of a judge's oath is not sufficient to ensure objectivity and independence where SIFE alumni are used as judges. The Executive Committee is asked to determine whether a set number of years since graduation is an acceptable solution and if so, six years is recommended. This length of time also appears appropriate because throughout all SIFE literature we refer to judges as "business executives." We know this past year, several judges were in entry level positions with their employers. An undergraduate out of school less than six years in unlikely to be a "business executive."

The first general area of recommendation identified by the task force concerned the judging of the overall competition, including selection, training, and objectivity of judges. This was a huge issue for me, because if SIFE was going to rig the results in the special competitions, why not the overall competition, too? Without a system of internal controls, who was to say that someone like Mat Burton wouldn't recruit a *ringer* judge (e.g., an alumni from XYZ university) to give a certain team (e.g., Chico State) absurdly low ratings? Or why not put a couple *extra*, fabricated ballots in the ballot box before they go to the judging room, staffed by … Mat Burton?

In fact, we had raised this concern with Larry Pinkerton. A few of the

Chico State presenters believed one of the judges in their semifinal round was also a member of Drury's business advisory board. They suspected this to be the case because Drury displayed a brief video clip during its presentations, and my students thought they recognized one of the female judges as a member of the Drury team's business advisory board.

I wouldn't have even dared to bring this up before the special competition fiasco, but now I firmly believed Mat Burton would stop at nothing in order to kiss his portly boss's ass, and to get a fat bonus along with it. It pained me to raise this issue with Drury's adviser, Robert Wyatt, but I was resolved to do anything it took to ensure my students didn't get jobbed any more than they already had. In the end, Pinkerton looked into this, but couldn't find any evidence to support the suspicions.

Milano's task force recommended that a judge's code of conduct be signed by each judge. SIFE's reply was to fully agree with the use of such a code, and that such a document would be implemented in the coming year.

But it was the special competition—not the overall competition—judging that gave rise to the formation of the task force. This caused the committee to call for an overhaul of the special competition of the judging process. The report stated, "According to SIFE leadership, the task of reviewing numerous submissions is too onerous to utilize 'business executives.' Coupled with the desire of the SWF to receive feedback on their submissions, the task is deemed by SIFE to be impossible."

The task force didn't buy Rohrs'—or SIFE's—explanation here. Instead, it said: "It is our recommendation that SIFE engage an independent organization to judge the submissions to special competitions and that each submission be commented on by the judges. Their assignment would be to select the best submissions to be awarded 'finalist' allowing 'business executives,' in a setting at the National Expo, to select the winners from the lists of finalists."

Before reading SIFE's lengthy reply to this recommendation, I shook my head. According to Tom, SIFE had been using young SIFE alumni and non-business leaders (e.g., Tom's retired military father) as judges for years, yet each year SIFE continued to claim that the special competitions were judged by business leaders. This was deceitful, and Rohrs had condoned (or maybe authorized) the deception.

But imagine the reaction if the Executive Committee fired Rohrs. How would they explain Rohrs' firing to the other 225 board members? Especially after the committee had, just a few months earlier, presented him with the keys to a customized Chevy Tahoe, inducted him into the SIFE Hall of Fame, and bestowed an endowment of $65,000 to provide a servant leadership scholarship in his name?[4]

Could you see the memo, "Sorry, fellow board members, Rohrs had absolutely no system of internal controls in place, so we let him go. Special competition results were manipulated and low-level SIFE alumni are judging the competitions, rather than business executives." This is the last thing that Milano and Moser and the KPMG folks wanted other board members to know. Many of the $25,000 dues-paying board members—a number of them KPMG clients—would have run from SIFE's turnstiles as a red-faced Milano and Moser watched them exit.

Aside from doing the right thing, why else hadn't SIFE's board gone after Rohrs the way Golden Key's board had gone after its CEO, James Lewis? Was Rohrs' head so far up Shewmaker's and Wal-Mart's ass that the rest of the board wouldn't dare challenge Shewmaker? Was Wal-Mart so invested in SIFE that letting Rohrs go would jeopardize its global growth—and management recruiting—strategy?

I scrutinized each of SIFE's replies to the Milano report with special interest.

"The use of special competitions has historically been driven by SIFE donor company requests," SIFE said. "Several problems have arisen from this approach: (1) the competition criteria are written to accomplish donor criteria/mandate and SIFE Teams haven't always been able to easily connect these back to the teaching principles established by SIFE; (2) these competitions usually have a very low participation rate; (3) since they are driven by donor sponsorship, they offer teams no stability in program development. They may be offered one year and then not the following."

From the get-go, sponsored special competitions were just another way to raise money for SIFE and heap recognition and praise on donors. With respect to the first problem, SIFE admitted that the *donor company* established the criteria, and that these criteria didn't connect easily to SIFE's teaching principles. Whose fault was that? SIFE should have said, "Thanks for your offer to support us, Company XYZ. We understand what you do, so let's work together to determine criteria that map onto your mission and our objectives."

This issue was a sore point for many leading Walton Fellows. We always suspected that donors wagged the tail, and those of us teaching at public universities were skeptical when any one company tried to establish undue influence over curriculum or extracurricular activities. Of course, SIFE had no problem with that, as long as the donor's check cleared.[5]

As for the second problem, SIFE was being contradictory here. Out of one side of its mouth, SIFE was saying, "The process is too onerous to utilize executives." Out of the other, it was saying, "The participation rate is very low."

SIFE's reply here is unadulterated bullshit. I recalled Mat Burton's email to Jill Zinke and me on May 20, 2003, explaining why Walton Fellows weren't provided feedback on special competitions. "We often receive more than a hundred entries in each special competition," he wrote. By now, I knew for a fact that only two special competitions had received more than a hundred entries in 2003, and neither of these was sponsored. According to Burton, judges for these competitions, who I now knew to be young SIFE alumni, "put in close to a full day reviewing these and making their decisions. Because of the volume of entries, it would be an overwhelming task for them to complete a written critique for each team."

Hey, Mat and Alvin, I have an idea. Why not use some of that extra $38,000 from Kauffman to do a professional job? Assume there are thirty legitimate entries for a special competition like Kauffman. With three judges equipped with a well-crafted judging rubric, each judge could read the executive summary for ten entries and rate the top three in his stack. Time on task—say, two hours. Now that the thirty entries have been winnowed down to just nine finalists, each judge can use the rubric to scrutinize the six other entries. Then, each judge ranks the entries number one to number nine.

Using a scoring system similar to the overall competition—where a team gets one point for a first place vote, two points for second place vote, etc.—the team with the lowest number of points wins. Time on task here—let's say, another two hours, giving us a total time commitment of four hours. This is no more than the time requirement for a CEO or senior business leader to judge one round of a regular competition. But, of course, special competitions were apparently so low on Rohrs' priority list that he didn't care how Burton got the job done—as long as he kept the donors happy.

As for the third problem—instability in program development due to donor wishes—this had nothing to do with who serves as a judge and how an entry is judged. This was fluff.

SIFE then presented the task force with a solution. Starting in 2004–2005, only four special competitions would be offered, with SIFE seeking sponsors for each competition. Each competition would align itself directly with SIFE's four overall criteria: market economics, entrepreneurship, financial literacy, and business ethics. The top projects at each regional competition, as selected by the overall competition judges, would then be invited to submit entries for the final phase.

This made perfect sense to me. Too bad it took Tom Payne, Chico State, Larry Pinkerton, Bernie Milano and his task force to help Rohrs come to such a common sense conclusion.

Chico State's influence had a bearing on two more issues identified by the task force. One issue addressed the concern over judging bias caused by relationship of a judge to a SIFE team. The task force recommended that judges complete personal data sheets that include university attended and year of graduation. Also, at the judges' orientation, each judge would be asked if they had a special relationship with any SIFE team in their assigned league. If so, they were to be assigned to a different league. SIFE agreed to this.

The second issue involved the need for greater clarification as to who can be involved in responding in the question and answer segment of a team presentation during the overall competitions. The report recommended that, when addressing judges' questions following the presentation period, any team member in the room may respond. They also specified that the Sam Walton Fellow may not respond to questions or otherwise coach the team in their responses in any manner. Again, SIFE agreed.

All told, I took some satisfaction knowing that Chico State had forced SIFE to begin cleaning up its act. But I was deflated and exhausted. SIFE wasn't going to fire Rohrs or Burton, and I was persona non grata with everyone at SIFE's home office in Springfield. Tom Payne was gone, as was Gail Beutler. I sent Al Konuwa a dejected email asking him for advice. I was about to throw in the towel.

"After ten years with SIFE," he replied, "you leaving at a time when you have made significant contributions to initiating processes for positive changes in the SIFE organization seem, to me, to be a bit premature."

He continued, "The (Milano) Task Force, in a large part, is a result of your suggestions. Leaving at this juncture, when we haven't had time to assess some of these recommendations may be what some folks, including Walton Fellows, want to see. There are not many DeBergs in SIFE; and like it or not, there is an appreciation for those, like you, who call an organization to its duties for accountability and change. Otherwise, a situation of the Emperor's New Clothes persists."

Al then addressed the SAGE program. "You need to take into consideration the growth of SAGE. In its early years, it is still cloaked in SIFE, which I see as continuing for the next couple years until SAGE enters its maturity phase," he advised. "The absence of your SIFE influence may hurt SAGE's potential, particularly in the international arena where you are beginning to make inroads."

Al's argument were persuasive. I needed at least one more year or so to get my SAGE ducks in a row before leaving SIFE. Christmas break was welcome. As the spring semester was about to begin, my attorney Jeff Carter received a final email from Larry Pinkerton, dated January 22, 2004. From SIFE's perspective, this was it—closure. The letter would either cause me to file a lawsuit or drop the matter. The email read:

Jeff,

I am authorized to provide the following additional information of steps taken by SIFE as a result of the concerns raised by Chico State:

- An independent investigator spent three months investigating each issue and reported to the SIFE Executive Committee.

His conclusions were that while there were errors of judgment there was no evidence that anyone at SIFE acted unethically. The results of this investigation were sent to the attorney for California State University Chico.

- A Task Force made up of faculty and board members headed by Bernie Milano President KPMG Foundation [*sic*] solicited input from all US faculty regarding recommendations on changes in competition procedures. These recommendations were presented to the SIFE Executive Committee on November 4. The SIFE staff is now implementing all of those recommendations approved by the Executive Committee.

- Special competition entry procedures have been changed internally at SIFE Headquarters to assure that every entry is initially logged in by the accounting department, then moved to University Relations and then to Development for distribution to the judges. It also requires all those who handle the entries to sign for each entry. This assures three points of cross checking by three different individuals to insure that every entry received is judged. These procedures also includes email notification of all teams whose entries have been received and posting of the receipt of all entries on the website so every team will know if their entry was received.

- An Official Rules Committee is being appointed by the Chair of SIFE so all future complaints about rules violations or improper procedures can be presented through a formal confidential review process.

I apologize for the delay in providing this information to you, but there has been a transition in the leadership of the Executive Committee of SIFE from Tom Coughlin to Robert Rich, Jr., and this has caused the delay.

I know how committed Curt is to SIFE and SAGE. His concerns have been very seriously addressed and brought positive reform.

Sincerely,

Larry Pinkerton

Jeff asked me if I wanted to pursue this any further, though he recommended against it. "Do you really want to get the university involved?" Well, no.

But Pinkerton's first bullet point said "there was no evidence that anyone at SIFE acted unethically." This was not factually correct. I knew we had strong evidence that Burton had intentionally inserted entries from one competition into another. Not to mention that SIFE had been deceitful for years, claiming in its handbook that special competitions were judged by a panel of business leaders when, instead, many of them were judged by young, and not so impartial, SIFE alumni, or retirees like Tom Payne's father.

I couldn't believe Rohrs and Burton were still SIFE employees. The situation dripped with sad irony—an international, nonprofit organization using university students to espouse a philosophy of business ethics when, at the same time, it was being led by ethically-challenged sycophants of SIFE's powerful board.

It gave me little comfort to learn that Rohrs had gotten quite a "tongue-lashing" from SIFE's Executive Committee at its August 25, 2003, meeting in Springfield.[6] But I did find a small measure of solace learning SIFE had hired a chief administrative officer whose main duty was to implement a set of internal controls. Clearly, Milano and his task force knew Rohrs needed help with internal controls. The board had to take action here, if for nothing else but to stave off a lawsuit.

As I had done with the incident three years earlier, I decided *not* to pursue further legal action. There was no need for a settlement here, because I didn't have a smoking gun proving SIFE intentionally lost the Chico State Kauffman entry. By nature, I am a positive person. By investing time, energy, and money to pursue the SIFE matter further would have cast a negative pall over my single-minded determination to make SAGE a model for education reform. I was zealous in my belief that SAGE could make a positive difference in the lives of teenagers.

Heeding Al's and Jeff's advice, I hung in there. I helped get the SIFE team off to a good start in the spring semester, and told incoming Chico State SIFE president John Van Dinther to pack his bags—we were heading for Manila. Bob Galindez had invited us to be special guests at the inaugural SAGE Philippines National Competition. We arrived in Manila late on the evening of Valentine's Day, February 14. Professionally, I had been bruised, but my personal life was about to get a whole lot better. I will never forget bringing Tricia chocolate and flowers just before the clock struck midnight. To this day, I am still buying her candy and flowers, but she loves designer handbags, high heels, and Kentucky Fried Chicken, too.

Prior to the SAGE competition in Manila, John and I visited Iloilo City and the Western Visayas. We led several SAGE workshops before returning to Manila. One of Bob's assistants took us to a tiny tropical island. Boracay is about two hundred miles south of Manila and only accessible by double-outrigger boats crafted after traditional fishing boats. No cars are allowed on the island, with ground transportation limited to *tricycles*—three-wheel motorbikes. The north shore of the island has a two-mile stretch of pure, packed white sand, perfect for jogging in bare feet. To top it off, one can buy live lobster on the beach and ask any local restaurant to cook it for you. With SAGE Philippines on board, I knew that someday I would return to this beautiful slice of paradise, with Tricia by my side.

The last couple days in Manila, John and I were honorary guests at the SAGE event. Dressed in our new tailor-made barongs, compliments of Bob and his SAGE advisory board, we watched as dozens of high school SAGE teams competed for the national title at a hotel on Rojas Boulevard.[7] All told, Bob Galindez did a superb job of organizing the competition. I was like a proud father watching SAGE grow before my eyes.

Upon returning to Chico, John recounted his experience to his SIFE lieutenants. Enthusiastically, they were determined to go for the gold again. But I, on the other hand, could no longer put my heart into it. The only thing that kept me going was to help Chico State students continue to do outstanding work—including SAGE, of course. Properly implemented, SIFE was a tremendous motivator for university students. The same was true for high school students.

On March 26, 2004, in our student union auditorium, we conducted the second annual SAGE USA tournament. On hand were Chico mayor Maureen Kirk and U.S. Congressman Wally Herger. Earlier in the day, both of them had served as honorary judges in the final round of the SAGE competition. A total of sixteen high schools were represented as $16,000 was handed out in scholarships and prize money.

Congressman Herger was in his ninth term as a member of the House of Representatives from the Second Congressional District in northern California. As a member of the tax writing Committee on Ways and Means, Herger also served on the powerful Subcommittee on Trade and the Subcommittee on Human Resources, of which he was the chairman. SAGE was starting to make some real connections.

Taking the microphone, Herger could hardly contain himself. "I was truly amazed with the passion and creativity of the students I met today," he said. "Whether they go on to pursue business or not, their participating in SAGE will instill in them lessons of teamwork, discipline, and ethics; all of which will pay generous dividends in the years to come."

Once again, the Fremont Business Academy from Oakland won the SAGE USA tournament, earning an invitation to the Second Annual SAGE World Cup. This year, we scheduled it for May in San Francisco, just before the SIFE USA expo in Kansas City set for May 23–25.

As we were selecting the USA's SAGE representative, nine more countries had launched the program. Miraculously, all but one of them found the funds to send their country champions to compete in California. On Thursday, May 20, eight delegations arrived at the Hyatt Regency San Francisco Airport to compete for the SAGE crown. The countries included Philippines, Poland, Tajikistan, Kazakhstan, China, Mexico, Ukraine, and Russia. The Philippines ended up taking the big trophy, with China coming in a close second.

With our best project hot off the burner, the Chico State SIFE team advanced to Kansas City a couple days later to compete in the SIFE USA nationals, for the eleventh year in a row. The five presenters adopted an international theme of *hope*—helping others pursue entrepreneurship. This was excellent. Our accrediting agency, the AACSB, was pushing colleges of business to include a heavier emphasis on global issues.

Courtney Kimball, a senior marketing and Spanish double major from nearby Yuba City, opened up: "Did you know that 50 percent of the people in South Africa live below the poverty line? And that they have a 37 percent unemployment rate? Or that the life expectancy is only forty-six years old? I am wearing a green tie today to symbolize our relationship with South Africa and how we are providing hope for their future."

Next up was Kristin Weil, a junior management major from Oceanside. "Did you know that the population growth rate in the Philippines is outstripping their natural resources, or that over 40 percent of the people live below the poverty line?" she asked. "I am wearing a blue tie today to symbolize our relationship with this beautiful country, and how we are providing hope for their future."

In turn, Kristin Demeduk, a senior from Tracy, focused on China. "Did you know that 1.3 billion people live in China, which is 20.3 percent of the world population? And 130 million people are unemployed and living below the poverty line—more than half the U.S. population! I am wearing a red tie today to symbolize our relationship with China."

Mollie Perlman then stepped forward. "Did you know that the distribution of income in Costa Rica between the wealthy and the poor is one of the worst in all of Latin America?" she asked. "I am wearing a white tie today to symbolize our relationship with Costa Rica."

Finally, bringing our program back home, Chico native Hannah Ortiz said, "I am wearing a California gold tie today, to symbolize our home state and how we are providing HOPE for the future of our children, not only in Butte County, but across the state." Hannah was a double major in accounting and marketing.

The presentation focused on Chico State's six main projects, trying to convince the judges that five factors set us apart from other teams. The areas were focus, entrepreneurship education, sustainability, collaboration, and integration. Would our approach take us back to the final stage?

The competition was getting harder every year. As usual, Chico State sailed through the first round on day one. But the next day, we got knocked out in the next round by the University of Arizona, which ended up placing first runner-up to Flagler College of St. Augustine, Florida. Drury University, yet again, made the final stage, taking third place honors. Flagler would represent the USA at the SIFE World Cup set for Barcelona, Spain, on September 22-24, 2004.

Supervising two dozen university students on a road trip is never easy, and when you count regional competitions, this was the twenty-second time I had done this in eleven years. I had one more year in me for SIFE, and I would do my best to expand SAGE throughout the world. On July 1, 2004, my sabbatical would begin, and I would devote all of my energy to SAGE.

Two years ago, I went to Amsterdam to inform SIFE World Cup participants about SAGE, and last year I went to Mainz. This year would be no different.

I booked my flight to Barcelona.

Chapter 17

Showdown in Barcelona

Tom Payne's major duty at SIFE, as the senior vice president, was to focus his efforts on recruiting a targeted list of fifty key undergraduate business schools. Alvin Rohrs assigned this task to him after SIFE's board determined that its number one strategic priority for 2003–2004 would be to increase market share of qualifying universities. The goal was to enroll thirty-five premier universities and coax at least twenty-eight of them to a regional competition.[1] Until now, only a few elite universities, like the University of Arizona, participated in SIFE and that was because they had an outstanding retail and consumer sciences program.

In 2004, SIFE reserved a special pot of funds to bring Walton Fellows and student leaders from targeted schools to observe the SIFE USA national exposition and the SIFE World Cup. Until his departure from SIFE, Tom's only job was to focus on the targeted fifty schools. I believed that the SIFE board's objective here was ultimately doomed to failure. Without a chance to publish in refereed journals, receive a reasonable stipend, or obtain release time from other teaching duties, most tenured or tenure-track faculty members from these universities would turn their nose up at the thought of receiving a paltry $1,000 Sam M. Walton Fellow stipend. And how excited could SIFE students from Carnegie Mellon or MIT or Harvard get when they told their dean that they prevailed over teams like Lubbock Christian or Drury University or Houston Baptist at a SIFE competition? This was hardly something that a prestigious university would want to proclaim to its illustrious alumni, who would be asking, "Why are we participating at an event with these types of universities?"

Going a step further, the reality was that hardly any elite universities would come close to winning the national event. The possibility of them prevailing over traditional SIFE powerhouses was practically zero. To win at SIFE, you needed to know how to play, and this meant a state-of-the-art multimedia presentation; dozens of sexy projects; and, in many cases, overly enthusiastic, yet robotic, student presenters who devoted a full semester to memorizing their script and rehearsing.

Not that my advice was ever sought or valued by SIFE anymore—I believed the way to attract such universities was curricular. If SIFE could be integrated into an entrepreneurship course, with service learning as part of the course, then faculty would be recognized for their efforts as part of the teaching load. Maybe they could even publish in academic journals. But changing the curriculum was a long-term proposition. As Woodrow T. Wilson, twenty-eighth president of the United States said, "It is easier to change the location of a cemetery, than to change the school curriculum."[2]

If the curricular route to adding elite universities to the SIFE network wasn't viable, then SIFE could take the extra-curricular path. But based on my experience early in my career at Arizona State, I knew that hardly any faculty at such universities would do this. Exceptions existed, of course, when a dean wanted to curry favor with alumni serving on SIFE's board of directors. In such cases, the dean could find some extra funds to pay an adjunct lecturer to assume the role of SIFE adviser, probably donated by the alumnus, himself.

All told, though, I really didn't care about SIFE's strategy anymore—I knew I was a short-timer. My focus now turned squarely on SAGE. I was interested in attracting any university to the SAGE network—big-name or small-time, secular or non-secular. Unlike SIFE, though, my strategy would be to go directly to students.

Early in the summer of 2004, I received an invitation to attend an August conference in Shanghai. The invitation was fortuitous because I had already begun making plans to go to Shanghai at Lili Qu's invitation. I had met Lili in Germany the previous October, and she had signed on to become the SAGE China national coordinator. She asked if I could come to Shanghai and visit several Chinese high schools.

The conference was coordinated by the Harvard Project for Asian and International Relations, known as HPAIR. HPAIR is a student-run organization of the Harvard University Faculty of Arts and Sciences. Its main role is to plan and deliver Harvard's largest annual student conferences in the Asia-Pacific region. As in prior years, HPAIR's conference in Shanghai promised to attract international students from top universities, along with renowned academics, business professionals, and political leaders. HPAIR's conference looked like an ideal opportunity to take the SAGE message directly to the world's brightest university students, so I applied for a visa and hopped on a plane to Shanghai on August 16.[3]

The theme of the conference was "The Once and Future Asia: Expanding Horizons, Historic Transitions," and took place at one of the world's tallest buildings: the beautiful, eighty-eight-story Jin Mao Tower. At the time, the tower was China's tallest building and the fifth tallest in the world. The anchor tenant was the five-star Shanghai Grand Hyatt, occupying floors seventy-nine to ninety-three. I decided to redeem some of my Hyatt frequent-stayer points.

At the conference, I met superb students from such universities as Oxford, Harvard, the University of Singapore, and many more. Three things quickly became apparent. First, China's economy was booming, and companies from around the world were racing to be part of the action. Among the companies represented were auto manufacturers and several fast-food giants like Yum! Brands, the owner of Taco Bell, KFC, and Pizza Hut.

Second, the discount retail industry also wanted a slice of the action in China, but French discount giant Carrefour, the world's second largest retailer, had been first to the punch in China in 1995 with Wal-Mart right behind in 1996. Wal-Mart was determined to change that. To no one's surprise, China was also on SIFE's list of priority countries.[4]

Third, the Chinese liked to joke that their form of doing business was *capitalism with a Chinese twist*. I took this to mean that the Chinese government was now encouraging private sector, free enterprise and entrepreneurship so long as such entrepreneurial entities had the central government's explicit or tacit approval. Given China's woeful human rights history and its public control of the media, I couldn't help but think that this probably was more like *Communism with a capitalistic twist*.

One unforgettable young man was Wang Lei. Lei, as he preferred to be called, was a doctoral candidate at Oxford University, and his hometown was Baoding, a city of over 1.5 million people about a ninety-mile train ride southwest of Beijing. He instantly liked the SAGE idea and asked if I might be able to travel to Baoding after the conference and meet some leaders there. "Sure," I said, "right after I finish my visits to the Shanghai schools with Lili."

Before meeting up with Lei, Lili had escorted me to seven high schools and a couple universities with new SIFE programs. One of the high schools was a girls-only private school with an emphasis on the arts. To be accepted to the school, a young woman needed to show a special aptitude in the arts such as dance, music, theatre, sculpting, or painting. During my presentation, the student leaders, numbering about thirty, sat solemnly around the large rectangular conference table. Their teachers, principal, and government liaison—always a government liaison—stood near the door.

After the presentation, the student president stood up and, in perfect British English, politely thanked me. Then, she asked, "Professor DeBerg, if we start a SAGE business at our school, how will we obtain the money to start our business?"

"Before I answer that," I smiled, "let me ask you two questions. What kind of business would you like to start, and where do you *think* you might get the money?"

She paused, put her finger to her chin, and looked to the ceiling. So did twenty-nine other pretty faces. Finally, she said, "Well, some of us would like to create a school calendar. I think that would be a good business idea."

Her peers nodded in agreement. "As for where we'd get the money—I think perhaps the ... *government?*"

What a teachable moment, and a learnable one for me, too!

"Your idea for school calendar is excellent," I said. "As for where to get the money, in the U.S., if a small business owner needs money to start a business, the government may loan her some startup funds if she qualifies." I was thinking of SBA loans and the awful amount of red tape it takes to get such a loan.

"But the government is the last place an entrepreneur would go," I continued. "If I were you, I'd think of ways that you could raise money at your school to obtain the start-up cash. Do you conduct a concert or performance for your relatives during the school year?"

"Yes, in the spring we invite our parents and grandparents to watch us perform and exhibit our art," she replied.

"Do you charge an admission fee?" I asked.

The girls gasped, in unison. They couldn't believe I said such a thing.

"Of course not, they're our relatives!" their leader cried.

Quickly, I recovered. "Oh, no, I'm not suggesting that you charge an admission fee in the spring exhibition," I explained. "What I am suggesting, though, is that you hold a separate exhibition in the fall, and make it a contest, like a talent show. For this exhibition, though, you *would* charge an admission fee."

I offered more advice. "You could advertise the event in the community, and let all of your classmates know that the best performances will share half the proceeds from the admission fees. Your new SAGE team would keep the other half to produce the calendar, which you can sell at a profit."

A collective light bulb seemed to light up the room. They liked my idea.

The following April, I would be on hand to watch their new SAGE team place third in the second annual SAGE China competition.

Upon my return to Chico, I found the 2004–2005 SIFE information handbook in my mailbox.[5] I read it with special interest because I expected to find SIFE's new policies and procedures described in the handbook. This is where the Milano task force recommendations would show up, I thought.

Sure enough, I found a few things to like. But I found a lot more things to dislike, and they seemed especially written to shackle aggressive Walton Fellows like me.

What did I like? There were now four special monthly competitions, with each competition aligned with SIFE's four specific educational topics. Regional tournament judges would also select the winner of each topic from their assigned league, with teams winning a $500 prize. These winners were then asked to submit a written, two-page summary of the project, to be judged by an independent panel of business leaders who would select the top three entries. I suspected that Bernie Milano himself would oversee the selection of business leaders, making sure to avoid using recent SIFE alumni as panelists.

What didn't I like? The list of dislikes was pretty long. On page eleven of the handbook, it stated, "SIFE Teams should be aware that unless they receive express permission to do so, they are not authorized to speak on behalf of SIFE or otherwise represent any SIFE national organization or the SIFE World Headquarters. In communication within the SIFE network or to outside interested constituencies, SIFE Teams are expected to make absolutely clear that they represent only the SIFE Team of their particular institution." I guess I wouldn't be doing any more guest speaking, like I had done with Denis Neveux in Paris.

Next, what about working with SIFE teams in other countries? "[Domestic teams] are authorized to conduct projects using the SIFE trademark in their home countries. They are also extended authorization to use the SIFE name and logo while conducting educational outreach projects outside their home country that have officially established SIFE national organizations, so long as they register their intended activities using the global outreach registration tool."

Ah, a new registration tool for SIFE to *track* teams doing work in other SIFE countries. So now, if Chico State SIFE wanted to encourage SIFE teams in other countries to start SAGE programs, we must first register. Well played, Alvin Rohrs.

Rohrs was now making up new rules to control Walton Fellows like me from working outside the country—he couldn't openly discourage me from doing this, but he could force me to register on his website, enabling him to track my every SAGE activity in countries where SIFE was operating. If I didn't register, he could cite my failure to do so as a violation of SIFE rules, and therefore sanction me. Rohrs should have been a lawyer. Wait a minute ... he was a lawyer!

Then, at the bottom of page eleven, "SIFE teams are not authorized to represent themselves as approved members of the SIFE network in any country outside their home country that does not have an officially established SIFE national organization. Requests for exceptions to this rule may be made to SIFE World Headquarters."

So, this means if my Chico State students and I go to Sierra Leone, a non-SIFE country, and want to call the SAGE program a Chico State SIFE project, I once again have two choices: (1) either get permission from SIFE or (2) refrain from calling it a SIFE project.

Bottom line here, if I wanted to operate SAGE in a SIFE country, I had to register it. If I wanted to operate SAGE in a non-SIFE country, I couldn't call it a Chico State SIFE project. Rohrs was smart, no doubt, and instead of being contrite about last year's transgressions in the Mat Burton affair, he was now even more emboldened to go after me—again. A violation of these new directives would be a violation of new SIFE policy. Clearly, he was setting me up for yet another fall. What a guy! A true servant leader.

I could read the handwriting on the wall. My question was: Which will come first, my resignation as a Walton Fellow or a pink slip from SIFE's new board chairman, Robert Rich? I smiled at at the thought of being fired from a volunteer position.

Another item inserted into the new handbook concerned SIFE's new policy about contacting board members or other SIFE teams. Ever since Chico State's first SIFE competition in 1994, SIFE would mail Walton Fellows a list of judges in their competition league and encourage us to write thank you letters. Of course, the further a team advanced, the more bigwigs would sit on the judging panel. When a team made the final round in Kansas City, almost all the judges were senior executives from SIFE board member companies. As usual, I would gladly thank them in my follow-up letter and at the same time, ask them if they'd be interested in judging a future SAGE tournament. Some board members, like David Bernauer from Walgreens, Joe Pedott of the Chia Pet fame, and Rieva Lesonsky of *Entrepreneur Magazine*, replied. They loved the SAGE idea and supported it.

Over the years I had built some social capital, and I had the email addresses of all of SIFE's board members. I wasn't hesitant about sending a rare—but relevant—email about how SAGE was targeting teenagers to become tomorrow's leaders, much like SIFE was targeting university students. Not surprisingly, many of them were keen to the idea, especially those who had witnessed the Chico State SIFE presentation with SAGE's name now highlighted throughout.

Other board members, however, weren't so receptive, especially now that SIFE, and Rohrs, had revised its policies. Now, with the new rules I was coming even closer to violating SIFE's brand.

I wondered if Jack Shewmaker was in this camp, too. Shewmaker's silence after the incident in 2000—and his silence during 2003, which included the Pinkerton investigation, the Milano task force and Merriman steering committee—was enough for me to know Shewmaker was no longer a friend. If Rohrs was whispering negative things about SAGE in the ear of the inner circle, was Shewmaker whispering a similar message in the other ear?

While Rohrs and his allies saw me as a Walton Fellow gone wild, I was heartened to know that others, like Al Konuwa, saw my actions as bold. Sure, I could understand how some would see my aggressiveness to be brazen. But I viewed myself as innovative and entrepreneurial—the same characteristics SIFE was espousing for its students.

Page twelve of the handbook also addressed SIFE's new policy regarding contact with other SIFE teams around the world. It stated: "One of the benefits of SIFE's recent growth and global expansion is the opportunity for networking and collaboration among members of the network. SIFE Teams are strongly encouraged to engage in sharing and exchanges with other teams. However, the SIFE World Headquarters and leadership of each SIFE country organization treat the privacy of their advisors and student members very seriously. Information about SIFE's privacy policy can be found on the SIFE website. This contact information is the property of each respective national SIFE organization and the SIFE World Headquarters and will not be provided to other SIFE faculty advisors or team members."

This was news to me. Off to the website I went where I found:

> The personal contact information provided to our organization is strictly confidential. At present, this information is only accessible by SIFE World Headquarters staff, members of the SIFE Board of Directors, and upon request by designated individuals at companies represented by members of the SIFE Board of Directors. The companies of SIFE Board members may not use this information for commercial purposes. Contact information includes name, title, address, phone and email.

In the old days, when I was a Walton Fellow in good standing, SIFE had freely provided me with a list of all participating schools, faculty advisers and their contact information. Many of the people now on the list of SIFE teams competing in the USA were from the thirty-five schools that Chico State had recruited as part of our Adopt-a-Rookie SIFE team campaign. In fact, SIFE provided veteran teams with a $1,000 stipend for each new team it recruited.

Now that SIFE was going global—and when a Walton Fellow like me was trying to expand his global network—SIFE was stomping on the brakes. Not only was the contact information of SIFE board members off-limits, but so, too, was the contact information of SIFE faculty and students from other countries.

The new policies on use of the SIFE trademark and contacting board members and other SIFE teams looked pretty harsh in general. But the next policy was clearly aimed at Chico State and SAGE. Two years earlier, recall, we had our first SAGE World Cup in Kansas City, and we received favorable publicity from the *Kansas City Star*. Also, Chico State SIFE had conducted SAGE workshops in Amsterdam and Mainz the prior two years.

Well, Rohrs (and his board) made sure this would never happen again, as spelled out on page thirteen:

> SIFE Teams that wish to organize events in the same metropolitan statistical area (MSA) at any time during or three days prior to and after an official event organized by the SIFE World Headquarters or any national SIFE organization must adhere to the following guidelines: (1) The SIFE Team may not offer invitations for its meeting to any official SIFE event attendee or group of attendees, other than their own team members, during the time that the attendee(s) has been invited to or is scheduled to participate in a function of the official SIFE event; (2) Members or constituents of the SIFE Team may not solicit financial support from any individual that is an official guest of the SIFE World Headquarters or any national SIFE organization; (3) The SIFE Team will notify the SIFE World Headquarters or national SIFE organization in advance of their meeting plans and invitation list; (4) The SIFE Team will not promote or respond to inquiries from

any member of the media in the MSA; and (5) The SIFE Team will not report any details of its meeting, activity, project, etc. in any official SIFE competitive event.

Any thoughts I may have had about bringing another group of Chico delegates with me to Barcelona in November were summarily quashed. The item that really jumped out was number four, where SIFE precluded a team from responding to inquiries from the media. Was this America? Was this how SIFE was now promoting free enterprise, by discouraging competition from an organization promoting youth entrepreneurship for high school students? And by forbidding its founder to talk to the media?

I could see Rohrs' point, though. Why let a renegade Walton Fellow from California piggyback on his event and let this fellow promote his own SAGE program when the board had clearly decided to support Rohrs' argument that SAGE should not be part of SIFE's future?

All told, SIFE's new policies would stop me dead in my tracks. Even though Mike Merriman's task force promised to include me in SIFE's future deliberations involving high school organizations, the new handbook made it clear that everyone wanted SAGE completely out of the picture.

At the time of the Pinkerton investigation in 2003, I believed Rohrs might be fired for his handling of the special competition kerfuffle. Now, the board had clearly decided to stick with him. Additionally, *they gave him a $10,000 raise.* Why?

In SIFE's IRS Form 990, its publicly available tax return for the year ended August 31, 2004, SIFE's revenues of $12,583,508 were up from $9,202,125 in 2003. Going into 2003, SIFE's initial fundraising goal was $10,700,000.[6] It didn't matter to Robert E. Rich, who was now the chairman of the SIFE board, that Rohrs had spent most of the last half of 2003 answering questions from Larry Pinkerton and Bernie Milano. What really mattered seemed to be the *money—money over ethics.* The more teams SIFE proclaimed to field—seventeen hundred colleges and universities and forty-two countries in its network—the more donors signed up. Rohrs exceeded his projected revenues by nearly $2 million, and he was compensated $279,000 for the year.[7]

Groan. The board was rewarding Rohrs for bringing home the bacon.

Here's how it worked for the board. Alvin discovers a breach of ethics by Mat Burton. Rather than disciplining Mat, Alvin tries to cover for him. The board finds out, and then slaps Alvin's hands and offers him a nice raise. Alvin presumably pays Tom Payne off as long as he goes away silently. Alvin tightens the controls, and SAGE's influence fizzles.

Where were the business ethics? My faith in the board was now zero. It wouldn't be long before a few key few members of SIFE's Executive Committee, including Tom Coughlin and Jack Kahl, would be confronted with their own ethical dilemmas. When the shit hit the fan for each of them, SIFE would be the least of their concerns.

Because I was still a Walton Fellow (*barely*) in good standing, I qualified to receive an official invitation to SIFE events. With SIFE's new rules and regulations in mind, I headed for Barcelona on November 21, 2004, to attend SIFE's fourth World Cup. Unlike the previous two years, I was traveling solo. This trip would mark my third and final SIFE World Cup. Instead of staying at the competition hotel, the Hotel Princesa Sofia, I met up with my friends from Poland, and we all chipped in to rent a beautiful apartment a few miles from the hotel.

My three days in "Barthelona," as the locals pronounce it, were filled with SIFE activities, of course, but before getting down to business, my friends and I took a tour of Spain's second largest city. To our delight, we were treated to the beautiful works of famous Spanish architect, Antoni Gaudi, especially the Sagrada Familia Roman Catholic church. Gaudi's architectural and engineering style was reflected in the religious images of so much of his work. Our tour bus also cruised by the 1992 Olympic stadium where, for the first time, the Olympic Games did not include a former Soviet Union republic, but did include a unified Germany and a post-apartheid team from South Africa.

By now, because of SAGE, I had friends from around the world and I was pleased to see many of them in Barcelona. Though I could no longer lead any workshops or anything else formally related to Chico State SIFE, I certainly could discuss one of Chico State's projects *informally*. I kept a high profile. Before and after presentations, I met with as many people as I could. Not at all to my surprise, whenever Rohrs, Nasby, or Burton made eye contact, they would quickly turn away. I was as welcome as a grizzly bear at a Sunday school picnic.

Strangely, I never saw Jack Shewmaker—he was on the program as the keynote speaker at a Global Leadership Summit on the morning of September 24. The purpose of the summit was to explore the topic of entrepreneurship.

At the end of the 2005 exposition, the SIFE World Cup Champion was announced—this time, it was a team from Australia, with the U.S. team from Flagler College coming in second. After the winners were announced and the confetti fell, the announcer invited all guests to a post-event party at a large nightclub on the city's waterfront. My Polish friends and I headed back to the apartment to change into some casual clothes. We arrived at the party about ten o'clock.

The party was rocking, loud speakers blasting to a virtual United Nations of ideological university students, faculty advisers, and country coordinators, jamming to the music played by a Spanish disc jockey. Like most college parties, it was so loud that you could hardly hear one another. Before I knew it, Volodymyr Melynk, SIFE's country coordinator from Kiev, Ukraine, was tugging on my sleeve.

"Can we step into the adjoining room and chat about SAGE a few moments?" he asked. "It's quieter in there."

About ten minutes into our conversation, someone tapped me on the shoulder. I turned around to see a big, imposing guy wearing a Toronto Maple Leafs hockey jersey.

"This is a private party—invited guests only. Take a hike," he said.

Melynk was aghast, and I was taken aback. This shit happened in the former Soviet Union. Was this a SIFE event, or a KGB event? In a flash I knew what was up.

But I played along. The dude was David Henderson from SIFE Canada, and Toronto was the host of next year's SIFE World Cup. The party was officially being hosted by SIFE Canada.

"You must be mistaken, my friend," I smiled. "I'm a Sam M. Walton Fellow from California, and I'm with the SIFE group." I dug into my pocket and retrieved my name badge. "Here, look," I offered.

"I know who you are," he growled, not bothering to look at my badge. "And I know why you're here. This is an invitation-only party, and you're not on the guest list."

I took a deep breath, exhaling slowly. "Look, you and I have never met before," I said softly. "And I'm sure this must be really uncomfortable for you to do someone else's bidding."

Just before Melynk and I went into the side room for privacy, I had seen Bruce Nasby come in the front door.

"I tell you what, I'll be happy to get up and leave without incident, but you've got to do one thing for me first," I said.

"What's that?"

"You've got to go back into the other room and tell Bruce Nasby that I'm happy to leave, but he has to tell me himself," I offered. "If you don't, I won't go voluntarily. You'll have to remove me yourself."

He blanched. Then he cleared his throat, leaned in, and less menacingly pleaded, "Hey, look, I don't want any trouble. Just do me a favor and promise me you won't use that four-letter word anymore."

I knew he didn't mean SIFE, nor did he mean fuck or duck.

"If someone asks me about SAGE," I said, "I'm going to answer them. In my country, we still have free speech."

"Well, we aren't in your country, and this is a private party. So you either promise you'll stop talking about you know what, or things might get pretty ugly."

Melynk whistled under his breath. "Volodymyr," I said, "maybe we can continue our conversation after the party is over."

"All right by me," he said.

We followed Henderson back into the main party room.

I consider myself to be a spiritual person, though not a religious one, especially after my youth pastor at the Tabernacle Baptist Church told me all religions other than Christianity were the works of the devil. Until this very moment in Barcelona, at age forty-eight, and at this juncture of my life, I truly didn't believe I had any enemies. Up until that point, let's just say that I had a serious *disliking* for Alvin Rohrs and Mat Burton.

Now, I am sorry to say, I felt nothing but vitriol. Joining Rohrs and

Burton on the list was Bruce Nasby. Two Bible school lessons from my youth came back to me, and I recalled the gist of Matthew 5:43-44: "Ye have heard that it hath been said, Thou shalt love thy neighbor, and hate thine enemy. But I say unto you, Love your enemies, bless them that curse you, do good to them that hate you, and pray for them which despitefully use you, and persecute you."

I also recalled the Golden Rule. The best way to love my three new enemies, I concluded, was to make SAGE a success. If, in turn, they hated me, so be it. And with that, I bid my friends in Barcelona a good night and headed back to Chico on September 25.

Though this was to be my last international trip as a Sam M. Walton Fellow and Chico State SIFE faculty adviser, I was about to start a SAGE journey that would take me to over twenty countries in the next seven years. Within a month, I had secured funding to finance the 2004–2005 SAGE program, with our two biggest grants coming from the Allstate and Walgreens Foundations. Another grant of $25,000 was received from the Earl Foor Foundation, a local foundation in Chico.

In Barcelona, the SAGE concept had been favorably received by a score of SIFE faculty and students from at least a dozen countries. Among them were Ghana and Nigeria, which I planned to visit in May. Now that SIFE had written new rules restricting SAGE's growth within SIFE's structure, I learned that Rohrs was going on the offensive.

On January 28, 2005, I received a fax from Kofi Obeng from the University of the Cape Coast. Kofi was a SIFE team leader there, and his father was the university chancellor. Kofi and his colleague, Seth Donkor, wanted to start a SAGE program in Ghana. Kofi shared a rambling email that he had received earlier that day from Sylvester John, SIFE's coordinator for Africa. The email revealed two things: SIFE's strategy to sever its relationship with SAGE, and John's disdain for paragraph breaks.

It is important for you to note that SAGE is one project of one SIFE Team, Cal State Chico. It is NOT a SIFE HQ endorsed program in any way, shape or form. This US-based team has embarked on this project and will present its impact at the USA National Competition. Note that only then will the judges evaluate the effectiveness of this project or if it even well meets SIFE criteria. It is also important for you to understand that the pressing needs of the communities in California may not be the same as those in Cape Coast and so what may be perceived as a valuable project in California may not be the same as those in Cape Coast and so what may be perceived as a valuable project by a California Team should not be automatically copied by your Team for local implementation, without seriously considering relevance, pressing needs and impact. I would also highlight the fact that whatever you do in terms of SAGE would be adding to the impact reported by Cal State Chico, so in essence your efforts and SAGE projects would be strengthening their program and worldwide reach, allowing them to be more competitive in the USA and/or World Cup. This would be a free service you will be providing them in a way and serving as their foot soldiers. A few teams have seen value in doing so whereas a whole lot of others have not and rather used their time and limited resources to focus on THEIR team's assessment of what is important in line with SIFE projects as it relates to their local community. Many teams have also felt that by embarking on a high school program that sounds similar to SIFE (SAGE) would confuse their local stakeholders and constituents. Other teams have also established a focused program in SIFE through the national SIFE office and SIFE world headquarters, and they feel that by embracing SAGE they may be 'serving two masters' because the people who manage SAGE are different and based in the USA with no local offices or significant local support. The aspect of SAGE high school national and international competition also creates a huge sense of confusion of many who are used to the competitive process of SIFE students being focused on university level. Finally the issue of best use of a Team's limited resources also comes into play in terms of getting high school students to a national competition and SAGE world cup. This requires significant funding much of which you would have to raise. This would clearly affect your ability to invest more resources into your other SIFE projects and getting ready for SIFE national competition and World Cup if you win. Many SIFE teams would not like a situation whereby they spend all their money on SAGE activities and as a result their other SIFE projects become weaker which results in them losing the competition or even not making enough resources to travel to the national and world cup competitions. So these are all very important things to think about and I would encourage you to carefully consider what you get yourself and your Team into. As you know, SIFE Teams do not have to embark on projects of other SIFE Teams because it is obvious that most SIFE Teams are just as smart as others in the US (or elsewhere) and can come up with their own projects without needing to copy or act as foot soldiers carrying out projects of other SIFE Teams.

I was offended—but not surprised—by John's email. Especially outrageous were John's references to Ghana SIFE students being *foot soldiers* for SAGE and *serving two masters*. He knew all about foot soldiers—he was a native of Sierra Leone, where for nearly a decade young boys had been recruited as foot soldiers by despots mining for blood diamonds. The bloody civil war in Sierra Leone had just ended in 2001, and to imply that Ghana SIFE students would be foot soldiers for Chico State was a ludicrous analogy. As for his "serving two masters" analogy, I was dismayed! If Kofi Obeng's SIFE team did not adopt SAGE, then John's analogy meant that they would continue to serve one master—SIFE. By playing the slave card, John inadvertently made SIFE—and Alvin Rohrs—the plantation owner.

Undeterred, Kofi Obeng and Seth Donkor promptly filed papers to make SAGE Ghana an official nongovernment organization incorporated in Ghana.

Chapter 18

Au Revoir, SIFE

===========

With no teaching duties for the entire academic year, I helped steer the 2004–2005 SIFE team in the right direction, at least when I was in town. But I was on the road a lot. In December, I headed back to China as Wang Lei's guest, making presentations at universities in Boading, Beijing and Dalian. The trip to Dalian was unforgettable. Lei and I bought train tickets in a sleeper car and made the overnight train journey from Beijing to Dalian in almost blizzard-like conditions. Our tiny cabin was packed with a dozen people. As Lei's guest, he gave me one of the cots and, dutifully, he watched over me as I slept. After the nine-hour journey we checked into a hotel and freshened up.

Dalian is a seaport on the Yellow Sea to the east, and is China's northernmost warm water port. Today it is one of China's most important cities, serving not only as an international shipping center but also is a regional financial base. A couple hours after our arrival, we made a presentation at Dalian University of Technology, the area's largest university and best known for its engineering and science programs. Meeting with the associate dean and a few faculty members, we focused our discussion on two issues: an upcoming entrepreneurship conference that we were planning for Chico in August, and SAGE.

Lei and I had come up with an idea to help fund the SAGE World Cup, which was scheduled for next August. Our plan was to recruit Chinese students and business leaders to come to Chico State one week prior to our SAGE World Cup in San Francisco to participate in an entrepreneurship conference featuring several of Northern California's most successful entrepreneurs. We were encouraged by the level of interest in such a conference wherever we went in China. The big problem, though, would be securing travel visas to the United States. It was a relatively easy task to obtain visas for students and educators, but not so easy for people in the private sector.

About this same time, Wal-Mart's vice chairman, Tom Coughlin, announced his retirement from Wal-Mart, to be effective on January 27, 2005. He oversaw Wal-Mart, Sam's Club, and Walmart.com. Coughlin, recall, was the SIFE chairman who had hired Larry Pinkerton to lead his special investigation into SIFE's special competitions.[1]

For years, Tom Coughlin had been battling it out with Lee Scott to become Wal-Mart's CEO, but Scott eventually won the battle in 2000.[2] Coughlin and Scott's differences came to a head at an October 2004 Wal-Mart board meeting. *CNN Money* later reported (February 18, 2009):

> Coughlin was frustrated that much of the meeting was spent discussing Wal-Mart's new environmental initiatives, rather than talking about business heading into the holiday season. After the meeting Coughlin, who didn't want to comment for this story, told Scott he was ready to retire and officially stepped down as vice chairman in January 2005, though he retained his board seat.
>
> That might have been the end of it if Coughlin hadn't used a Wal-Mart gift card to buy contact lenses. The $100 card was part of an All Star program to reward lower-level employees. According to Wal-Mart, the home office was tipped off to Coughlin's use of the card when a salesclerk at the store called headquarters to inquire about the program. The home office employee could not understand why Coughlin would be using such a card and alerted corporate fraud, which launched an investigation.
>
> Coughlin was forced to resign from Wal-Mart's board in March 2005, and the company accused him of stealing as much as $500,000 by filing fake expense reports and cashing in bogus gift cards. Coughlin has said that he used the money to finance covert anti-union activities. Wal-Mart says it knew nothing about such a program. Coughlin later pleaded guilty to wire fraud and tax evasion and served twenty-seven months of house arrest. And in August (2009), Wal-Mart agreed to pay Coughlin $6.75 million to settle a lawsuit it brought against him to void his retirement

package, which according to regulatory filings was valued at $17 million.[3]

In his last year, Coughlin's annual salary was reportedly $1.03 million and he had received $3 million in bonuses and other income. According to SEC filings, he held about $20 million in company stock.[4] In a February 14, 2005, article in *Drug Store News* entitled "A Tribute to Tom Coughlin: A Legacy of Leadership," the article said, "When it came to the company's culture, Coughlin believed fervently in the concept of servant leadership, which is the foundation of Wal-Mart's operation and approach to decision-making."[5]

There it was again, servant leadership. Since the time he announced his retirement in December 2004 until March 2005 when he resigned from the board, Rob Walton and Lee Scott sang Coughlin's praises. He was a talented leader; he had great relationships with associates; he had achieved one of the most successful business careers anyone could imagine. But then came March.

Why would Coughlin do this? In a subsequent July 2006 article entitled, "From the Boardroom to the Courtroom," *IBmag.com*, one of northeast Ohio's business magazines, commented on the Coughlin case:

> While it may seem baffling, it's not uncommon for those with millions of dollars at the highest levels of power to abuse their privileges. "What I've found in dealing with high-profile people is that it's a gradual transformation to where they've rationalized in their minds that somehow this is OK," says Alex Johnson, a former FBI special agent and thirty-year veteran of white-collar crime investigations. "They feel they're entitled to this and that whatever they're doing is just a bonus that they deserve."[6]

Had Coughlin recently graduated from the Alvin Rohrs School of Servant Leadership? His behavior wasn't like that of Leo the servant, serving his associates before himself. Tom Payne and I had a chat about this, and Tom told me that he had heard from his contacts at SIFE's office in Springfield that "they were all praying for Coughlin."[7]

By early April, 2005, I had helped our Chico State SIFE team get ready for regionals, which would take place in Los Angeles. This would be my last SIFE regional competition. Our two main projects, again, were the Youth Entrepreneurship Camp and, of course, SAGE. SAGE had grown from one to six states in the U.S. and from seven participating countries to eleven globally. In the annual report, we said, "We have built our SAGE business by offering customers quality service at the lowest of all prices—they are free. Our services are free because university students can make a difference by giving back to their communities while attending college through community service learning." If nothing else, I would go out with a bang, letting my students be the voice for SAGE.

We won our regionals for the twelfth straight year. Sample comments from judges included: "SAGE recognizes the need to start SIFE at the high school level"; "You do an excellent job of teaching younger students the entrepreneurial skills to successfully compete"; and "Teaching high school students is a great help in preparing them for the future."

When I read these comments, I thought of Sylvester John's silly email to Kofi Obeng on January, 28, 2005, where he implied that the needs of the Ghana community may not be the same as the California community. When it comes to youth entrepreneurship and civic engagement, there are no geographical boundaries.

Throughout the school year, Chico's SIFE students had been corresponding closely with SAGE friends in a long list of countries from Australia to Zimbabwe. Our new SAGE national coordinators were planning to expand SAGE into their countries. Observing my Chico State SIFE leaders, I felt a tremendous sense of pride. For many of them, I could see their worldview expanding from an organization-based model to a humanitarian one.[8] Their world began to reach beyond the windshields of their cars.

As the team began preparing for the SIFE USA expo, I continued globetrotting. On April 26, 2005, I flew back to Shanghai where I met Tom Payne. On Thursday, April 28, Tom and I took a train to Su Zhou [sue joe] to visit a university. We were like two little boys pedaling a couple old clap-trap rental bikes navigating the crowded streets to see a wonderful outdoor museum called Lion's Head.

Tricia and I were growing closer and closer. I had been to the Philippines for ten days in February 2005, helping Bob Galindez with SAGE and meeting Tricia in Boracay on two consecutive weekends. I sent an email to Tricia, "The bikes were way too small for us, with our knees coming up to our chin with every cycle. Tonight, we took the train back to Shanghai and checked into the Renaissance Hotel in the Pudong District, near the Jin Mao Tower."

Two days later, on April 28, we attended the SAGE China tournament. Tom had graciously agreed to be a SAGE judge. As was the case with the Philippines last year, I couldn't stop grinning the entire time with six brave Shanghai teams competing.

After the day's event, Tom and I were sitting in the hotel's executive lounge when I stumbled on an April 18, 2005, article in *Fortune* magazine about Wal-Mart, entitled "Bruised in Bentonville." The article started out by explaining Wal-Mart was the world's largest company, with annual sales of $288 billion and profits of more than $10 billion. But it was now facing battles on many fronts, especially those dealing with sex discrimination lawsuits, union fights, and wage and pay disputes. Near the end of the article, Lichtenstein's name popped up.

> The University of California at Santa Barbara hosted a conference last April titled "Wal-Mart: A Template for 21st-Century Capitalism?" As you might imagine, the discussion was in no way Wal-Mart friendly. The conference's organizer, Nelson Lichtenstein, proposed this central thesis: Throughout U.S. history there has usually been one dominant company that essentially sets a benchmark living wage for the American worker. "Today that company is Wal-Mart, but its pay is so low, it can't be considered a living wage," Lichtenstein says.
>
> On this point, Wal-Mart management says, there is a tradeoff. The more than a million Americans working at Wal-Mart are paid wages that might be higher, but if they were, Wal-Mart's goods would cost more, to the detriment of the 296 million of us who can shop at Wal-Mart. There is something coldly reductionist, though, about Wal-Mart's paying its workers so little that the only store where they can afford to shop is Wal-Mart.[9]

This was fascinating. As Tom was checking his email and taking care of other business on the Internet, I decided to do a Google search on Lichtenstein. I learned he was a history professor from University of California, Santa Barbara, and he specialized in American political economy. Much of his work centered on Wal-Mart and its role in modern-day capitalism. At UCSB, he was also the director of the Center for the Study of Work, Labor and Democracy. Soon after learning about Lichtenstein, I happened to see him in a recorded June 9, 2004, interview on PBS's *Frontline*. Lichtenstein had compared the Wal-Mart model of employment to that of General Motors.

"When you had a job at General Motors, it was a lifetime job," he said. "It was a high-wage job, and there were often many, many benefits attached to it."

Lichtenstein said the Wal-Mart model of employment, based on low wages, low skills, low benefits and rapid job turnover, is becoming the template for American firms to follow, but this model is eroding the American middle-class standard of living.

"What I think is the road forward here," he argued, "is we want to take the efficiencies that have been generated by Wal-Mart—and they are real efficiencies—and we want to shape them and control them and regulate them in such a way that the benefits of these are distributed widely throughout the society, within the firm between its managers and its employees, and then in the rest of the United States as well."[10]

I wondered if Lichtenstein might want to be my guest at the SIFE USA National Exposition coming up in Kansas City in a few weeks, May 22–24. I hunted down his email address at the UC website and shot him an email. I introduced myself as an accounting professor at CSU, Chico, and also a Sam M. Walton Fellow. Did he know what SIFE was? Did he know that Wal-Mart was one of its biggest sponsors? This would get his attention, I thought.

In a few minutes, I received a return email, and yes, he was very interested, and yes, indeed, he would like to observe the SIFE event. I directed him to SIFE's online registration site.

He asked when we might have a phone conversation. I told him that

I'd be returning to the U.S. the next day, but would only be around for a couple days before catching a flight to London. We agreed to talk the next night, before I took off again. I was traveling to Sierra Leone but had to connect in London for two nights. Ironically, Sierra Leone was Sylvester John's home country—home of real foot soldiers in the 1990s.

One night later, on May 3, we talked for about an hour. Lichtenstein had heard about SIFE but didn't know much about it. I gave him the short version of my history with SIFE, and about Tom's whistleblowing.

After the call, he sent me an email. "Do you think Mr. Payne might be willing to talk to me about SIFE's history and its relationship to Wal-Mart and other mass retailers?" he asked. "Was he involved with SIFE for several years? I want to understand the organic relationship between SIFE and the recruitment of lower level management for the mass retailing sector. This strikes me as something genuinely new in how college students move into industry. Plus the aggressive move by SIFE into Asia needs exploration."

As for Tom talking to him, I doubted it. Tom was tight-lipped and had maintained a low profile.

A week later, Lichtenstein sent me an email saying his request to be an observer had been denied by SIFE. Tim Clow, now managing director of SIFE's U.S. program, said that because UC, Santa Barbara, didn't have a SIFE program, "we regretfully inform you that you have not been approved to attend."

I emailed Nelson, expressing my regret that he wasn't going to get a close-up view of SIFE and Wal-Mart's unique recruiting pipeline in action. "Good morning, from a humid, and very poor, Sierra Leone," I wrote from its capital city, Freetown. "No chance of any Wal-Marts coming here soon."

I then referred to Tim Clow's letter, denying his admission to the Kansas City event.

"SIFE implements rules as it goes, usually to retain control and power over the actions of aggressive (e.g., entrepreneurial) faculty members like me. SIFE's agenda in Kansas City feels very similar to a Wal-Mart annual meeting, complete with a SIFE cheer ("Students in free enterprise, success is where we specialize!"). Lots of rally cries and inspirational speeches, with one or two always coming from Jack Shewmaker and one or two from Jack Kahl. A few Walton Fellows and I refer to this as the Jack and

Jack Show. And near the end, Alvin Rohrs always gets up in front of the audience and literally cries, thanking everyone for how much they are doing to change the world."

Lichtenstein wanted to know more about how SIFE was putting up road blocks for SAGE.

"Many of SIFE's new policies are related to restricting my use of SIFE as a tool to promote a Chico State SIFE project called SAGE," I wrote. "SAGE is why I am in Sierra Leone."

I continued, "SIFE's fear of SAGE, I think, stems from the fact that they view SAGE as (1) not in line with SIFE's priorities, (2) confusing the SIFE "brand" (Alvin Rohrs always refers to SIFE as though we are a manufacturing entity who needs to trademark and brand our product), and (3) [this is the big one] an ultimate competitor for SIFE's funds."

To date, the only SIFE-affiliated companies contributing any substantial funds to SAGE were Walgreens and Joe Pedott's company, JEI Enterprises in San Francisco. Joe is the marketing genius behind the famous Chia pet.

My five-day stay in Sierra Leone was similar to my first trip to South Africa—I couldn't possibly get over the jarring reality of abject poverty. The revolting stench, awfulness, and downright inhumane conditions of so many people—many of them missing one or more limbs—was almost too much to bear. I learned that often, during the Sierra Leone war, captors would ask their victims if they preferred a *short-sleeve* or a *long-sleeve*. Their answer determined if their arms were macheted above or below the elbow. World travel most assuredly was expanding my worldview.

For people inclined to cry frequently or pray often, I would ask that a few tears and prayers be reserved for countries like Sierra Leone.

My host in Sierra Leone was Francis Horace Dove-Edwin, a member of the 1999 champion SIFE team at Chico State. His nickname was Tipeps (pronounced Tee Peps), and he was well-known wherever he went. Tipeps had been a world-class sprinter, representing his country in the 1992 Olympics. At one time, he held one of the world's fastest times in the 100 meters, clocking in at 10.14 seconds. He had asked me to come to Sierra Leone to try to launch SAGE in his home country.

The last day, after four days of nonstop meetings with government officials, school leaders, and the media, we were winding down. Tipeps and I decided to eat a late lunch at a Lebanese café. We entered it about 2:30. The restaurant was empty, except for one table occupied by two Sierra Leonean men and two Americans—a woman and man. We all exchanged nods, and the Americans smiled at me. It took me a split second to recognize Angelina Jolie, who was in Sierra Leone on a humanitarian mission for the United Nations. After their group finished lunch they walked by our table on the way out. Tipeps couldn't contain himself, and he asked for a picture. "Sure," she smiled, though a bit reluctantly. I took Tipeps' camera and shot a couple photos.

"Would you like one, too?" Jolie asked me, certain of my answer.

"No," I surprised her. "Just meeting you has been a pleasure."

Off they went. The next day, I flew back to California.

I only had about two weeks to help the Chico State SIFE team make its last trip to Kansas City with me as its faculty adviser. Our delegation of about fifteen students and a few business advisers arrived at the Kansas City Marriott late in the afternoon on May 22, and I headed straight for the Walton Fellow dinner and reception in the Colonial Ballroom. I took an empty seat at a table occupied by Sylvester John and his South Africa SIFE coordinator, William Essiam. They were caught off guard, and clearly not happy to see me.

"So, Sylvester, you don't want Ghana SIFE students to *carry water* for Chico students?" I asked. "Just what do you mean by that?"

He hemmed and hawed, and said something about how SAGE would give us an unfair advantage if we called it a SIFE project. I decided to enlighten him.

"A few years ago, before you joined SIFE and before SIFE truly went global," I said, "did you know that *Business Week* sponsored a SIFE competition for Best Education Project? The main criterion was how well the project could be implemented nationally."

No, he said he didn't know this, but it didn't matter. "If our SIFE teams in Africa, or anywhere else, devote resources to SAGE, it will take away from their SIFE resources."

"It's not about resources," I countered. "It's about university students wanting to help younger students become entrepreneurs, develop leadership skills, and go to college."

He raised his voice, much to the discomfiture of other Walton Fellows seated at the table. "You are totally missing the point." He slammed his fist to the table. "Your SAGE program is confusing. It is leading to confusion with the SIFE brand."

"I am tired of hearing SIFE talk about its brand," I said, equally as loudly. "We are not Coke or Pepsi or McDonalds. SIFE is about faculty and students teaching about entrepreneurship and creating value."

Using another memorable word from his January missive to Kofi, I added, "And we certainly are not about serving our *masters* at Wal-Mart or Sam's Club or RadioShack."

The keynote speaker, coincidentally, was Doug McMillon, executive vice president of Sam's Club, the nation's largest members-only warehouse club with more than 46 million members. McMillon would later become Wal-Mart's president and CEO, starting January 31, 2014.

I was on a roll. "The main problem SIFE has with SAGE is that I started it, and Alvin doesn't want anything to do with SAGE or with me."

I didn't say it, but I thought it: at this point in our relationship, who could blame Rohrs for wanting me completely out of his life? I had caused him a lot of extra work.

John continued to recite the points he made in his rambling email to Kofi Obeng. I can't remember how the conversation ended, but it was somewhat along the lines of my telling him that he was so full of shit that one could give him an enema and send him home in a shoebox.

The next day, the Chico State SIFE team presented without any problems. That night, though, we learned that we had been edged out in the first round by Anderson University of Indiana.

For the last time, I would console my SIFE team. But I felt a strange lightness. This was it. No more Kansas City, and no more listening to SIFE cheers, Jack and Jack speeches, or Alvin Rohrs' call to SIFE's monied altar. Again, I took comfort in reading the judges' feedback forms, especially as the comments pertained to SAGE. Samples:

- "SAGE is a great program. We need to get more high schools involved!"
- "Super job with SAGE!"
- "SAGE is a good activity. Keep it going. Try to get it into more states."
- "Global SAGE is outstanding! What an accomplishment!"
- "Very strong communication of the institutions that support the global economy. These concepts are taught at the MBA level. Good job!"
- "A lot of lives have been touched by your efforts—how does it feel to be a "blessing" in the lives of others?"
- "Teaching the teacher is very important—until the teacher understands, it is impossible for them to effectively teach others. Global SAGE is a very effective activity. Excellent work—you are carrying out some very worthwhile activities benefiting many people."
- "Great programs! You are making a positive impact! Keep striving to reach more people with your message."
- "Global SAGE is a winner!"

Strangely, for the first time I remember Jack Kahl was absent from a national SIFE expo. Mr. Duck Tape wasn't a main center of attraction.

Kahl was fun, loud, gregarious, and loved to be around students. Each year, including 1999 when I was the proud recipient, he personally presented the unusually long titled "Jack Kahl SIFE Leadership Award to the Sam M. Walton Fellow of the Year." However, Kahl had other more pressing matters to attend to this year.

A year earlier in 2004, Kahl had written *Leading from the Heart: Choosing to be a Servant Leader.* A slim primer on leadership, at only 110 pages, it was chock full of quotes, anecdotes, and sage nuggets based on his experience as the Top Duck at Manco for nearly thirty years. Interwoven throughout the book were stories of what Kahl had learned from Sam Walton.

In the acknowledgements he wrote, "To Sam Walton, whom I was lucky enough to call a friend for 16 years. Thanks, Sam, for teaching me that what my mother and father did around our kitchen table as I grew up was how you approached running your great Wal-Mart Company. ... I knew from your example that I could build any size business as long as I remembered what I learned from my parents, as well as the great lessons learned from you, Jack Shewmaker, Tom Coughlin, and so many others."[11]

The book, co-authored with former Manco associate Tom Donelan, was quite well-written. I was especially surprised to see that chapter one was preceded by my one of my favorite passages from a book by James Michener. The passage, as extracted by Kahl and Donelan, reads:

> If a man happens to find himself—if he knows what he can be depended upon to do, the limits of his courage, the positions from which he will no longer retreat, the degree to which he can surrender his inner life to some woman, the secret reservoirs of his determination, the extent of his dedication, the depth of his feeling for beauty, his honest and unpostured goals—then he has found a mansion which he can inhabit with dignity all the days of his life.

But the entire passage, which I knew by heart, includes a preceding paragraph:

> For this is the journey that men make: to find themselves. If they fail in this, it doesn't matter much what else they find. Money, position, fame, many loves, revenge are all of little consequence, and when the tickets are collected at the end of the ride they are tossed into the bin marked FAILURE.[12]

Like so many modern disciples of the servant leader management philosophy, Kahl couldn't help but include a shout-out to the Big Guy on page two:

> Jesus Christ said, "Many are called, but few are chosen." In the case of leadership we could say, *many are called, but few choose.* Many people study leadership, but too few dig deep inside themselves and make a choice to serve their team from the very heart

of who they are. I hope this book will show you how important it is to do just that.

Humans are frail, and we all make mistakes. When I dig deep inside myself, I sometimes find an abrasive, curt, cynical, and sarcastic person. I try to overcome these character flaws each day. In spite of these flaws, it is generally not in my nature to kick a man when he is down.

But it is also in my nature to call a spade a spade. In life, we all make choices and decisions that we later regret, and there are times when what we say is the opposite of what we do. When I teach business ethics in my classes at Chico State, I let my students know that a man's true character can be revealed by the way he acts when no one is looking.[13] Also, I challenge students to ask themselves the following questions to help them confront an ethical dilemma: (1) Is this action or decision legal? (2) Would I be proud to tell my parents about this action or decision? (3) Would I be able to look myself in the mirror if I do this? If a student answers no to any of these questions, I tell them, "You shouldn't carry out the action, even if there are harsh consequences. Always remember—your integrity is more important than making money."

For decades, Jack Kahl had been a model of citizenship and civic engagement in the Cleveland community. His definition of social responsibility went way beyond just respecting the law. Some of these actions included donating large sums of money to charity and providing customer service beyond industry standards.[14] But in 1999 he had a weak moment—a weak moment of greed—and in 2004 the FBI came calling.[15]

The FBI wanted to know if Kahl had received any insider tips from an Ohio State marketing professor, Roger Blackwell, on September 20, 1999. Kahl had purchased fifteen thousand shares of stock in a company called Worthington Foods for $186,000.[16] For him, this was a small trade. Soon thereafter, Kellogg's bought Worthington Foods, and Kahl reaped a $168,000 profit from the sale of the Worthington stock. Again, this was pretty much chump change for Kahl. At first, Kahl denied receiving any insider tips. The next day, though, he reconsidered and called his lawyer to tell him that he had lied to the FBI.

During the SIFE event in Kansas City in late May of 2005, Kahl wasn't able to free himself to attend. Instead, he was on the witness stand in U.S. District Court in Columbus, Ohio, as a prosecution witness in Blackwell's trial. Kahl was promised immunity if he testified against Blackwell. During the second week of the trial, Kahl took the stand. The story was fascinating, and sad. In a May 27 article by Ted Wendling of *The Plain Dealer* bureau of Columbus:

> Kahl said he regretted the purchase almost instantly, realizing that he was jeopardizing his sterling reputation in Cleveland for a pittance. Kahl, who sold his duct tape company in 1997, said he routinely made stock trades involving more than 100,000 shares and millions of dollars. "Why did I buy the stock? is the question I've asked millions of times," Kahl said. "Greed, I guess, or stupidity."
>
> "One night of not being forthright with them was one night too many for me," Kahl said. He said he had decided to come clean even though "I saw loss of reputation, I saw probably having to go to jail—everything I saw was bad." Defense attorney Dan Costello hammered on Kahl about his deal with the government, saying authorities had given him a "get-out-of-jail-free" card in exchange for turning on a close friend. "You can call it what you want," Kahl retorted, adding that he had no idea when he first admitted lying to the FBI that he might avoid prison.[17]

In the end, Blackwell was fined $1 million and sentenced to six years in prison. Kahl walked free. More than a year later, Kahl reflected on his ordeal in the July 2006 issue of *IBmag.com*:

> "I didn't want to leave this life as a coward," he says. "If you make a mistake, then stand up as a man and admit it. I did that and immediately I was at peace." Less in the limelight these days, Kahl still runs his leadership development and consulting firm, Jack Kahl & Associates, and promotes his book, *Leading from the Heart*. Some have even suggested he write a book about his experiences throughout the scandal. "I don't want to make a business

out of talking about it," he says. His advice for others is simple: Stock tips are overheard all the time, but it's better to let it go in one ear and out the other, he says. If you think it's something you shouldn't do, then don't do it.[18]

Jack Kahl, I think to this day, is a good and decent man. He has lots of friends—for sure, though, it is pretty obvious that he needs to be a bit more selective. Roger Blackwell didn't turn out so well. And Tom Coughlin wasn't quite the servant leader everyone made him out to be. I still find it hard to swallow when I remember one of Kahl's lines at Kansas City a couple years earlier, when he said, "Alvin Rohrs is like a brother to me." Really?

Nelson Lichtenstein and I kept in touch. He even interviewed me for his forthcoming collection of essays entitled *Wal-Mart: The Face of Twenty-First Century Capitalism*. When I let him know about the Kahl story, he sent me an email.

> It is remarkable. But then again, hypocrisy is plentiful, in academe as well as in business. I think SIFE merits a story, not really because of the corruption at the top, although that adds interest, but because of its success as an alternate pathway into management for thousands who would not have gone to get an MBA. If a kind of institutional networking/corruption is all part of this, well, that is the way of the world. Deals are made in the Harvard Commons Room as well as at Kansas City. When Kahl got that call from the Ohio State professor it was no more remarkable than the things he must have discussed at various SIFE/Wal-Mart cocktail parties along the way. I don't mean to be too cynical, but I think the Wal-Mart/Vendor/SIFE relationship needs a lot of looking into and given the closeness and the pressures and the power relationships, the situation must be just ripe for all kinds of deals, payoffs, backscratching, etc.

He signed off with an amusing reference to the fact that I was the 1999 recipient of the Jack Kahl SIFE Leadership Award. "Be sure to keep the plaque on prominent display."

Thus, my twelve-year stint as a Sam M. Walton Fellow came to end.

Just one day after returning from Kansas City, I received a registered letter from Robert E. Rich, Jr., CEO of Rich Products Corporation. Rich Products, founded by Robert E. Rich, Sr. in 1945 is the largest family-owned frozen foods manufacturer in the U.S. It now generates over $2.6 billion in annual sales. The younger Rich, a former professional hockey player, is now at the helm of the family company. He is also president and CEO of the triple-A baseball team in Buffalo. Rich Products, of course, is a big supplier for Wal-Mart and Sam's Club.

What started in 1993 with a personal letter from Sam Walton's son, S. Rob Walton, was now ending with a letter from SIFE's new board chairman. Dated May 25, 2005, Re: Termination of Faculty Advisory, the letter said:

Dear Dr. DeBerg:

Please be advised that effective immediately you will no longer be allowed to participate in SIFE activities as a faculty advisor or Sam Walton Fellow. This decision was made by the Executive Committee of the SIFE Board of Directors on May 23, 2005. This decision was based on conduct, activities and statements contrary to the best interest of SIFE.

Even though you will no longer be a Faculty Advisor or Sam Walton Fellow, we want to maintain the relationship with California State University - Chico. We will be communicating with California State University - Chico to ensure this continuing relationship and finding your replacement.

Please cease representing yourself or SAGE as having any relationship with SIFE. If you continue to believe it necessary to promote SAGE by speaking negatively of SIFE, you should use care not to defame SIFE, its board, officers, employees or representatives.

Sincerely,

Robert E. Rich, Jr., Chairman, SIFE Board of Directors

Rich had beaten me to the punch. I had planned to submit my

resignation to SIFE as soon as our new dean, Dr. Willie Hopkins, arrived on campus in early June. Somehow, though, knowing SIFE's true colors, I took a perverse sense of pride in being fired. Rich's last sentence cautioned me to "use care" not to defame SIFE. I read that and thought, SIFE should also use care not to defame SAGE.

It was now official—SIFE had divorced me. And with that, SIFE had hoped to divorce SAGE, but there were some courageous SIFE teams out there who saw the nobility of our mission. My sabbatical was coming to an end soon, and I had a few more big trips to make before summer's end.

Before leaving Chico, I prepared an email. I wanted one more opportunity for Walton Fellows to consider starting a SAGE program, even though SIFE was making it difficult for them to embrace it.

For the most part, my involvement with SIFE has been a fun, exhilarating and fulfilling ride. The most satisfaction has come from seeing students who started with SIFE with very low self-confidence and self-esteem, only later watching them grow as they discovered untapped talents as leaders, team members and community servants. In essence, SIFE helped them find a "home" on campus. Simultaneously, SIFE allowed me to find an "academic home," too, because it provided me with a structured outlet to pursue my interests in community service learning. I will always treasure the time I spent with students in being their SIFE adviser.

Like many of you, I have been at the SIFE game for a long time. I started in fall 1993 and now, twelve years later, the road has officially come to an end. I wish you all very well as you continue your SIFE journey, and do know that even though I have had many differences with SIFE management, I have always believed in SIFE's mission.

Here are just a few areas of concern for me:

1. There is a need for more "transparency" in the judging process of special competitions (especially after the discovery that four universities won prize money for a com-

petition they hadn't even entered in 2003); rather than terminate or demote the perpetrator, he was promoted; the whistleblower is no longer with the SIFE. Some of you may recall that this led to the creation of the Bernie Milano task force on policies, rules and procedures. Also, even though SIFE touted these special competitions as being judged by a panel of business executives, in reality, several of these competitions were judged by very recent SIFE alumni who had little experience in the working world.

2. With glaring weaknesses in special competition judging, I saw a need for better rules in judging the overall competition. This includes the need for a judging rubric that makes it clearer for judges to interpret what is, and what is not, a quality SIFE project.

3. There is a need for some real representation by Walton Fellows and/or faculty advisers on the Executive Committee of the Board, rather than restrict membership only to donor members (after all, SIFE is a college student organization whose success largely rests on the commitment of its faculty advisers).

4. There is a need for more diversity on SIFE's Board of Directors, and the need for more diversity in the make-up of the Board to include more non-retail companies.

5. There is evidence that SIFE is becoming an autocratic, centrally-planned organization (e.g., new rules and "protocols" were adopted last year governing SIFE teams' relationship with the media and board members; timing of projects; scope of projects; "registering" global projects) rather than a free flowing organization consistent with the notion of *free enterprise*.

6. There is an unwillingness of SIFE to "audit" the veracity of some of the elite SIFE team projects, and to provide guidelines on what is a SIFE "planned, organized and delivered" project as opposed to merely a SIFE "affiliated" project.

7. There is a tendency for SIFE Headquarters to seek and receive government assistance, based on its relationship with federal legislators.

8. There is a tendency for SIFE to become an "invited guests only" club rather than present itself to the world as a student organization willing to stand up and invite constructive criticism. This was evidenced by SIFE's denial of Dr. Nelson Lichtenstein, a nationally-renowned scholar in economic history who is also well-respected for his constructive criticism of modern-day retailing (including Wal-Mart), as one of my guests to the 2005 USA SIFE competition in KC a few weeks ago.

Addressing the email to over six hundred Sam M. Walton Fellows in my database, I hit the send button.

Au revoir, SIFE. And may the SAGE wind blow.

Part III

THE

REDEMPTION

THE THRILL OF VICTORY
One outstanding SAGE team from Nigeria, the Government School from
Junior Secondary School in Jikwoyi Village, won top honors in the best Social
Enterprise category at the 11th annual SAGE World Cup in Abuja, Nigeria.
Photo courtesy of Robert J. Best.

NIGERIA SHINES IN SAGE COMPETITION
Based on its outstanding performance at the SAGE 2011 World Cup, the
Government Secondary School from Jibi Village was awarded this van from the
First Lady of Nigeria, Mrs. Dame Patience Goodluck Ebele Jonathan. Pictured
is Curt DeBerg. Photo courtesy of Agwu Amogu.

Chapter 19

Role Models

━━━━━━━

Ideally, I would have resigned as a Walton Fellow before Robert Rich's letter landed in my mailbox, but I felt I owed it to our incoming dean that I was going to step away from SIFE. When Willie Hopkins interviewed for the dean's position a few months earlier, he had pointed to our SIFE program as an area of excellence that prompted him to interview. So, because of this, I wanted to explain my reasons to Dean Hopkins before officially stepping down.

After spending twelve years helping Chico State students complete projects and travel to competitions, it came as a huge relief to put SIFE behind me—as best I could. In Chico, SIFE had become a household name and I was known as the SIFE guy. Also, now that SAGE was up and running, I found myself telling the same story over and over. Though I was no longer affiliated with SIFE, I was now focusing on a new high school organization named SAGE.

One key person helped me officially start SAGE in 2002—Rob Best. Rob is a handsome, six-foot three-inch basketball junkie from Southern California who had been on the Chico State SIFE team in 1999 and 2000. He played briefly for the Chico State basketball team, but the head coach didn't appreciate Rob's affinity for three-point rainmakers instead of working the ball into the low post—to the bigger men. The coach, Puck Smith, was a decorated old-time Army guy, winning a Bronze Star medal and Medal of Valor as a long range reconnaissance ranger. Smith believed that the best basketball approach started inside the paint and worked out.

Rob, being a pure shooter, did not believe in this philosophy. His reasoning: why not drain a three-pointer if you could make it 40 percent of the time, as opposed to a two-point field goal 50 percent of the time? Do the math, Rob implored his coach.

Puck did the math, and decided Rob's best place on the team would be right next to him on the bench. Knowing that he wouldn't get much playing time, Rob promptly hung up his basketball shoes and signed up for the Chico State SIFE team. At the SIFE expo in Kansas City May 2000, the same event that the "incident" occurred, Rob met a fellow SIFE student from Lexington Community College in Kentucky: Sarah Myers.

Two years later, I was on hand to watch Rob and Sarah get married in the atrium of the Kansas City Marriott. Sarah's father, a renowned photographer who had done work for *National Geographic*, would soon take Rob under his wing and teach him the nuances of photography. Before long, Rob was an expert with a camera.

After graduating from Chico State, Rob spent a short time with me at Yeardisc in the summer and fall 2000. When Yeardisc became a victim of the dot-com bubble, Rob went to work for a financial services company in Santa Monica as its director of operations. As SAGE was morphing from Cal-High SIFE into SAGE in the summer of 2002, Rob made it clear that he wanted to be part of it.

I jumped at the chance to bring him aboard. Rob is incredibly good with students, quick with a joke, and quicker with a smile. But these aren't his greatest attributes. His greatest strengths are his attention to detail and his willingness to provide constructive criticism even when it hurts.

From 2002–2007, SAGE had been an operating fund within the Chico State University Foundation. In early 2008, however, we obtained our charter from the state of California and incorporated as a nonprofit organization. Soon after, we obtained our 501(c)(3) letter from the IRS proclaiming SAGEGLOBAL as a tax-exempt, nonprofit corporation. Now, donors had a choice. They could make tax-deductible contributions directly to our company—or make the check payable to the university. In 2008, I officially became the CEO of the new company, and Rob became the COO.

As my sabbatical leave of absence was coming to an end on June 30, 2005, I was busy securing travel visas and making flight arrangements for another trip to Africa. This time, my destination was Ghana first, and then on to Nigeria. On June 21, I boarded a flight to Amsterdam, connecting to Accra, Ghana. Arriving about ten o'clock that evening, I was greeted by three enthusiastic alumni of the University of the Cape Coast.

Cape Coast is about a two-hour drive southwest of the capital city of Accra. The group was led by Kofi Obeng, whose father was the vice chancellor at the university. Accompanying Kofi were Seth Donkor and Leeford Hope. Before they graduated, all three were active members of the Cape Coast SIFE team

As in previous trips to Africa, I again had a hard time reconciling the beauty of the surroundings with the pervasive poverty. The land seemed to be plush with natural resources, such as gold, bauxite, timber, and cocoa, but the average person outside of Accra lived in dilapidated, adobe-hut villages. With a population of about 20 million people and a land size similar to the state of Oregon, Ghana has a tropical climate.

Kofi, Seth, and Leeford took me to a surprisingly nice hotel near Elmina Beach, which is part of Ghana's Gold Coast region. Elmina is home to one of Cape Coast's two famous trading posts. One of the trading posts, the Elmina Castle, served as a launching point for Portuguese and Dutch slave traders from the mid-1600s to the early 1800s. In 1871, the fort became a possession of the British Empire, with Britain granting independence to the Gold Coast in 1957. The castle is now recognized as a World Heritage site by UNESCO.

The other trading post, the Cape Coast Castle, also engaged in the slave trade. It is now included as a UNESCO historical site, and is most famous for its dungeon and Door of No Return, usually the last stops on the guided tours. From the Door of No Return, slaves were led to awaiting ships. Not long after taking office in 2008, President Obama took his family to Ghana—his tour of the Cape Coast Castle was one his most impressionable stops.

My new SAGE friends from Ghana arranged for a private tour of both castles. Also, Kofi arranged for a visit to the rope bridges at Kakum National Park in the tropical rain forest, with the bridge suspended about 110 feet off the ground. After the trip to the rain forest, Seth and Leeford took me on an unforgettable rickety drive north to the famous Ashanti Kingdom.

Between visits to potential SAGE schools and to the offices of local government officials, I had a chance to jog on the beautiful beaches east of the hotel. Both mornings, a long line of people were queued up, extending from the beach far out into the blue shallow waters of the Atlantic Ocean. Together, they retrieved a huge fishing net, pulling it in hand over fist. Teamwork in action—fascinating. The fascination, however, was colored by the large amount of garbage that had been thrown into the ocean and washed ashore. Environmental stewardship education was needed in Cape Coast.

My trip to Ghana was successful. As I boarded the plane, Kofi and Seth proudly showed me the newly printed certificate from the Ghana government recognizing SAGE Ghana as an official NGO. Kofi and Seth promised to bring a SAGE delegation to our third annual SAGE World Cup, set for San Francisco two months later.

My next stop was Abuja, Nigeria. On June 29, I was greeted at the Abuja airport by a quiet, stocky gentleman in his mid-thirties. His name was Agwu Amogu (pronounced ahh-goo ahh-moe-goo). Ken Schoolland, a professor of economics and political science at Hawaii Pacific University, had met Agwu at an economics conference a year or so earlier, and Ken had told Agwu about SAGE. Ken was also the Walton Fellow at Hawaii Pacific. He and I had become acquainted in Kansas City over the years. A staunch libertarian, Ken is the author of an economics education book called *The Adventures of Jonathan Gullible: A Free Market Odyssey*.

Agwu was enthralled by the idea of youth enterprise and competitions. He and I instantly hit it off. He agreed to take me to Kaduna, a city about two hours north of Abuja. Kaduna was the host city for the inaugural SAGE Nigeria tournament, which would take place in a few days under the direction of a young university lecturer, Lateef Latopa.

Lateef was the SIFE adviser to the Nigerian SIFE champion in 2005, from Kaduna Polytechnic University. He had learned about SAGE from the Nigerian delegation in Barcelona in the fall of 2004, and saw it as a solid project for his SIFE students. Lateef had arranged for three local high schools to compete in the tournament on July 2 on the university campus. A few days before I arrived, though, Lateef sent me an email.

Curt, I understand SAGE and I am ready to promote it within

the limit of my ability. Some people are afraid of the spread of SAGE; that is why they see SAGE as a threat to SIFE. I have seen and got the message. Attempt has been made to intimidate me because of SAGE but I will always refuse to be intimidated. You will need to educate some people here about SAGE and SIFE. Lots have been said about you in order to discredit you. I'm just keeping you abreast so that you can prepare your facts.[1]

I was a bit taken aback by this. SIFE was intimidating him because of SAGE?

Interesting. I shot back an email, "Your concerns about SIFE and its relationship to SAGE are valid. Attempts to discredit me are not surprising, given the lengths SIFE has taken to discourage SAGE the past several years."

I continued, "For twelve years, I have been a tremendous supporter of SIFE's mission, and I saw how that mission could be transferred to the high schools. Because SIFE refused to work toward this goal, my students and I met an unmet need (e.g., SIFE criterion #2), and are quite willing to share this program for the betterment of youth around the world. I look forward to clearly differentiating SAGE from SIFE with your interested stakeholders; and after meeting me and hearing from me directly, I want to build a trusting relationship between SAGE Nigeria and SAGE Global. I look forward to meeting you, Lateef, and appreciate the risk you are taking even by associating with me and SAGE. Do know that I believe in total transparency, and my goal is to spread entrepreneurship education and community service across the world."

Agwu and I arrived in Kaduna, the night before the tournament, and stayed at a flea-bite hotel with a plastic ten-gallon bucket and dipping cup for a cold shower. Other features included closets with doors hanging haphazardly by one screw from the hinges and reading lights with no light bulbs. Air conditioning? Not even a consideration.

The next day, we met Lateef at the auditorium on campus, and he informed us of a problem.

"The university won't let us use the generator to turn on the electricity unless we buy diesel fuel," he said.

Stepping into the sweltering, dimly-lit auditorium, we found three teams of about fifty students each, all seated together wearing their matching school uniforms. One team green, another red, and the other blue. Patiently, they waited for us to turn on the air conditioner and, hopefully, connect their PowerPoint presentations to a live socket. Lateef informed me that I'd need to come up with about fifty bucks to buy the fuel. Transaction completed, the electricity and air were turned on and the show began.

Dick Vitale, the famous basketball color analyst, would have described it thus: *awesome, baby!* The winning team was from nearby Gray's Academy, a private school on the outskirts of Kaduna. One of Gray's winning projects was the Rural Empowerment Initiative, where the students introduced a program to a remote village of the Kaduna North Local Government, called Doka Village. SAGE students taught the villagers how to extract milk and make cake out of soya beans. As a result, four of the villagers had started a business and were now generating profits.

Another business was REAL BIZ, where the students used their school's bakery to start a business making bread to serve at breakfast time. The students wrote a business plan and submitted it to school administrators, who approved it. The students appointed a manager, accountant, supervisor, and sales personnel, and had several "bread-making days."

One of the seven judges recruited by Agwu was a member of Nigeria's House of Representatives, the Honorable Abdul Oroh, from Edo State. After the tournament, Oroh said, "This program has the potential to change the face of education in Nigeria, and I am pleased to offer my support."[2]

As was the case with Ghana, my trip to Nigeria was a success.

As much as I wanted to let go of SIFE, though, I really couldn't, because SIFE wouldn't let go of me—or SAGE. On July 15, Peter Anyansi, country coordinator and CEO of SIFE Nigeria, wrote a lengthy memorandum to all of Nigeria's SIFE teams with a priority level listed as "High." The memo started: "As we begin a new SIFE program year in Nigeria it is important that I officially communicate SIFE Nigeria's position regarding SIFE Teams' involvement with outside organizations. This is especially pertinent given the fact that SIFE Nigeria has observed certain things taking place that may create serious confusion and misrepresentation of its aims, goals, overall organization philosophy."[3]

Uh-oh.

"It is important that I start off by stating clearly that SIFE Teams are encouraged to identify credible community and business partners with whom they can deliver SIFE projects and activities," Anyansi continued.

Key word: *credible*. What makes someone a credible partner? Who decides who is credible or not? Is the determination of credibility by decree from SIFE World Headquarters?

Next, Anyansi said, "For many years SIFE Teams all around the world have worked with community groups, business organizations, government agencies, academic institutions, and other credible organizations like Junior Achievement. So long as the activities of SIFE Teams are in line with the mission and objectives of SIFE, these partnerships are encouraged and worthwhile."

There it was again, the word *credible*. JA's mission was to ensure that every child have a fundamental understanding of the free enterprise system. Its vision was to educate and inspire young people to value free enterprise, business, and economics to improve the quality of their lives. SAGE's vision, by contrast, was to improve the quality of life worldwide through socially-responsible entrepreneurship and community service.

Anyansi went on to warn Nigeria SIFE advisers to be careful when using the SIFE trademark and logo. He also scolded those faculty members and/or SIFE students who were actively promoting and developing other organizations, making unauthorized contacts with businesses and institutions inside and outside Nigeria through the SIFE Nigeria network.

Then, the SAGE connection. "This has resulted in the direct and indirect association of the SIFE Nigeria logo and name with that of their own organizations and as a result SIFE Nigeria stakeholders are misinterpreting things and making wrong assumptions on whom these individuals truly represent. This is even graver in cases where the new organizations have been modeled off the SIFE program including the use of SIFE Nigeria methodologies, terminologies, and in some cases even materials. One can clearly understand why SIFE Nigeria would not want its logo or name associated with these organizations and the confusion this may cause for many stakeholders and supporters of SIFE Nigeria."

There was little doubt that Anyansi was getting his directions from SIFE's headquarters in Springfield. He was parroting the same words I had heard from Sylvester John, Bruce Nasby, and Alvin Rohrs. His memo sounded a lot like the memo Bruce Nasby wrote to SIFE's country coordinators on December 31, 2002.

According to SIFE, we were causing confusion. We weren't exactly pouring Pepsi drinks into Coke cans, though, nor putting Whoppers inside Big Mac boxes. For crying out loud, we were targeting high schools students, and we wanted them to learn about entrepreneurship.

Then came Anyansi's official pronouncement. "I am hereby officially making it clear to SIFE Nigeria Teams and SIFE agents that associations and partnerships with other organizations, though encouraged, must be done in a manner that clearly respect the rules and regulations of SIFE as well as demonstrates the independence and non-connectivity of both organizations. A policy of full disclosure to the Country Coordinator/CEO must always be practiced by SIFE Teams/Agents regarding their dealings with other organizations."

Translation: if you are a SIFE Nigeria team and you want to start a SAGE program, you must disclose this to headquarters so that they can … *ban it*. Free enterprise? Hardly. In order to respect governing rules and regulations, a free society means that those who are governed have a say in how and by whom those rules and regulations are promulgated. Once again, SIFE faculty advisers had virtually no role in creating the rules and regulations to which they were expected to adhere. They were dictated to, from above—from their *masters*. Not exactly *servant* leadership.

Near the end of the memo, Anyansi stated, "It has become necessary to highlight one particular organization, Students Advancing Global Entrepreneurship (SAGE), which appears to be built off the SIFE model and targets secondary school children. This organization was launched by a former SIFE Faculty Adviser in the USA as a project under the umbrella of his SIFE Team. It appears that this organization's strategy has been to grow and develop off the backbone of the SIFE international network by using SIFE to gain access to its members and then encouraging these members to affiliate with its cause and organization. It is important to mention that, for various serious reasons, the founder of this organization was officially dismissed from the SIFE network by the SIFE World

Headquarters Board of Directors and as such is no longer a SIFE faculty adviser or member of the organization."

Yes, I had been officially dismissed for serious reasons. Given my history with SIFE, especially as it related to possible litigation, SIFE couldn't comfortably go on the attack against me until it had covered all its bases. The Pinkerton investigation long since completed, my SAGE presentation in Cleveland to Mike Merriman's high school steering committee a distant memory, and the Milano internal controls report duly filed, the board of directors was finally in a position to sever me from the organization, followed by an all-out attack on SAGE, most likely under Rohrs' direction.

Anyansi then went good cop.

"It has been brought to my attention that SAGE has been established in Nigeria and is working to develop a national network. I wish them well and all the best in their efforts," he offered.

But then bad cop again.

"However, given the potential for confusion and misinterpretation of both SIFE Nigeria and SAGE, it is hereby being officially announced that SIFE Nigeria Teams are not permitted to partner with or engage in any activities with SAGE using the name of SIFE Nigeria. This means that there can be no project affiliation whatsoever between any SIFE Nigeria Team and SAGE, under the SIFE Nigeria banner. This new policy is effective immediately. Note that there is nothing preventing SIFE Nigeria Teams from engaging in SIFE-like projects involving secondary schools if you choose to do so. This is nothing new as SIFE Teams around the world have been doing so for more than a decade. However, you do not have to do them in the name of SAGE nor under that organization's umbrella. You could choose to do so on your own and coin your own name for the project (e.g. Junior SIFE or Kids in Free Enterprise, etc.)."

Finally, the last paragraph: "I would like to stress that, though I have highlighted one organization, this is not meant to discourage SIEF [*sic*] Teams from partnerships and collaborations. There are many credible organizations in Nigeria with whom you can partner while maintaining your independence and direct affiliation with SIFE Nigeria."

SAGE had established its credibility, as evidenced by its support from several companies and foundations. Most of these supporters weren't even affiliated with SIFE. Moreover, my experience with the FIPSE grant in the 1990s encouraged academicians to share successful best practices, to be adapted and disseminated. Now that it was completely independent from SIFE, I thought SAGE should have been seen as even more credible. The memorandum from SIFE Nigeria Headquarters discouraged and denounced a successful program, and its real message was clear—SIFE teams must refrain from adopting or adapting SAGE or suffer the consequences.

The memo was contradictory and pejorative—possibly even defamatory. By highlighting one organization—SAGE—the memorandum did indeed discourage SIFE teams from partnerships and collaborations. It sent a message: if your SIFE team is innovative, if your SIFE team has an adviser who questions authority, if your faculty adviser would like more input into the rules-making process, if your SIFE team develops a substantial program of national or international scope—then SIFE HQ will sanction you.

Of course, Nigeria wasn't the only country to get this message. In all, SIFE was in thirty-two countries now, and friends like John Thornton of Australia and Bob Galindez of the Philippines let me know they were receiving occasional reminders from Bruce Nasby to steer clear of SAGE. If any SIFE teams dared touch SAGE, they would now be violating SIFE policy, unless they coined a different name and hid their actions from SIFE brass.

Upon my return to the U.S., I had only a few weeks to get ready for the third SAGE World Cup in San Francisco. One week prior to the tournament, though, Wang Lei and I planned to conduct the entrepreneurship conference in Chico, which we dubbed the Entrepreneurial Leadership for Business Advantage—ELBA—conference. The two main goals of the conference were to introduce the international participants to leading entrepreneurs and business leaders in northern California and to exchange ideas for possible import/export opportunities.

Over one hundred delegates from five countries had registered, but we eventually had to settle for about sixty-five. The U.S. Embassy in China was a real stickler with visas, and ultimately all Chinese business and industry guests were turned away. Only students obtained visas. Nonetheless, we enlisted about forty Chico-area entrepreneurs to make presentations and establish new international business contacts.

Even with the smaller number of expected guests, the ELBA conference in Chico was a success. Delegates from Ghana, South Africa, Sierra Leone, China, and the Philippines brought a rainbow of cultural diversity to our sleepy little city, which is quite slow and laid-back when the university isn't in session. Highlights included presentations by the founders of two of Chico's most successful businesses, the Sierra Nevada Brewing Co., maker of its famous pale ale, and Computers for Classrooms, a prime example of a social enterprise. The mayor welcomed the group, and on Sunday we treated everyone to an outing on two houseboats at nearby Lake Oroville and a minor league baseball game in Chico that evening. On the last morning of the ELBA conference, we had a rousing sendoff at the Holiday Inn by local business leaders who were part of the Chico Economic Planning Commission.

On August 11, we all headed for San Francisco to meet up with the SAGE World Cup delegates. Teams from eight countries competed: USA, Poland, Ghana, South Africa, Russia, Tajikistan, China, and Ukraine. Every team made its presentation in English before dozens of judges from academia, nonprofit organizations, and the business sector.

"All of the presentations were outstanding," noted Beth Mazak of Junior Achievement's home office in Colorado Springs, who was among the judges. "The presenters demonstrated a creative use of technology, and their hardbound annual reports were of professional quality. JA Worldwide looks forward to supporting SAGE and the advancement of global entrepreneurship."

Interesting comment, seeing how Peter Ansanyi specifically referred to JA as a credible organization while precluding Nigerian SIFE teams from collaborating with SAGE. What if JA and SAGE formed a partnership, I wondered? Would JA then go on SIFE's "not credible" list?

As it turned out a few months later on September 22 and 23, JA invited me to its headquarters in Colorado Springs to make a presentation about SAGE. After my visit, JA asked for a formal proposal for a possible partnership. JA was especially intrigued by our use of university mentors to help high school entrepreneurs, and they wanted to know more about our global network. Eventually, we decided not to become partners, but JA certainly hadn't questioned our credibility. I wondered if Bruce Nasby, a former JA executive in the Los Angeles office, had put a negative bug in JA's ear. Life goes on.

The winning SAGE team in San Francisco came from Specialized Secondary School #17 in Odessa, Ukraine, led by Olga Azarova. A tall, elegant woman in her early forties, Olga had been the faculty SIFE adviser at a university in Odessa. She wasn't unlike most of the SAGE country leaders in attendance.

Most of SAGE's country leaders, like Olga, were current SIFE advisers, former SIFE national coordinators, or recent graduates of universities with a SIFE team. In spite of SIFE's not-so-hidden efforts to prevent SIFE teams from starting SAGE programs, these people forged ahead anyway—excellent role models for future youth in their programs.

Two of the Ukraine team's most impressive projects included the production of a four-color magazine and the formation of a popular music band. Finishing behind Ukraine were teams from China and South Africa.

Another SAGE judge was Chico State's new dean, Willie Hopkins. "When you see young people put together business plans and operate businesses, when you see them benefit their communities through business, you cannot but feel optimistic about the future," noted Hopkins. "These young people are ready, before high-school graduation, to contribute meaningfully to their communities. They have learned self-reliance, undoubtedly the most important skill with which they could graduate from high school. They have also learned the importance of operating business in a socially-responsible manner."[4]

The same day the third annual SAGE World Cup started, on Friday, August 11, 2005, former Wal-Mart executive and SIFE board chairman, Tom Coughlin, faced a maximum of twenty-eight years in prison on one count of filing a false tax return and five counts of wire fraud, with a maximum possible fine of $1.35 million. Instead, U.S. District Judge Robert Dawson sentenced him to twenty-seven months of home detention and five years of probation. In addition, he was sentenced to a $50,000 fine and another $400,000 in restitution. Based on a doctor's recommendation,

Coughlin avoided a prison sentence because of poor health.[5]

A few weeks earlier, on December 15, 2005, former Ohio State marketing professor Roger Blackwell's trial ended. He was sentenced to six years in federal prison and a $1 million fine for his role in the insider trading scheme with Jack Kahl, also a former SIFE chairman.[6]

While SIFE board members Coughlin and Kahl were dealing with their ethical issues, KPMG, one of SIFE's sponsors, had its own ethical matters to resolve. Two weeks after our event, on August 29, nine KPMG partners and senior executives, including the former deputy chairman, were criminally indicted in a matter involving a conspiracy to commit tax fraud (none of the nine people served on SIFE's board). KPMG's problems started when whistleblower Michael Hamersley reported the misconduct in 2003. Though neither Tom Moser nor Bernie Milano was part of the conspiracy, KPMG eventually admitted criminal wrongdoing in helping wealthy clients evade $2.5 billion in taxes. The firm agreed to pay $456 million in penalties, an almost unheard amount for a business whose primary operating activity is to serve the public with its certified audits.[7]

Coughlin had provided a clue about Wal-Mart's human resource problem in his October 6, 2003, story in *Business Week*: "If the company can maintain its current 15% growth rate, it will double its revenues over the next five years and top $600 billion in 2011. That's a very big if—even for Wal-Mart. Vice-chairman Coughlin's biggest worry is finding enough warm bodies to staff all those new stores."

This was hardly a new problem for Wal-Mart, as author Lichtenstein noted:

> In the early 1980s, Wal-Mart faced a recruitment crisis. With more than a hundred new stores opening each year, the company had to hire or promote upwards of a thousand managers or management trainees to staff them. Wal-Mart faltered. Recruitment from within meant the promotion of a lot of women, which ran headlong into those Wal-Mart family values that tilted toward small-town patriarchy.
>
> So Wal-Mart looked to the universities to recruit a new generation of managers. But here they faced another problem. Few

freshly minted MBAs were going take an arduous assistant manager job, and even the undergraduate business majors at the big
schools became frustrated when they found that Wal-Mart had
little use for their accounting and marketing skills. The solution
was to search for a fresh cohort of management trainees in the
denominational colleges and the branch campuses of the state
universities, where diligence, Christianity, and modest career expectations were already the norm. Wal-Mart wanted the B and C
students, the organization men, the undergraduates who were the
first in their family to take college courses.[8]

SIFE, therefore, was a pipeline for warm bodies to propel Wal-Mart's
projected growth. The ideology and culture of Wal-Mart's managerial
ethos—as well as that of other retail businesses—was best perpetuated by
SIFE-educated managers as compared to graduates of traditional MBA programs or campus recruiting offices. But this meant, of course, that Walton
Fellows drink Rohrs' *brand* of servant leadership Kool-Aid, the same brand
espoused by its most influential board members, almost all of whom were
aging white men in their 50s and 60s. I may have been an aging white man
in 2005, but I was no longer going to drink the SIFE Kool-Aid.

Most SIFE advisers lining up to support SAGE were not conformists,
either. These were the type of people who I wanted to serve as role models
for teenagers, not as servant leaders for college students.

Coughlin, Kahl, and dozens of KPMG partners had witnessed the SIFE
presentations made by idealistic young advocates for free enterprise. These
power brokers from the business world showered students and their faculty
advisers with appreciation and recognition, as is the way of servant leaders,
in spite of the fact that students were not paid for their services. In fact,
many paid their own way to competitions. Further, Walton Fellows like
me often spent exponentially more than our $1,000 stipend to operate
a SIFE team. With enough appreciation and recognition, people will do
extraordinary things to please their servant leader.

I drew parallels to Sam Walton's management philosophy, one that
helped quell employees' efforts to unionize. As Bethany Moreton said:

In the early 1980s, when Wal-Mart's fame was still largely regional, an interviewer asked Sam Walton to summarize the single most important lesson he had learned through his Arkansas retail career. Walton did not hesitate: his business taught him that "all of us like to be recognized and appreciated and need to feel like the roles we play or what we do is important." This sentiment found its formal codification in a sign hanging over one entrance to the home office. "Through these doors pass ordinary people on their way to accomplishing extraordinary things." For all its obvious instrumentality, the phrase that Wal-Mart made famous was more than an off-the-rack slogan of spin. To many observers, it seemed self-evident that the way to value work was to reward it concretely with security, high wages, and benefits. To the extent that the average Wal-Mart job offered none of these, critics pointed out, the corporate cheerleading for its front-line workers was hypocritical. When low-wage employees expressed loyalty to Wal-Mart, the same critique was at a loss to explain it.[9]

When I had my breakfast meeting with Jack Shewmaker in May 2000 at the Kansas City Marriott, I had been a Walton Fellow in his good graces. In a way, I was like one of his loyal Wal-Mart associates accepting very low wages for extraordinary effort—and many people, including colleagues and my brother Craig thought I was crazy. Unless Shewmaker was being disingenuous when he suggested that I become a global ambassador for SIFE, I think he saw me as a poster boy for SIFE's global strategy. And, at the time, I was thirsty to please. Pass the Kool-Aid.

But after the incident with SIFE in summer 2000, along with my aggressive attempts to rally Walton Fellows to push for a greater role in SIFE's policies, I think Shewmaker began to see me as Alvin Rohrs did—as a meddling organizer. Nelson Lichtenstein reported that Shewmaker didn't take kindly to union organizers:

> As the National Labor Relations Board would later note, Jack Shewmaker, one of Walton's rising stars, had been overheard telling the store manager Robert Haines that "if he caught any em-

ployees with union cards, he should fire them even if he had to hire all new employees."[10]

Wal-Mart and SIFE's brand of servant leadership was effective. Heap on enough praise, give an award, present a plaque, and people will walk miles without shoes for you. Having been through what I had been through with SIFE, I could better relate to the employees of the profitable Wal-Mart store in Jonquiere, Quebec, shut down in May of 2005 when workers tried to unionize.[11] Because of my aggressive actions to enlist other Walton Fellows to help shape SIFE's managerial policies, Rohrs—and Shewmaker—had likely come to view me as a unionizer of Walton Fellows. And I certainly didn't fit the mold of their ideal Walton Fellow—I wasn't politically conservative; I wasn't religious; and I certainly wasn't a conformist.

Ironically, in 2005, SIFE teams were judged on four major criteria. The last criterion required students to demonstrate effectiveness in practicing business ethics in an ethical and socially responsible manner. Businesses can write ethical codes of conduct, but one of the most important factors guiding employee behavior is the behavior of its leader—the role model. What lessons were SIFE students learning from Coughlin, Kahl, and KPMG? I vowed to do my best to recruit leaders to the SAGE organization who could provide a better lesson.

After the San Francisco SAGE World Cup, I returned to Chico to start the fall 2005 semester. For the first time in thirteen years I was beginning a semester without being the SIFE adviser. I wondered if this would affect my ability to recruit Chico State students to become SAGE mentors. With no opportunity to showcase their presentation skills at a competition, I anticipated there might be a fall-off in interest.

But I was wrong. Though Mollie Perlman had graduated, students like Allison Smith and Carol Furtado recruited other students to become SAGE mentors. I was still able to offer bonus points or academic units as part of a student's service-learning activities. And in some cases, I could offer leaders a small scholarship from an endowment provided by a donor to the university.

On April 28 and 29, 2006, we conducted the SAGE California event in Los Angeles, with an outstanding team from Santa Monica High School advancing to the upcoming national SAGE USA competition in New York City. In the Big Apple, the Santa Monica students squeaked by an outstanding team from Buffalo, New York, which had been mentored by a SIFE team from D'Youville College.

D'Youville College's brave faculty adviser was Pete Eimer. Pete and I had met in Kansas City the previous May. His SIFE team had always come close to cracking into the top echelon of teams, but unlike teams such as Drury and La Sierra, D'Youville didn't quite have the same flash and—*inauthenticity*—as the top teams. Pete had become aware of the SAGE program through my posts on a listserv that I had created for other Walton Fellows and, like me, he taught financial accounting. The listserv, from Rohrs' perspective, must have looked like another example of my heretical unionizing activities.

SIFE hadn't been as aggressive about its SAGE stance in the U.S. as it was in other countries, but active Walton Fellows knew SAGE should be avoided. Nonetheless, SAGE appealed to Pete and he wanted his two daughters to participate. Molly was a senior and Bridget a freshman. Both girls were enrolled at Holy Angels Academy, an all-girl Catholic high school. Pete's wife Betsy was supportive, too. Over Memorial Day weekend at the end of May 2006, they drove down to New York City with about ten girls and an equal number of parents to participate in the SAGE USA event.

Pete and I became instant friends—he loved sports, especially hockey. He had been a star player at Canisius College in Buffalo, he liked to drink a pale ale now and then, and best of all, he was committed to youth enterprise. "Though Santa Monica prevailed this year, we'll be back again next year," he said as we knocked down a couple cold ones after the winners were announced.

The host of the SAGE USA event was Kingsborough Community College in Brooklyn. To our good fortune, two enthusiastic experts accepted our invitation to be keynote speakers. One speaker was Gretchen Zucker, director of Youth Venture, which is a program of the well-known international Ashoka Foundation. The other speaker was Jerr Boschee, founder of The Institute for Social Entrepreneurs. Both Gretchen and Jerr would have a big impact on SAGE down the road. Starting in fall

2005, Youth Venture would provide our SAGE teams with grants of up to $1,000 to fund social enterprises. In 2007, Jerr Boschee became chairman of the SAGE board.

Throughout the 2005–2006 academic year, the Chico State SAGE leaders and I had been working closely with Lili Qu, SAGE China national coordinator. We had chosen Shanghai to be the 2006 SAGE World Cup host city. On my previous two trips to Shanghai—the last one when Tom Payne and I had visited in early May 2005—I decided that the famous Peace Hotel on the Bund would make an ideal venue, and Lili agreed. In exchange for SAGE's pledge of $15,000 to help defray the costs, and for my pledge to help her staff the event by bringing three experienced Chico State students to lead the way, we booked the hotel and got to work.

On August 1, 2006, Allison Smith, Carol Furtado, Anthony Mellow, and I boarded a plane from San Francisco to Shanghai. Crossing the international date line, we arrived a day later, on August 2, and had just one day to help Lili and her crew prepare for the fourth SAGE World Cup. Rob Best met us at the Peace Hotel's legendary jazz bar, with his photo equipment in tow.

The Peace Hotel has two buildings—the North Building, at ten stories, was completed in 1929, and the South Building, at six stories, was completed in 1908 as the Palace Hotel. The buildings are separated by Nanjing Road, Shanghai's busiest street. The SAGE competition took place August 4–5 in the North Building of the hotel. All meals and hotel rooms for our event, however, were in the South Building, and our delegation made frequent trips crossing Nanjing Road. The hotel overlooks the Huangpu River. Lili and I had hired a cruise boat to take the entire delegation on a riverboat cruise following the awards banquet on Saturday night.

As it turned out, the team from Santa Monica prevailed as the fourth SAGE World Cup champion. The student team had generated over $20,000 in profits by operating the school cafeteria, and the students demonstrated their civic engagement by researching proposed state legislation to limit unhealthy foods on campus. The students met with the school board, organized debates about student rights, and created a business plan to turn a teachers' lounge into a new lunch spot carrying healthy sandwiches and salads. They promoted the importance of healthy eating with a March for

Fitness campaign, aptly held in March.

A year earlier, at the third SAGE World Cup in San Francisco, we started something that has been a big hit ever since. We asked each SAGE team to come prepared not only for the competition, but also for what we call *country day*. We wanted everyone to get to know each other by making a presentation or performing a dance routine unique to their country. Since then, the day has become one of the highlights of SAGE World Cup. The Russians performed a ballet, the Ukrainians handed out a community cake, the Ghana boys performed a coming-of-age dance, and the Koreans came with five percussion instruments and played them with perfection.

The USA team from Santa Monica showed the delegates how to do the Electric Slide dance choreographed by director/dancer Ric Silver. Chris Peterson was among the Santa Monica students. After the event, Chris reflected on his experience in an article published by the *Santa Monica Daily Press*:

> "We toured the city, went to a museum, the Yuyuan Garden, a silk-making factory, took a tour of McDonald's and (saw) a really cool acrobatic show," Peterson wrote in an e-mail two days after the event, which concluded Sunday. "The food was ... different, to say the least. Coke tastes different. It's nothing like the Panda Express of the United States. The culture is different, as well. Everybody works, it's like work ethic is in their blood. We passed this place the first night that some people were working on. There was nothing inside of it, just people and lights at work. The next day, it was a shoe store, open and ready for business. I have so much respect for the other teams for all the hard work they put in to get them to the final competition and I especially have respect for the entire SAGE organization," Peterson added. "I think it's a great opportunity for high school students to show their entrepreneurship skills and I am really honored to have been introduced to such an organization."[12]

As in prior years, the competition was fierce. The team from Ukraine came in second, China came in third, and surprisingly, Nigeria finished fourth. This was Nigeria's first year competing, because Gray's College students could not get their visas in time for the 2005 event. In 2006, the team representing Nigeria was a junior secondary school near Abuja. Junior secondary schools are the equivalent of junior high schools, and almost all the team members were thirteen or fourteen years old. Creativity and innovation starts young, and the youngsters from Nigeria made a statement that they were taking SAGE very seriously.

One interesting issue involved South Africa, which had brought two SAGE teams to Shanghai. Two separate regions of South Africa had conducted SAGE competitions, but the distance between Bloemfontein in the Orange Free State and Cape Town on the Western Cape had prevented our regional coordinators from conducting a national event. As a result, I had to make two painstaking decisions: should one team be allowed to compete, or both? If only one, which team?

My decision led to a debate among the two regional coordinators as to which team was the official SAGE South Africa champion. I wanted to declare them co-champions, but this wasn't satisfactory to either party. Another option was to let them go head-to-head against one another to determine a country champion before the overall competition, but the team from Bloemfontein had arrived late due to weather conditions. This was no longer an option.

In the end, I let both teams compete without declaring one or the other champion or cochampion. But both regional coordinators were concerned that if one of the teams advanced to the final four and the other didn't, how would they explain this to their funders? Funders for each team were under the impression that each team was the country champion. How would they explain that a South Africa team made it to the final four if it wasn't their team?

International diplomacy was needed. When other countries learned that two teams from South Africa were competing in the overall tournament, they believed that this unfairly favored them. If South Africa could bring two teams, why couldn't they?

While the judges deliberated, I went to the jazz bar for a drink. I needed it. Never before had I cheered that a SAGE team would *not* make it to the next round, but in this case … if neither team finished in the top four, the problem would be solved. If one or both made it, I had a big problem on my hands. Thankfully, the judges solved the dilemma—neither South African team advanced.

As the CEO of a relatively new international nonprofit organization, I was now in the catbird's seat. I was getting a fast lesson on how important it is to be fair, while balancing the often competing desires of teachers, coordinators, and funders. The South Africa situation had to be addressed on the fly. After considering all viewpoints, I was the only one who could make the final call.

And as much as I hated to admit it, I was now empathetic—albeit begrudgingly—to Alvin Rohrs' position with SIFE. His problem, though, was his undying attention to funders and scant attention to Walton Fellows.

That night, 180 people boarded the cruise boat at The Bund's main docking station across from the hotel, and delegates from eight countries sailed up and down the Huangpu River, mesmerized by the skyscrapers to the east—the Pudong District—and the bustling hub of old Shanghai to the west.

The South Africa situation got me thinking. Why not bring two teams from each country in the future? Our board would meet in a few months, and I brought this up. Together, we agreed that, starting with the 2007–2008 academic year, a country would be permitted to bring a second place team and its champion team. On the first day of the event, we would conduct an elimination round for second place teams. The winning team would get a shot at winning it all by getting a berth in the overall competition. This way, more teens could avail themselves of their first international travel experience, if the country could afford to bring more than one team. Thanks to the South Africa situation, what could have been a disaster turned out to be a learning moment.

Santa Monica's performance drew headlines back home. On October 25, 2006, the Santa Monica SAGE team was featured on the front page of the business section of the *Los Angeles Times*. The headline, STUDENTS SCORE HIGH IN THE ART OF FREE ENTERPRISE, was followed by the following lead paragraph:

At Santa Monica High School's homecoming game Friday night, a team will be awarded championship rings during a half-time ceremony. But tackles and touchdowns aren't behind the honors. The students are being recognized for winning an international business competition held in Shanghai by Students for the Advancement of Global Entrepreneurship, or SAGE.[13]

The article featured SAGE and Junior Achievement. SIFE may not have believed SAGE to be credible, but the *LA Times* did.

Halfway down, it quoted me: "I want these youth to think not only about how to make money but how they can improve their community." The article ended by saying that I had "created the SAGE program to bring [my] philosophy of service-oriented entrepreneurship to high school students."

The media were now starting to grab hold of my idea to link social enterprise and service learning. I loved this. Unfortunately, this idea wasn't as easily grasped by colleagues in higher education.

As the publicity came rolling in, we created the new SAGE handbook for 2006–2007. Two big changes were introduced into the handbook. First, the criteria changed. The three main criteria now involved creating and operating a least (1) one new commercial business, (2) one social venture and, if the team was a veteran SAGE team, (3) demonstrating the continuation of at least one commercial business from the prior year. The third criterion was a way for us to engineer sustainability into the team projects. We didn't want students to view their SAGE activities simply as another class project; instead, we wanted them to start thinking in a longer time horizon, like a real business. The second change was because Jerr Boschee, who had joined our board of directors, started a special competition for teams that created the most innovative social enterprises. Jerr and his family donated $3,500 for prize money to the top three teams at the SAGE World Cup.

Jerr was now in his late sixties. He had spent the past twenty-five years as an advisor to social entrepreneurs in the United States and abroad. He was a world traveler, delivering seminars or conducting workshops in forty-two states and fifteen countries. He had long been recognized as one of the founders of the social enterprise movement worldwide. He created The Institute for Social Entrepreneurs in 1999. His resume was impressive, and his credentials have garnered invitations as a guest lecturer at academic institutions such as the University of Oxford, the University of Cambridge, Carnegie Mellon, Northwestern University, Stanford University, and many others.

If that wasn't impressive enough, he had also been an executive for a Fortune 100 company and a national nonprofit. In addition, he had been the managing editor for a chain of newspapers, a Peace Corps volunteer, and a frequent writer, speaker, and trainer in the social service and public policy arenas.

In short, Jerr was the perfect fit for our board and he joined our other seven board members. Two of the board members, Rieva Lesonsky and Joe Pedott, were also SIFE supporters. Other board members included attorney Van Ajemian; former Walton Fellow Al Konuwa of Butte College; Ed Byers, principal at the San Francisco office of Deloitte; and former SIFE student at Chico State, Allison Steltzner. Dick Steltzner, as you recall, was grooming Allison to take over her family's wine business in Napa.

Our board had a blend of private sector and nonprofit sector leaders. Jerr's expertise in social enterprise blended nicely with the commercial expertise brought to the table by other board members. I was now in a better position to grow SAGE, relying on an unpaid staff of volunteers who loved SAGE as much as I did. These volunteers were Chico State university students. The older students represented an untapped battalion of service providers to an army of teen entrepreneurs.

These teens—our world's future entrepreneurs—were encouraged to be innovative and creative in seeking financial profits, with an eye toward making the community better through their commercial and social enterprises. I wanted to help youth become future leaders—not servant leaders, mind you, but leaders who believed in what Paul Hawken believed, which merits repeating: "The ultimate purpose of business is not, or should not be, simply to make money. Nor is it merely a system of making and selling things. The promise of business is to increase the general well-being of humankind through service, a creative invention and ethical philosophy."[14]

Chapter 20

An Untapped Army

AACSB International—The Association to Advance Collegiate Students of Business—is the international accrediting agency for colleges of business. The AACSB, created a special task force in 2006 which culminated in a report that addressed how business education may be able to contribute to a more peaceful world.[1] Because private sector businesses seek new opportunities and markets, they are innovative in finding effective solutions that transcend personal and cultural differences. Creating new value—wealth—"can inspire collaboration between strangers, and sometimes even between those who might have regarded each other as enemies. Once people work together and learn that people are essentially the same, regardless of their backgrounds, making war is likely to become far less attractive than making money."[2]

This was good news; such a report could help spread my message of social entrepreneurship and service learning. My accounting colleagues thought I was a bit out in left field. Instead of focusing my research on financial markets and international accounting standards, my career interests, since coming to Chico State, had been finding innovative ways to motivate students to learn. Instead of shutting my door and conducting empirical research, I was happier in the classroom and in the community.

Early in the fall of 2006, I was excited to receive an email inviting me to a peace through commerce conference at the University of Notre Dame entitled "Partnerships as the New Paradigm." The invitation read: "At the founding of the United Nations in 1945, political and business leaders as well as scholars shared the conviction that commerce could play an important role in fostering peace. This conference will bring together academics, corporations, NGOs and government leaders. It seeks to advance the understanding of the role of business in society and to encourage new and more effective partnerships. The conference also hopes to lay the foundation for new courses in business schools on the subject of peace through commerce."

Using my university business faculty travel fund allocation, I booked my flight to South Bend, Indiana. The two-day conference was enlightening—I had the chance to meet world leaders in business, government, and the nonprofit sector. One such leader was Bruce McNamer of TechnoServe. I had met a colleague of McNamer's in Ghana in 2005. His name was Nick Railston-Brown, the director of TechnoServe's Ghana office. Nick joined SAGE's global advisory board in December 2005.

At the Notre Dame conference, McNamer and I discussed how programs like SAGE could work with TechnoServe. Its mission was to help entrepreneurs in poor areas of over twenty developing countries create income. TechnoServe's guiding philosophy was that poverty can be abated by unleashing entrepreneurship as a force to overcome inertia, stagnation, and the status quo. McNamer was attracting some attention. In 2006, TechnoServe was named by the Geneva-based Schwab Foundation for Social Entrepreneurship as one of its outstanding social enterprises. A couple years later in 2008, Google.org would provide TechnoServe with a $3 million grant to expand its private-sector development work.

One of the best things coming from the conference was it made me aware of the UN's ambitious Millennium Development Goals (MDGs) initiative. By way of background, on September 8, 2000, the UN General Assembly passed resolution 55/2 called the Millennium Declaration, which outlined eight MDGs to be met by 2015. The overarching goal was to eradicate extreme poverty and hunger. Other goals included: achieving universal primary education; promoting gender equality; reducing child mortality; improving maternal health; combating HIV/AIDS, malaria and other diseases; ensuring environmental sustainability; and forming global partnerships for development. The resolution, signed by 189 heads of state, was a compact between the world's major economic players. Wealthy countries pledged resources, and developing countries pledged to improve policies and governance, and to increase accountability.

The AACSB's special report acknowledged that it could not mandate university business faculty to change what they teach or how they go about it. However, it sent a powerful signal to faculty by stating "not all professors are eager to expand their teaching styles and content to include more than the narrow core of disciplinary content. The good news is that many are already doing so and that a host of emerging forces and support systems may help to ensure more."[3]

The report and the conference got my head spinning. The powerful AACSB was giving business deans the green light to support faculty like me. The report gave my work more credibility. Also, for untenured faculty and adjunct teaching professors, they could now justifiably pursue projects like SAGE without negatively impacting their tenure and promotion prospects. If social enterprise, as a discipline, and service learning, as a teaching strategy, had been questioned by administrators previously, the Peace through Commerce report now gave faculty some leverage to experiment. Down the road, I believed, the AACSB report could help SAGE grow.

After the conference, I considered how I might introduce the MDGs into the SAGE program. I believed that there could be far greater impact by teaching teenagers—rather than university students—how to start social ventures to address the goals. With SAGE, I could reach a larger number of young people—most of whom had not yet formed cultural, religious, or ethnic stereotypes. As I saw it, SAGE teens were an untapped army of future social entrepreneurs and socially-responsible commercial entrepreneurs.

Further, I could make an impact on the university students who signed up to become SAGE mentors. Using the same analogy, university student mentors represented another untapped army—an army of service providers, acting as role models for their younger protégés.

As the 2006–2007 academic year came to an end, Harvard University's most famous dropout, Bill Gates, was invited to give the commencement speech to the Harvard graduating class. He informed his audience that he was very appreciative of the things he learned during his brief stay at Harvard, he left "with no real awareness of the awful inequities in the world—the appalling disparities of health, and wealth, and opportunity that condemn millions of people to lives of despair. ... I left campus knowing little about the millions of young people cheated out of educational opportunities here in this country. And I knew nothing about the millions of people living in unspeakable poverty and disease in developing countries. It took me decades to find out."[4]

According to Gates, one of the challenges for him and his wife Melinda was to find an answer to this question: How can we do the most good for the greatest number with the resources we have? Through the work with their foundation, the two Gates learned how millions of children in developing countries were dying from diseases that are no longer a problem in developed countries. They realized that neither the free market nor the government was addressing this problem effectively.

Gates came to believe the best way to address this challenge is through what he coined *creative capitalism*, whereby businesses can make a profit by serving the needs of the poor. He also called for more citizen activism. Individuals can make a difference if they press government to make poverty-alleviation a priority. However, Gates insisted, before business and government will change their behavior, individuals like those at Harvard must turn their *caring* about the problem into *acting* on the problem. Near the end of his speech, Gates left Harvard faculty, alumni, and students with this question: "Should our best minds be dedicated to solving our biggest problems?"

Not long before Gates gave his speech, we conducted our SAGE California event in Southern California. Santa Monica again prevailed, narrowly out-pointing a team from Benicia High School, about forty miles northeast of San Francisco.

Generously, Ed Byers, one of our SAGE board members, arranged for the Deloitte offices at New York's World Financial Center, to host the SAGE USA event in May. A week after the New York event, I filed a report summarizing the results on the *Huffington Post* website.

"One of the best weapons against terror is youth empowerment through education, and SAGE is part of the secret arsenal," Major Miemie Winn Byrd, Deputy Economic Advisor, U.S. Pacific Command, told me after she served as a judge/panelist at a recent SAGE competition in Los Angeles. Byrd is now one of our biggest fans. "It's time to let the secret out of the bag," she said.

After the NYC competition, team photos were taken next to the 9/11 Memorial and fire station on Liberty Street, which is the southern border street where the Twin Towers collapsed. The photo of the winning team was taken with a U.S. flag. According to Klass, "The flag was lent to us by a firefighter that survived the collapse of the World Trade Center Towers. He told us his story and was very proud of the flag and what it represents! He wished us well in representing the USA at the world competition!"

SAGE's combination of social entrepreneurship, service learning and interscholastic competition is potent. It is a powerful new education model whose time is come.[5]

My philosophy for SAGE had been evolving over time. By now, it was markedly different from Rohrs' philosophy for SIFE. Aside from his evangelical, tearful exhortations while shaking the money tree to drum up funds, Rohrs had always been quite good at keeping a low profile about his personal beliefs. A Google search turns up a few glowing articles about his role with SIFE, but the articles did not reveal much about the man himself.

Ken Schooland, a libertarian, of Hawaii Pacific forwarded a revealing email to me. A year earlier, Rohrs had sent Ken a note defending SIFE's rationale for seeking, and winning, a federal grant. The email shed some light on Rohrs' worldview. Ken had been upset when he learned that SIFE was chasing federal funds, and he let Rohrs know that he was unhappy that SIFE had won a $250,000 grant. The grant proposal, submitted, to the U.S. State Department's Office of Education and Cultural Affairs, was supported by Congressman Roy Blunt from Missouri.

Blunt, recall, was the former president of Southwest Baptist University, Rohrs' alma mater and former employer. Springfield, SIFE's home office, was in Blunt's district. The grant, awarded in August 2004, was to be used to create an international exchange program for SIFE in India, Malaysia, and the USA. Funding for the program was "specifically allocated for programs that promote peace and prosperity. *Out of 123 applicants, SIFE was the sole recipient.*"[6] SIFE, in the past, had discouraged SIFE teams from seeking government funding, but now SIFE was seeking it. The proposal submitted to the State Department was either very, very compelling, or … SIFE had some extremely helpful friends in Washington.

SIFE had hired a well-connected SBU alumnus, Shane Schoeller, to help SIFE raise federal funds. Schoeller, who would later go on to be elected to the Missouri House of Representatives, had worked as a field representative for Senator John Ashcroft right after graduating from SBU. Later, he became a legislative assistant to Congressman Blunt, working under Blunt's longtime chief of staff, Gregg Hartley.

When SIFE received the grant, Ozarks Public Radio station KSMU reported, "In announcing the grant, Southwest Missouri Congressman Roy Blunt said the money is an investment which nourishes capitalism and will help Islamic countries resume their role as players in the world economy. The grant will provide global business internships and cultural exchanges between twenty-six U.S. students and thirteen students each from India and Malaysia."

Again, the irony was laughable. Rohrs, for years, had discouraged SIFE teams from seeking public funds from state or federal coffers. This mindset was reflected in the "Halt the Deficit/Reduce the Debt" special competitions. Apparently, federal spending on these types of educational programs was considered anathema to red-state advocates of the limited role of government—at least when Democrats controlled the White House.

Unlike Ken Schooland and other libertarian Walton Fellows, I was not opposed to federal support, having won a FIPSE grant in the mid-1990s. Also, in the late 1990s, I submitted a grant proposal to the U.S. Department of Education's FIPSE program to advance community service learning for business students. Though we made it through to the final round of review, an accomplishment in itself given the number of applicants, we weren't invited to the final round. Unlike SIFE, I didn't have many friends in Washington. Had we won the $200,000 grant, I told my SIFE team that we wouldn't highlight this at SIFE competitions because we knew that SIFE's philosophy, shared by many of SIFE's CEO-judges, discouraged teams should from seeking public funding.

But with SIFE's—and Wal-Mart's—international growth plans, and with George W. Bush taking the White House in 2000, applying for federal funds to advance SIFE's mission, apparently, was no longer an ideological problem. By 2005, Blunt was the acting House majority leader. As Springfield's representative in Washington, he was on a first name basis with one of Washington's most powerful lobbying firms, Cassidy & Associates—in fact, one of Cassidy's senior executives was Blunt's former chief of staff, Gregg Hartley.[7] SIFE cut Cassidy a check for $80,000 for six months of work to lobby Blunt for support. It was $80,000 well spent.

A January 29, 2006, article in the *Boston Globe* cited the SIFE grant as an example of how lobbyists with inside ties to congressmen get their pet pork projects earmarked in federal budgets. I still had a friend or two at SIFE's home office in Springfield, and I received some email correspondence between Tom Payne and one of SIFE's senior staffers, Cathy Ashcraft. Ashcraft was the senior financial person at SIFE, and my friend asked if she had read the *Boston Globe* article.

"Yes, interesting week last week," she said. "Also made the Miami newspaper (nearly the same article as the Boston paper). All these basically tied to Roy Blunt ... not really flattering."

Tom replied with some chit-chat, and said, "I hear morale is at an all-time high at SIFE."

Ashcraft replied, "It is ???????? Hehehe. Our philosophy is the book, *Good to Great.* ... I can hardly keep a straight face. Going to go visit Mr. Coughlin inside when he goes ?????????"[8] She was referring to Tom Coughlin's pending sentencing for wire fraud and filing a false tax return.

On May 28, 2006, Ken Schooland sent me an email. "Here is the letter from Alvin Rohrs about government funding for SIFE being for national defense! Outrageous, huh? This will surely cause people abroad to be wary of who's behind SIFE and for what purposes." The letter, dated May 12, was sent from SIFE staff member Jane Owen on behalf of Rohrs:

Subject: Response to Congressional Funding
From The Office of Alvin Rohrs, President & CEO
Ken,

As the CEO of Students in Free Enterprise for 20 years, and as a student of the Austrian School of Economics, I understand your concern about our efforts to secure funds for SIFE from the government.

Even under the Austrian school, one of the legitimate and appropriate uses of government funds and rationale for taxing citizens is to provide for the common defense. On September 11, 2001 it became very clear that the defense of America couldn't be achieved by only protecting our physical borders. The only thing more painful that day than watching the death and destruction in America was watching people especially young people in other parts of the world cheering that death and destruction.

Why did they cheer? One of the reasons is the frustration they felt over the disparity between the prosperity of Americans and them. This frustration leads to hopelessness that leads to anger. Why are they hopeless? Because they do not understand why America is prosperous. They do not understand that America's prosperity is a result of economic freedom—free enterprise—the market economy that unleashes the entrepreneurial spirit.

We can defend America through military action after this anger has been channeled into more terrorists, more bombs and more death and destruction. Or we can defend America by defusing this anger by teaching the rest of the world how to become prosperous through market economies and entrepreneurship.

Using government money to teach free enterprise may seem like an oxymoron but it isn't. As more and more of America's leaders learn about SIFE, our mission and our successes, more and more of them see SIFE and our efforts to teach prosperity to the world as a real tool for Peace, and as a key component of America's national defense.

The funds being requested for SIFE are to fund an annual gathering of SIFE students from across America and around the world to teach them entrepreneurship and market economics, and to give them an opportunity to learn from each other and about each other. The goal is to send hundreds of students back to their countries and communities equipped much better to teach the hope that comes from learning how to create wealth and prosperity. Some of these funds are also going to be used to teach market economics and entrepreneurship in greater depth to those leading SIFE in other countries, thereby bringing more economic freedom and prosperity to those countries.

Taxing citizens to spend money to provide for the common defense is the most legitimate function of government. Using some of those funds to convert our enemies who threaten us into our friends who respect us is a legitimate and appropriate function for SIFE USA.

I hope you can now better understand why an avid free marketer like me would accept and seek government money to support SIFE. If not, please give me a call and I would be pleased to discuss this with you.

I wondered if Rohrs now supported the Peace Corps?

At first blush, Rohrs was using similar logic as the AACSB's. After all, what could be wrong with giving students a more global worldview through an international exchange program? To the extent this could mean a better understanding of free markets, which could lead to more prosperity, which could mean less war, which could mean more peace ... well, then, the grant could just as easily been requested from the Department of Defense. But, hey, if you have Shane Schoeller on the payroll and Gregg Hartley as your lobbyist and your district's powerful U.S. Congressman Roy Blunt in Congress, why not just go for an earmark from the Department of State?

There were several holes in Rohrs' arguments. First, his rationale reminded me of Ivan Illich's "To Hell with Good Intentions" speech, with U.S. students traveling abroad to teach economic freedom and entrepreneurship, and international students traveling to the U.S. to learn how to understand why America is prosperous.[9] According to Rohrs, this international exchange program would help convert our enemies. To say the least, this was patronizing.

Second, Rohrs asserted that one of the reasons people cheered after 9/11 is because of their frustration over the disparity between the prosperity of Americans and themselves. This reminded me of the "envy" interview Matt Lauer had with Mitt Romney in January 2012:

Lauer: When you said that we already have a leader who divides us with the bitter politics of envy, I'm curious about the word envy. Did you suggest that anyone who questions the policies and practices of Wall Street and financial institutions, anyone who has questions about the distribution of wealth and power in this country, is envious? Is it about jealousy, or fairness?

Romney: You know, I think it's about envy. I think it's about class warfare. When you have a president encouraging the idea of dividing America based on 99 percent versus one percent, and those people who have been most successful will be in the one percent, you have opened up a wave of approach in this country which is entirely inconsistent with the concept of one nation under God. The American people, I believe in the final analysis, will reject it.[10]

Alas, the class warfare argument—this was standard fare for the Right. The logic: people from other countries are envious of us because of our success. They dislike us because we are *prosperous*. Not because we espouse democracy for all countries except those who supply us with oil; not because we implore other countries to conserve while we consume much more energy per capita.

If Rohrs was going to link his SIFE grant request to national defense and homeland security, his argument would have been much stronger if he listened to people like Major Miemie Winn Byrd, deputy economic advisor, U.S. Pacific Command. Byrd was a member of SAGE's board of directors, and she was a prolific thinker and writer in the area of government's role in counterterrorism efforts. In a 2006 article in *Joint Force Quarterly*, Byrd explained how U.S. government, in general, and the U.S. military, specifically, can adopt a comprehensive U.S. counterterrorism strategy that includes "economic policies that encourage development, more open societies, and opportunities for better living. Igniting and sustaining economic growth in the poorest areas require creativity and cooperation."[11]

She described how the U.S. military had begun cooperating with cross-disciplinary organizations such as the United Nations Development Program, governmental aid agencies, and other militaries, NGOs, and private businesses. Byrd termed these new partnerships as "civil-military operations" and indicated that "few are aware that the U.S. military conducts a variety of humanitarian assistance and civic action projects around the globe. ... Projects include building schools, hospitals, roads, and community centers; digging wells and irrigation ditches; conducting water sanitation projects; providing rudimentary health care; and training local medical personnel."[12]

The U.S. military's actions were exactly in step with the AACSB's peace initiative, as well as C.K. Prahalad's call for multinational companies to change their business models to target those at the bottom of the pyramid.[13] Byrd said, "Based on the new cooperation between the Armed Forces and USAID, the Economic Advisor's Office at U.S. Pacific Command now recognizes an opportunity to alleviate poverty and create sustainable economic growth in areas that are vulnerable to terrorist influence. ... This will require fresh thinking by all parties. The 9/11 Commission criticized U.S. government agencies for their lack of imagination prior to the attacks in New York and Washington. In the post-9/11 world, we have no choice but to think creatively if we are to win the fight against rising terrorist threats."[14]

Like other organizations whose traditional activities are now blurred by new goals and objectives, the military faces significant challenges. According to Byrd, "It suffers from all the obstacles that most bureaucratic organizations confront in regard to systems, structures, entrepreneurial thinking, policies and procedures, people, and culture."[15]

What? The U.S. military lacks entrepreneurial thinking? Maybe Rohrs should have been encouraging more entrepreneurial-minded SIFE students to join the military rather than accept federal funding for a free enterprise mission to India and Malaysia. These bright, young, future Wal-Mart managers could teach our generals a thing or two about free enterprise and entrepreneurship.

A third reason why Rohrs' argument was weak can be gleaned by reading the works of Peruvian economist Hernando de Soto.[16] De Soto argued that free market capitalism has not been the answer for the world's most impoverished people. It is not because there is a lack of entrepreneurial spirit or drive in undeveloped countries—rather, the major impediment is their inability to produce capital, which is the lifeblood of the capitalistic system. Without legal title, land dwellers are unable to borrow money using property as collateral.

De Soto pointed out that capitalism is viewed by many developing countries as "an apartheid regime most cannot enter. There is a growing sense, even among some elites, that if they have to depend solely and forever on the kindness of outside capital, they will never be productive players in the capitalist game."[17] Without legal property systems that can convert their cash and labor into capital, it is "senseless to call for open economies without facing the fact that the economic reforms underway open the doors only for small and globalized elites and leave out most of humanity. At present, capitalist globalization is concerned with interconnecting only the elites that live inside the bell jars."[18] Legally-recognized property systems and enforceable contracts were needed to unlock the mystery of capital.

DeSoto also correctly noted that people in developing countries understand entrepreneurship very well, but physical, legal, and political barriers prevent them from, as Rohrs would say, unleashing the entrepreneurial spirit. Jeffery Sachs pointed out several specific barriers: lack of infrastructure to link people to markets, which is largely a failure of government to provide adequate transportation and education; cultural or religious norms, which often block the role of women; physical geography; large families; and trade barriers imposed by other countries, which are often politically-driven.[19]

About the same time the $250,000 grant was announced, SIFE snagged another big grant. This time, though, it was for $750,000. The liberal press got hold of this. The January 29, 2006, article in the *Boston Globe* led with:

> Members of Congress inserted a record number of pet projects in last year's budget, feeding the burgeoning Washington lobbying industry that lawmakers in both parties insist they want to reform. Congress, which spent $10 billion on 1,439 such projects in 1995, ran up $27.3 billion for a record 13,997 such projects—known as earmarks—last year, according to the nonpartisan Citizens Against Government Waste. A *Globe* review of Senate records

shows that the secretive earmark process has also become a boon for lobbyists, who sell clients on their ability to persuade members to insert pet projects into the budget.

And later in the article:

The Globe review found that lobbyists arguing for the projects often have close connections to the members of Congress they are pressuring for cash. Many have worked on Capitol Hill—including directly for the lawmakers they are lobbying—and others contribute to the members' campaigns." She then quoted Keith Ashdown, vice president for policy at the nonpartisan Taxpayers for Common Sense. "If you don't have the money to hire a lobbyist, especially a former appropriations staffer, your chances of getting federal dollars are thrown through the window."

Then, she pointed out SIFE's good fortune.

One of the lobbyists listed on the case is Gregg L. Hartley, Blunt's former chief of staff. Last year, the group was rewarded with a total of $1 million in grants in two separate spending bills.

A week after the *Boston Globe* article, *salon.com* featured another unflattering article, providing more details of Blunt's cozy relationship with Cassidy—and SIFE:

If you go to the Web site of Cassidy & Associates, Washington's second-largest lobbying firm, you can find a description of Gregg Hartley, the firm's vice chairman. He is described as a lobbyist with connections to Blunt and other GOP leaders "unsurpassed by any other group or individual in Washington."

"I'm working with a group of people that I know," boasts Hartley, who was Blunt's closest advisor for the better part of 18 years before becoming a lobbyist.

Such credentials have given Hartley an impressive array of

clients, corporations and trade groups who were served well by Blunt when he was DeLay's second in command until late last year, according to documents obtained by Taxpayers for Common Sense, an advocacy group that opposes excess government spending. After Ocean Spray Cranberries hired Hartley, Congress instructed the U.S. Department of Agriculture to buy more than 34 million pounds of cranberries to stabilize their price. After the Dairy Farmers of America hired Hartley, Congress extended a $22 million program to provide foreign "dairy development" assistance. After a pro-capitalist student group, Students in Free Enterprise, hired Hartley, Congress showered the group with government subsidies of near socialist proportions—$750,000 for capital improvements to the group's Missouri headquarters.[20]

The *Washington Post* piled on with a March 27, 2006, article. The headline was, PROPOSALS CALL FOR DISCLOSURE OF TIES TO LOBBYISTS: LAWMAKERS MAY BE FORCED TO DETAIL CONTACTS, CASH RECEIVED. Weisman described how lawmakers channel special interest groups, like SIFE, to lobbyists to help "secure home-district pet projects, or 'earmarks,' and in turn, those lobbyists can send part of their fees back in the form of campaign contributions."[21]

Weisman pointed to several examples, and again, SIFE was among them.

Last year, Missouri-based Students in Free Enterprise hired Gregg Hartley, a former chief of staff to House Majority Whip Roy Blunt (R-Mo.), to help diversify its funding base, said Michelle West, the group's spokeswoman. Students in Free Enterprise paid Hartley $80,000 for the first six months of the year, according to lobbying records, and quickly secured $750,000 to expand its Springfield headquarters, and another $250,000 through the State Department to continue an international student exchange program. In an interview, Blunt said he recommended that the group hire a lobbyist after they asked, but he said he did not recommend Hartley. He did not have to. The leaders of Students in Free Enterprise knew Hartley as well as they knew him, Blunt said.

The left-leaning *Boston Globe* and *Washington Post* were critical, but so was the political right. For example, Republican U.S. Representative Jeff Flake from Arizona listed the SIFE earmark in his weekly posts "Egregious Earmark of the Week: $750,000 for Free Enterprisers in Mo." His April 13, 2006, note said, "By serving up this generous helping of pork, Congress has told these 'students in free enterprise' to throw away their Adam Smith textbook." Flake added, contemptuously, "There's such a thing as a free lunch after all."[22] The bill passed the House on November 18, 2005, and was unanimously approved by the Senate the same day. President Bush signed the bill into law on November 30.

The negative publicity didn't stop SIFE from going after more federal funds. According to the Office of Management and Budget, SIFE received another $2,976,000 grant to develop SIFE programs in the Middle East from the Agency of International Development. Apparently, earmarks are bad when Democrats are in the White House. Not so much, though, when Republicans run the show.[23]

What a far cry from the days when SIFE encouraged its teams to enter the Jules and Gwen Knapp Foundation Halt the Deficit/Reduce the Debt Special Competition. The sole judging criterion was, "How effectively did the SIFE team educate their community on the federal budget deficit and national debt and their impact on nation's economy?"

Cynically, I wondered if Rohrs and the SIFE board might now be considering new competition judging criteria for USA SIFE teams, like "How effectively did the SIFE team use its lobbying budget to win federal funding for its pork-barrel projects?" Or "How effectively did the SIFE team prevent international skirmishes by inculcating the principles of free enterprise into the hearts of its local citizens?" or "How effectively did the SIFE team teach these citizens to stop lying on the couch to unleash their entrepreneurial spirit?"

Nelson Lichtenstein had maintained a friendly correspondence, and I sent him an email updating him on SIFE news. I thought he'd get a kick out of learning about the pork-barrel money SIFE was raking in. On June

2, 2005, he replied:

> I agree that is pretty funny invoking national defense for getting a government grant. Why not say, hey, here is some money, let's take it.
>
> Equally interesting to me was Rohrs' invocation of the Austrian school of economics. Does this mean that he is a scholar and lecturer on Hayek and Schumpeter and von Mies? Is SIFE itself "Austrian?" And despite all the invocation of spreading "free enterprise" education, what does that mean really? A defense of the World Bank and the IMF "Washington consensus" abroad? Or at home, how political does this get? In favor of open borders for immigrants, China in the WTO, an end to the multifiber agreement, against zoning regulations, or is it all kept a bit vague and upbeat (i.e., an entrepreneurial spirit will fulfill the American dream, both personally and for the country)?
>
> I've just been through the *2004* (SIFE) *Yearbook* which was sent to me by Tim Clow when they rejected my attendance. There were a lot of pictures of happy people but I could not figure out the content of the various educational projects. There were few examples offered.
>
> Also, insofar as the real point of SIFE is to staff lower level management at retail stores, one can see a logic to why Walgreens and Radio Shack are so active. Both those companies have about 5,000 stores and each one needs a manager and an assistant.

A week before the 2007 SAGE World Cup, scheduled for Odessa, Ukraine, August 3–6, I flew to Moscow where Irina Dannikova and her husband, Sergei, picked me up at the Moscow airport and drove me to Tula. As in other countries like Ghana and Nigeria, I had come to Russia to make presentations to government agencies and local high schools.

Tula is a city of about half a million people, approximately 120 miles directly south of Moscow. An ironworking center, it is most famous as the first armament factory in Russia. Irina and Sergei lived in a tiny, four hundred square foot flat typical of about 95 percent of all Russians. The inside was quite comfortable, but the outside of the building and staircase reminded me of the inner-city slums I had seen on television, like the Baltimore tenements depicted in the HBO series *The Wire*. Lots of graffiti; heavy doors with secure locks; repulsive garbage strewn about in front of the entrance; dilapidated playground equipment; nonworking elevators; missing tiles. I saw very few residential houses, but with the 1991 collapse of communism, Irina told me that more and more people in the upper class were building single-family summer homes.

The next morning, the first order of business was to stand in a long line at the municipal office and register my presence in Tula. Strange, I thought, this would be like out-of-town guests visiting me in Chico having to register with our local police station.

"Our government likes to keep track of our foreign visitors," Sergei said.

Later that day, I asked Sergei and Irina if I could go for a jog through the park. They looked at each either, eyebrows raised. "Yes, you can go to the park and exercise, but please, please stay on the main road. If something should happen to you, we would get into trouble. The local government makes us responsible for your well-being."

Communication was difficult. While out and about, Irina had arranged for an interpreter, Alexander, who accompanied us to all meetings. Alexander was twenty-three years old, and he spent several years as a child and teenager in the United Kingdom and Austria. His parents were both English teachers, and his father also worked as an interpreter at the Russian embassies in London and Vienna. Thankfully, when Alexander wasn't with us, Irina spoke and understood enough English for us to get by.

Two full days were spent in Moscow. On the first day, we had two meetings. The first one was at the Ministry of Education, and what was scheduled for thirty minutes ended up being two hours. It went well. The deputy minister and her assistant especially liked SAGE's global aspect and dual emphasis on environmental stewardship and social entrepreneurship. They didn't seem very excited, though, about the civic engagement part. Needless to say, I didn't play it up.

Meeting number two was a strikeout. Given that the location was directly across from the old KGB building and next to a huge statue of Karl Marx, I probably shouldn't have expected too much. The organization was called Apora, and it represents small and medium sized businesses in Russia. The two representatives assigned to the meeting weren't there on their own volition, but appeared to attend by order from the executive director, who wasn't present. They clearly weren't interested in learning about SAGE.

After the second meeting, my hosts took me on a driving tour of Moscow, highlighted by a stop at the Novodevichy Cemetery southwest of Moscow's center. A few months earlier in April, Boris Yeltsin was laid to rest here after a state funeral attended by Mikhail Gorbachev and Vladimir Putin. Also in attendance were British Prime Minister John Major, former Polish president Lech Walesa (who helped end communist rule in 1989 as the leader of the Solidarity movement), and former U.S. presidents Bill Clinton and George H.W. Bush.

Yeltsin, Russia's first democratically-elected president who oversaw the breakup of the Soviet Union, is considered much more of a hero in modern-day Russia than Gorbachev. Many of Russia's most famous writers and artists are buried at Novodevichy, as are a few other notable political leaders like Nikita Khrushchev. However, most Soviet leaders, including Joseph Stalin, have been buried in the Kremlin Wall. Vladimir Lenin's body lies in a mausoleum on Red Square.

As we ambled through the cemetery, I thought how the Cold War had ended only sixteen years earlier, and how programs like SAGE could help usher in a new generation of entrepreneurs. I also reflected on the AACSB's Peace through Commerce task force, which understood the importance of social capital when it suggested that when people work together for a common cause, regardless of backgrounds, war is less likely and making money is more likely. These were exciting times.

Before 1991, entrepreneurship was illegal in Russia. The government assigned jobs and individuals took what they got. Now, the government was encouraging innovation and risk-taking, within boundaries. The media were still controlled by the Kremlin, and any form of dissent of Putin's policies was asking for trouble. When topics like these came up, Irina and Sergei talked in hushed tones even in their own apartment.

Early in the morning on August 1, 2007, my two Russian hosts and I climbed into Sergei's car. We drove southwest all day through the Russian countryside, crossing the border into Ukraine in the early evening. We had driven about five hundred miles, and it reminded me of driving through the wheat fields of Nebraska—except there were no family farms and hardly any buildings, a product of decades of collective farming. The next day, we pointed straight south for a three hundred-mile drive from Kiev, and pulled into Odessa in mid-afternoon.

We went directly to the Black Sea Hotel in downtown Odessa. As we checked in, we noticed dozens of teens milling in the lobby and throughout the hotel. The fifth annual SAGE World Cup 2007 was about to begin.

Chapter 21

Humanitarian Capitalism

The 2007 Odessa SAGE World Cup champion was Junior Secondary School from Jikwoyi Village, about fifteen miles southwest of the center of Nigeria's capital city of Abuja. The young entrepreneurs manufactured chalk and candles, selling the chalk to nearby school districts and marketing the candles to villagers. Many parts of Jikwoyi Village, which I would visit four years later, had no electricity and for those who did have power, frequent outages were the norm.

Odessa, Ukraine, was an elegant host city for our fifth SAGE world event. The citizens were smart and cultured. After the results were announced, Olga Azarova and her husband Andrig hosted all two hundred delegates to a banquet and dance at a beach resort on the north shore of the Black Sea, ending with an incredible fireworks display.

The night was magical. Teens from around the world danced and celebrated. The Brazilian youth taught the Samba; the Ukrainians performed their traditional folk-stage dances; a member of the Russian delegation entertained us with her beautiful ballet; the Nigerians showed grace and rhythm with their acrobatic dance steps; the Chinese dancers were softer and gentler, using their body to express thoughts and feelings to communicate everyday life. No one had an agenda—no one was trying to convert anyone else to their brand of religion, politics, or economic theory. I couldn't help but marvel that our SAGE teens were born about the same time the former Soviet Union disbanded in 1991, when entrepreneurship in a market economy was nonexistent.

Earlier in the day, all of the national coordinators or their representatives met in the hotel and plotted strategy for next year. Jerr Boschee, our newest board member, sat in on the meeting. The biggest agenda item was to decide the location of the 2008 world event. Nigeria and Brazil both wanted to host. Agwu Amogu argued that it would be good for us to come to Abuja in order to attract more attention to other African countries, and he had strong support from the minister of education. Magdiel Unglaub, on the other hand, countered that Brasilia or Rio de Janeiro would be a better host city because he had a large corporate sponsor willing to foot most of the tab.

After a long debate, we voted—six votes for Nigeria, six votes for Brazil. Everyone looked to me to make a decision, but before I did, I asked Jerr for input. He sided with Nigeria, given that Nigeria had been in the SAGE program for three years, while Brazil was new to SAGE. In fairness, Nigeria should get the nod, he said, and I agreed.

Jerr and his family had created a special competition for SAGE teams competing at our world event called The Arthur Boschee and Evelyn Ball International Awards for Social Enterprise. Starting in 2007, the top three social enterprises would earn special prize money of $2,000, $1,000, and $500. In Odessa, the first place team was from Ateneo High School in Manila, Philippines. The Filipino students utilized recycled tarpaulin that had been used for political and corporate advertising on gigantic freeway billboards. The tarpaulin was turned into designer bags, which were cut and sewn together by unemployed seamstresses. Local artisans painted logos and signs.

In Jerr's view, the business was an ideal social enterprise—it made a profit, employed the unemployed, and had an environmental sustainability component. He viewed SAGE as an excellent organization to articulate his view of social enterprise. Much debate continued to center around how, precisely, to define social entrepreneurship. Example questions: must a social enterprise be profitable, or can innovators and risk takers in the *nonprofit* world be considered social entrepreneurs? Can someone who addresses a problem unique to a small community be considered a social entrepreneur? How does one measure the success of a social enterprise, if profitability is secondary to solving a social problem? Like Jerr, I saw SAGE as a way to clarify the meaning of social entrepreneurship and to be one of the world's first organizations to teach this new topic to youth.

But SAGE wouldn't only teach it. We would provide an avenue for youth to actually start social enterprises, or start traditional commercial enterprises that took the issue of social responsibility seriously. Social entrepreneurship,

I believed, could lead to a new form of capitalism, which I had begun to use in speeches and presentations. I called this *humanitarian capitalism.*

Chico State's College of Business was seeking reaccreditation in 2007, and on January 25, 2008, Dean Willie Hopkins received a letter from the AACSB informing him that we had maintained our precious rating. In the second paragraph, nine items were listed for special commendation as a strength and effective practice. The second item on the list was SAGE.

As decided a year earlier, the next SAGE World Cup took place in Abuja, Nigeria, July 21–27, 2008. The top four teams advancing from the preliminary round were from Singapore, South Korea, Nigeria, and the United States. The USA team, represented by Santa Monica High School from California, earned the right to represent the USA by winning the SAGE USA tournament in Cincinnati in May. In Abuja, the Jikwoyi team from Nigeria once again took first place, South Korea took second, the USA earned third place honors, and Singapore came in fourth.

A new feature at the 2008 World Cup was a special competition sponsored by the founders of one of California's most respected businesses, Sierra Nevada Brewing Co. A model humanitarian capitalist and winner of several corporate social responsibility awards, Sierra Nevada was cofounded by Ken Grossman in 1981. His wife, Katie Gonser, had learned about SAGE through Chico State's Center for Environmental Literacy. She requested a lunch meeting, and I walked away with a $10,000 check to sponsor eight new awards, one for each of the eight Millennium Development Goals. Every year since then Katie and I have repeated our lunch meeting. I update her on SAGE and she writes another check. Prior to each world cup event, SAGE teams are asked to submit a summary of their social enterprise if it meets one of the MDGs. Even though a SAGE team may not place in the overall competition, they now have a chance to win prize money in Jerr's special competition and the Grossman special competitions.

In addition to the cultural day, a highlight of the Nigeria tournament was a trip to Ushafa Village, made famous when Bill Clinton paid a historic visit in August 2000. Ushafa is a picturesque little village about twenty-five miles north of the heart of the Abuja city center, and it is best known for its beautiful pottery studio and shop. Like most of the small villages in

Nigeria, Ushafa was off the grid. No electricity, filthy sanitary methods, shoeless children—a wakeup call for all SAGE students and chaperones from more prosperous homes.

The village chief invited Rob Best and me into his home where he proudly displayed photos of him, together with President Clinton. Clinton, dressed in a beautiful robe, was bestowed with the title of honorary chief. Along with his daughter, Chelsea, they donned the traditional chieftain attire. "We want to help you build your economy, educate your children and build a better life in all the villages of this country," Clinton told the throng of villagers gathered outside the chief's home during his visit.[1]

SAGE continued on a shoestring budget. Our entire staff, including myself, consisted of volunteers. Our main funders were the Allstate Foundation and Wells Fargo, along with Joe Pedott's foundation. Their contributions were just enough to cover food and hotel for our delegates. Incredulously, teams found a way to get to our World Cups. Airfare was the responsibility of each individual country, and I was extremely grateful for the dedication of our SAGE regional and national coordinators. For SAGE to succeed, local buy-in was a necessity. The private sector and the public sector had to support local SAGE programs or they couldn't participate in the crowning event of the year.

SAGE was not a social enterprise—yet—because we relied entirely on the generosity of donors. Instead, the state of California listed us as a charitable corporation. SAGE was not a charity, in my mind. We were a groundbreaking, international youth education program that received official recognition as a 501(c)(3) entity, SAGEGLOBAL, in 2008.

As SAGE watched its every penny, nickel and dime, SIFE continued to live in a relative lap of luxury. According to its tax returns filed with the IRS, SIFE earned over $13 million in 2005, almost $12 million in 2006, over $13 million in 2007, and almost $14.5 million in 2008. It certainly didn't hurt that they had some power brokers in Washington. SIFE issued the following press release on August 26, 2008, with the headline, "Top Executives Visit SIFE World Headquarters for Building Dedication."[2]

Springfield, MO – Executives from around the world gathered

in Springfield today for the dedication of the expanded Robert W. Plaster Free Enterprise Center at the Jack Shewmaker SIFE World Headquarters. With state of the art meeting facilities and technology, as well as expanded office space, the Plaster Center will make Springfield the physical and virtual hub of communications for SIFE's worldwide network of students, academic professionals, and industry leaders.

"We are honored to host so many great friends of SIFE at this new facility today," said Alvin Rohrs, President and CEO of SIFE. "Without their support, SIFE would not be possible. We thank them for their collaboration in this effort as we give university students the tools to make a real difference in their communities."

A ribbon cutting kicked off the event followed by a dedication program featuring remarks by Doug Conant, President & CEO, Campbell Soup Company; Robert Plaster, Chairman, Evergreen Investments LLC; Jack Kahl, President & CEO, Jack Kahl & Associates (Former Founder & CEO, Manco Inc.); Jack Shewmaker, Executive Consultant, J-Comm, Inc. (Former President & CFO, Wal-Mart); John Ashcroft, Former U.S. Attorney General; Congressman Roy Blunt; and State Representative Shane Schoeller. The program concluded with the Board Room being named in honor of Alvin Rohrs, who has served as SIFE's CEO for 25 years.

Familiar names jumped out at me, especially John Ashcroft and Roy Blunt. And though I didn't know it at the time, Shane Schoeller was the former Blunt staffer who was a SIFE paid consultant to help Rohrs get a total of $1 million in federal grants a few years earlier. Tom Coughlin probably would have been there, too, if he hadn't been under house arrest after pleading guilty to stealing money, merchandise, and gift cards from Wal-Mart.

I shook my head when I saw that the board room was named after Rohrs. Once again, was this an example of servant leaders keeping their egos in check? Also, I couldn't understand why SIFE's board was investing so much money in brick and mortar and "a highly motivated staff of more than sixty professionals."[3] Bear in mind, the vast majority of SIFE's *operations* took place on university campuses, led by outstanding students and dedicated faculty advisers. SAGE's home office, by contrast, consisted of my tiny office on the third floor of Tehama Hall at Chico State. Our highly motivated staff had a payroll totaling exactly zero.

Near the end of 2008, the economic recession took a toll on everyone. SIFE's contributions dropped to $11.2 million in 2009, but bounced back to $12.9 million in 2010. As for SAGE, our World Cup tournament took place in Brasilia in July of 2009, but because of a budget shortfall, we couldn't provide as many amenities as in prior years. We bounced back in 2010 when we traveled to beautiful Cape Town, South Africa. In 2011, we made some significant changes to our structure, which were implemented for our ninth annual SAGE World Cup in Buffalo, New York.

In 2009, instead of inviting first and second place teams from each country to participate in the World Cup, we created two separate categories of competition. Our thinking was heavily influenced by Jerr Boschee, who had now become SAGEGLOBAL's chairman. Each country could still bring two SAGE teams, but each team had to be a champion in its respective category. For example, a SAGE team could choose to compete in one of two separate competitions: the socially-responsible business (SRB) competition or the social enterprise business (SEB) competition.

Our handbook pointed out that SRBs are always legally structured as for-profit businesses; they do not directly address social needs through their products or services or through the numbers of disadvantaged people they employ. Instead, they create positive social change indirectly through the practice of corporate social responsibility. Examples of such practices include paying equitable wages to their employees; using environmentally friendly raw materials; providing volunteers to help with community projects.

Our definition of a SEB, unlike some other leading thinkers in the social enterprise area, included a provision that required the enterprise to seek at least 50 percent of its financial support from an earned revenue strategy.

For most of his career, Jerr had worked hard to define social enterprise. Some writers have taken a large-scale view of social enterprise, while others have adopted a narrower view. For example, in a spring 2007 article in the *Stanford Social Innovation Review*, Roger Martin, dean of the University of Toronto's business school, and Sally Osberg, CEO and president of the Skoll Foundation, adopted a macro perspective. They defined a social entrepreneur as someone who "should be understood as someone who targets an unfortunate but stable equilibrium that causes the neglect, marginalization, or suffering of a segment of society; who brings to bear on this situation by his or her inspiration, direct action, creativity, courage, and fortitude; and who aims for and ultimately affects the establishment of a new stable equilibrium that secures permanent benefit for the targeted and society at large."[4]

This somewhat lengthy definition is similar to David Bornstein's definition. Bornstein authored a book in 2004 entitled, *How to Change the World: Social Entrepreneurs and the Power of New Ideas.* According to Bornstein, social entrepreneurs are transformative forces who, systemically, shift behavior patterns and perceptions. Social entrepreneurs are "people with new ideas to address major problems, who are relentless in the pursuit of their visions; people who simply will not take no for an answer; people who will not give up until they have spread their ideas as far as they possibly can."[5]

Gregory Dees, widely recognized as one of the first leaders of the social entrepreneurship movement, is more inclusive in his definition of social entrepreneurship. In Dees' view, a social entrepreneur is someone who makes an impact, be it small-scale or large-scale. Dees said, "My feeling is that entrepreneurship lies in behavior: how innovative and resourceful people are, their willingness to do what it takes to have the impact, and their determination to make it happen. This kind of behavior can happen in many venues and on many levels, on a small or a large scale." Dees' definition of social entrepreneurship, unlike SAGE's, included innovative leaders of nonprofit organizations.[6]

Jerr and I believed that entrepreneurs need to earn money, and before any entrepreneur can make a positive impact on society—small or large—they must first arrive at the belief that they can address an unmet need. SAGE is an incubator for entrepreneurs. Through SAGE, today's youth—tomorrow's commercial and social entrepreneurs—can be exposed to entrepreneurship as teenagers, through nontraditional course content in the schools and innovative teaching. Examples of course content include courses in commercial and social entrepreneurship, which are becoming more and more popular. Their popularity will grow as more entrepreneurially-minded teachers are trained in the area. Examples of new teaching approaches include service learning and finding ways for students to be more civically engaged, and relying on technology to "flip" the classroom, where classwork becomes homework and homework becomes classwork.

As leading social enterprise thinkers like Jerr were educating the public about the meaning of social enterprise, entrepreneurial giants like Microsoft's Bill Gates and Whole Foods' John Mackey were coming up with their own definitions of a new form of capitalism. Gates called his version *creative capitalism* and Mackey referred to his version as *conscious capitalism*.

Gates opened a can of worms. His form of capitalism is based on a system whereby a corporation's good deeds are recognized by the market, and rewarded with higher prices.[7] Profits and recognition? Many leaders, like Warren Buffett, applauded. Others, though, like economist William Easterly, were critical. What incentives would corporations have to devote some of its most valuable resources to solving problems that wouldn't directly add to the bottom line? Easterly's view was consistent with Nobel economist Milton Friedman's assertion that a business's only social responsibility is to maximize profits for its shareholders.

Unlike Gates' creative capitalism, Friedman's and Easterly's view is classical capitalism. Both Friedman and Easterly were in the same camp. Corporations that give money to the poor, they contended, do so because they are simply responding to consumer demand. Such *corporate philanthropy* is merely a token, though, and is not enough to make a real dent in poverty. What Gates said struck an emotional chord to the bleeding-heart liberal in me, but it sounded pie-in-the-sky to my alter ego: the more conservative CPA and accounting professor.

Mackey's definition was consistent with the notion of sustainability that had become popular a year or two earlier. Andrew W. Savitz wrote a book in 2006 called *The Triple Bottom Line*, which describes a sustainable business as one that "creates profit for its shareholders while protecting the environment and improving the lives of those with whom it interacts."[8] Unlike Gates, who seemed to be prescribing a new form of capitalism that would tackle poverty based on profits and recognition, Mackey's conscious capitalism sees classical capitalism as doing a good job in addressing poverty—or at least a better job than any other economic model. Also, as a libertarian, he wants to keep government interference to a minimum.[9]

Subscribers of Mackey's conscious capitalism would recognize that a corporation's role is to optimize value for all of its major stakeholders, not just shareholders. These stakeholders include employees, suppliers, customers and the community at large. In an October 2005 article in *Reason* magazine, Mackey said, "To extend our love and care beyond our narrow self-interest is antithetical to neither our human nature nor our financial success. Rather, it leads to the further fulfillment of both. Why do we not encourage this in our theories of business and economics? Why do we restrict our theories to such a pessimistic and crabby view of human nature? What are we afraid of?"[10]

So, we have three types of capitalism—classical, creative, and conscious. Classical capitalists, with a single-minded determination to maximize financial profits, have what Giacalone and Thompson call an *organization-centered worldview*. Historically, business educators and practitioners have operated from this worldview.

Proponents of creative and conscious capitalism, on the other hand, have a *human-centered worldview*. Here, business ethics, social responsibility, and sustainable business practices are part of an organization's core goals. Individuals with this worldview see the possible redeeming values of business.[11]

What kind of company is Wal-Mart? In a 2006 cover story in *Fortune* magazine, Gunther described how Wal-Mart's CEO, Lee Scott, was leading the way for his company to become a better corporate citizen. Gunther reported that Wal-Mart had developed "sustainable value networks" which share ideas, set goals and monitor progress in its environmental and social efforts. [12]

Was Wal-Mart's ostensible new desire to save the planet after decades of so-called efforts to pave the planet, a real shift in its business model? If so, Wal-Mart's shift may reflect the business model envisioned by Paul Hawken, where marketplace competition is not between a company wasting the environment versus one that is trying to save it. Hawken's ecological,

competitive model was intriguing: "Corporations can compete to conserve
and increase resources rather than deplete them."[13] He called for businesses
to implement better designs and processes that require it to reuse, recycle,
and reclaim the natural resources that it consumes in the manufacture and
distribution of its products. In this competitive environment, companies
that sell products would also be responsible for the product when it
becomes waste. Here, retailers like Wal-Mart would become *de-shopping*
centers where consumers would return durable products like refrigerators,
televisions and automobiles, and the retailer would be responsible for the
costs to dispose or salvage them.

While the Wal-Mart of the future may not become a de-shopping
center, one can get an idea of its new philosophy when it comes to re-
cycling materials. Like a true free market capitalist, Scott told Wal-Mart
employees in fall 2005, "If we throw it away, we had to buy it first. So we
pay twice—once to get it, once to have it taken away. What if we reverse
that? What if our suppliers send us less and everything they send us has
value as a recycled product? No waste and we get paid instead?"[14]

As Lee Scott was beginning to see the pecuniary virtues of environmental stewardship in the fall of 2005, he was confronted with some bad
news. As the *New York Times* reported not long before this book was going
to press, Wal-Mart allegedly tried to cover up bribery and corruption in
Mexico. The front-page story, VAST MEXICO BRIBERY CASE HUSHED UP
BY WAL-MART AFTER TOP-LEVEL STRUGGLE, reported on the newspaper's
months-long investigation into the Wal-Mart scandal, purportedly involving $28 million in bribes paid to Mexican civil authorities and lawyers in
order to speed up expansion into Wal-Mart's most lucrative international
market. Rather than authorize a full, independent investigation, Scott
"rebuked internal investigators for being overly aggressive."[15] In February
2006, Wal-Mart transferred control of the investigation over to a gentleman named Jose Luis Rodriguezmacedo, an executive with Wal-Mart de
Mexico. Rodriguezmacedo was one of the key figures being investigated.

According to the article, "Wal-Mart typically hired outside law firms to
lead internal investigations into allegations of significant wrongdoing. It did
so earlier in 2005, when Thomas M. Coughlin, then vice chairman of Wal-
Mart, was accused of padding his expense accounts and misappropriating

Wal-Mart gift cards."[16]

Ironic. Wal-Mart hired an outside law firm to investigate Tom Coughlin much the same way SIFE's board, under Coughlin's direction, hired Larry Pinkerton's law firm to investigate SIFE and the special competition snafu in 2003. But when it came time for Wal-Mart to adhere to its "much publicized commitment to the highest moral and ethical standards," Lee Scott and his fellow servant leaders got out the broom.[17] Such matters were better swept under the rug.

Companies like Wal-Mart rely on a servant leader management philosophy that heaps praise and recognition on its employees—which for many employees was sufficient for them to remain loyal to their boss even though wages and working conditions were below par. This paternalistic form of servant leadership is not unlike a husband recognizing and appreciating his wife in exchange for her continued devotion to him—or SIFE appreciating its faculty advisers by calling them Sam M. Walton Fellows and providing a modest $1,000 stipend and an indirect link to some of the nation's top retail executives. Was Lee Scott a servant leader? Was Tom Coughlin a servant leader, or a self-serving selfish leader? What about Jack Kahl? Roger Blackwell?

And what about Jack Shewmaker? I had climbed to the top of SIFE's recognition ladder, where I soared, ever so briefly, with the top eagle. The "incident" in the summer of 2000 and the special competition *glitch* required that I hire an attorney to defend my reputation. I looked around, but the big eagle was gone. Quickly, I fell. Then, in 2005, I was fired before I resigned. A rise, and then the fall.

The title of this book indicates that my journey with SIFE included a rise, fall, and ultimately, *redemption* as a Sam M. Walton Free Enterprise Fellow. Redemption? *Webster's Dictionary's* definition for *redeem* include "to make good by performance." How have I made good by performance since leaving SIFE in 2005?

My redemption, I believe, is based on three legs of the same stool: a business philosophy of humanitarian capitalism; a teaching philosophy that includes social enterprise and service learning; and a determination to provide students with a human-centered worldview. The stool is called

SAGE.

Humanitarian capitalism can lead to more prosperity not only for those who already enjoy prosperity, but for everyone. These capitalists will start two types of businesses: socially responsible commercial enterprises, like those recommended by John Mackey, and businesses that are social enterprises, like Muhammad Yunus' Grameen Bank.

Mackey's conscious capitalism comes closest to humanitarian capitalism, except unlike Mackey and tea party supporters (but like Gates), I believe government must play a key role, especially in areas of poverty, education, health care, energy, and the environment. As William Easterly points out, "In a democratic society with institutions that protect the right of private property and individual economic freedom, governments face the right incentives to create private sector growth. We can envision a world in which governments do provide national infrastructure—health clinics, primary schools, well-maintained roads, widespread phone and electricity services—and they do provide assistance to the poor within each society."[18]

When I teach my introductory accounting students, I teach them that the fundamental accounting equation is Assets – Liabilities = Owners' Equity. In other words, a company's net financial assets are equal to its financial value. The real accounting equation, I tell my students, is A + B + C = Value. A is for financial assets, B is for brains, and C is social capital.

If an entrepreneur is going to truly make a positive impact in the world, all three ingredients are needed. The ABCs of my social capital equation is what SAGE is all about. SAGE encourages teenagers to start commercial and social enterprises with a triple bottom line mentality. University students guide their younger protégés as part of a service-learning program. And when we conduct our national and international SAGE tournaments, all students are exposed to youth with different cultural, religious, and ethnic backgrounds, thereby expanding their worldview and adding to their social capital.

Researchers in sociology and political science have attempted to measure social capital. For example, Smith described how Transnational Social Movement Organizations (TSMOs) are building social capital globally, linking local problems to global initiatives. Her work has direct implications for the AACSB's peace initiative in that "the presence of transnational organizations, prepared to organize global campaigns and strategically link local conflicts with global policy processes, enable these global/local links to be made."[19]

TSMOs create common interests among otherwise diverse members by relating various local problems to common, global problems. With the communication tools like Facebook and Skype in place today, social capital can be created without face-to-face contact. Smith said that "the ability to engage in such transnational dialogue—either face-to-face or via newsletter or via e-mail—is a necessary component for the formation of social capital and for the strengthening of a global civil society," and led her to conclude that "transnational social movement mobilization promises more than any other contemporary trend to help break down rather than reproduce existing global inequalities."[20]

Robert Putnam, who authored *Bowling Alone* in 2000, noted that communities and organizations can be more productive "when there's a pattern of connectedness, where people trust one another and behave in a responsible way toward one another." How connected one is in a community or organization alludes to the strength of one's network, and the associated norms of reciprocity which, according to Putnam, means, "I'll do this for you now without expecting any favor back immediately from you, because down the road you'll do something for me and we'll all be connected anyhow."[21]

Putnam also distinguished between two types of social capital: bonding social capital, which links you to people like you, and bridging social capital, that links you to people unlike you. Whereas the former can be good, or bad (e.g., racist or ethnocentric organizations), social capital's greatest potential in the twenty-first century is to connect people who are not alike. Putnam concluded, "Let's pay special attention to bridging social capital. Let's rely heavily on the ideas of younger people because they are likely to have the ideas that fit the way the twenty-first century will be."[22] This, in essence, is what SAGE is all about.

What *isn't* SAGE about? Nonprofit organizations are not social enterprises and their founders are not social entrepreneurs. Innovative public sector managers are not social entrepreneurs. Individuals who start mom and pop ventures with little risk and little innovation are not social entrepreneurs. SAGE enterprises must earn revenue and they must be innovative.

SAGE is not about any one leadership style—whether it be from a secular leader like Steve Jobs, a creative capitalist like Bill Gates, a conscious capitalist like John Mackey, or a self-proclaimed servant leader like Alvin Rohrs, Jack Kahl, Tom Coughlin, or Sam Walton. Each leader, in his own way, does his best to convince their workers that they are serving a higher purpose. But, please, keep God and political ideology out of the workplace—and out of SIFE, especially as was the case with SIFE in its first thirty years.

Sam Walton got it right in his autobiography in 1992 when he said, "In all likelihood, education is going to be the issue we focus on most. It is the single area that causes me the most worry about our country's future. ... Frankly, I'd like to see an all-out revolution in education. We've got to target inner-city schools and the rural poverty pockets and figure out a way to make a difference."[23]

If humanitarian capitalism and social entrepreneurship are to take root, we need to change our education system. The system needs to start with teens, or younger, tapping into their creative potential as soon as possible in order to give them the best opportunity to lead a happy life. University students, like those who participate in SIFE, are already on the fast-track to a successful career. It's the teenagers who are most at-risk, and that's why I think SAGE provides a better platform to do more good for more people.

Because most schools don't teach entrepreneurship, education leaders must do a better job of including it in the curriculum. This requires finding the right courses and the right teachers. The latter is harder than the former. Most high school teachers are risk averse, and many of them have selected education as a career in order to avoid risk—and entrepreneurial thinking. Universities, therefore, must change their teacher credentialing programs to encourage more risk-takers who want to teach entrepreneurship.

So much of a young person's academic life is devoted to thinking inside the box. Students sit in rows, most listen to their teachers for fifty minutes, and for many, they game it with the teacher in order to maximize their grade with minimal effort. Textbooks contain extraneous material that students never use. After fifty minutes, the bell rings and they're off to another class. Students pass through grade levels based on age, not on subject mastery. SAGE is different, and we give students more freedom to shoot higher in a contextual learning environment. As *New York Times* columnist Thomas Friedman said:

> Give young people a context where they can translate a positive imagination into reality, give them a context in which someone with a grievance can have it adjudicated in a court of law without having to bribe the judge with a goat, give them a context in which they can pursue an entrepreneurial idea and become the richest or the most creative or most respected people in their own country, no matter what their background, give them a context in which any complaint or idea can be published in the newspaper, give them a context in which anyone can run for office—and guess what? They usually don't want to blow up the world. They usually want to be part of it.[24]

Instead of competing for grades, we ask students to compete against other's SAGE teams based on their creativity. Mohammed Yunus states: "I can picture local, regional, and even global competitions, with hundreds of thousands of participants vying to create the most practical, ambitious, and exciting concepts for social businesses."[25]

SAGE is part of Yunus's picture. After our SAGE World Cup tournament in Nigeria in 2008, our next five events were in Brasilia in 2009, Cape Town in 2010, Buffalo, New York, in 2011, San Francisco in 2012, and Abuja in 2013. Scenes such as the one in Odessa in 2007 have been repeated in each country, and my reward is witnessing the growing rainbow of colors as seen in the costumes, dances, flags, faces, and enterprises of the participating teens.

I think Sam Walton was a genuine servant leader, in the way Robert Greenleaf meant it to be without bringing Jesus into the equation. Walton led by example. I love the quote in Walton's autobiography: "A lot of people think it's crazy of me to fly coach whenever I go on a commercial flight, and maybe I overdo it a bit. But I feel like it's up to me as a leader to set an example. It's not fair for me to ride one way and ask everybody else to ride another way."[26] The best leaders, truly, do so by example.

I think Sam Walton would support the theory of humanitarian capitalism, especially considering his prediction about the future of business. "In the future, free enterprise is going to have to be done well—which means it benefits the workers, the stockholders, the communities, and, of course, management, which must adopt a philosophy of servant leadership," Walton said. He cautioned management about becoming too greedy. "Recently, I don't think there's any doubt that a lot of American management has been too far toward taking care of itself first, and worrying about everybody else later."[27]

Again, though, I come back to the big eagle. What about Jack Shewmaker? He, too, was a servant leader—in most respects. I was on my way to Belfast, Northern Ireland, on November 18, 2010, enjoying a coffee and checking my email at the Houston airport when I received a note that Shewmaker had died of a heart attack the night before at age seventy-two. Included in his obituary was the note, "Throughout their lives, Jack and Melba Shewmaker remained true to their small-town values and embraced the role of servant leaders in all their endeavors." [28]

A wave of emotions overcame me. He had been a mentor at one time, and I respected him greatly. Up until his death, Shewmaker would remain an active member of SIFE's board of directors, serving on its powerful Executive Committee. And until 2008, he served on Wal-Mart's board. Without doubt, he was a passionate advocate of free enterprise, an ardent subscriber to servant leadership and, as SIFE's patron saint, he was Alvin Rohrs' entrée into the executive suites of hundreds of corporate sponsors. When I first became acquainted with him in May 1994, and up until his death, I had no reason to question Shewmaker's unequivocal commitment to youth and to service.

After his retirement, he traveled the world to support SIFE's mission. He truly loved students. Servant leadership, as he outwardly practiced it, appeared to be genuine and sincere in a manner consistent with Robert Greenleaf's secular definition of servant leadership. Part of his philosophy, however, included loyalty, right or wrong, to someone who I knew, firsthand, to be disingenuous and insincere. To the very end, Shewmaker remained loyal to Alvin Rohrs, so much that SIFE's board of directors, under Shewmaker's guiding hand, created the Alvin Rohrs Servant Leader Scholarship and named the board room after Rohrs at SIFE's expanded Jack Shewmaker SIFE Worldwide Headquarters.

Like SAGE, SIFE recently has made some big changes, too. Notably, starting in the 2010–2011 year, SIFE changed its judging criteria from seven criteria to just one criterion. In a press release dated August 9, 2010, SIFE announced that there would now only be one judging criterion in the overall team competition. The new criterion read: "Considering the relevant economic, social and environmental factors, which SIFE team most effectively empowered people in need by applying business and economic concepts and an entrepreneurial approach to improve their quality of life and standard of living?" Prior to the change, it was difficult for most teams to meet all seven criteria unless they had a large number of SIFE students, deep pockets, or both.

I read the new criterion carefully. Amazing—SIFE was now encouraging its teams to empower people in need. This sounded a lot like Bill Gates' creative capitalism.

"This change in criteria directly connects our mission to the work of our student teams and it distinguishes SIFE as an organization that is using the positive power of business to improve lives and strengthen communities," said Rohrs in the press release. "Building on our strategy to continually enhance the relevance and impact of our program, this criterion provides teams with a clear and compelling mandate, while still preserving their opportunity for creativity—a longstanding hallmark of the SIFE program."[29]

According to the release, the updated criterion took more than a year and the process involved the participation of a wide variety of stakeholders. Stakeholders included global staff, country leaders, faculty advisors and members of the International Advisory Council of Board Chairs. The end product was then presented to Executive Committee of the SIFE worldwide board of directors for consideration and final approval. This certainly wasn't the same SIFE operating model when I was a Sam M.

Walton Fellow. The organization appeared to be changing for the better.

SIFE also changed its mission statement "to bring together the top leaders of today and tomorrow to create a better, more sustainable world through the positive power of business." This was a good sign, I thought. Who could argue with a better world? Sustainability? Positive power of business? Not me. Could SIFE, like Wal-Mart, be embracing Mackey's conscious capitalism?

SIFE's special competitions have been replaced by "project partnerships" with sponsor companies or organizations such as the U.S. Chamber of Commerce, Campbell's, HSBC, Lowe's, and Unilever. Each sponsor offers prize money or scholarships to teams that meet specific criteria. For example, Campbell's has a competition called the Let's Can Hunger Challenge, with prizes going to SIFE teams that "demonstrate a comprehensive approach to addressing hunger including; raising awareness, translating awareness to action in the form of urgent hunger relief, and empowering those in need to defeat the cycle of hunger." All entries are submitted online and, ostensibly, judged by representatives from the sponsor.[30]

SIFE's changes weren't all good. Starting in 2010–2011, stipends for Walton Fellows were cut to $500, and in 2011 they were dropped altogether. They also discontinued paying for hotel rooms at regional competitions. If SIFE was Tom Sawyer, then SIFE teams were Tom's friends getting whitewashed.

The biggest SIFE change of all, though, was announced by Donna M. Patterson, president of SIFE USA, via email to all Sam Walton Fellows on April 13, 2012. The subject read, "SIFE Rebranding and Name Change." The email read:

> As part of a multi-year strategic review, the SIFE worldwide board of directors has decided to explore the opportunity of changing the organization's name to better support our mission and ability to build a global brand. This is an exciting time as we seek to preserve and strengthen the core values that have guided SIFE to this point, while also telling a more complete and compelling story—one that will lead us into the future and serve as a platform for greater growth and impact.

We need your help and are inviting members of the SIFE network from around the world to develop suggestions for what our new name should be. Please watch this video message from the President and CEO of SIFE Worldwide for more information about this decision and how you can participate in the process: www.youtube.com/watch?v=WOJ80MKWmBA

You can also visit www.sife.org/nameideas for more information and to submit your ideas. The deadline for submissions is Monday, April 30.

After all these years of Rohrs' trying to build SIFE's "brand," SIFE was now changing its name. Was *free enterprise* not such a good sell anymore to prospective donors in, say, Saudi Arabia? Qatar? China? Sweden? I checked out Rohrs' eight-minute video on YouTube.

"We started out as an advocacy organization that promoted ideas." Rohrs said. "We've become an action organization that uses ideas to improve people's lives." A bit later he added, "While we think we're doing a great job of changing the world and changing lives, the visibility of what we do doesn't match the impact of what we do."

Advocacy, all right—SIFE had started out by promoting ideas that trumpeted right-wing Republican dogma and Christian servant leadership.

The 2011 SIFE World Cup took place in Kuala Lampur, Malaysia, October 3–5. A year earlier, a smiling Bruce Nasby gleefully signed a contract with the secretary general of the Minister of International Trade and Industry, with the Malaysian government pledging RM1 million as a hosting grant, worth about $320,000.[31] A total of thirty-seven countries participated with Germany taking top honors, followed by Zimbabwe, Puerto Rico, and Guatemala. SIFE reported revenue of $12,800,000, and had seventy-five full-time employees. At the closing ceremony, a videotaped message from Secretary of State Hillary Clinton announced a partnership between SIFE and the U.S. Department of State, with Washington, D.C., as the SIFE World Cup 2012 host.[32] KPMG was also announced as the main sponsor.

I was somewhat surprised to see Clinton's endorsement, but not completely. When she was the first lady of Arkansas, she had been the only woman member of Wal-Mart's fifteen-member board of directors. She served for six years, from 1986 to 1992. In a May 20, 2007, feature article in the *New York Times*, Clinton is shown in a picture seated between Jack Shewmaker and David Glass on her right and Sam Walton on her left. At the time, Shewmaker and Glass were fighting it out to become Walton's heir apparent to Wal-Mart. Though critical of Wal-Mart during her husband's presidency, she maintained "close ties to Wal-Mart executives through the Democratic Party and the tightly knit Arkansas business community. Her husband, former President Bill Clinton, speaks frequently to Wal-Mart's current chief executive, H. Lee Scott Jr., about issues like health care and even played host to Mr. Scott at the Clintons' home in New York last July for a private dinner."[33]

By contrast, the 2011 SAGE World Cup was hosted by Canisius College in Buffalo, New York, at the end of July. National champion teams from eighteen high schools representing twelve countries competed in our ninth annual tournament. The four countries advancing from the preliminary round to the overall final round of the SRB competition were Canada, China, Nigeria, and Ukraine, with Nigeria emerging as the champion. In the SEB competition, the Jikwoyi team from Nigeria prevailed again. Along with Nigeria, the three countries advancing from the preliminary round to the overall final round of the SEB competition were Canada, South Africa, and the United States. Jikwoyi's winning SEB business consisted of an environmental intervention project designed to help convert biodegradable waste into organic fertilizer. SAGE reported revenues of about $150,000 with no full- or part-time employees.

Without question, SIFE has made an indelible impression on my Chico State students during the twelve years I served as the Sam M. Walton SIFE Fellow. In the fall of 2011, I sent an email to some of the leaders from the past asking them to reflect on their SIFE experience. Kelby Thornton, now a senior manager for Chevron in Australia, said, "SIFE was a very grass roots movement when I joined. The programs were driven by the students who wanted to give back to their community. This was an integral part of my Chico State experience for over three years."

Suzanne Cozad, who works for Hewlett-Packard as a manager of sales operations, wrote, "SIFE was a true game changer for me. It really broadened my view of entrepreneurship and how business has an effect on so many aspects within a community. Personally, SIFE really enriched my experience at Chico and I truly believe was pivotal to the success I have achieved professionally."

When I asked Dawn Houston, now an attorney at Berliner Cohen in San Jose, about her overall impression of her SIFE experience, she replied, "It was my favorite part of my Chico State experience. Through SIFE, I gave back to the community, helped underprivileged kids, learned valuable presentation and management skills, and obtained friendships, travel, and networking that I would have never experienced otherwise."

Chris Coutant, the long-haired political science major who was leader of Chico State's first SIFE team in 1994, is now a senior manager for Oracle. He wrote, "I have a strong belief that if it wasn't for SIFE, and my experiences with SIFE, I would not be where I am today. I will always believe that SIFE allowed me to take my degrees and experience to the next level in my career."

How high is up for SAGE? There are 193 countries in the United Nations, with the addition of South Sudan in 2011. By the year 2015, I dream we will be in forty countries. In the past year we have added Kazakhstan, Pakistan, Japan, Vietnam, and the United Arab Emirates to our growing network. As I write this in February 2014, we have twenty-one registered countries, and expect at least fifteen of them to travel to our next world cup, with Moscow, Russia, serving as the host city on August 8–13, 2014. SAGE doesn't operate from brick-and-mortar buildings or enjoy the luxury of full- or part-time staff; instead, we rely on the resources provided by Chico State and a dedicated staff of alumni and current student volunteers.

SAGE, itself, is not yet a social enterprise; rather, it's still a charity. But starting in spring of 2012, we have created a one-semester course for teens called Turning Risk into Success, which we hope to market through traditional means and electronically. We also offer teacher training workshops because most high school teachers have no training in entrepreneurship.

Without SIFE, I would never have started SAGE. I am eternally grateful I became a Sam M. Walton Fellow in 1993. If I hadn't become a Walton Fellow, I don't think I could have found an outlet to combine my interest in social entrepreneurship and community service learning. As far as servant leadership, I see many virtues in it as a management philosophy, so long as it isn't explicitly or implicitly linked to religion, or to any particular political ideology.

In fact, I like the overarching philosophy of servant leadership in that loyalty to an organization can be earned through sharing, involvement, recognition, and appreciation. I have seen how great managers share their power by creating an environment where employees are involved in decision making. By honoring subordinates with deserved awards and plaques, a culture is created that "we're all in this together." As a result, the organization becomes a better place to work, and all boats rise.

But I seriously question self-anointed servant leaders who take home exorbitant executive salaries at the same time their employees are living in virtual economic slavery. I don't ask these people, "How high is up?" Instead, I ask, "How can you sleep at night?" And I also ask, "*How much is enough?*"

SIFE changed its name to *Enactus* on September 30, 2012.[34] Moving from a brand of free enterprise toward a brand of entrepreneurship, Rohrs said, "We needed a name that reflected that uniqueness. Something that captured the entrepreneurial spirit that fuels everything we do. We were also eager to create a name that reflected how global this organization has become. Entrepreneurial action is not something that is relevant to a single culture or nationality. What we do is just as powerful in Shanghai as it is in Sao Paulo, just as transformative whether we are in San Francisco or Sydney."

Notably, SAGE has put entrepreneurship front and center since 2002. Now, more than ten years later, Enactus jettisons the SIFE name and puts entrepreneurship front and center, too. I find it a bit ironic that for over a decade Rohrs, Nasby, and other SIFE executives have criticized SAGE for copying SIFE. Now, though, SIFE rebrands itself to include entrepreneurship as its strategic focus.

Imitation is the best form of flattery.

Donna Patterson, whose title changed from president of SIFE USA to president of Enactus United States, sent out another email to all Walton Fellows on March 18, 2013, detailing more changes in the USA program. She informed faculty advisers that SIFE would no longer be hosting regional competitions. Replacing the regional competitions would be "two or three intensive Fall Leadership Conferences with Career Fairs at a time when our Partner Companies are even more actively seeking new talent." The leadership conferences, she said, would help Enactus teams launch their annual program "inspired by powerful lessons in servant leadership, best practice sharing, and networking opportunities with other Enactus students and our corporate Partners." There it was again—*servant leadership*. Rohrs must have had his fingerprints all over this email.

The retired Walton Fellow who forwarded Patterson's message said, "I wonder if [SIFE/Enactus] is having a financial squeeze. They have grown into a bureaucracy, in my humble opinion. Not like the good old days. Or, maybe it's just me growing old."

Patterson claimed that there were a few reasons for the change. For one, she said that many faculty advisers had expressed a desire to have more time to achieve their outcomes and prepare annual reports and presentations for competition. Another reason, she stated, is that regional winning teams would no longer "have two competition trips to fund and two times out of classes at critical periods in the academic year."

Certainly, hosting a dozen or more regional competitions is costly. The main reason for the change, I could only guess, is that donor companies didn't want its managers taking so much time off to judge Enactus events, when just two or three career fairs would do the trick at a much lower cost. And such change wouldn't affect any salaries in Enactus' home office, especially those of Rohrs, Nasby, and Burton.

How high is up for SIFE? I hope "up" is as high as Jack Shewmaker dreamed it might be. I believe SIFE's mission is noble, and by the looks of the recent changes to the mission statement and judging criteria, there is a chance that SIFE's current board *might* be driven by humanitarian capitalists. Maybe, just maybe, Wal-Mart and its vendors are truly beginning to embrace corporate social responsibility and sustainability. But to the extent that they continue to trust Alvin Rohrs to be its CEO—well, I have a hard time swallowing this. But—gulp—if push came to shove, I would lay down my sword with Rohrs if it meant that SIFE would embrace SAGE, and encourage SIFE students—or whatever SIFE's new name—to mentor SAGE teenagers.

My redemption as a fallen Sam M. Walton SIFE fellow has been SAGE. A program like SAGE focuses on training young entrepreneurs because, for many, their creative energy has not been dampened by life's harsher realities. Between four and five billion people in the world live on less than $2 a day. Though their individual incomes are small, P.K. Prahalad's book summarized the untapped market here by the title of his book, *The Fortune at the Bottom of the Pyramid*. For companies that want to tap into this fortune, Prahalad indicated market development at the bottom of the pyramid can create millions of new entrepreneurs at the grass roots level—from women working as distributors and entrepreneurs to village-level micro enterprises. He emphasized that "entrepreneurship on a massive scale is the key."[35] SAGE is my attempt to create such scale.

It really is too bad that Alvin Rohrs and I have clashed over the years, but it's not over yet. Maybe someday we can get together and link SAGE teens with university mentors who are truly an untapped army of social entrepreneurs and service providers. Alvin, let's talk.

Epilogue

The Golden Rule

It had been six years since my last leave of absence from Chico State. But in the spring of 2011, I was happy to learn my sabbatical request had been approved. There were two official objectives of the sabbatical: first, to pursue my interest in spreading SAGE to the Middle East; and second, to travel to London to learn more about the standard-setting process of the International Accounting Standards Board. And there was one unofficial reason—to start writing this book.

The first ten chapters of this book were written in the Middle East, mostly in Bahrain, in September and October of 2011. At the end of August, I met my girlfriend Tricia in Athens for a ten-day holiday in the Greek Islands, and then we flew to Bahrain. Tricia had been working in Bahrain the past two years as a contracts manager for a large utility company in Saudi Arabia. Her office was in Bahrain, rather than Saudi Arabia, because Saudi Arabia had strict restrictions forbidding women to work.

For the first four weeks in Bahrain, a tiny island country of only 1.2 million people, my daily schedule was routine. I would drive Tricia to work each morning, starting on Saturday, corresponding to the Saudi workweek. Then, I would return to our sixth-floor apartment in the village of Burhama and write for a couple hours. To keep the creative juices flowing, I'd go for a jog and lift some light weights, and then write a while longer.

Burhama was considered to be a hot spot, and authorities had set up traffic checkpoints in key traffic areas around the circle that was previously home to the Pearl Roundabout. After the spring uprising in 2012, the government destroyed the roundabout, erasing the city's most famous landmark in order to quell public demonstrations. Almost every night, we would see a few Shiite anti-government demonstrators protesting the Sunni-led government right outside our apartment building. Shiites make up about 70 percent of the population but have very little representation

363

in senior government and the military. No matter where I jogged, I would find anti-monarchy graffiti on building facades. The next day it would be painted over with white paint by the police. The situation was quite tense, but I never felt threatened.

Before the civil unrest, Bahrain's economy was booming. New skyscrapers were under construction, but the turmoil halted most of the construction in its tracks. Capital does not flow to hot spots.

On a Wednesday morning, near the end of September, I flew to Dubai where I met with our newly-enlisted Middle East SAGE coordinator, Aman Merchant. Aman and I had met at the Princeton Club in New York City in July, just before the SAGE World Cup in Buffalo, and he was working hard to launch SAGE in the United Arab Emirates. Tricia joined me on Thursday night. For the next two days, she and I took in as much of Dubai as we could.

We were awestruck by Dubai's wealth—much of it ostentatious. I decided to break my piggy bank and treat Tricia to dinner at the top of the Burj Al Arab, which is one of the most luxurious hotels in the world. Most of us have seen pictures of its stunning design, shaped to resemble a billowing spinmaker sail. It's a seven stars hotel with 202 double-floor suites—each suite has its own private butler.

The day after dining at the Burj Al Arab, we visited the Burj Al Khalifa Tower in downtown Dubai. Khalifa is the tallest building in the world, opened on January 4, 2010. It sits next to the world's largest shopping mall, the Dubai Mall. At this point in my life, my good fortune of becoming a university professor and SAGE coach had allowed me to see life's extremes, from the most destitute in countries like Sierra Leone, Nigeria, and the Philippines, to the most affluent in the Arabian Gulf.

Aman promised to do his best to bring a SAGE team from Dubai to the tenth SAGE World Cup in San Francisco the next year, and we bid him goodbye. In October, now back in Bahrain again, my same weekly routine continued. But for the next three weekends out of four, Tricia and I flew to Doha, Qatar, where she had accepted a temporary consulting position. While Tricia was working, I would explore Doha for a couple hours and then come back to the hotel to continue writing.

A smaller version of Dubai, Doha is no less bustling. With a population of less than one million citizens, the majority of Doha's residents are expatriates, all coming to Qatar to take part in its explosive growth, driven by its bountiful oil and natural gas. Unlike Dubai, Doha is not a tourist destination, although tourism is bound to increase now that Doha has won the rights to host the 2022 FIFA World Cup.

Each morning I would jog along the scenic Doha Corniche, which is a promenade along the waterfront that runs parallel to Corniche Street. Forty years ago, this area was an empty stretch of walkway with only one tall building, the Sheraton Hotel. Today, Corniche Street is a major road connecting the West Bay business district to the south part of the city leading to the airport. The street is now lined with sparkling new skyscrapers, each seemingly trying to outdo the other for architectural flair. Surrounding the new buildings are swarms of monoliths in the making.

From my hotel room I witnessed a forty-story building under construction while I wrote, adding floors like building blocks. As I finished chapter nine, I felt like I had finished building my own floor. A couple weeks later, I finished chapter ten—another floor. I had outlined the book to be twenty-one chapters, and I wondered if I would ever be able to finish. The mental discipline it took to write this book reminded me of the physical fortitude of training for a marathon when I was a doctoral student at Oklahoma State University.

After I left SIFE in May 2005, I knew I would someday chronicle my experiences as a Sam M. Walton Fellow. I had been toying with the title for a long time. Somehow, I couldn't get Jack Shewmaker's "How High Is Up?" speech out of my mind. He made the speech in Kansas City in May 2000—and without doubt, it had left an indelible impression. The euphoria I experienced in guiding Chico State to the SIFE USA national championship in 1999 had been the highest point of my career. I didn't know it then, but the ceiling had been reached with SIFE. There would be no more up.

SIFE had some great ideas and successful strategies, and I used them. Much as Jack Shewmaker's evangelical passion for SIFE gave him a reason to circumnavigate the world with a purposeful mission, my devotion to SAGE would take me to the far corners of the world, not as a tourist, but also with a higher purpose. When Shewmaker died on November 17, 2010, I knew I had to write this book, sooner than later. And the title was a no-brainer.

At a January 2011 SAGE board meeting at the Deloitte offices in downtown San Francisco, Jerr Boschee and Joe Pedott pulled me aside and asked if I could somehow reconnect with SIFE. "Curt, we agree with you, there is an untapped army of university students who would be great role models for teens. Are you sure you can't settle your differences with Rohrs?" they asked.

Too often, nonprofits that ought to work together don't, because of egos, funding bases, or slightly different missions. SAGE and SIFE were meant for each other, especially now that SIFE was beginning to subscribe to humanitarian capitalism, at least on paper. So I said yes to Jerr and Joe, and wrote the following letter on February 24, 2011:

Dear Alvin,

I hope this note finds you and SIFE doing well.

It has been a long time since we communicated, and, although we have had our differences in the past, I would like you to know that I believe in SIFE. It is an organization that has a tremendous positive effect on university students, positively impacts those in the community who are served by SIFE students, and provides businesses that hire SIFE students with a bright and enthusiastic set of new hires that have unique potential to become tomorrow's business leaders committed to social responsibility.

I noted two recent changes to SIFE's mission statement: To bring together the top leaders of today and tomorrow to create a better, more sustainable world through the positive power of business; and implementation of a single judging criterion that rewards SIFE teams to empower people in need by applying business and economic concepts and an entrepreneurial approach to improve their quality of life and standard of living.

These two changes reconfirm SIFE's alignment with SAGE's mission: To help create the next generation of entrepreneurial leaders whose innovations and social enterprises address the major unmet needs of our global community. SAGE is currently operating in eight U.S. states and 21 countries, impacting about 5,000 teens per year.

SAGE teens are a natural training ground for future SIFE students, and I would like to pursue a conversation whereby we could work together as organizations. To this end, I would be most happy to travel to Springfield in the next month or so to discuss this with you in person. Let me know what day might be best for you.

Also, I would like to personally invite you and SIFE's board members to come to Chicago as my personal guest to be an honorary judge/observer at the SAGE USA Tournament on May 27–28, 2011. The event is hosted by the University of Illinois-Chicago.

Rohrs never replied.

Just before leaving Bahrain at the end of October, I Googled the words "How High Is Up?" just to see if Shewmaker had written any articles or documented speeches with this phrase. To my surprise, I found a link on YouTube. The video contained a thirteen and a half minute video uploaded by SIFE on May 12, 2012, right after showing it at the SIFE USA competition in Minneapolis. Like all of SIFE's media, the video was slick and well-produced.[1]

After his introduction, Shewmaker—to resounding applause—strolled to the center of the stage, wearing a crisp red tie, white shirt, and black business suit, with arms swinging, then both thumbs up. He bellowed, "I'm excited! How about you? Are you excited?"

He then asked, somberly, "Will you accept my challenge to make a difference in the lives of others throughout the world? (pause) Yes? Please say yes!" Great applause.

The video cut away to Rohrs in a studio wearing a SIFE black polo shirt, talking about how SIFE wouldn't exist without his mentor. "There is one person without whom SIFE wouldn't exist today. We wouldn't be international. And without the hard work done by that person over a lot of years to build a good foundation, we wouldn't be able to go on without him. And that person is Jack Shewmaker."

Rohrs went on to explain that SIFE only had eighteen enlisted schools in 1982. About two years later, Bill Seay, one of SIFE's founders who had joined the Wal-Mart board of directors in 1984, asked Sam Walton to support SIFE. The video continued with Shewmaker and Rohrs telling the story about Walton asking Shewmaker to lead Wal-Mart's involvement with SIFE, and Shewmaker became the chairman of SIFE's board. At the first meeting, Shewmaker challenged the board to help SIFE grow, and he asked, "How high is up?" In his first year as SIFE's chair, SIFE grew from twenty-two to sixty-five schools.

As Rohrs talked, the camera occasionally cut away to still photos of Shewmaker chatting with students or celebrating with jubilant SIFE teams. Returning to Rohrs, the camera switched between frontal, color head shots to an occasional black and white profile of Rohrs.

The video was outstanding. The tribute was moving. But the cynic in me couldn't help but think how Rohrs and Nasby would use this as a fundraising tool.

A little over nine minutes into the video, Shewmaker said, "When I discovered that I could become more successful simply by making my goal to make others successful, that is—that's SIFE." That sentence, I think, summed up Shewmaker's philosophy of servant leadership.

Rohrs said Shewmaker made him a better leader. He went on to explain how Shewmaker was instrumental in taking SIFE global in 1999.

In another story Rohrs recounted a SIFE board meeting at Wal-Mart's corporate office in Bentonville. "Jack stood up and he said, 'I want you to understand how I stand on this position. I grew up in Dallas County in Missouri. Some of my classmates who were my best friends lived in houses with dirt floors. We were a poor county. Fortunately, I had a good family. I got a good education, and I lived in the country that gave me the opportunity to reach up to my full potential.'"

Rohrs continued to reflect on his memories of Shewmaker. According to Rohrs, Shewmaker said, "I want young people around the world to have that same opportunity. I have now traveled the world and everywhere I go I talk to young people and I realize that they are as smart as I was—they are as hard-working as I was—but a lot of them are in places where they don't have the opportunity that we have in this country. I want to find a way to share that with them."

If SIFE isn't the organization that can do that, Rohrs recalled Shewmaker saying, he would find another place to invest his time and money. With Jack's endorsement, the board unanimously agreed to expand globally. Rohrs said, "Without Jack Shewmaker stepping up that day and saying what he really believed, and putting his reputation on the line, SIFE would never have gone international. Without him, it would have taken years and probably never would've happened."

Then the video went back to Shewmaker's speech. "You can contribute to the success of the world by coming together in a way that us older people haven't been able to do. Accept the challenge. Do what you can and care about others. God bless you all."

At twelve minutes, the video showed Rohrs with tears welling in his eyes. "Jack shared with me, in my last phone call with him, [the details of] his last conversation with Sam Walton," Rohrs' voice cracked. "Jack knew this was going to be his last conversation with Sam Walton, one of the things Sam said was, 'Jack, let's keep this SIFE thing going. It's good for America, and it's good for the world.'"

Rohrs, now choking back tears, bravely continued to narrate. "Well, in that conversation I had with Jack just a week before he passed away— neither one of us had a clue it was going to be our last conversation—he said, 'Alvin, this SIFE thing, let's keep it going. It's even more important for America and more important for the world than it's ever been.'"

The camera cut back to the black and white profile of Rohrs at 12:37. The last minute of the video took my breath away. Now breaking up, Rohrs sputtered, "So as I think about Jack and all that I learned from him, I think the question that we all need to ask ourselves about SIFE and about ourselves, how high is up? So, Jack, we're going to keep this SIFE thing going and we're always going to ask the question, 'How high is up?'"

The video ended with Shewmaker in a position I had seen at least a dozen times over the years—behind a podium at a SIFE conference, with a gold eagle in front—both arms outstretched, fists clenched, jaw firm. A man changing the world.

In his soft Ozarks drawl, Shewmaker said, "We are still a young organization, but I have to believe that somewhere one of those students is going to make a huge difference in the world. I would like to be there, yeah, but I probably won't. But the fact of the matter is, it's a pretty good feeling thinking that you might have helped them along the way to better understand what happens and to change the world."

When I saw that Rohrs had used Shewmaker's, "How high is up?" question to pay tribute to his mentor, I had mixed feelings. When my book is published, I wondered, will Shewmaker's family think I am being disrespectful? Let me be clear: the title was chosen before I saw the video, and in no way do I want the Shewmaker family to think I am capitalizing on Shewmaker's tagline.

In a way, Jack Shewmaker reminded me of my father. He was strong. He talked straight, worked hard, made smart decisions, and loved young people. Unlike Shewmaker, though, my dad came from a poor farm family and only had an eighth grade education.

In my research for this book, I looked for evidence that Shewmaker viewed himself as a Christian servant leader. Only a few clues could be found. I found a link on Southwest Baptist University's website where Jack Shewmaker had been a guest lecturer in a business program called "Integration of Discipline with Faith and a Biblical Worldview." The purpose of the program was to take a "College-wide approach toward the integration of Christian themes." With such an approach:

> [O]pportunities are increased for teaching character traits consistent with a biblical basis. By hearing, seeing and experiencing these themes during their courses of study at SBU, students will leave with a unified sense of Christ-centered ethics that were reinforced in their business classes."

SBU alumnus Alvin Rohrs was also listed as a guest lecturer. In the role of guest lecturer, Shewmaker and Rohrs were asked to:

> share their testimonies with advisees and with classes in an appropriate and balanced manner. In an effort to encourage dialogue

and in hopes of ingraining Christian perspectives in business and computer science students, the College has adopted Psalm 15 as a guiding principle for our students. The College is specifically dedicated to producing 'Psalm 15 Professionals' for servant leadership roles in business and computer science.[2]

Shewmaker, I learned, was a member of Bentonville's First Baptist Church. However, his funeral service took place at the Fellowship Bible Church in Rogers on November 22, 2010. His obituary said he and his wife "embraced the role of servant leaders."

Fellowship Bible Church? That sounded familiar. I picked up Bethany Moreton's book, and found the following passage:

> If a single church could capture the religious transformation of the Ozarks during Wal-Mart's rise, a strong argument could be made for Fellowship Bible Church of Northwest Arkansas. The church home of many Wal-Mart executives, as well as management from Tyson Foods and other national powerhouses based in the retailer's backyard, Fellowship was at once an explicit companion to Wal-Mart, an inheritor of a specific regional religious history, and an active innovator of novel trends in postwar Christianity.
>
> [A]cross an oceanic parking lot and [b]olstered by a 10-million-dollar expansion, its campus in 2008 included offices, children's centers, and missionary housing. The worship center measured over 40,000 square feet and filled to capacity three times every Sunday. At the rear of the cavernous auditorium a team of volunteers managed the AV booth, projecting images and texts onto an enormous screen to accompany the sermon. In place of hymnals, the video screen provided the words to songs. An impressive choir was a regular feature, but worship included interpretive dance or a visiting Ukrainian orchestra. Between services, members milled about the mall-like foyer, drinking cappuccino from the coffee bar and looking over the new inspirational CDs for sale.[3]

Shewmaker's final service, I imagined, must have resembled a Wal-Mart annual meeting or a SIFE expo. He would have liked that. Grand. Video. Music. High tech. The church, too, I imagined, may have been a much grander version of the Jack Shewmaker SIFE World Headquarters in Springfield, Missouri.

I decided not to seek an agent or a publisher for this book until I was nearing the finish line, because I wanted to get most of the story in my word processor first. In my view, there are several potential audiences, but I had to ask myself first, is this book a memoir? In a way, yes, but after I read a recent review in *The Economist*, this gave me pause. The review said, "Few memoirs are worth reading. When they are not tawdry opportunities to air grievances, settle scores, or rationalize errors, they tend to be tales of adversity with a triumphant twist."[4] The review said that a good memoir, while written from a personal perspective, does not make the author the center of attention.

I hope readers find this book to be a good memoir. I would like to think that this book is a tale of adversity with a happy ending. The center of attention, I hope you have found, is SIFE, along with Alvin Rohrs, Bruce Nasby, and Mat Burton. By recounting my experiences, this book is also an exposé of SIFE.

SIFE stakeholders deserve to know who is leading SIFE, or as it is now called, Enactus. As I've said many times, SIFE's mission has been a noble one, especially the revised mission adopted in 2010. But I firmly believe SIFE's leadership needs to be held more accountable, and its operations need to become more transparent. After all, SIFE faculty advisers are somewhat like Wal-Mart store managers. They work really hard to organize and motivate a team. In SIFE's case, faculty no longer receive any financial compensation, and students have never been paid.

This book is also educational. One target audience includes university educators who want to learn more about how social enterprise and service learning can be a potent combination for a new form of capitalism—what I call humanitarian capitalism. Professors and management theorists interested in leadership style and philosophy would also find this book to be of interest, I think. Servant leadership as explained by Robert Greenleaf is not the same as the Christian-based servant leadership as espoused by Alvin Rohrs.

Last, anyone who is interested in Wal-Mart and its management and growth strategy will find this book to be revealing. SIFE's growth, in a way, has mirrored Wal-Mart's. Wal-Mart continues to fill entry-level management positions with recent SIFE graduates. One can view SIFE as a low-cost vendor of managerial talent. In exchange for Wal-Mart's annual donations to SIFE, SIFE offers companies like Wal-Mart a direct pipeline to young, idealist talent that shares Wal-Mart's culture of servant leadership.

I returned to Bahrain at the end of March in 2012 to visit Tricia over my spring break. Serendipitously, on Monday, March 19, 2012, I received an automatically forwarded email from SAGE's website. The email from Mutya Salen said, "I'm a former coach of one of the teams in the SAGE Philippines in 2009. Now I am a business studies teacher here in Bahrain and I would like my students to join in the SAGE program. Is there any chance for us to participate in 2012 cup?"

She referred to herself as a coach. Nice. I could relate.

Two days later, Tricia and I paid a personal visit to her school where I presented to four teachers and about fifteen students, all between the ages of thirteen and fifteen. The girls all wore burkas, the full body cloak worn by Muslim women.

"Won't girls be prevented from traveling to a Western country?" I asked.

Mutya replied, "Not from this school. We are much more progressive."

"But can you fund a team to bring to the U.S?" I pressed on.

"We will bring many people in our delegation. The only problem is that the parents may want their children to stay in a five star hotel," said another teacher.

What a world. Affluent Middle Eastern children would interact with some of the world's most underprivileged. They would learn from each other. They would become friends. They would compete in a friendly atmosphere. And they would think twice before recommending that their parents go to war.

In his 2004 book, *How to Change the World: Social Entrepreneurship and the Power of New Ideas*, David Bornstein said:

[P]eople who solve problems must somehow first arrive at the belief that they can solve problems. This belief does not emerge suddenly. The capacity to cause change grows in an individual over time as small-scale efforts lead gradually to larger ones. But the process needs a beginning—a story, an example, an early taste of success—something along the way helps a person form the belief that it is possible to make the world a better place. Those who act on that belief spread it to others. They are highly contagious. Their stories must be told.[5]

SAGE helps teens form the belief that it is possible for them to make the world a better place, not only for themselves but for their fellow man. The SAGE experience begins with small-scale efforts by teenagers, and provides them with an early taste of success. It also provides a stage where they can describe their successful business and social ventures to others. And for those students who are exceptionally creative and innovative, a national and world stage is offered. SAGE provides an avenue by which their stories can be told. It provides a formula for education and economic reform that so far has proven to be successful; now approaching our twelfth SAGE World Cup, we are showing real results in how we have helped to change the lives of teenagers.

My dad didn't have the same opportunities as Jack Shewmaker—or me. I bet my father was a lot like those poor friends Shewmaker had as a kid growing up in Dallas County, Missouri. I bet my dad and Jack would have liked each other.

Even though my father was raised by strict Baptist parents, he was not evangelical. He liked to play poker; he delighted in practical jokes; and he loved shooting baskets with my brothers and me. He also enjoyed a thick steak and a cold beer.

But my dad was spiritual. Though he rarely attended church, he left it up to us, my brothers and me, to decide if we wanted to go. He lived by the Golden Rule: to treat others as you wish to be treated. Dad had only two simple rules in our household: never lie, and never cheat.

When I go jogging through the majestic Bidwell Park in Chico,

California, there's a grove of towering oak trees about two miles east of one-mile bridge. I worship here in silence, twice a week, all by myself. I call this place My Father's Cathedral.

Through my father's example I will continue to lead SAGE.

What a world.

Acknowledgements

Many people have made this book possible.

To all Chico State SIFE alumni, your dedication to the community is evidenced by the quality of the projects you completed. You enthusiastically embraced the concept of service learning. By the same token, members of the Chico State SIFE business advisory board deserve recognition. At the top of the list are Ken and Barbara Derucher, Abe Baily, Judy and Gary Sitton, Cliff Neill, Tim Colbie, David Bunganich, Mary Ginno, and Tom Dwyer. Also, thank you, Dr. Manuel A. Esteban, former president of CSU, Chico, and Rick Vertolli, computer graphic artist extraordinaire.

I would like to thank all SAGE national coordinators for their tireless commitment to youth entrepreneurship. Continental coordinators especially deserve applause: Agwu Amogu of Nigeria, Basil Burke of Jamaica, Olga Azarova of Ukraine, Irina Dannikova and Maria Olshanskaya of Russia, Bob Galindez of the Philippines, Aman Merchant of the United Arab Emirates, and Pete Eimer of the United States.

A big shout-out goes to all current and former SAGEGLOBAL board members and officers: Jerr Boschee, Ed Byers, Van Ajemian, Al Konuwa, Joe Pedott, Matt Enstice, Rieva Lesonsky, Miemie Byrd, Allison Steltzner-Sharp, and Richard Davis.

Eight Chico State alumni have done Herculean work for SAGE since it was founded in 2002. I gratefully acknowledge the work of Rob Best, Carol Furtado, Liz Wendorf, Allison Smith, Blake Garcia, Rob Martinez, Daniel Fearing, and Max Frederick. Your collective commitment to the SAGE vision has kept us going for the past eleven years.

George Rogers, retired from the Chico State College of Communications, is a superb videographer. George, thanks to you and your wife, Cecelia, for those wonderful Sunday morning brunches.

Our biggest SAGE financial supporters have kept the SAGE flame burning. Thank you, Katie Gonser and Ken Grossman, Kenny Pasternak, Kishawn Leuthauser, Donovan Davis, Timothy Jones, Matt Cervantes, Joe Pedott, Dan Elkes, Elfrena Foord, Mark Sewell, Matson Sewell, Lisa Sewell, and Wally Marshall.

All current and former SAGE students and their teachers deserve special recognition.

Two academic giants deserve applause. Professors Nelson Lichtenstein of UC Santa Barbara and Edward Zlotkowski of Bentley College have each provided critical input and encouraging words.

Tom Payne remains my good friend. His input for this book was invaluable.

We all need coaches and mentors. In high school, Superintendent Jim Slade provided a guiding hand, as did Coach Greg Schmidt and Coach Dick Null. High school English teachers Doug Johnson and Dan Smith taught me the pleasures of English literature and grammar. High school friends Scott Slade, Paul Kammarmeyer, Dave Fields, Bruce Jongerius, Harold Hommes, and Lynne Megan helped shape an entrepreneurial attitude that formed the basis for SAGE.

My mentor as an undergraduate at the University of Northern Iowa was Dr. Darrel Davis of the University of Northern Iowa. Dr. Don Hansen guided me as a graduate student from dissertation idea to finished product at Oklahoma State University.

Three college friends have remained lifelong pals. Bright Ebenezer, from Stockholm, gave me the first real taste of what it means to have a global worldview. Brad Billings introduced me to my first walleye and northern expeditions to Canada. And who would have thought that Joe McLaughlin, the seventh floor Bender Hall renegade, would become a lawyer?

Early in my career, when I was a CPA with Ernst & Whinney, I became friends with an entrepreneur and free-spirit extraordinaire, Dirk Van Slooten. Dirk and I shared great times while playing backgammon in Oklahoma, Minnesota, Texas, Nevada, Mazatlan, and Puerto Vallarta. Though he is no longer with us, Dirk's spirit lives on in the eagle's eye. He, too, helped shape my entrepreneurial zeal.

My housemates in Des Moines, Iowa, while working with Ernst & Whinney in the early '80s, made my two years as a CPA much more pleasurable in spite of the long hours during tax season. Thanks, Tim Hermsen, Steve Marlow, Rich Johnson, and Chris Lang.

Two Arizona State colleagues also deserve credit for making my early career as an accounting professor so pleasurable. Steve Kaplan and Phil Regier, I will never forget our long runs along the Salt River Trail.

Friends in Chico have kept my spirits up as I slogged through the last several chapters of this manuscript. Thanks, again, to Dave Bunganich and his wife, Lori. Dave makes the best chicken piccata in the world. Also, thanks to Marilyn Maghetti for her positive comments and attitude.

My poker colleagues in Chico have provided a welcome reprieve from the daily professorial work of teaching, research and service. Thanks, Kenny Chan, Shekhar Misra, Marc Siegall, Jim Sager, Chet Cotton, Jeff Wei, Rico Cuneo, and Richard Davis. Richard, a former Sam M. Walton fellow, is one of my best friends. We often share a boat on our Canadian fishing trips.

Many other current or former Chico State professors have also provided inspiration. Thanks, Ken Chapman, Gail Corbitt, Jim Connolly, Amy Griffin, and Rob Burton. Rob has written a book about Sierra Nevada Brewing Co., and he has provided insight as we sipped an occasional pale ale or pilsner at the local pub and restaurant.

A big thank you to Elizabeth Quivey for designing the cover of this book and serving as a copy editor. I would also like to express my gratitude to my publisher, Larry Jackson.

Justin and Kate Steltzner of Napa, California, along with our mutual friends from Ottawa, Ontario, Sean Moore and his wife, Anne Carlyle, have listened to my story as we sipped fine merlot in Mendocino the past couple years. Thanks for listening.

I also want to express my gratitude to my beautiful stepdaughter, Julie Connolly Morrison, who now is an entrepreneur herself in Truckee, California. Also, thank you to my stepmother, Don Nita DeBerg, who made my dad's last few years on this sweet earth such happy ones.

Family members that keep me in check are my three brothers, Craig, Jarvis, and Del. Thanks, dear brothers and fellow Minnesota Twins fans. Also, thanks to their wives, Gloria, Mary, and Karen, along with nephews CJ, Will, Philip, Jakob, Henry, Drew, and niece, Chandler.

And of course, I wouldn't be here if it weren't for my mom, Ruby, of

Sioux Falls, South Dakota.

I especially thank Tricia Mendoza for all she's given. You're beautiful, Tricia. *Mahal kita.*

References

Endnotes

Prologue
HOLD ONTO YOUR SOCKS

1 According to its website, the Retail Industry Leaders Association was established in 1969 as the Mass Retailing Institute. It became the International Mass Retailers Association in 2004. See http://www.rila.org/about/who/Pages/default.aspx.

2 SIFE Yearbook '99, An Evening of Celebration, "Message from the Chairman and President," p. 1.

3 Information obtained from Wal-Mart's annual report for the year ended January 31, 1999, http://?media.corporate-ir.net/media_files/irol/11/112761/ARs/1999_annual report.pdf.

4 For a detailed account of SIFE's history, see Bethany Moreton's, *To Serve God and Wal-Mart: The Making of Christian Free Enterprise*. I've drawn extensively on this reference, especially chapters nine and ten, in my research about SIFE's genesis in Texas in 1975 and its move to Missouri in 1982.

5 All financial numbers for SIFE, including compensation of its senior officers, were obtained from GuideStar, a database for nonprofits. Their website is http://www.guidestar.org/.

6 Of course, no one can possibly know exactly what Alvin Rohrs or Bruce Nasby was thinking in Orlando, when the Chico State SIFE team made its presentation in 1999. This is merely my opinion of what they were likely thinking. Based on my previous and future interaction with these men, as described later in this book, I will leave it up to the reader to decide if the scenario I have painted here is plausible.

Chapter 1
TO BE A SAINT, A SINNER OR A TEACHER?

1 To learn more about service learning, go to http://www.learnandserve.gov/about/service_learning/index.asp.

Chapter 2
FREE ENTERPRISE "COACH"

1 The purpose of *Fortune* magazine's sixth annual Education Summit in Washington, D.C., in September 1993 was to share ideas on how to better educate tomorrow's workforce. About 260 executives, educators, and politicians attended.

2 Wingspread Group on Higher Education. 1993. An American imperative: higher expectations for higher education. The Johnson Foundation.

3 To learn more about Jules Knapp, visit http://www-news.uchicago.edu/releases/06/060210.knapp.shtml.

4 Two books were very useful in my research for this book. Both books detail the relationship between Wal-Mart and SIFE, and how both organizations relied on the management philosophy of servant leadership to motivate employees and volunteers. The first book is *To Serve God and Wal-Mart: The Making of Christian Free Enterprise*,

by Bethany Moreton (2009), Harvard University Press: Cambridge, MA. The second book is *The Retail Revolution: How Wal-Mart Created a Brave New World of Business*, by Nelson Lichtenstein (2009), Henry Hold and Company: New York, NY.

5   From this point forward, the term service learning is not hyphenated when used as a noun. However, when used as an adjective, as in "service-learning activity," the term is hyphenated.

Chapter 3
KANSAS CITY, HERE WE COME

1   Rick Alm, "One of KC's Top Conventions Says Farewell," *Kansas City Star*, May 20, 2006.

2   Richard J. Laird was a Sam M. Walton Fellow at Lubbock Christian University for several years, leading his team to four national championships in 1988, 1990, 1991, and 1992. Shortly after his team's last championship, he joined the SIFE staff in Springfield, Missouri. I sent Laird an email on October 1, 2011, asking him for his recollection of prayers offered at SIFE events. On October 3, 2011, he replied, "I do not believe that Alvin ever led a prayer at any of SIFE events. I know I did at several and other SIFE fellows did. He always was afraid that someone would be offended. Alvin only cried at convenient times to appeal to donors."

3   See *To Serve God and Wal-Mart: The Making of Christian Free Enterprise*, by Bethany Moreton (2009), Harvard University Press: Cambridge, MA, and *The Retail Revolution: How Wal-Mart Created a Brave New World of Business*, by Nelson Lichtenstein (2009), Henry Hold and Company: New York, NY.

4   See Moreton, pp. 189–192 and pp. 200–210 for background information on Alvin Rohrs. Also, see John Kerr, "Pass It On: Minister's son Alvin Rohrs likes to joke about how inept he once was at spreading the gospel of free enterprise," *Inc.*, December 1, 1995, accessed March 1, 2013, at http://www.inc.com/magazine/19951201/2515. html; and Carol Cook, 2009 "12 People You Need to Know: Alvin Rohrs, At the doorstep to the world," *sbj.net*, last accessed March 1, 2013, at http://sbj.net/main. asp?ArticleID=83917&SectionID=48&SubSectionID=108&S=1.

5   "Gene Taylor National Free Enterprise Center Dedication," University Archives, Hutchens Library of Southwest Baptist University, Bolivar, Missouri (1982), cited by Moreton, chapter 10, footnote 56.

6   Moreton, p. 187.

7   Ibid, p. 191.

8   Jack Shewmaker tribute video: http://www.youtube.com/watch?v=2XkaoUun0yg. Last accessed March 1, 2013.

9   Moreton, p. 192.

10   Rohrs' fundraising efforts haven't slowed since 1994. In the article by Carol Cook, 2009 "12 People You Need to Know: Alvin Rohrs, At the doorstep to the world," Cook said, "Rohrs spends about 80 percent of his time fundraising, with the rest divided between strategic planning and administrative leadership duties."

11   Shewmaker tribute video: http://www.youtube.com/watch?v=2XkaoUun0yg. Last accessed March 1, 2013.

12   Many books have been written about Sam Walton, Wal-Mart and its executives, but one of the best to provide a detailed account of Jack Shewmaker's career at Wal-Mart is Bob Ortega's, *In Sam We Trust: The Untold Story of Sam Walton and Wal-Mart and the World's Most Powerful Retailer*, 2000, Times Business: Random House.

13   "Jack Shewmaker: Lessons I've Learned Along the Way," in Career Connections, SIFE, 2008. Last accessed March 1, 2013, at http://d3jdp1eztxtcv.cloudfront.net/ documents/global/jackshewmakerInterview1.pdf.

14 "Wal-Mart's Shewmaker Honored at Gala Dinner," *Discount Store News*, May 23, 1988.

15 Moreton, p. 197.

16 Ibid, p. 202.

17 Ibid, p. 203.

18 Jack Shewmaker's obituary can be found here: http://www.stockdalefuneral.com/ Obituaries/Obituary_Shewmaker_Jack.html. Last accessed March 1, 2013. Also, for another article chronicling Shewmaker's life can be found at "Remembering a Legendary Retailer," by David Pinto, December 13, 2010, *MMR: Mass Market Retailers*. Last accessed March 1, 2013, at http://massmarketretailers.com/inside-this-issue/news/12-13-2010/remembering-a-legendary-retailer.

19 Moreton, pp. 215–216.

20 From http://www.sifeaustralia.org.au/library/SIFE_History.pdf, accessed September, 2011. The site is no longer active. Hard copy in author's possession.

21 According to KPMG's website: "Globally, KPMG has been a major sponsor of SIFE since 1990." China has received great attention from KPMG. Most recently, "For the academic year 2010–2011, 79 KPMG China staff from 9 offices volunteered to be business advisors for 82 SIFE projects," and its partners and senior managers also have served as judges in SIFE competitions." See http://www.kpmg.com/cn/en/whoweare/ corporate-social-responsibility/key-partnerships/pages/partnerships-sife.aspx, last accessed April 9, 2012.

22 Jack Kahl described his friendship and business relationship with Sam Walton, Jack Shewmaker, Tom Coughlin, Wal-Mart, and other retail executives in his 2004 book (with Tom Donelan), *Leading from the Heart: Choosing to be a Servant Leader* (Westlake, OH).

23 More information about Kahl's youth and relationship to Jack Shewmaker, Sam Walton and Wal-Mart can be found at, "Parents, Sam Walton Helped Duck Tape Maker's Success," by Lana F. Flowers, *The Morning News*, last accessed from http:// www3.samsclub.com/NewsRoom/Press/Print/383 on March 1, 2013.

24 "On Competition's Cutting Edge," *Industry Week*, September 20, 1999.

25 *Leading from the Heart*, p. 106.

26 Ibid, p. 110.

27 Information contained in Chico State's 1994 special competition entries, in author's possession.

28 *Everybody Counts: A Report to the Nation on the Future of Mathematics Education*, National Academy Press: Washington, D.C., 1989.

29 Lichtenstein, Nelson (2010). *The Retail Revolution: How Wal-Mart Created a Brave New World of Business* (p. 82). Macmillan. Kindle Edition.

30 This passage was contained in the first paragraph of the dust jacket to Moreton's book.

31 Moreton, p. 92.

32 Ibid, pp. 101–102.

33 *Wal-Mart: The Face of Twenty-First-Century Capitalism*, 2006. Editor: Nelson Lichtenstein. The New Press: New York.

Chapter 4

SERVANT LEADERSHIP, SIFE, AND THE BIG THREE

1 Information about Wasilla Bible Church can be found at its website, http://www. wasillabible.org/wbc/. Last accessed on March 1, 2013.

2 In a May 3, 2007, presidential debate, three Republican candidates stated that they did not believe in evolution. A June 11, 2007 article from the Gallup News Service, entitled, "Majority of Republicans Doubt Theory of Evolution," by Frank Newport, it said, "The majority of Republicans in the United States do not believe the theory of

evolution is true and do not believe that humans evolved over millions of years from less advanced forms of life. This suggests that when three Republican presidential candidates at a May debate stated they did not believe in evolution, they were generally in sync with the bulk of the rank-and-file Republicans whose nomination they are seeking to obtain. Independents and Democrats are more likely than Republicans to believe in the theory of evolution. But even among non-Republicans there appears to be a significant minority who doubt that evolution adequately explains where humans came from. The data from several recent Gallup studies suggest that Americans' religious behavior is highly correlated with beliefs about evolution. Those who attend church frequently are much less likely to believe in evolution than are those who seldom or never attend. That Republicans tend to be frequent churchgoers helps explain their doubts about evolution. The data indicate some seeming confusion on the part of Americans on this issue. About a quarter of Americans say they believe both in evolution's explanation that humans evolved over millions of years and in the creationist explanation that humans were created as is about 10,000 years ago." Last retrieved on March 1, 2013, from http://www.gallup.com/poll/27847/majority-republicans-doubt-theory-evolution.aspx.

3 To see the full text of Palin's comments, go to http://www.marklevinshow.com/Article. asp?id=2303165&spid=32364. Last accessed on March 1, 2013.

4 The transcript for Palin's speech can be found at http://www.npr.org/templates/story/ story.php?storyId=94258995, last accessed March 1, 2013.

5 "A Servant's Heart," by Peggy Noonan, September 5, 2008, *Wall Street Journal.*

6 I will go into more detail about conscious, creative, and humanitarian capitalism in chapter twenty-one.

7 Moreton, p. 177.

8 Ibid, p. 178.

9 Ibid, pp. 107–110. For more information about Greenleaf and servant leadership, see the following link: http://www.greenleaf.org. Last accessed March 1, 2013.

10 Robert K. Greenleaf, *The Servant as Leader,* 1970.

11 Moreton, pp. 179–180.

12 Years later, I would see Jack Shewmaker do the same thing by honoring and recognizing a member of the service staff working at a luncheon for Sam M. Walton Fellows at the Marriott in Kansas City. After Shewmaker recognized one person, the audience responded by giving a standing ovation to the entire staff.

13 Moreton, p. 180.

14 Moreton, p. 181, citing Harold F. Boss, *How Green the Grazing: 75 Years at Southwestern Life,* 1903–1978 (Dallas: Taylor Publishing Company, 1978), p. 285.

15 Ibid, p. 174.

16 The banner page at Southwest Baptist University's website proclaims, "Since 1878, Southwest Baptist University has been a Christ-centered, caring academic community preparing students to be servant leaders in a global society." See http://www.sbuniv. edu/aboutsbu/, last accessed April 11, 2012.

17 "The Perfect Executive," by James F. Hind, *Wall Street Journal,* December 18, 1989, p. A20. In this article, Hind also said, "Practicing servant leadership does not mean that you cast aside personal ambition and career goals. But ambition is healthy only when worthwhile goals are achieved; not at the expense of others, but with their help. As a servant leader, Jesus even lowered himself to wash his disciples' feet, considered to be the most menial task of that day. But it gained even more respect and loyalty of his followers—and vividly reminds us of the power of humble service to others."

18 Stephen Koepp, with B. Russell Leavitt, "Make That Sale, Mr. Sam," *Time,* May 18, 1987, p. 54.

19 "Top Executives Visit SIFE World Headquarters for Building Dedication," March 26, 2008, press release, *last* accessed on April 11, 2012 from *http://www.sife.org/aboutsife/ News/Pages/TopExecutivesVisitSIFEWorldHeadquartersforBuildingDedication.aspx.*
20 *Leading from the Heart,* by Jack Kahl, with Tom Donelan. 2004, pp. 51–52.
21 http://www.linkedin.com/in/bnasby, last accessed April 12, 2012.
22 Hard copy documentation from SIFE in author's possession.
23 "Pass It On," by John Kerr, December 1, 1995. *Inc.* As of April 12, 2012, the SIFE website listed Rohrs' 505 active US teams under its "Quick Facts," but a count of their "active teams list" only totals 400. In any case, projections for 1,000 active SIFE teams in the US by the year 2000 was more than optimistic. But even though SIFE's growth in the US may not have met Rohrs' expectations, the fact that SIFE is now present in thirty-nine countries is remarkable. Clearly, SIFE's growth strategy since 1999 has been focused in the international arena.
24 Ibid.

Chapter 5

GO YE FORTH AND PREACH THE GOSPEL

1 Document in author's possession.
2 Chico State SIFE newsletter, spring 1995, in author's possession.
3 *The Work of Nations: Preparing Ourselves for 21st Century Capitalism,* by Robert B. Reich, Alfred A. Knopf, 1992.
4 1994/1995 Chico State SIFE annual report, in author's possession.
5 Robert Wyatt became president of Coker College, a small college of about 1,100 students in Hartsville, South Carolina, on July 1, 2009. His biography can be found here: http://www.coker.edu/static/robertwyatt/index.html, last accessed March 2, 2013. According to "New Coker president calls for redefining education," by Jim Faile in *SCNOW* (March 26, 2010), Wyatt was officially inaugurated as Coker's president on Friday, March 25, 2010. Jack Shewmaker, a "longtime friend and colleague," introduced Wyatt by saying, "He believes in God. He believes in his family, and he supports his family in all the right ways."
6 Information about the NFIB can be found at its website, http://www.nfib.com/about-nfib, last accessed on April 13, 2012.
7 Extracted from the 1995/1996 Chico State SIFE annual report, in author's possession.
8 The title of the course is *Business and Computer Literacy in the Community.* The syllabus is in the author's possession, and is available upon request.
9 Illich's address was made to the Conference on InterAmerican Student Projects in Cuernavaca, Mexico, on April 20, 1968. The address can be obtained at http://www. swaraj.org/illich_hell.htm, last accessed on March 2, 2013.
10 "The Role of Service-Learning Programs: CAS Standards Contextual Statement," Council for the Advancement of Standards in Higher Education, from http://www. cas.edu/getpdf.cfm?PDF=E86EC8E7-9B94-5F5C-9AD22B4FEF375B64, last accessed on March 2, 2013.

Chapter 6

NEARING THE SUMMIT

1 Information obtained from the following websites: (a) http://www.walmartstores. com/AboutUs/7603.aspx and (b) http://pressarchive.net/libpa/wal-mart. Last accessed March 4, 2013.
2 Email in author's possession.
3 To learn more about CALWORKS, visit http://www.dss.cahwnet.gov/calworks/ default.htm. Last accessed April 15, 2012.

4   Email correspondence in author's possession.

5   To learn about the center of retailing at the University of Arizona, visit http://
    terryjlundgrencenter.org/history.html. Last accessed March 4, 2013.

6   Per http://www.fundinguniverse.com/company-histories/WalMart-Stores-Inc-Com-
    pany-History.html, accessed on March 4, 2013, Wal-Mart's "overall net sales typically
    had risen 25 percent or more per year in the 1980s and early 1990s. For fiscal years
    1996, 1997, and 1998, however, net sales increased 13 percent, 12 percent, and 12
    percent, respectively. The company was beginning to reach the limits of expansion in
    its domestic market. This was reflected in the scaling back of the Wal-Mart discount
    store chain, which reached a peak of 1,995 units in 1996 before being reduced to
    1,921 units by 1998. The company staked its domestic future on the Wal-Mart Su-
    percenter chain, which was expanded from 34 units in 1993 to 441 units in 1998.
    Most of the new Supercenters—377 in total—were converted Wal-Mart discount
    stores, as the company sought the additional per-store revenue that could be gleaned
    from selling groceries. Meanwhile, the Sam's Club chain was struggling and was not as
    profitable as the company overall. As it attempted to turn this unit around, Wal-Mart
    curtailed its expansion in the United States; there were only 17 more Sam's Clubs in
    1998 than there were in 1995."

7   For an excellent discussion of Wal-Mart's history in California, see Nelson Lichten-
    stein's *The Retail Revolution*, pp. 229–234, Kindle edition.

8   Wal-Mart's annual report for fiscal year ended January 31, 1998, trumpeted, "With
    more than 600 units in seven countries and another 50 to 60 new units planned for
    fiscal 1999, the International Division plays a key role in the Wal-Mart organization.
    Five years into our international expansion, operating profits from the International
    Division were $24 million in fiscal 1997 and $262 million in fiscal 1998." The annual
    report for fiscal year ended January 31, 2012, international sales in a total of 27
    countries had soared to $125 billion. Net sales, overall, for the company were about
    $118 billion with net income of $3.5 billion. Compare this to year ended January
    31, 2012, when net sales overall were $444 billion and net income was $15.8 billion.
    Mexico, China, and the United Kingdom contributed the highest dollar increases to
    Walmart International's net sales growth. By far, Mexico was the strongest country,
    with 2,088 retail, wholesale, and restaurant units. The next closest country was the
    UK at 541.

9   "Shewmaker: Retailers Need Global Outlook to Compete in Ever-Shrinking
    World Market," June 8, 1998, *Discount Store News*, last retrieved from http://www.
    walmartstores.com/sites/annual-report/2012/WalMart_AR.pdf on March 2, 2013.

10 For a biography of Coleman Peterson, go to http://investing.businessweek.com/
    research/stocks/people/person.asp?personId=12436835&ticker=BBW:US&previous
    CapId=122203&previousTitle=BUILD-A-BEAR%20WORKSHOP%20INC. Last
    accessed March 2, 2013.

11 "The Wal-Mart Annual Meeting: From Small-Town America to Global Corporate
    Culture," *Human Organization* 57(3): pp. 292–299, 1998.

12 Lichtenstein, p. 79, Kindle edition.

Chapter 7
WORLD CHAMPIONS

1   Merriman now works in the venture capital arena. He is an operating partner of
    Resilience Capital Partners. His profile can be found at the company website, http://
    www.resiliencecapital.com/team/Michael-Merriman/index.php, last accessed March
    2, 2013.

2 In a letter jointly signed by Merriman and Rohrs in the first page of the *SIFE Yearbook '99*, SIFE claimed 139 members of the board. The yearbook is in the author's possession.

3 Hard copy of email is in the author's possession.

4 See SIFE tribute video to Jack Shewmaker to learn more about Shewmaker's quest to build SIFE globally in the late 1990s: http://www.youtube.com/watch?v=2XkaoUun0yg, last accessed March 2, 2013.

5 Per page 5 of the *1999 SIFE Yearbook*, "SIFE was given the green light by the Board of Directors to cultivate SIFE Global. SIFE Global has made dramatic strides in its second full-year effort. This year, 53 Global Teams competed in their countries, and 10 competed at the SIFE International Exposition."

6 Per page 10 of the *1999 SIFE Yearbook*, "Thanks to the introductions made by SIFE's former Board Chairman, Jack Shewmaker, plans are underway to develop SIFE Australia. Mr. Shewmaker has helped pave the way in developing relationships with Woolworths, Ltd. and the Australian Retailers Association. Both organizations have agreed to assist with funding for SIFE Australia. We are also looking forward to having SIFE organizations in Uzbekistan, Ukraine, Malaysia, and Argentina."

7 Ibid, page 3.

8 Robin Anderson is now the dean of the School of Business at the University of Portland. His biography and curriculum vitae can be found at http://www.up.edu/dir/directory/showperson.aspx?id=000752484. Last accessed on March 2, 2013.

9 As Rohrs recounted in the tribute video to Shewmaker, "If SIFE isn't the organization that can [become global]," Rohrs recalled Shewmaker saying, then Shewmaker said he "would find another place to invest my time and money." Thus, with Shewmaker's endorsement, the SIFE board unanimously agreed to expand globally. Rohrs said, "Without Jack Shewmaker stepping up that day and saying what he really believed, and putting his reputation on the line, SIFE would never have gone international. Without him, it would have taken years and probably never would've happened."

10 The Coleman Foundation, based in Chicago, was established in 1951. See http://www.colemanfoundation.org/, last accessed on March 3, 2013.

11 Dees, J. Gregory. "The Meaning of Social Entrepreneurship." Original Draft: October 31, 1998. Reformatted and revised: May 30, 2001. Retrieved from http://www.caseatduke.org/documents/dees_sedef.pdf, last accessed on March 3, 2013.

12 Vertolli is now the department chair of Animation on the Oakland campus of the California College of the Arts. His biography can be found here: http://www.cca.edu/academics/faculty/rvertolli, last accessed April 16, 2012.

13 The full text of the article can be found here: http://www.csuchico.edu/pub/cs/spring_99/departments/index.html, last accessed on March 3, 2013.

14 See Moreton, pp. 173–175 for a description of the College of the Southwest SIFE team's activities in 1989. The College of the Southwest is a small Christian college from Hobbs, New Mexico.

Chapter 8
HOW HIGH IS UP?

1 For fiscal year ended August 31, 1999, SIFE reported revenues of $5,337,004. Expenses were $4,690,200, for a net gain of $691,617. Alvin Rohrs was paid direct compensation of $236,816 and Senior Vice President Bruce Nasby was paid $188,417. Additional employee benefits were $48,321 to Rohrs and $31,981 to Nasby. This information was taken SIFE's IRS Form 990, last retrieved from http://www.guidestar.org on April 16, 2012.

2 *SIFE Yearbook '99*, page 1, in author's possession.

3 Under the "Foundation Initiatives" tab at the KPMG Foundation's website, SIFE is listed first, and KPMG proudly proclaims that it "has a multiyear investment in SIFE of $50,000 annually, and worldwide, KPMG practices provide more than $250,000 annually." Joining Bernie Milano on the board today is KPMG partner Shaun Kelly. Last accessed on March 3, 2013, at http://kpmgfoundation.org/foundinit.asp.

4 "No Stopping Wal-Mart," by Tom Gascoyne, October 30, 2003, Chico News & Review. http://www.newsreview.com/chico/no-stopping-wal-mart/content?oid=27756, last accessed March 3, 2013.

5 For a detailed account of Roger Corbett's career at Woolworths, including his association with Wal-Mart and Jack Shewmaker, see an interview of "Roger Corbett—Mr. Woolworths," by Julia Baird, Sunday, July 23, 2006: http://www.abc.net.au/sundayprofile/stories/s1694291.htm, last accessed March 2, 2013. Another insightful article referencing Shewmaker and Corbett's relationship is "Shewmaker at the Top of His Game," by David Pinto, in Mass Market Retailers, September 17, 2001. The article can be found here: http://www.highbeam.com/doc/1G1-79026457.html, last accessed March 2, 2013.

6 Another article providing more details about the Shewmaker/Corbett relationship is "The Corbett-Shewmaker Connection," by David Pinto, Mass Market Retailers, June 28, 2004. The article can be found here: http://www.highbeam.com/doc/1G1-118686733.html, last accessed March 2, 2013.

7 "SIFE Nears 25th Anniversary of Preparing Future Business Execs," by Debbie Howell, June 21, 1999, *Discount Store News*.

8 Moreton, p. 181.

9 Tom Payne and I had become friends and in our phone conversations I asked him why SIFE always reported such big numbers. He told me that it was to impress the board. Keeping the board happy meant that donor money would keep flowing into SIFE's treasury.

10 Lichtenstein, p. 79, Kindle edition.

11 "SIFE History," downloaded from the SIFE website on January 31, 2004. Hard copy in author's possession.

12 Hard copies of all email references are in author's possession.

13 In the book, *Sam Walton: The Inside Story of America's Richest Man*, by Vance H. Trimble, Dutton, 1990, the author cites an essay written by Jack Shewmaker in the April 1987 issue of the company magazine, *Wal-Mart World*. One can glean insight into Shewmaker's leadership philosophy when he prodded associates to do better: "Not because we want to be bigger than our competition, but simply because the opportunity is there and in the process of reaching our potential, we can make a good thing better for a lot of people … and better than any of us have dared to imagine! The new Associate Incentive Bonus program is a fantastic opportunity to get involved in the real issues and challenges facing your store, warehouse or operating unit! I wonder how much we could learn? … how much each of us could improve? … how much each of you could earn in bonuses? … and how far Wal-Mart could go? … If (or perhaps I should say when) we all make a commitment to involvement in reaching our goals—not just for ourselves, but for others", p. 225-226.

14 In a September 18, 2000, article in *Arkansas Business*, the top 109 wealthiest Arkansans was listed. The Walton family (Helen, Rob, Jim, Alice, and John) was ranked first, at $108 billion. Jack Shewmaker was ranked sixteenth with $213 million of Wal-Mart stock. Article last retrieved March 3, 2013 at http://www.thefreelibrary.com/Wealthiest+Arkansans.-a065653911.

Chapter 9
HOW LOW IS LOW?

1   This story was recounted in a tribute to Shewmaker, "Remembering a Legendary Retailer," by David Pinto, *Mass Market Retailers*, December 13, 2010. Last accessed on April 18, 2012, at: http://massmarketretailers.com/inside-this-issue/news/12-13-2010/remembering-a-legendary-retailer.

2   This conversation with Alvin Rohrs took place on June 20, 2000. My brother Craig urged me to keep detailed notes of every conversation, and to email the contents to Rohrs immediately after the conversation. All conversations between Alvin Rohrs, Gail Spradlin, and Mike Merriman have been similarly documented, with physical and email copies in the author's possession.

Chapter 12
STAYING THE COURSE

1   This quote was last retrieved from http://www.goodreads.com/author/quotes/23041. John_Wooden?page=2 on March 3, 2013.

2   "Basketball's Coaching Legend," Interview of John Wooden, February 27, 1996, Academy of Achievement, last accessed on March 3, 2013, at http://www.achievement.org/autodoc/printmember/woo0int-1.

3   Per Guidestar's website at http://www.guidestar.org, for the fiscal year ended August 31, 2000, Rohrs earned $132,555 in compensation and $78,884 in employee benefits. The previous year, before the dotcom bubble burst, he earned $177,816 in regular compensation and $48,321 in benefits. However, he also received an additional $59,000, which is most likely a bonus.

4   Page 13, *SIFElines*, fall 1995, in author's possession.

5   2000-2001 *SIFE Handbook* in author's possession.

6   *Bowling Alone: The Collapse and Revival of American Community*, Putnam, Robert D., 2000, Simon & Schuster, New York, NY.

7   2000-2001 *SIFE Handbook*.

8   "Updating CSU, Chico's Strategic Plan for the Future," May 2006, p.5. Last accessed March 3, 2013, at http://www.csuchico.edu/prs/documents/strategicplan5_06.pdf.

9   Ibid, pp. 8–9.

10 A lead gift is the first major contribution to start a major campaign to raise funds for a specific purpose. The gift is usually accompanied by a request urging like-minded donors to make similar contributions.

11 See http://www.droidmatters.com/news/steve-jobs-we-have-always-been-shameless-about-stealing-great-ideas/ for a video of Steve Jobs making this quote. Last accessed March 3, 2013.

12 "A Service-Learning Kaleidoscope of Insights: Conversations with Mihaly Csikszentmihalyi, Theorist/System Change Artist; Bernard Milano, Practitioner/Foundation Leader; and John Saltmarsh, Historian/Service-Learning Educator," by Marilyn L. Taylor (Interviewer). *Academy of Management Learning & Education*, SPECIAL ISSUE: SERVICE-LEARNING 4(3): pp. 363–376.

13 "Developing Personal Competencies through Service-Learning: A Role for Student Organizations," with Gail L. Cook, Alfred R. Michenzi, Bernard J. Milano, and D.V. Rama," fall 2003, volume 5, *Advances in Accounting Education*: pp. 99–119.

Chapter 13
THE SAGE BABY

1   *The Ecology of Commerce: A Declaration of Sustainability*. Paul Hawken. Harper Collins, New York, NY. 2003, p. 1.

2   *The New Webster Encyclopedic Dictionary of the English Language*, published by Consolidated Book Publishers: Chicago, 1971, p. 740.

3   In Vance H Trimble's biography, *Sam Walton: The Inside Story of America's Richest Man*, Dutton Books. 1990, p. 222, Trimble recounts Shewmaker's exit from Wal-Mart. "Jack Shewmaker was doing some serious thinking. From the first he had set his sights on being able to retire at age fifty. He wanted to be free to travel, to see the world. His mother had hoped, too, to do that. Her death shook him. Now she never could, his sister Mary Lou reminded him. Jack's wife also was pressuring him to quit working 'before it's too late.'" P. 222.

4   The first order of business for the year, we agreed, would be to notify existing Cal-High SIFE teachers that we had changed our name to SAGE. California teams could, in the transition year, continue to refer to their programs as Cal-High SIFE, but that they should take special note that this would be the last academic year that they could do so.

5   Ibid, p. 115, Kindle edition. Lichtenstein cited his source for this quote "The Real Deal; As President and CEO of Wal-Mart's U.S. Operations, Cleveland Native Tom Coughlin Guides the Biggest Company in the World," by as Michael McIntyre, *Cleveland Plain Dealer*, Sunday magazine, March 4, 2013.

6   Wal-Mart Annual Report 2002, last accessed from http://www.walmartstores.com/Media/Investors/2002_annualreport.pdf, on April 21, 2012.

7   Lichtenstein cited his source for this quote, "The Real Deal; As President and CEO of Wal-Mart's U.S. Operations, Cleveland Native Tom Coughlin Guides the Biggest Company in the World," by as Michael McIntyre, *Cleveland Plain Dealer*, Sunday magazine, April 28, 2002.

8   "Is Wal-Mart Too Powerful?" *Business Week*, October 6, 2003.

9   A biography of Roy Blunt can be found at his website, http://blunt.senate.gov/public/index.cfm/biography?p=about-the-senator, last accessed March 4, 2013.

10 See Blunt's February 12, 2003, resolution to Congress here: http://books.google.com/books?id=mWUkdSooqZOC&pg=PA3700&lpg=PA3700&dq=Carol+Hymowitz+SIFE+2003&source=bl&ots=AOaxm7TjrW&sig=aZq6_wiNgO7cHAwj_lnU-ApTi0Cg&hl=en#v=onepage&q=Carol%20Hymowitz%20SIFE%202003&f=false, last accessed March 4, 2013.

11 SIFE's financial information obtained from the http://www.guidestar.com.

12 The video, entitled "Student Entrepreneurs Change Their Community," can be found here: http://www.edutopia.org/student-entrepreneurship-high-school-video, last accessed April 22, 2012.

13 Drury University's vision statement today includes: "With abiding commitments to our heritage and with renewed commitments to the global community and innovative teaching and scholarship, Drury will be a premier university where the finest teacher/scholars and professional staff educate students to become engaged, ethical and compassionate citizens for servant leadership in communities characterized by change, complexity and global interdependence." Last accessed at http://www.drury.edu/multinl/story.cfm?ID=22104&NLID=123 on March 3 2013.

14 "A Tribute to Alvin Rohrs," *SIFE USA Yearbook: 2002-2003 Special Report*, p. 9.

15 Ibid, p. 64.

16 Ibid, p. 9.

17 "Student Capitalists are Ready to Face Off," by Rick Alm, *Kansas City Star*. May 9, 2003.

18 "SIFE Champions Will Be Getting Taste of Morning Glory," by Rick Alm, *Kansas City Star*. May 14, 2003.

19 The *SIFE USA Yearbook: 2002-2003 Special Report*, pp. 68–69, lists Coors and Philip Morris USA as members of the Director's Club, with a contribution between $25,000–$49,000. British American Tobacco was listed as an Enterpriser's Club member, with a contribution of between $50,000–$74,999.

Chapter 14
LOWER

1 The *SIFE USA Yearbook 2002–2003 Special Report*, p. 6, includes SIFE's mission, vision, philosophies, and three guiding values. The first guiding value is, "We encourage SIFE students to learn that the best way to help people long-term is through free enterprise, practiced ethically and correctly." The second guiding value is, "We believe that in a market economy, a business cannot succeed long-term without practicing good business ethics, honesty and integrity towards its customers, associates, shareholders and community."

2 Email from Gail Beutler to Tom Payne, sent Thursday, May 19, 2005, at 10:24 a.m. In author's possession.

3 Per phone conversation with Maggie Kenafake of the Kauffman Foundation on Friday May 30, 2003.

4 See Note 1 above.

5 This memo was faxed to the author on September 22, 2003.

Chapter 15
LAWYERING UP, ENCORE

1 "Ozarks Influential," *Springfield News Leader*, by Karen E. Culp, May 21, 2003.

2 "Independent Program Puts College Students on Leadership Path," by Carol Hymowitz, *Wall Street Journal*, January 14, 2003.

3 Information about Pinkerton and his law firm can be found at http://www.pinkertonfinn.com/, last accessed March 5, 2013.

4 The seven members were: Bharat Desai, Chairman and CEO, Syntel, Inc.; John Griffin, VP of Global Accounts, AT&T Corp.; Richard J. Hynes, Sr. VP, Alberto Personal Care Products; Toney R. McCollum, VP, Trade Development, The Gillette Company; Thomas O. Minner, President & CEO, Champion Performance Products LLC; Stennis Shotts, VP of Sales, Coca-Cola Enterprises, Inc.; and Paul A. Stroup, III, Chairman & CEO, Lance, Inc.

5 "Dishonor Society," by Andrew Brownstein, *Chronicle of Higher Education*, March 22, 2002. Article last accessed at http://chronicle.com/article/Dishonor-Society/18357 on March 5, 2013.

Chapter 16
LOVE ON THE RHINE RIVER

1 Ultimately, in 2006 Germany's business culture was too much for Wal-Mart, and the world's largest retailer packed its bags and said *auf wiedershehen*. See *The Retail Revolution*, by Nelson Lichtenstein. 2009, p. 181 and 187. Kindle edition.

2 "Eligibility Procedures and Accreditation Standards for Business Accreditation," AACSB International–The Association to Advance Collegiate Schools of Business. April 25, 2003. Document can be retrieved from http://www.aacsb.edu/accreditation/standards-busn-jan2012-with-Track-changes.pdf. Last accessed on March 16, 2013.

3   The task force report is in the author's possession.

4   Facts taken from *SIFE USA Yearbook 2002–2003 Special Report*, in author's possession.

5   As Bethany Moreton said in her book, *To Serve God and Wal-Mart*, p. 199: "The key to attracting financial support, SIFE's leaders understood, was lavishing honors and attention on businessmen who had felt themselves unfairly maligned in the 1970s. In this they built on the techniques developed by schools like Harding and John Brown University. Awards multiplied at a brisk clip, and were seldom confined to a single recipient. Regional competitions and even individual rounds of judging within them bore the names of friendly corporations. These honors complemented the major gateway to sponsorship, the invitation to potential sponsors to serve as 'distinguished judges.' The attention frequently paid off handsomely: The conservative Adolph Coors family—foundational backers of the Heritage Foundation, the Committee for the Survival of a Free Congress, and other key institutions of the conservative ascendancy—came on board as sponsors of the magazine *SIFE Lines* after careful courtship. In a pattern repeated by Wal-Mart, Coors gave generously to SIFE both through the company itself and through the family's philanthropic foundation."

6   According to Tom Payne, he and Dick Laird often shared information. Laird was on friendly terms with one of SIFE's board members, and some of what Laird learned from the board member, he passed along to Payne.

7   A barong is an embroidered garment and in Filipino culture it is formal attire for men. Always worn untucked, over an undershirt, it is very light and airy.

Chapter 17
SHOWDOWN IN BARCELONA

1   This information, in the author's possession, was provided by a SIFE board member. The information included an approved budget for fiscal year ended August 31, 2003; an eleven-year financial summary; and details of SIFE's seven strategic priorities. The priorities were: Market share of qualifying universities worldwide, long-term financial sustainability, global expansion and organization (country growth), alumni, diversity, position and visibility, and infrastructure support. Also included was a report from SIFE's development office, which included financial goals, including donor retention and new contributions.

2   Typing this quote in a search engine yields several sources attributing this to Woodrow Wilson. One such website is http://www.searchquotes.com/search/Technology_Curriculum/, last accessed on March 6, 2013.

3   For more information about HPAIR, visit their website at http://www.hpair.org, last accessed on March 6, 2013.

4   By August of 2006, Carrefour would have seventy-nine stores in thirty-two Chinese cities, while Wal-Mart would have fifty locations in thirty cities. In 2005, Carrefour's sales in China were $2.2 billion, compared to $1.2 billion for Wal-Mart. Information retrieved from "Carrefour vs. Wal-Mart in China," by Bill Belew, *Zhong Hua Rising*, August 9, 2006. Article was last retrieved from http://www.zhonghuarising.com/2006/08/carrefour_vs_walmart_in_china.html, last accessed on March 6, 2013.

5   A copy of this handbook is in the author's possession.

6   Per SIFE's Development Office Report. See note 1.

7   Form 990 for 2003 shows that Rohrs earned a total of $278,767—$159,360 in compensation and $119,407 in employee benefits.

Chapter 18
AU REVOIR, SIFE

1   For an excellent discussion of Tom Coughlin's career at Wal-Mart, and his subsequent guilty plea to tax and fraud charges, see Nelson Lichtenstein's *The Retail Revolution*, pp. 114-117, Kindle edition.

2   "Changing of the Guard at Wal-Mart," by Suzanne Kapner, February 18, 2009, *CNN Money*.

3   "Former Wal-Mart Boss Sentenced to 27 Months of Home Detention," August 11, 2006, *Associated Press*. Last accessed on March 7, 2013, at http://www.foxnews.com/story/0,2933,207989,00.html.

4   Tom Coughlin and Jack Kahl, interestingly, had other things in common. Besides their Wal-Mart affiliation, both men were former chairmen of SIFE's board, and graduated from St. Edward High School in Lakewood, Ohio. St. Edward is a Catholic boys high school. One of its core beliefs is "servant leadership as a way of life for all our community members" (per http://alumni.sehs.net/?page=About_MissStatement), last accessed on March 7, 2013.

5   See note 3.

6   All quotes in this chapter, including email quotes, are included in author's files.

7   For an excellent discussion comparing the organization worldview (OWV) with the humanitarian worldview (HWV), please see R. Giacalone and K. Thompson, K. R. (2006). "Business Ethics and Social Responsibility: Shifting the Worldview." *Academy of Management Learning & Education*, 5(3), 266–277.

8   "Bruised in Bentonville," by Andy Serwer, April 18, 2005. *Fortune Magazine*.

9   "Interview: Nelson Lichtenstein," *Frontline*, June 9, 2004. Last accessed at http://www.pbs.org/wgbh/pages/frontline/shows/walmart/interviews/lichtenstein.html on March 7, 2013.

10 *Leading from the Heart: Choosing to be a Servant Leader*, by Jack Kahl (with Tom Donelan). 2004

11 *The Fires of Spring*, by James A. Michener, Fawcett Crest, NY, 1949.

12 Legendary basketball coach John Wooden was famous for his quotes. One of my favorites is, "The true test of a man's character is what he does when no one is watching." Many of my teaching principles are based on the teaching of the great Wizard from Westwood.

13 To learn more about Jack Kahl's history and background, see "Parents, Sam Walton Helped Duck Tape Maker's Success," by Lana F. Flowers, *The Morning News*, 2005, last accessed on March 7, 2013, at http://www3.samsclub.com/NewsRoom/Press/Print/383. Also, see "Interview with Jack Kahl," by Kris Woods, October 1999, last accessed on March 7, 2013, at http://emergingleader.com/article11.shtml.

14 "Friend Says OSU Prof Gave Illegal Stock Trip," by Ted Wendling, May 27, 2005. *Plain Dealer Bureau*.

15 See "Blackwell Suggests Ex-wife Spread News of Deal, by Kevin Kemper, June 7, 2005, *Business First*, last accessed at http://www.bizjournals.com/columbus/stories/2005/06/06/daily10.html?page=3 on March 7, 2013, "OSU professor sentenced for insider trading," December 16, 2005, *The Plain Dealer;*

16 See Wendling article, note 14.

17 "From the Boardroom to the Courtroom," *IBmag.com* (Northeast Ohio's Business Enthusiast), July, 2006.

Chapter 19
ROLE MODELS

1 Email received from Lateef Latopa on June 28, 2005.
2 Press release, "SAGE High School Students from Kaduna Going to USA for World Cup Competition," July 6, 2005.
3 The author has a copy of this email memorandum in his possession.
4 Quote included in *SAGE Information Handbook, 2005/2006*.
5 "Wal-Mart Legend to Serve Sentence Confined to Home," by Ann Zimmerman, August 12, 2006, *Wall Street Journal*, last accessed at http://online.wsj.com/article/SB115530259301833293.html, on March 8, 2013.
6 "Former OSU Prof Loses Appeal of Insider Trading Conviction," by John Kroll, March 12, 2007, *The Plain Dealer*.
7 "KPMG to Pay $456 Million for Criminal Violations," August 29, 2005, Internal Revenue Service. Last accessed March 7, 2013, at http://www.irs.gov/uac/KPMG-to-Pay-$456-Million-for-Criminal-Violations.
8 Ibid, p. 79.
9 Moreton, Bethany. *To Serve God and Wal-Mart: The Making of Christian Free Enterprise*. Kindle edition, p. 102.
10 Lichtenstein, Nelson (2010-06-08). *The Retail Revolution: How Wal-Mart Created a Brave New World of Business* (p. 123). Macmillan. Kindle edition.
11 "Wal-Mart to Close Store in Canada with a Union," by Ian Austen, February 10, 2005, *New York Times*. Article retrieved from http://www.nytimes.com/2005/02/10/business/worldbusiness/10cmart.html.
12 "Say Again: Echo Team is the Tops," by Kevin Herrera, August 8, 2006, *Santa Monica Daily Press*.
13 "Students Score High in the Art of Free Enterprise," by Cyndia Zwhalen, October 25, 2006. *Los Angeles Times*. Last accessed March 8, 2013, at http://articles.latimes.com/2006/oct/25/business/fi-smallbiz25.
14 Hawken, P. (1993). *The Ecology of Commerce: A Declaration of Sustainability*. Harper Collins, New York, NY, p. 1.

Chapter 20
AN UNTAPPED ARMY

1 Association to Advance Collegiate Schools of Business Accredited Schools of Business (AACSB). 2006. *A World of Good Report: Business, Business Schools and Peace*. Report of the AACSB International Peace through Commerce Task Force.
2 Ibid, p. 7.
3 AACSB report, p. 11.
4 "Remarks of Bill Gates, Harvard Commencement 2007," June 7, 2007, *Harvard University Gazette Online*, http://news.harvard.edu/gazette/story/2007/06/remarks-of-bill-gates-harvard-commencement-2007/. Last accessed on March 9, 2013.
5 "A Secret Weapon Against Terror: Educating Youth through Social Entrepreneurship," posted June 18, 2007, at *Huffington Post*. Copy in author's possession.
6 "SIFE Gets Funding for International Program," by Mike Smith, August 26, 2004, KSMU Ozarks Public Radio, last accessed at http://ksmu.org/article/sife-gets-funding-international-program on March 9, 2013.
7 "Congressional Pet Projects Boom—In Secret Lobbyists with Hill Ties Key to Record Funding," by Susan Milligan, January 29, 2006, *Boston Globe*. Article last accessed on March 9, 2013, at http://www.boston.com/news/nation/washington/articles/2006/01/29/congressional_pet_projects_boom_in_secret/.

8 Email dated February 6, 2006, in author's possession.

9 Illich's speech can be found here: http://www.swaraj.org/illich_hell.htm. Last accessed March 9, 2013.

10 NBC *Today Show*. See http://globalgrind.com/node/824023. Last accessed March 9, 2013.

11 Byrd, M. W. 2006. "Combating Terrorism: A Socio-economic Strategy." *Joint Force Quarterly*, 41(2), 15–19. Article last retrieved on April 27, 2012, at http://business.highbeam.com/435059/article-1G1-152196880/combating-terrorism-socioeconomic-strategy.

12 Ibid.

13 Prahalad, C. K. 2005. *The Fortune at the Bottom of The Pyramid: Eradicating Poverty through Profits*. Upper Saddle River, NJ. Wharton School Publishing.

14 Byrd. 2006.

15 Ibid.

16 De Soto, H. 2000. *The Mystery of Capital: Why Capitalism Triumphs in the West and Fails Everywhere Else*. New York, Basic Books.

17 Ibid, p. 209.

18 Ibid, p. 227.

19 Sachs, J. 2005. *The End of Poverty: Economic Possibilities for Our Time*. New York, NY. The Penguin Press.

20 "Rolling with Blunt: A Missouri Republican Is Poised to Replace Tom Delay at the Party's Helm—And Carry On Delay's Tradition of Enriching His Friends," by Michael Scherer, February 2, 2006. *Salon.com*. Article last retrieved on March 9, 2013, at http://www.salon.com/2006/02/02/blunt_4/singleton/.

21 "Proposals Call For Disclosure of Ties to Lobbyists Lawmakers May Be Forced to Detail Contacts, Cash Received," by Jonathan Weisman, March 27, 2006. *Washington Post*.

22 "Egregious Earmark of the Week: $750,000 for Free Enterprisers," posted on Congressman Jeff Flake's Web page on April 12, 2006.

23 See http://earmarks.omb.gov/earmarks-public/earmarks/earmark_229374.html. Last accessed on March 31, 2013.

Chapter 21

HUMANITARIAN CAPITALISM

1 "Clinton visits Nigerian village," Sunday, 27 August, 2000, *BBC News*. Last accessed on March 9, 2013, at http://news.bbc.co.uk/2/hi/africa/898450.stm.

2 Last accessed on April 27, 2012, at http://www.sife.org/aboutsife/News/Pages/TopExecutivesVisitSIFEWorldHeadquartersforBuildingDedication.aspx. Copy in author's posession.

3 At the time, SIFE's website claimed more than sixty staff members. The same number is reported in 2013. See http://enactus.org/who-we-are/staff, last accessed March 9, 2013.

4 Martin, R. and Osberg, S. 2007. "Social Entrepreneurship: The Case for Definition." *Stanford Social Innovation Review*, Spring: 29-39.

5 Bornstein, D. 2004. *How to change the world: Social entrepreneurs and the power of new ideas*. New York, NY. Oxford University Press, p. 1.

6 Fulton, K. 2006. "The past, present and future of social entrepreneurship: a conversation with Greg Dees," Monitor Institute, Duke Center of the Advancement of Social Entrepreneurship, Gathering of Leaders, New Paltz, New York. http://www.caseatduke.org/documents/deesinterview.pdf, last accessed March 9, 2013.

7 For an outstanding series of essays about creative capitalism, including Gates, Buffett, Easterly, and Friedman, see *Creative Capitalism: A Conversation with Bill Gates,*

Warren Buffett, and Other Economic Leaders, edited by Michael Kinsley, 2008. Simon & Schuster.

8   *The Triple Bottom Line: How Today's Best-Run Companies Are Achieving Economic, Social And Environmental Success—And How You Can Too*, by A. Savitz and K. Weber, 2006. John Wiley & Sons.

9   Compare John Mackey's philosophy with Hernando de Soto, who said, "I am not a die-hard capitalist. I do not view capitalism as a credo. Much more important to me are freedom, compassion for the poor, respect for the social contract, and equal opportunity. But for the moment, to achieve these goals, capitalism is the only game in town. It is the only system we know that provides us with the tools required to create massive surplus value. From De Soto, H. 2000. *The Mystery of Capital: Why Capitalism Triumphs in the West and Fails Everywhere Else*. New York, Basic Books, p. 228.

10 "Rethinking the Social Responsibility of Business: A Reason Debate Featuring Milton Friedman, Whole Foods' John Mackey, and Cypress Semiconductor's T.J. Rodger. *Reason*. October 2005.

11 A comparison of the organization worldview (OWV) with the humanitarian worldview (HWV) is made in R. Giacalone and K. Thompson, K. R. (2006). "Business Ethics and Social Responsibility: Shifting the Worldview." *Academy of Management Learning & Education*, 5(3), 266–277.

12 "The Green Machine," by M. Gunther, August 14, 2006. *Fortune*, pp. 42:57.

13 Hawken, P. (1993, p. 13). *The Ecology of Commerce: A Declaration of Sustainability*. New York, NY. Harper Collins.

14 Ibid, p. 48.

15 "Vast Mexico Bribery Case Hushed Up by Wal-Mart after Top-Level Struggle," by David Barstow, April 21, 2012. *The New York Times*.

16 Ibid.

17 Ibid.

18 *The Elusive Quest for Growth : Economists' Adventures and Misadventures in the Tropics*, paperback edition 2002, by William R. Easterly, The MIT Press, p. 290

19 *Global Civil Society? Transnational Social Movement Organizations and Social Capital*, by J. Smith, in B. Edwards, M. W. Foley, & M. Diani, Beyond tocqueville: Civil society and the social capital debate in comparative perspective. 2001, p. 200. Tufts University, University Press of New England.

20 Ibid, p. 206.

21 *Bowling Alone: The Collapse and Revival Of American Community*, by R.D. Putnam. 2000. Speech on Social Capital Presented to the Commonwealth Club of California. Copy of speech in author's possession.

22 Ibid.

23 Sam *Walton: Made In America, My Story*, by Sam Walton (with John Huey). 1992, Doubleday, p. 237.

24 Friedman, T. 2005. *The World Is Flat: A Brief History of the Twenty-first Century*. Farrar, Straus and Giroux, New York, NY, pp. 458-459.

25 Yunus, Muhammad 2007. *Creating a World without Poverty: Social Business and the Future of Capitalism*, p. 230.

26 Sam *Walton: Made In America, My Story*, p. 256.

27 Ibid, pp. 253-254.

28 "Obituary: Jack Clifford Shewmaker," *News-Leader.com*, last accessed March 9, 2013, at: http://www.legacy.com/obituaries/news-leader/obituary.aspx?n=jack-clifford-shewmaker&pid=146704911.

29 "SIFE Announces Improved Program Focus," August 9, 2011. Copy in author's possesion.

30 A description of these partnerships can be found at http://enactusunitedstates.org/project-partnerships, last accessed March 9, 2013.

31 "2011 SIFE World Cup Determined," August 11, 2010, last retrieved April 28, 2012, from http://www.sife.org/aboutsife/News/Pages/2011SIFEWorldCupLocationDetermined2010.aspx. Also see http://blog.miti.gov.my/?p=1701 and http://www.utusan.com.my/utusan/info.asp?y=2010&dt=0707&pub=Utusan_Malaysia&sec=Dalam%5FNegeri&pg=dn_10.htm, last retrieved March 9, 2013.

32 To see this video, about one and one half minutes long, go to http://www.youtube.com/watch?v=4lIBXpRxOaY. Last retrieved March 9, 2013.

33 "As a Director, Clinton Moved Wal-Mart Board, but Only So Far," by Michael Barbara, May 20, 2007, *New York Times.*

34 See http://enactus.org/rebranding/sife-changes-their-name-to-highlight-a-deep-commitment-to-entrepreneurial-action/#.UGmi61HxPhc. Last retrieved March 9, 2013.

35 *The Fortune At The Bottom Of The Pyramid: Eradicating Poverty Through Profits,* by C.K. Prahalad, C.K. 2005, p. 2. Upper Saddle River, NJ. Wharton School Publishing.

Epilogue
THE GOLDEN RULE

1 The video can be found here: http://www.youtube.com/watch?v=2XkaoUun0yg, last retrieved March 9, 2013.

2 Information about SBU's integration of Christian themes into its business courses, see http://www.sbuniv.edu/cobacs/faith_integration.htm, last retrieved March 9, 2013.

3 *To Serve God and Wal-Mart,* Bethany Moreton, 2009, pp. 96–97.

4 "Joan Didion Memoir: Kind of Blue," November 2, 2011, *The Economist.*

5 *How to Change the World: Social Entrepreneurs and The Power of New Ideas,* by David Bornstein. 2004. New York, NY. Oxford University Press, p. 282.

CPSIA information can be obtained at www.ICGtesting.com
Printed in the USA
LVOW07s2320030814

397252LV00002B/6/P